Conservation Skills for t

Conservation Skills for the 21st Century provides a much-needed update to the original *Conservation Skills* volume, presenting an overview of current issues facing conservators of historic and artistic works.

Beginning with the basics – why the past is important, as well as an overview of the nature and history of conservation – the book allows the reader to develop a holistic appreciation of the subject. As with the first edition, this volume assists with the development of judgement in conservation students and young professionals. A selection of new case studies representing issues conservators are likely to face in the 21st century illustrates the crucial considerations that must be made when proposing and executing a conservation treatment. Incorporating recent developments and use of new technologies in conservation processes, the book also covers topics such as conservation ethics; recording and documentation; investigating and cleaning objects; stabilisation and restoration; values, decision-making, and responsibilities; preventive conservation; approaches to the treatment of working and socially active objects; sustainability in conservation; and the conservator's role as advocate.

With detailed case studies and written in a clear, accessible style, *Conservation Skills for the 21st Century* remains essential reading for student conservators and conservation professionals around the globe working across a wide range of conservation disciplines.

Chris Caple is Emeritus Reader in Archaeological Conservation having been director of the Durham University postgraduate programme in artefact conservation 1988–2018. Author of 7 books including the first edition of *Conservation Skills: Judgement, Method, and Decision-Making.* He is currently writing up his archaeological excavations at Nevern Castle.

Emily Williams is Associate Professor of Archaeological Conservation at Durham University where she directs the MA in the Conservation of Archaeological and Museum Objects. Prior to this she was the Senior Conservator of Archaeological Materials at the Colonial Williamsburg Foundation. She has worked at museums or sites in Australia, Belgium, Bermuda, Egypt, Iraqi Kurdistan, Syria, Tunisia, and Turkey.

Conservation Skills for the 21st Century

Judgement, Method, and Decision-Making

Second Edition

Chris Caple and Emily Williams

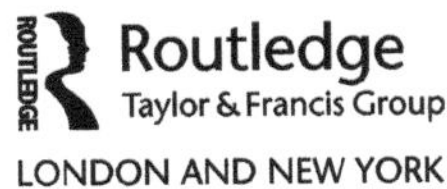

LONDON AND NEW YORK

Designed cover image: Durham Cathedral Galilee Chapel – Roundel created in the 19th century composed of fragments of the original 13th–15th century stained glass windows of Durham Cathedral. Installed in 1963 in the central window on the west side of the Galilee Chapel, Durham Cathedral. Photo: Chris Caple.

Second edition published 2023
by Routledge
4 Park Square, Milton Park, Abingdon, Oxon, OX14 4RN

and by Routledge
605 Third Avenue, New York, NY 10158

Routledge is an imprint of the Taylor & Francis Group, an informa business

First edition published by Routledge 2000

British Library Cataloguing-in-Publication Data
A catalogue record for this book is available from the British Library

Library of Congress Cataloging-in-Publication Data
Names: Caple, Chris, 1958- author. | Williams, Emily, 1969- author.
Title: Conservation skills for the 21st century : judgement, method, and decision-making / Chris Caple and Emily Williams.
Other titles: Conservation skills | Conservation skills for the twenty-first century
Description: Second edition. | Abingdon, Oxon ; New York, NY : Routledge, 2023. | "First edition published by Routledge 2000." | Includes bibliographical references and index.
Identifiers: LCCN 2022055705 (print) | LCCN 2022055706 (ebook) | ISBN 9780367443313 (hbk) | ISBN 9780367443320 (pbk) | ISBN 9781003009078 (ebk)
Subjects: LCSH: Antiquities--Collection and preservation. | Historic sites--Conservation and restoration. | Cultural property--Protection. | Historic preservation.
Classification: LCC CC135 .C29 2023 (print) | LCC CC135 (ebook) | DDC 363.6/9--dc23/eng/20221130
LC record available at https://lccn.loc.gov/2022055705
LC ebook record available at https://lccn.loc.gov/2022055706

ISBN: 978-0-367-44331-3 (hbk)
ISBN: 978-0-367-44332-0 (pbk)
ISBN: 978-1-003-00907-8 (ebk)

DOI: 10.4324/9781003009078

Typeset in Times New Roman
by MPS Limited, Dehradun

Contents

Figures

Preface

The first edition of this book, *Conservation Skills: Judgment, Method and Decision-Making,* set out to introduce emerging conservators to the process of conservation decision-making, to look at the balance of skill and judgement that informed the process and to explore where various options, such as partial cleaning of archaeological iron artefacts or the full restoration of a painting, might lie within that spectrum. The book tried to appreciate that conservation was still a developing subject, emerging from different material/museum collection disciplines (fine art, furniture, sculpture, industrial, archaeology, natural history, etc.) and to consider how consistent conservation principles could be applied to different objects in a collection, whether they were 5,000 or 50 years old, static or working, plastic or cast iron.

Nearly 23 years later, the field of conservation has changed significantly. How we conserve objects (the skills part of conservation) has changed as new technologies have been introduced but many of the goals remain the same. Where the field has experienced more profound change is in the areas of what we conserve and why we conserve it. The importance of values was just beginning to be explored when the first edition of the book was written. Increasingly, their role in informing statements of significance guides decisions about what will be conserved and which aspects of an object's history are privileged and retained during treatment. Objects are conserved because they matter to people, they connect people with their past (both real and imagined). As conservators and others have explored these connections, it has become increasingly apparent that who we are conserving for matters as well. Cultures throughout the world now draw upon conservation, adding ideas taken from their own traditions of caring for ancient and valued artefacts. This is enriching the subject, allowing engagement with a broader set of ideas, approaches, artefacts, and heritage and subtly reshaping the discipline. As a result, it seemed the right time to update *Conservation Skills* and to reflect some of the changes and challenges to the field that are emerging in the 21st century.

Like the first edition, this volume is intended primarily to help orient those new to the field but we hope that it may also serve as a useful tool for those who have been in the field for a number of years and for curators, archaeologists, and those engaged in allied professions. Although many of the ideas in the book are universal, we acknowledge that the examples given are drawn largely from those we are familiar with and are limited by our own reading and experience working in Britain, the United States and Europe. We have used the terms 'object' and 'artefact' synonymously to refer to all things which are not buildings, monuments, or landscapes and have made an effort to broaden the scope of the case studies offered so that they now range from wall paintings to statues, leather bags to woven baskets; from the artistic to the functional.

We would like to thank the many people who played a role in developing the ideas and case studies highlighted in the first edition of the book. In addition, we are deeply grateful for the help that John Watson, Carolyn Riccardelli, Lisa Young, Mary Brooks, Kate Ridgway, Lynn Grant, Angelika Kuettner, Molly Gleeson, Johanna Rivera, Felicity Turner, Crista Pack, Bob Kentridge, Ida Hovmand, Louise Mumford, and Jenny Arnsby have given us in preparing this edition. We would also like to thank the many conservators whose work (both in the lab and in journals, books, and conference papers) has inspired and challenged us. Your work defines and shapes the field.

Chris Caple & Emily Williams

1 Reasons for Preserving the Past

The Importance of the Past

Before discussing how we preserve the past, or even what parts of the past we should preserve, it is essential to answer the question, why is the past important? Human perception is based on our previous encounters with the physical world; we understand the world around us through correlating our present perception with past experiences. Therefore, a personal past is essential to us. As social beings, humans require points of contact (shared experiences and mutual beliefs) as a basis for communication. Our past also provides us with a wider sense of belonging, often manifested in an interest in our ancestry or the maintenance of traditions from a long-departed homeland. A poignant example of this can be found in tokens from London's Foundling Hospital. In the 18th century, mothers sometimes abandoned children that they could no longer care for at the door of the children's home. They frequently left them with an object, a token such as an engraved or split coin, button, a scrap of fabric, a pendant, or a lock. If the mother's fortunes improved, she could reclaim her child either by successfully identifying the token left with the child, or by presenting a matching part, such as the key that fit the lock left with the child or the other half of the split coin. These tokens were the only link to the child's earliest identities and connected the child to their past. Remembering a visit to the hospital, Robert Cox, a former pupil stated

> I was taken up to the Picture Gallery and ... beside the pictures on the wall were two or three showcases ... There was all little tokens in there ... bits of ribbon, bits of lace, buttons, bits of material, bits of tickets, coins ... I knew instantly that these were things that ... mothers had left to be able to identify their child by ... I suppose they all hoped at some stage ... I was just transfixed by this ... I kept wondering what my mother had left with me. Not realising, at that stage, that that system had finished years before ... It was just a heart-breaking moment.
>
> (Foundling Museum n.d)

Like individuals, groups may cherish a past; indeed, many define themselves and their traits or qualities by reference to their past. Thus, regiments record their battle honours, sports teams record their victories, and nations erect monuments to celebrate individuals and momentous events in their past. Many cultures start their pasts with a creation myth – a narrative of the past that explains the world they inhabit. Names from these creation myths are often given to features of the landscape through which

DOI: 10.4324/9781003009078-1

members of that society move as a means of explaining and claiming them (Layton 1994). For example, the name of the Welsh mountain Cadair Idris translates as 'Idris' Chair' referring to a mythological giant who was said to have used the mountain as his throne, explaining its shape. The giant Idris was skilled in poetry, astronomy, and philosophy (valued Welsh traditions) and is often conflated with the early Welsh prince, Idris ap Gwyddno (also known as Idris Gawr or Idris the Giant) who won an important battle against the Irish and whose military prowess was worthy of emulation. Thus, the name not only connects an existing story to an origin myth but also reinforces societal values and offers tips for survival or integration in the present. Similarly, 'songlines' or dream tracks, associated with the ancestral past known as 'the Dreaming', continue to connect modern Aboriginal Australians with their land and guide their travels across it.

In Western European society, creation stories and the biblical narratives that replaced them were challenged by Enlightenment era beliefs that sought to create a single provable past – '*the* past' – based on physical evidence and reason. The past has many forms: oral history, written history, buildings, landscapes, objects, pictures, memories, sounds, smells, tastes, people, etc. In creating our own personal pasts, we often experience all or many of these elements together and they remain connected in our minds; however, we engage with '*the* past' primarily in two forms, as the physical remains of objects and sites and as narratives.

Remains (Objects and Sites)

Physical remains, often referred to as material cultural or as 'tangible cultural heritage' (UNESCO 2020), may include archaeological sites, monuments, and functional and decorative objects. These are often seen as primary sources (documents) that can objectively be read to understand events in their creation, working life, and the society that made and used them (Lipe 1987; Jones 1990, Caple 2000; Caple 2006; Watson 2010). Many objects are complex and have been altered over the years for a variety of motives and it is important to remember that past interventions can distort how we perceive them in the present (Genbrugge 2017; Case Study 1A: De Walden helmets). For example, St Wenceslas' helmet consists of an early 10th century cap consistent with Wenceslas' life; however, the rim and nasal, with Christian imagery, were likely added later in the century as support grew for the saint's cult (Vlasatý 2019). Since objects and sites act as mnemonic devices, every time we encounter them, they bring the past to mind. Physical 'touchstones' of the past may therefore be created to provide authority or to point to early periods or to commemorate past events (memorials); for example, at the Step Pyramid of Djoser in Saqqara, a symbolic south tomb alludes to older dynastic burials in Upper Egypt and speaks to Djoser's role in unifying Egypt (Baines 1994: 134), similarly war memorials give physical presence to past triumphs and losses.

Narrative

A narrative may be a myth or tradition, oral or written history, museum label, guidebook, or other account of the past that relates physical remains to a wider understanding of events in the past. Objects of the past always have a narrative, even if it is simply a date or an association with someone in the past. The narrative provides a context beyond that of the object's immediate surroundings. Through the narrative, people interpret and appreciate an object's previous existence (its past) and connect its physical remains to a societal past. The more detailed and engaging the narrative, the more important (valued) the object will appear. Narratives contain:

- *Facts:* Details about composition, date, manufacture, discard and use recovered from the object, its context and contemporary sources. Conservators may play a key role in revealing and adding facts to narratives due to their intimate engagement with the objects they work on.
- *Interpretation:* Deductions made from the facts that draw the meaning or role of the object into a wider understanding.

Whenever a narrative is presented, facts may be selected or elided, and the narrative biased consciously or unconsciously. To be accepted, narratives must normally fit the 'established' view of the past. However, narratives are adjusted to fit new evidence or an 'improved' understanding of the past. Recently, many museums have revised the narratives about ethnographic objects to incorporate traditional forms of knowledge associated with their source communities.

The power of narrative can be seen in the project *A History of the World in 100 Objects*. Initially a radio programme created by the BBC and the British Museum, where objects were used as engaging mnemonics that drew listeners into stories and explanations of the past, the project later developed into a book (MacGregor 2012) and a touring exhibition.[1] It was very popular and drew people to the British Museum to see the real objects; however, the initial trigger was the narrative.

Heritage and the Past

Heritage can be defined as something inherited or passed on from a previous generation. Although heritage may be experienced personally, its focus is on communal or group memory and on rendering the past useable in the present (Lowenthal 1996; Harrison 2013). Like historians, heritage practitioners create narratives about the past; however, there are some differences between them. The work of historians explores and explains the past but focuses on verifiable facts usually contained in written documents. It seeks to create a detailed authoritative version of the past. Heritage, on the other hand, is 'an actively constructed understanding, a discourse about the past that is ever in fluctuation' (Moody 2015: 113). Lowenthal (1996) illustrated this by citing the example of the Tiv tribe in Nigeria who first recounted their tribal genealogy and account of their past to anthropologists over 50 years ago. The anthropologists' written record (or history) no longer corresponds to the present-day genealogy and account of their past told by the tribe. Over the intervening years, the narrative has changed. The members of the tribe adapted and amended the record to reflect changes and to ensure that the past continued to serve the needs and purposes of the present. The line between history and heritage is not a sharp one. It is blurry. History museums are part of the heritage industry and historical facts underpin many heritage narratives. The difference between the two lies in how the past is used. While all elements of the past are historical, only some are heritage. Heritage is a product of selection and designation by a group or society.

Cultural heritage is the legacy of human creativity and expression that is inherited by the present from the past. It is composed of both tangible elements (physical artefacts, buildings, works of art, and written words) and intangible elements (customs, traditions, performances, beliefs, and rituals). Tangible and intangible heritage are not mutually exclusive; both can be present in a single artefact. For example, a mask can be both a tangible wooden structure and the manifestation of a supernatural entity (Seip 1999).

Heritage is established and maintained through three processes:

- *Identification:* This may include research to discover as much information or evidence as possible. Linked to notions of authenticity and truth.
- *Preservation*[2]*:* The idea of heritage as an inheritance from the past is important since it carries with it the idea that as we inherited these things, we should also pass them on and that we should ideally pass them on in similar or better condition. For many this is seen as an important social responsibility. Preservation is a process that aims to protect the object for the future. In 2001, UNESCO adopted the *Universal Declaration on Cultural Diversity,* which states in Article 7 that: 'heritage in all its forms must be preserved, enhanced and handed on to future generations as a record of human experience and aspirations, so as to foster creativity in all its diversity and to inspire genuine dialogue among cultures' (UNESCO 2001).
- *Presentation:* Making cultural heritage and information about it accessible to the public. Traditionally, this has been done through physical display or performance. Digital technologies offer opportunities for virtual displays allowing heritage to be presented in ways that might not be possible otherwise. Displays select some of the 'truths' about the object and through the narrative (verbal or written), or the nature of the display, emphasise and communicate them. It is necessary to evaluate displays critically as those who control the means of presentation have the power to intentionally or unintentionally bias the narrative presented.

Today, the processes of identifying, preserving, and presenting heritage are often undertaken by large interdisciplinary teams that may include architects, archaeologists, exhibit designers, curators, fundraisers, historians, conservators, security professionals, collections care specialists, and others. Collectively, these individuals are often referred to as heritage professionals and the industry within which they work is referred to as the heritage sector. In 2019, in England alone, it was responsible for employing 464,000 and contributing nearly 2% to the nation's gross value added or GVA (Historic England 2019).

Modernisation has meant that many connections with the past have been lost. People increasingly live away from larger family units and as a result, traditions (or intangible heritage) and heirlooms (tangible heritage) may not be handed down; new technologies are replacing older methods of working and multi-storey buildings in newly created cities often replace vernacular forms of architecture (Figure 1.1). In periods of change, the new (what is unknown) can be threatening and the past (what is known) is reassuring. As vestiges of the past become scarcer, they are valued more highly. Traditional food and music are sought and objects that were once seen as old become 'collectible', 'vintage', and 'antique'. Heritage becomes a poultice for the trauma of loss and the disturbance of the new. Consequently, people attempt to collect and preserve the past; to freeze it. This is not a new phenomenon; writers in Imperial Rome sought the certainty of the earlier Republican Age. However, what we consider 'our' or 'the' heritage varies from one individual to another and from one group to another. It can be deeply personal, which leads to conflict and to 'contested heritage'. Dominant groups

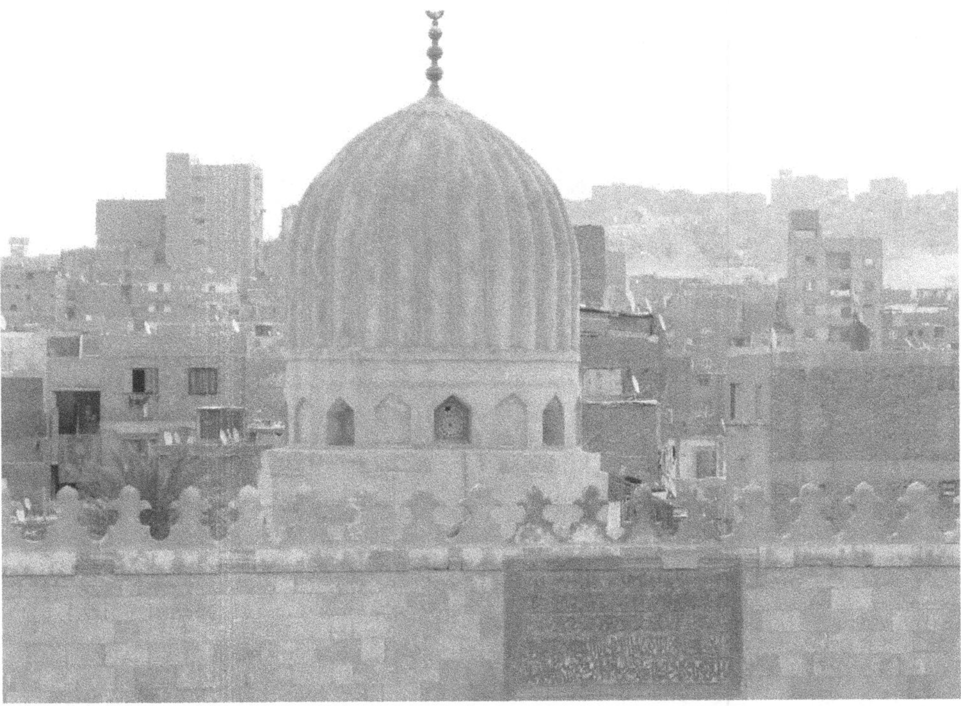

Figure 1.1 The 15th century Khanqah (a Sufi ritual space) and Mausoleum of Sultan Farag ibn Barquq, once isolated in Cairo's Northern Cemetery is now encroached on by modern, often unpermitted, structures. Felicity Turner.

may portray other groups as lacking a past. They may appropriate elements of another group's heritage as a means of controlling that group. Heritage can therefore be a cultural process through which individuals and social groups express, contest, and expand their power (Ireland and Lydon 2005). Thus 'heritage' although tied to an individual's need to have a past, goes beyond it and becomes an essential component of social and political organisation (Kavanagh 1990; Fowler 1992).

Valuing the Past

Cultural heritage survives when it is deemed valuable to succeeding generations or when it is buried or otherwise hidden. When its value is higher in another form, for example as a raw material, it is altered. Thus, bronze statues are melted down when their value as scrap is greater than the memory of the individual they portray (Figure 1.2). The value of the past is relative. It is dependent on economic circumstances, geography, cultural background personal experience, religious beliefs, academic training, etc. William Stukeley (1743) recorded an early example of the differing values inherent in an object. The late 17th and 18th centuries saw both the wholesale destruction and the simultaneous recording of the prehistoric stones (sarsens) at Avebury. Stukeley, an 18th-century English antiquarian, observed a local man, Tom Robinson, and his accomplices breaking up sarsens. They dug pits beneath the stones, lit fires in the pits, heated the stones,

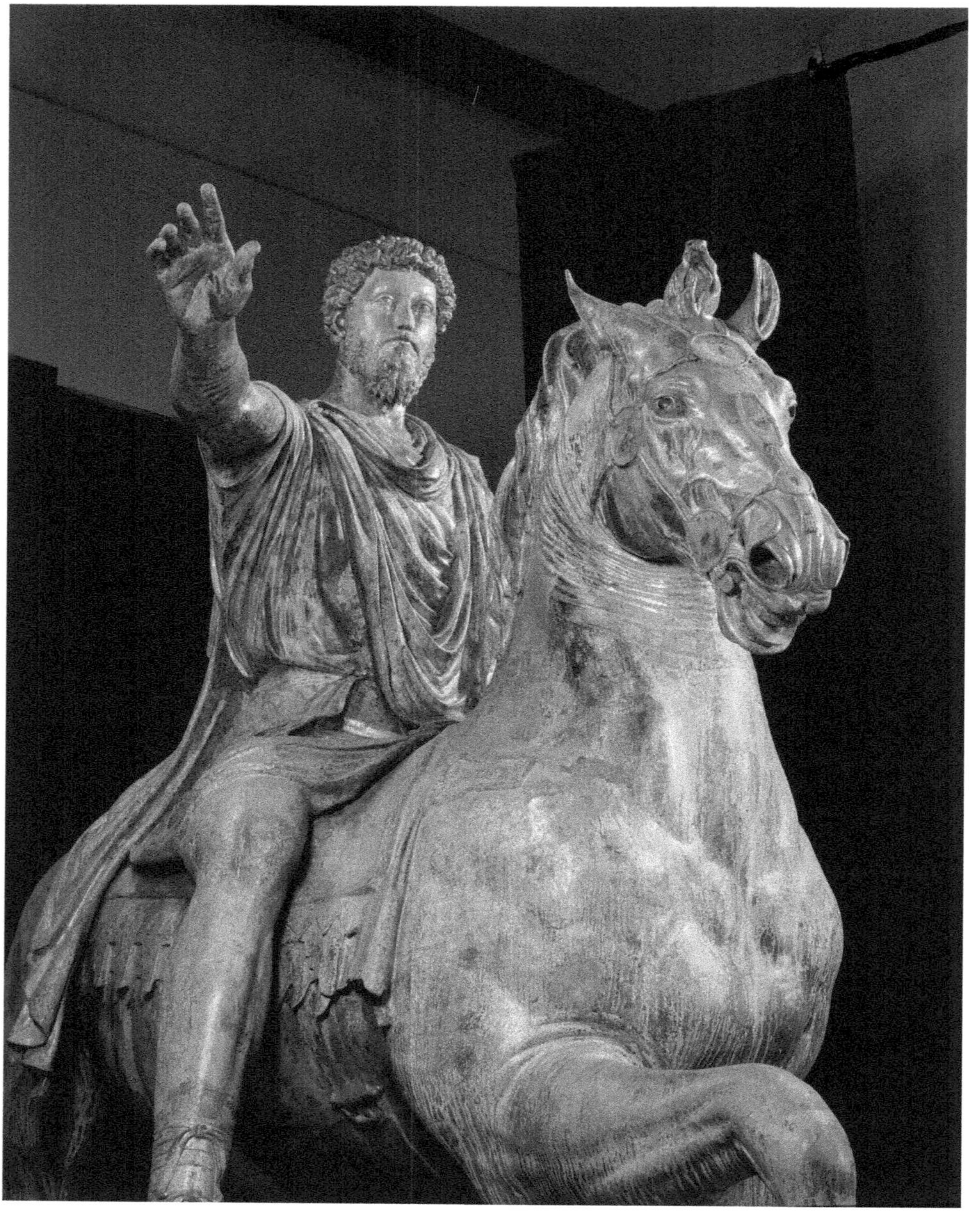

Figure 1.2 Initially one of at least 22 similar statues of its type, the equestrian statue of Marcus Aurelius, a Roman Emperor, is today the only surviving example. Later Roman Kings and Pontiffs, believed erroneously that it depicted Constantine, the first Christian Emperor. Therefore, they valued the statue and preserved it. © Sovrintendenza Capitolina – Foto in Comune.

shattered them by throwing cold water on them, and then collected and sold the fragments as building stone (Stukeley, 1743: 15). For Stukeley, who recorded what remained, the stones had value for their connections to the past and the ways in which they fuelled his antiquarian imagination; for Robinson and his helpers, the stones had value as a raw material – a single stone broken up in this manner provided enough building material for an entire cottage (Stukeley 1743: 31). Robinson also valued the cleared land for growing crops (Stukeley 1743: 22). For Stukeley, an Anglican cleric, Robinson's actions may have seemed even more objectionable because he was a member of a dissenting community (Edwards 2004), demonstrating how complex values can be and how they can be influenced by seemingly unconnected beliefs. With no way to settle their differences, all that remained to Stukeley was to pillory Robinson in his writing.[3]

Today, museums and heritage agencies carry out conscious valuation processes to ensure that valuable heritage is not lost, to clarify which aspects of the past are important, and to justify allocating resources to their preservation. In 1903, the art historian Alois Riegl identified three values (measures of importance) that he felt were key to the identification and preservation of artistic and historic works (Stanley Price *et al.* 1996): age value, historical value, and commemorative value. Each of these values could, he argued, be further qualified by two additional values: use and newness. Thus, an old and historic building, such as Hagia Sofia in Istanbul, may be valued for its age, its ability to document key historic moments, and its continued use to the community. In seeking to preserve it, all three values must be considered, or the essence of the building may be damaged. The notion of values gradually found its way into the preservation field. In 1964, the Venice Charter noted that the aim of restoration was to 'preserve and reveal the aesthetic and historic value … based on respect for original material and authentic documents' (ICOMOS 1965). This rather narrow view of values, which focused on maintaining the authenticity of the piece through the materials it was made from, was augmented in 1979 by the Burra Charter, which recognised a new class of values – cultural values (ICOMOS Australia 1979). Cultural values were defined as the 'qualities for which a place has become a focus of spiritual, political, national or other cultural sentiment to a majority or minority group' (ICOMOS Australia 1999). Over the intervening years, a number of different values have been identified. Mason and Avrami (2000) included historic, aesthetic, social (or civic), spiritual (religious), symbolic (identity), research, nature, and economic values in their list. In practice, several values are often grouped together under one 'master' value term, such as 'communal value', which may encompass financial value, use value, social and religious value (English Heritage 2008).

It is important to note that

- Values can be subjective and culturally dependant (Figure 1.2).
- Values can be measured and expressed in different ways, including financial (monetary value), visitor numbers (popular value), citations or references (impact value), emotional response (aesthetic value), etc.

The value of objects changes over time. A generalised curve of the changing overall value of objects over time can be derived (Figure 1.3), highlighting three distinct phases.

When clearly articulated, values help identify the aspects of an object or monument that are particularly important and/or preservation worthy, i.e. the fabric, appearance, context, location, and/or use. The individuals, groups, and corporate entities holding

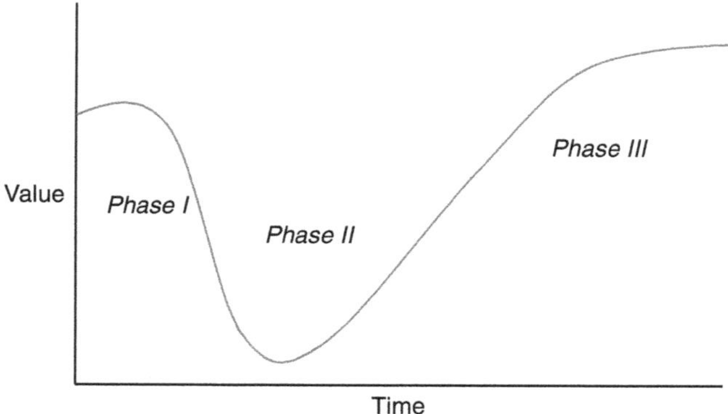

Figure 1.3 Time-value curve applicable to almost all artefacts. In Phase I, objects have an initial value based largely on their functionality. This declines as the objects wear, decay and grow older. In Phase II, objects are old, broken and obsolete. They have little value beyond the recyclable materials they contain (high for gold jewellery, low for most things). Most objects cease to exist. By Phase III, a few objects survive, slowly acquiring value due to their increasing age, scarcity and mnemonic function. Conservation and restoration activities enhance their (many) values (Thompson 1979; Ashley-Smith 1999; Waller 2003; Hucklesby 2005; Strlic *et al.* 2013; Thompson 2017). Chris Caple.

and articulating these values are referred to as stakeholders. Values are summarised and communicated through a 'statement of significance', which can be created for sites, monuments, and objects. English Heritage (2008) defines the 'significance' of a place as its capacity to provide physical evidence of the human past (evidentiary value); its associations with people and events and how these connect the past with the present (historical values); the sensory and intellectual stimulation the place provides (aesthetic value); and the meaning the place holds to the lives of those living there, using it and who have experienced it (communal value).

Once significance has been established the next steps are to identify the obligations arising from its significance, such as identifying the physical condition and any future resource needs, as well as any resources, opportunities, and constraints that might be present (ICOMOS Australia 2013). The final step is to prepare a management plan, including priorities, resources, responsibilities, and timings and then implement that plan. Values and significance can inform planning at the level of a single artefact (Russel and Winkworth 2009) or on a national level (Kirby Talley Jr. 1999).

Establishing the significance of a place (or object) is not an entirely objective process. As Riegl noted in 1903, 'it is modern viewers rather than the works themselves by their original purpose that assign meaning and significance to a monument'. Heritage agencies frequently engage with stakeholders (community members, politicians, business leaders, and heritage groups as well as others) to explore the values of an object or place. But who is a valid stakeholder? Does anyone with an opinion get a voice, or should there be some test of validity or worthiness before you can be considered a stakeholder? How can we successfully negotiate unequal power structures and recognise that some stakeholders are very powerful, and some may be acutely unempowered? How frequently should the group of stakeholders be reconstituted? If consensus is achieved one year, how soon can it be revisited if there is a dissenting voice or finding? Since values may be measured in different ways it can be difficult to balance them to reach a conclusion (Mason and Avrami 2000: 25). Unfortunately, in these situations monetary concerns may trump other units of measurement and impact which elements are seen as most significant.

Devaluing the Past

Identifying, preserving, and presenting heritage emphasises its value for 'our' identity and can make it a target for those wishing to undermine or eliminate that identity. This may be tactical or punitive. In 1944, the Nazis purposely destroyed Warsaw as a punishment for the Warsaw Uprising (Chamberlin 1979). During the Bosnian war, Serbian Nationalist forces deliberately targeted libraries and archives seeking to destroy historical records that might offer written proof that non-Serbians once lived in the area. The communal records of over 800 Muslim and Croat (Catholic) communities were destroyed. In 1993, the Stari Most Bridge in Mostar, which was commissioned in 1557 by Suleiman the Magnificent and connected disparate Christian, Orthodox, and Muslim communities, was destroyed by Croat nationalist forces as a way of excising that shared cultural heritage and peaceful coexistence. In an interview about the bridge's destruction, a militiaman serving in the forces of Mate Boban, a Croat Nationalist warlord, noted that 'it is not enough to cleanse Mostar of the Muslims … the relics must also be destroyed' (Riedlmayer 1994: 3).

The idea of excising the past and 'killing memory' (Riedlmayer 1994) is not a uniquely modern concept nor is it solely associated with ethnic cleansing. It can be carried out for political and religious reasons as well. In ancient Egypt, Thutmose III ordered the obliteration of the name and image of Hatshepsut, the powerful eighteenth-dynasty queen who had usurped his throne and declared herself Pharoah (Quirke and Spencer 1992). In ancient Rome, the 'damnatio memoriae' (condemnation of memory) punished tyrants, traitors, and state enemies; their images and any inscriptions mentioning them were destroyed. After the fall of Baghdad in 2003, the statue of Saddam Hussein in Firdos square was toppled, decapitated, jumped, and stomped on, and then dragged through town and beaten with shoes. The physical indignities enacted on the statue, which served as a surrogate for Hussein's own body, allowed Iraqis to express their anger at their treatment by his regime.

Changes in religious belief often lead to iconoclasm (the rejection or destruction of religious images as heretical). As Christianity spread across Europe, many temples and their contents were destroyed or converted to churches to demonstrate the vanquishing power of the new God. In areas that later came under Muslim rule, these same churches were converted to mosques. For Hagia Sophia in Istanbul, this meant that the iconostasis, altar, ambo, and baptistery were removed, figural mosaics showing Christ, Mary, and saints and angels were plastered over and a minbar, mihrab, and minarets were added. When Turkey embraced secular governance in the 20th century, the plaster was removed, and the mosaics revealed again. During the Reformation, protestants destroyed or damaged many Catholic statues, paintings, and books that they felt were idolatrous. Often this damage corresponded to existing corporal punishments for crimes (Graves 2008).

Occasionally, wars throw up icons such as the bombed shell of Coventry Cathedral or the Genbaku Dome in Hiroshima, which are preserved to remind subsequent generations of the destructive power of wars. Such monuments are rare; typically, the debris from conflict is swept away. Humanity seeks to tidy away its messes. Order imparts a sense of inevitability to the outcome, but it also wipes away trauma; therefore, preserving damage can be an important element in acknowledging historical events.

The fact that heritage is never universally shared makes it vulnerable. Dominant groups may valorise and protect their heritage, while subordinate groups may lack the power to advocate for theirs. Similarly, the sense that something is not one's own heritage (and therefore not relevant or valuable to one's identity) may lead to acquiescence to, or participation in, its destruction or to the failure to use valuable resources to preserve it.

Authenticity

Authenticity, value, and preservation are tightly linked. We preserve objects because we believe they are genuine in some way: a 'real example' of a medieval castle or of a painting by Van Gogh. What makes an object authentic is tied to both its tangible aspects (materials and manufacturing techniques) and its intangible aspects (historical, aesthetic, and spiritual values). For example, when we assess the authenticity of a painting, we look for evidence that the paints used and the ways they are handled are consistent with the period in which the artist was working and the style of their work and that the aesthetic qualities of the work accord with those attributed to the artist.

Authenticity is a concept that we deploy unthinkingly in our everyday lives. We speak about things having an authentic look or flavour and we purchase certain brands because they are the 'real thing' as opposed to others which we deem to be counterfeit. Authenticity can seem straight forward and yet in a preservation context it is a problematic and much debated concept (Muñoz Viñas 2005; Gordon *et al.* 2014; Scott 2016). What is the authentic state of an object? Is it the pristine condition it was in when it left its maker's hand? Is it the state it achieves after it has been in use for many years? Or is it the possibly corroded or misshapen state in which we now see it? If we intervene, are we restoring it to a more authentic aesthetic version or acting to stabilise its current state, which may more truthfully reflect its use and history? For objects that have had a long history of use, adaptation, and repair this becomes more difficult to determine. HMS *Victory*, Nelson's flagship at the Battle of Trafalgar, was initially commissioned in 1765 and had several refits prior to playing its part at Trafalgar in 1805. In 1812, it was refitted again and substantially updated. Around this period, it also began a gradual shift from a replaceable warship to the status of 'national icon and tangible memorial to Nelson and Trafalgar' (Wessex Archaeology 2015: 12). A plaque was added to the quarterdeck where Nelson fell and to the cockpit on the orlop deck where he died, and his funeral barge was stored on the ship. Further refits, an early conservation campaign to return it to its 1805 appearance, repairs after the ship was rammed by another ship, bomb damage in the Second World War and a major battle with fungal attack and death watch beetle all followed. This raises the question of how much of what we see today is Nelson's ship? Recent work suggests that much of the lower decks (including the orlop deck), the keel assemblage and elements of the longitudinal bow structure are 18th and early 19th century but that the most visible parts, the hull framing, and upper decks largely post-date 1922 (Wessex Archaeology 2015). Does that make the ship less authentic?

Western tradition places a premium on the authenticity of the materials. Material authenticity is seen as conveying an objective truth to the object that endures long after interpretations have changed. Objects are sometimes viewed as documents that can be unlocked and read through the study of their material constituents (Caple 2006; Watson 2010). The emergence of fields such as conservation science, technical art history, and archaeometry speaks to the importance of these concepts in Western thinking, but it is also reflected in the notion that a key part of the conservator's job is to facilitate the 'legibility' of the object. Other approaches to the relationship between authenticity and preservation exist. In Japan, the Ise Jingū temple and its ancillary shrines are dismantled every 20 years and rebuilt at great cost to exacting historic specifications. The current Ise Jingū temple dates to 2013 and is the 62nd iteration of the temple. The rebuilding process celebrates the idea of perpetual renewal, presenting a site that is both new (in material terms) and ancient (in terms of form). Additionally, it celebrates the perpetuation of craft knowledge and the transmission of these skills – the 20-year renewal cycle being shorter than one generation (Sand 2015) – in a way that is echoed by the tradition of designating craftsmen who epitomise perfection in a craft idiom as 'living national treasures'. Both these practices root authenticity not in materials but rather in form, craft skills, and other intangible criteria.

The Nara Conference held in 1994, examined the question of authenticity and resulted in the production of the Nara Document on Authenticity (ICOMOS 1994). Although it has not resolved all the issues surrounding authenticity, it is widely seen as expanding the definition of the term and of opening the heritage field to a more multicultural and multivocal approach.

Preservation Mechanisms: Legislation, Preservation in Situ, and Collection

Once the values associated with an item of cultural heritage (building, object, landscape) are established, it is common to begin to think about how they can be preserved. This typically occurs through one of three mechanisms – legislation, preservation in situ, or acquisition – which one is chosen often depends on the size of the object and its location.

Legislation

Laws have been developed by different societies over time to protect things that are valued, from human life to heritage. Initially, significant monuments and landscape features valued by a community may become the focus of traditions, which protect them from harm. Children raised within the community learn the traditions and thus this social protection effectively preserves the heritage. Aurel Stein, in his 1903 accounts of his journey through central Asia to China, recorded an example of such social valuation:

> Shami Sope, a withered old man of about ninety, had heard from his father and grandfather, who had both died at a great age, that the little mound had ever been respected by the folk of Somiya as a hallowed spot not to be touched by the plough share. Some unknown spirit is supposed to have sat upon this spot, and evil would befall those who should touch the ground. The name of the saint is forgotten … But the people of Somiya never pass without saying a prayer.
>
> (Stein 1903: 265–266)

As societies grow both in terms of population size and geographic range and an increasing number of individuals are unaware of local tradition, laws are created to provide protection. In Europe, heritage legislation principally developed in the 19th century (Cleere 1984; Caple 2016: 144–156). Such laws were often created as new nations were establishing themselves and seeking not only to assert a claim to the land but also to define membership within the nation. Greek legislation passed in 1834, only four years after Greece won independence from Turkey, succinctly expresses these nationalistic aims 'all objects of antiquity in Greece being the productions of the ancestors of the Hellenic people, are regarded as the common national procession of all Hellenes' (Cleere 2002). Heritage legislation was not always popular since it was perceived as curtailing the rights of the landowners. In the case of England and Wales, where a land-owning class controlled the government, the first heritage protection was the 1882 Ancient Monuments Protection Act, which was voluntary for landowners with ancient monuments on their land (Breeze 1993; Champion 1996). Only when centralised governments became stronger in the 20th century and the threats to a nation's heritage were more immediate was more powerful protective legislation passed. In England and Wales, the 1913 Ancient Monument Consolidation and Amendment Act, was passed shortly after Tattershall Castle – 'the finest piece of medieval brickwork in England' (Pettifer 2002: 145) – was sold with the intention to demolish parts of it and rebuild them in the United States (Thompson 2006: 49–59; Thurley 2013: 72–75). Even then, the legislation only protected specific ancient sites, which were added to a national schedule or list; the ground and its contents continued to belong to the landowner. This practice continues today and explains why activities such as metal detecting flourish in Britain, where private landowners possess all the rights to the land and everything found on it but are often illegal in countries where the state maintains a claim of ownership on resources, including archaeological ones (Thomas and Stone 2009).

As awareness of the archaeological past grew in the late 20th century, and its loss due to development (i.e. housing, infrastructure, industrial cf. Coles 1987; Darvill and Fulton 1998) became a source of public concern, governments faced an increasing (and often unwelcome) financial burden to excavate and protect the archaeological past. At the same time the wider social principle of 'the polluter pays' was becoming established. Applied to heritage protection, this principle establishes that archaeological remains have a value to society and if threatened with disturbance (pollution) then the developer (the polluter) should avoid them, if possible. If it is not possible to avoid them, the developer must compensate society by creating a detailed record, which is normally achieved through funding the excavation of the site, the study of the finds and the publication of the results. This approach became enshrined in legislation as early as 1974 in the United States (Archaeological Resources Protection Act). In Europe, the 1992 European Convention on the Protection of the Archaeological Heritage (Valletta) required all countries in the European Union to develop relevant legislation (Willems 2008). These developments led to the establishment of the commercial archaeology industry (also known as CRM – Cultural Resource Management). This industry unearths millions of artefacts every year that are subsequently deposited in museums.

Legal protections have theoretically resulted in millions of artefacts still buried in the soil being preserved in situ and protected by law from damage and loss by anything other than a detailed and approved archaeological excavation, although instances of illegal disturbance and looting occur in most countries. Buried artefacts typically decay extremely slowly since they near equilibrium with the surrounding environment; however, there is still a measurable loss of artefacts (Rimmer and Caple 2008). Practices such as aerating the soil through ploughing and the use of fertilisers are believed to increase the corrosion rates of buried metal artefacts (Fjaestad *et al.* 1998; Galliano *et al.* 1998; Pollard *et al.* 2004, 2007). For objects preserved in waterlogged, desiccated, or frozen conditions any disturbance of the burial environment, such as drainage, irrigation, or global warming, will lead to active decay of the preserved remains (High *et al.* 2016, 2018; Peacock and Callanan 2018). Legislation whilst protecting sites and their buried objects from deliberate damage by humans has no jurisdiction over subsoil chemistry and millions of objects may be lost, even from familiar ancient monuments, without ever having been seen.

Preservation in Situ[4]

Most buildings are preserved in situ[5] (Figure 1.4). This occurs for practical reasons, such as size and cost, but also because the context of a building remains crucial to understanding its role. To protect standing structures as well as excavated archaeological ruins, a range of options are available:

- Standing buildings (with a roof on) are costly to care for in the long term, consequently the building must either have an appropriate continued use or an organisation committed to its care. Some form of restoration and adaption is usually required. Considerable efforts are often taken to accurately preserve the historic character of such structures.
- Ruins are normally conserved to a state where they can survive with low-level maintenance; for example, ensuring that they are physically stable and can shed water effectively, that cracks and other faults are corrected, and that vegetation is removed. Attempts to use shelters over ruins can be intrusive and are often unsuccessful in the longer term, though they may facilitate excavation (Atalay *et al.* 2010; Caple 2016: 439–449).
- Reburial takes advantage of the fact that decay rates under the soil are often much lower than those above ground.[6] Although it is desirable to make excavated remains accessible, often heritage authorities must choose between an active, and potentially costly, conservation and restoration programme and preservation, which may be most effectively achieved through reburial. The location of the site, its accessibility, its durability, and its significance as well as the potential costs of conserving the remains play into this. Reburial is standard practice on many archaeological sites, especially those with waterlogged deposits. Recognising that cycles of decay, conservation, and exposure can cause damage and that upkeep is costly to maintain, some long-exposed sites have been reburied or partially reburied (Ford *et al.* 2004). Recent decades have seen increased efforts to monitor and even control burial conditions (Corfield *et al.* 1998; Williams 2012; Caple 2016: 383–395; Case Study 1B: The Laetoli footprints).

Successful preservation in situ is always supported by legislation, which creates a legal framework that supports the protection of the site from deliberate human damage. This may occur at an international level (through conventions such as the World Heritage Convention), at a national level (through national laws) or at a local level

	Approach	Sites
Preserved	Sites remain unexcavated	Unexcavated sections of Pompeii, Italy Tomb of Emperor Qin Shi Huang, China
	Reburial; backfilled sites after excavation	Rose Theatre, London San Diego Presidio, California, USA
	Reburial; backfilled sites occasionally unearthed	Woodchester, Gloucester, England Rock art sites in Scandinavia
	Above ground ruins left 'as found'	Wigmore Castle (most of it)
	Temporarily protected (roofed) site 'as found'	Flag Fen
Part Preserved, Part Restored	Stabilised ruins	Machu Picchu, Peru Coventry Cathedral (Medieval), England Mycenae, Greece
	Stabilised ruin with associated museum	Paestum, Italy Skara Brae, Orkneys, Scotland
	Stabilised ruin with (1) projected outline of the original building (2) small section restored	Benjamin Franklin's House, Philadelphia (1) Knossos, Crete (2) Great Zimbabwe(2) Pompeii (excavated), Italy (2)
	Stabilised ruin beneath roof or substantial shelter	Casa Grande, Arizona, USA Fishbourne Palace, Sussex, England Villa Romana del Casale, Piazza Armerina, Sicily Çatalhöyük, Turkey
	Ruins incorporated within later structure (1) or garden /landscape (2).	Theatre of Marcellus, Rome (1) Roman Baths, Bath, England (1) Fountains Abbey (Medieval) & Studley Royal (18thcentury)(2)
	Anastylosis	Library at Ephesus, Turkey Temple of Trajan, Pergamon, Turkey
Restored	Restored Ruins	Cardiff Castle & Castell Coch, South Wales. Temple of Hatshepsut, Deir el Bahari, Egypt Colonia Ulpia Traiana, Xanten, Germany
	Relocated Buildings	Abu Simbel, Egypt Temple of Dendur, Metropolitan Museum, New York Skansen, Stockholm
	Reconstructions	Colonial Williamsburg, Virginia, USA Biskupin, Poland Stari Most (bridge at Mostar), Bosnia Herzegovina

Figure 1.4 Examples of different approaches to preserving and displaying ancient remains, based on Stubs 1995. Chris Caple.

(through city or county ordinances). Preservation in situ is not always a viable option. If a building is at risk, it may be necessary to relocate it as was the case between 1964 and 1969 when the Temple of Abu Simbel was relocated to save it from the construction of the Aswan High Dam.

Collection

Portable objects, such as paintings, statuary, furnishings, and personal adornments, are typically acquired and displayed in personal collections or in those of museums. The physical manifestation of collecting has formed the basis of most of the world's museum collections and has consequently been defined and studied by many authors (Belk 1994; Pearce 1994; Pomian 1994; Belk 2014). Motives that have contributed to the creation of collections include:

- *Belief:* Many sacred sites retained collections of artefacts, often in a secure location or treasury, that embodied important tenets of the faith (i.e. relics) as well as objects that were also offered to the shrine as dedicatory items or expressions of the congregant's beliefs. Examples include the Athenian treasury at Delphi constructed to hold votive offerings to the God Apollo, the Toji treasure house in Kyoto, which houses the collection of the widow of the Japanese emperor Shomu (724–756 AD), the shrine at Mashhad, which houses objects related to the Muslim martyr Alī al-Ridā, (765–818 AD) and the treasury at Aachen Cathedral (Lepie and Minkenberg 2013). Other beliefs, such as the importance of civic engagement and democratic representation, have led to the creation of collections and museums (The Colonial Williamsburg Foundation, Williamsburg VA).
- *Control:* When the past can be collected and understood, it can be used to provide explanations. Since the past gives rise to the present, being able to explain the past makes it possible to explain, influence, and justify the present. In the 19th century many emerging states established national museums, a trend which has continued into the 20th century. Such national collections not only highlighted the origins of nations through their collections, but also frequently laid claims to territories both at home and abroad through their collections and served as a form of propaganda for the country. More recently, the reliance of many modern museums on donor funds has raised questions about who controls the ways collections are used and what stories are told about the past (Kilian 2002). To quote George Orwell, 'Who controls the past, controls the future; who controls the present controls the past' (Orwell 1949).
- *Curiosity:* Gaudy, symmetrical, outsized, and interesting items attract attention. Collections of the unusual formed the basis for the 'cabinets of curiosities' created in the 16th and 17th centuries, which often mixed myths with reality incorporating tokens of mythical creatures such as mermaids, unicorns, and barnacle geese. These collections established by Europe aristocrats and wealthy merchants were designed to fascinate themselves and their visitors. Collectors, including Ole Worm (1588–1654) of Copenhagen, Athanasius Kircher (1602–1680) in Rome, and the Tradescants in England (1570–1662), studied their collections as a means of explaining the world, publishing books, and opening museums to share their curiosities with others. After their deaths, many of these collectors bequeathed their collections to the towns, learned societies or universities, which were springing up around Europe. A number of these private collections eventually formed the basis of national museums. For example, Worm's collection become part of the Danish Royal Collection (Figure 1.5) and later the Danish National Collection.

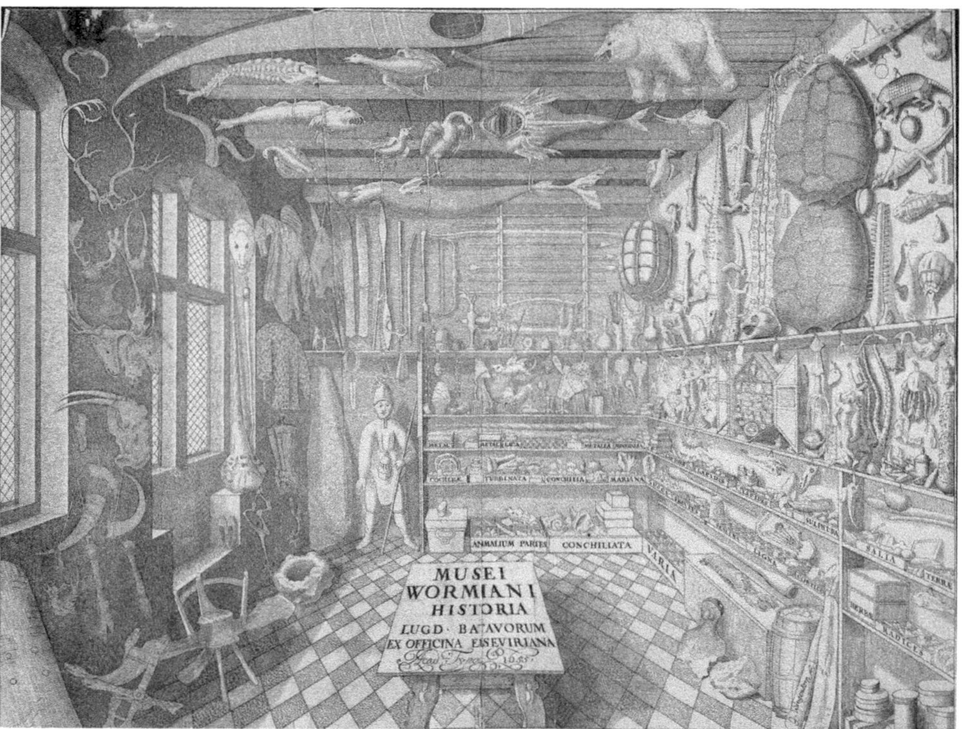

Figure 1.5 Frontispiece of Museum Wormianum (pub) 1655. The assortment of objects exhibited illustrates the eccentric nature of cabinets of curiosities. ©Trustees of the British Museum.

- *Understanding* (scholarship): Objects are collected to study what they are, how they relate to one another and to the world at large, as well as so that they can be ordered and classified. In the sixth century BC, Ennigaldi-Nanna, the daughter of Mesopotamian king Nabonidus, created a collection of ancient objects, together with inscribed clay cylinders which may be interpreted as labels, in a building which has been interpreted as a school or museum, the first example of a collection used to educate others (Remer 2020). In the 18th and 19th centuries, there was an interest in categorising natural-history specimens, resulting in the foundation of many modern sciences such as geology, zoology, and botany. Concepts such as evolution, genetics, natural selection, adaptation, stratigraphy emerged to explain the observed differences. In the latter half of the 19th and early 20th century, museums began to open as places of self-education. Natural history, ethnographic and science museums, and museums/galleries devoted to 'good' art and taste (such as the Victoria and Albert) were seen as a means of educating the populace.
- *Nostalgia:* The notion that the past is fleeting and that if it is not captured and frozen, important lessons will be lost is a powerful motivator for collecting objects from the recent past. Nostalgia for a 'lost' rural way of life led to the founding of the first open air museum at Skansen in Sweden in 1891. Similarly, as industries close, there is often a campaign to preserve worksites and materials associated with them.

For example, the Historic Whaling Station in Albany preserves the last Australian shore-based whale processing factory and a whale chasing ship, while at the Big Pit National Coal Mining Museum in Blaenavon, Wales 'the tunnels and buildings that once echoed to the sound of the miners now enjoy the sound of the footsteps and chatter of visitors from all over the world' (Big Pit National Coal Museum n.d.). The goal of such collections is to elicit an empathetic and emotional response from the museum visitor as well as impart an understanding of a past way of life. They seek to convince the viewer that these aspects of the past are important and part of a communal heritage. In 1858, the Mount Vernon Ladies' Association (MVLA) purchased and began restoring George Washington's home. This effort like many other preservation initiatives was characterised by a form of 'personalism' that stressed the idea that human attachments (both material and immaterial) were worth noting and nurturing, and that they provided intimate links to the past that could be used to educate (Lindgren 1996).

- *Aesthetics:* Works of art on canvas or paper, sculpture, glass, ceramics, textiles, photographs, and buildings are all more likely to be saved if they appeal to the aesthetic sensibilities of the collector. In some instances, such as the Victoria and Albert Museum, collections of 'good art' were amassed explicitly to demonstrate to the masses what 'good taste' was.
- *Monetary worth:* The value of objects that are rare, well-known, beautiful, or associated with famous/infamous people, events, and places is expressed in financial terms. Today many objects are collected, wholly or in part, because of their financial value. Some are seen as investments and retained in bank vaults. The works of an artist invariably rise in value and are more assiduously collected after their death. The emergence of a 'valuable' past has given rise to fakes and forgeries (Jones 1990).
- *Memories:* Retaining an object may remind someone of another person or of a particular aspect of their personal past and often accounts for the short-term survival of an object, often something small and of little monetary value (e.g. a grandfather's medals, a toy from childhood or a souvenir from a holiday).
- *Age:* Places and objects are valued for their age. Initially, age veneration may have been tied to ancestor cults (Schwartz 2013). Some ancient objects, such as Roman coins found in Saxon graves, were retained as personal mementoes and apotropaic charms (Knight *et al.* 2019). That something has survived a long time suggests that it is valuable, powerful, different from the norm, and important to others. In 1819, the artist Charles Willson Peale painted Yarrow Mamout's portrait because Peale believed Mamout was 140 years old, and Peale was seeking to understand the personal traits that supported long life.

Collections are rarely built through one motivation alone and two or more may be at play during the acquisition of a given object.[7] What frequently unites even disparate collections is the desire to own and display the materials in them.

Biases in Collections and Displays

In placing objects of the past on view, curators and collectors seek to convey their own understanding (beliefs) regarding the past (or present). The authenticity of objects and the fact that they are regarded as 'the real thing' makes such displays convincing. Exhibits are frequently regarded as educational and impartial depending on the extent to which the viewer subscribes to the viewpoint of the display. However, various elements of the display process and of the survival of objects can introduce dissonances and biases. For each item that has survived to be collected, many more have been lost to natural decay processes or to human actions (including but not limited to iconoclasm). As a result, what we see may not represent all that was made. A number of factors have helped to bias the shape of collections:

- *Decay bias:* Some materials such as wood, textile and leather decay quickly and as a result are under-represented in collections. Other materials such as ceramic, stone, and many metals do not decay as quickly and survive much better; consequently, they are over-represented in museum collections. Rare survivals in waterlogged or frozen conditions demonstrate that the majority of objects in the Stone Age and Bronze Age were organic and yet museums are filled with tens of thousands of stone and bronze axe heads and only a handful of wooden items.
- *Collection bias:* Collectors often preferentially acquire and study small decorative objects or high-value items such as paintings or jewellery. Larger, more mundane, or undecorated objects are frequently under-studied and consequently rarely collected. Similarly, the desire to 'complete' a set and acquire an example of each item of a type (for example coins or stamps) may motivate some collectors (and curators) leading to more complete holdings in those areas. This can lead to an unrepresentative overvaluing or undervaluing of portions of a collection.
- *Temporal bias:* The more distant a society is in terms of time or social geography (different social systems) from the modern period, the less likely we are to be able to correctly explain how and why the objects were used. This may make collecting an item less desirable and impact its long-term retention and survival. Our perception of the distant past is primarily through fragmentary archaeological remains that must be interpreted through written or pictorial records. Therefore, the truth about the past is relative; some interpretations are considered more accurate than others. It is obvious that the less functional an object, the older it is and the more numerous the phases of use and reuse, the greater the difficulty in accurately interpreting it. Thus, prehistoric monuments or ritual objects that were used for a long time will be particularly hard to accurately interpret (Chippindale 1983).
- *Social bias:* Collecting cannot be easily divorced from its social context. Collectors, especially publicly funded institutions, may avoid acquiring and/or displaying objects that are blasphemous, racist, or pornographic, although as with many things the definition of these terms depends on the beholder. An excellent example is the controversy over Robert Mapplethorpe's photographs in the late 1980s. For some, the works were beautiful celebrations of the human body, others deemed them obscene. Deaccessioning policies, the deliberate targeting of elements of collections because they run counter to beliefs, and repatriation and restitution all have the potential to alter the face of collections. Again, the context is dependent on one's viewpoint. While repatriation of objects to indigenous communities has been welcomed by many as an indicator of respect and inclusion

(Ford *et al.* 2004; Turnbull and Pickering 2010; Cuno 2012; Pouliot *et al.* 2017), it has been critiqued by others for curtailing scholarly access (Hunt 2001).

- *Presentation biases:* Displaying many similar objects is perceived to imply that minor variations between similar objects are important. A single object displayed alone invites the visitor to see the object as a work of art with meaning in its form, colour, and decoration. When an object is displayed as part of a diorama the object is seen as important in terms of its function and its association with the objects around it, but such displays often group disparate objects together and may have no relation to the actual or known history of the object. Similarly, the limited space on museum labels or explanation panels necessitates the selection of some information about the object and the omission of other aspects. What is exhibited (and how) depends on the purpose of the display, museum policy, the personal bias of the curator, the state of knowledge, what is fashionable in museum/academic circles at that time and what is socially acceptable to display in a public place.

The public views museum objects selectively and fit them into existing knowledge frameworks (Chapter 10). Consequently, they frequently ignore objects and information that do not fit into their existing pattern of understanding. They literally cannot make sense of them, having no hooks on which to hang this information. Dioramas, didactic panels, videos, and other tools that integrate the new object or information with their existing knowledge help to bridge this gap and build a more holistic view of the past. The more complete and detailed people's views of the past the easier they find it to add existing information and thus to 'decode' museums (Kavanagh 1990; Pearce 1990) and ancient monuments.

Since heritage is linked to memory, the past on view is the past that we feel is important to remember but it is important to note that our notions of what is important change with time. Thus, objects are constantly re-examined and new information and meaning ascribed to them. In 1919, a statue of Lincoln was given to the citizens of Manchester in England by an American, Charles Phelps Taft. The statue celebrated the fact that, after receiving a letter from Lincoln 'to the Working Men of Lancashire' during the American Civil War, they had refused to spin cotton from the Confederate South. In 1986, the statue was refurbished, and the dedicatory inscription was altered to read 'to the Working People of Manchester' Lowenthal 1996). This modification reflects the political correctness of the late 20th century, Lincoln's words have been rewritten and there is a danger that they may be mistaken for the original. John Bintliff (1988) pessimistically noted that such actions put us at risk of 'self-projection onto an essentially unknowable past'.

To preserve the past successfully, we must be able to successfully define why it is valued, be cognizant of the factors that have influenced its survival to date and look critically at our motivations for preserving and displaying it. We should also be aware of how our actions may transform the object and potentially act against our aims. In the next chapters we will discuss the way in which conservation emerged as a profession, look at its nature and ethics and then examine key actions that conservators undertake before ultimately considering some of the emerging challenges that conservators face in the 21st century.

1A Case Study: The De Walden Antique Helmet Collection (Wollny 1996)

Thomas Evelyn Scott Ellis, 8th Baron Howard de Walden and 4th Baron Seaford, came of age in 1901 and inherited his full titles and estates, making him a wealthy young man. Subsequently, he built up a considerable collection of weapons and armour with a particular emphasis on the classical period. There is little information about how he acquired the objects, which he initially displayed at his home in Kilmarnock and after 1911 in Chirk Castle in Wales, where he lived for most of his life. After his death in 1946, his collection passed to the National Museum of Wales. He wrote to the director of the museum, Sir Cyril Fox, 'there are certain pieces you may not wish to have, such as a few oriental specimens and several specimens of doubtful authenticity'. We do not know how many objects were held back on these grounds, but the bulk of the collection was deposited with the museum. In 1990, Kate Hunter, the museum's antiquities conservator, surveyed and repackaged the 136 objects of the collection. Amongst the most notable pieces were a number of copper alloy helmets that appeared to be fragile and either corroded or patinated and there was evidence that many had been crudely 'restored'. Eight of the helmets were recorded and investigated in greater detail over the next decade (Figure 1.6).

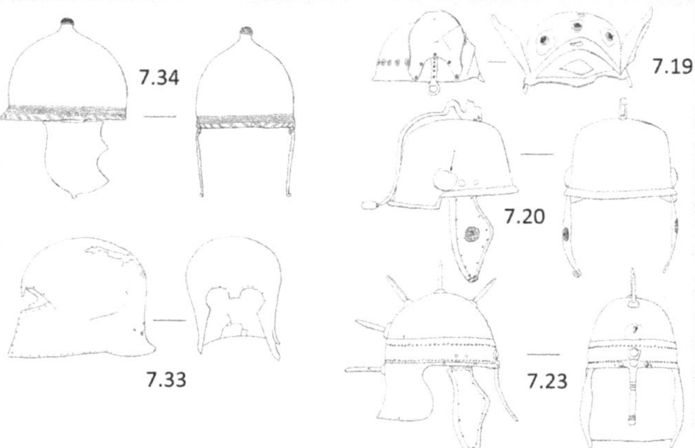

Figure 1.6 Helmets from the De-Walden Collection in the National Museum of Wales. National Museum of Wales. Redrawn by Yvonne Beadnell from Wollny 1996.

De Walden Collection No. 7.33

This helmet has the rounded open-fronted skull form of the Corinthian helmet frequently depicted as worn by Greek hippolytes. The nose-guard is broken off, as is the front of the left-side protective neck guard. Cracks on the top of the helmet had been crudely repaired with a cement-like gap filler and internal supports of adhered textile and metal were visible. X-radiographs indicated that the helmet had been formed from a single piece of metal. Many small indentations, hammer marks from extensive shaping, were visible. Around the eyeholes and the lower edge of the helmet were numerous regular small holes for the attachment of internal and edge padding. Metal analysis revealed that the helmet was made of a typical ancient bronze with 8.6% tin. Fourier transform infra-red (FTIR) spectroscopy analysis confirmed the presence of normal copper-alloy corrosion products principally malachite plus traces of chrysocolla. Chrysocolla (copper silicate) is rarely seen in copper corrosion crusts but is a commonly used artist's green pigment. This object is almost certainly an original Greek helmet with 19th-century restorations.

De Walden Collection No. 7.34

This helmet, which has a roll-formed rim and cheek pieces, has a top that curves upward to form a knop in a form identical to that used by early Republican Roman legions circa 400 BC. X-radiographs showed the slight irregularities of hammer marks present on the main part of the helmet, which was formed from a single piece of metal. The cheek pieces have many small bubbles apparent in the metal suggesting they were manufactured through a poor-quality casting process. Metal analysis revealed that the helmet was made of a typical bronze with 7.7% tin, the cheek pieces of a leaded tin bronze containing 5% tin and 5% lead – a typical casting metal composition with a raised lead content. The form, methods of manufacture and composition of this object clearly suggest that it is an original unrestored object.

De Walden Collection No. 7.19

This helmet has an inverted shallow bowl with a pair of ears or wings riveted to the side. No comparable examples are in any other museum collections. The metal is thin (0.55 mm thick) and the top of the helmet is cracked with small pieces of the metal missing. The metal was analysed revealing that it was composed of a 35% zinc brass. The Romans, the first civilisation to make extensive use of brass, only achieved brass with zinc contents of up to 30% due to technical limitations in the cementation process (Craddock 1978). Brass with 35% zinc was only seen in Europe after the 17th century (Pollard and Heron 1996); therefore, this object is a modern (19th century) forgery.

De Walden Collection No. 7.20

This helmet consists of an inverted basin with deep sides. On top of the helmet is a damaged sinuous figure forming a crest probably initially in the form of a hippocamp or centaur and curved cheek pieces, attached through hinges, to the sides of the helmet. This form of helmet is not readily paralleled by any known ancient examples. X-radiographs revealed that the helmet was of unusually poor construction formed by a shallow bowl soldered to a ring of sheet metal to for the sides. Analysis of the metal revealed that it was composed of a 5–10% tin bronze, consistent with ancient metal. Analysis of the corrosion products using FTIR identified copper acetate (verdigris) as one of the principal minerals present. This is an extremely rare corrosion product, which hardly ever appears in normal burial conditions. Since it can form very quickly, in a matter of weeks or months and looks like many more natural slowly formed corrosion products such as malachite, it is frequently deliberately created by forgers to make new objects appear corroded and ancient. Therefore, it appears likely that this object is either a modern (19th century) forgery or a pastiche, composed of several pieces of ancient metal, which have been formed into a helmet and re-corroded.

De Walden Collection No. 7.23

This helmet forms an inverted basin, which curves down the back of the head with a line of five, originally six, square-section spikes with domed bases protruding 50–60 mm from the central line of the helmet. There is a thin nose-guard and hinged cheek pieces attached to the sides. Again, no comparable example of this helmet can be found from antiquity. X-radiography revealed that the helmet was formed from a shallow cap with a series of four bands of metal soldered to each other to form the deep sinuously contoured sides of the helmet (Figure 1.7). The whole helmet had also been split along the crest, presumably to assist in inserting the spikes and then soldered back together. This helmet, formed of ten separate plates soldered together, was an extremely weak form of construction, which would have provided little practical protection for the wearer. Analysis of the metal composition revealed that the sheet metal of the helmet was low tin bronze, and the spikes were of leaded bronze, compositions consistent with an antique origin. Based on the unusual form and weak construction the helmet is probably a modern forgery or a pastiche using ancient pieces of metal.

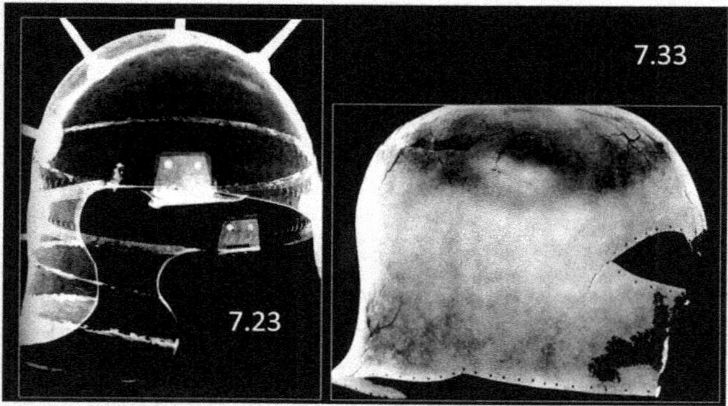

Figure 1.7 X-radiograph of two of the De Walden Helmets in the National Museum of Wales. National Museum of Wales. From Wollny (1996).

Lord Howard de Walden, a collector fascinated with the study of arms and armour, amassed a varied collection of ancient helmets while recognising that some items may not have been original. Modern analytical techniques, a clear set of comparable analyses to known ancient artefacts and an understanding of ancient technology and the practices of 19th century forgers have enabled modern investigators to reach a judgement about which objects in this collection are fakes (7.19), which are probable fakes or pastiches (7.20, 7.23), and which are likely to be genuine (7.33, 7.34). This same set of knowledge and skills has enabled other helmets to be authenticated, such as the Yarm helmet, which was felt to be of dubious origins when it entered a museum collection and later shown to be a genuine Viking helmet and only the second to be excavated (Caple 2020b).

Lord Howard de Walden's collected some original objects from antiquity, but his interest and wealth also unintentionally promoted a market in fake artefacts. Forgeries, present even in antiquity (Jones 1990), are carefully executed to meet the tastes and expectations of potential purchasers. De Walden's fakes reflect rather romantic Victorian notions of the past with winged helmets (7.19) and helmets with cruel and vicious spikes (7.23). When collecting, cataloguing, researching, preserving, or explaining the past it is always necessary to investigate objects closely to ensure that an accurate picture of the past (history) is drawn rather than a modern-day fiction.

1B Case Study: The Laetoli footprints (Agnew and Levin 1996; Demas *et al.* 1996; Agnew and Demas 1998)

In 1978–1979, Dr Mary Leakey uncovered footprints left by three australopithecines in the bedrock at Laetoli in Tanzania. The footprints are 3.6–3.75 million years old and constitute the earliest and most important evidence of bipedalism in early hominids. The tracks had been made, together with those of numerous animals, in wet volcanic ash that had then set hard so preserving the impressions. The footprints run in two tracks for over 27 m and contain over 70 individual prints. The principal track was made by a large individual with a stride length of 0.87 m, a smaller individual walked beside it. A third individual followed the pair, walking in the footprints of the large individual. These impressions showed that the feet which made them had raised arches, rounded heels, pronounced balls, forward pointing big toes and were thus very similar to a modern human foot. They demonstrate that bipedalism was almost fully evolved in early hominids of this date and was one of the earliest human traits to develop (Renfrew and Bahn 1991). Evidence of movement and soft-tissue form are extremely rare in the study of early hominids, which is normally confined to the study of small scraps of fossilised bone.

After the footprints had been excavated, fully recorded and casts had been taken, the tracks were covered over with loose soil capped with a layer of boulders to prevent damage to the site by the feet of cattle and elephants. In 1992, the condition of the trackway was reassessed. The boulders had created shade and a condensation trap, which had led to the growth of acacia trees whose roots were now found to be damaging the footprints.

In 1992, the options for preserving the footprints were considered:

- It would be very costly to lift and transport all the footprints for storage or display, in a museum. There was no museum big enough in Tanzania and thus a new one would need to be built.
- As part of the cultural heritage of the people of Tanzania, removal outside the country would neither be permitted nor was it desirable.
- The rock which contains the footprints is friable, so lifting and transporting it would create a substantial risk to the well-being of these fossils.
- Creating open shelters to protect remains in situ has been shown not to work well and to consume scarce resources (Agnew 2001). Exposed or sheltered sites degrade very quickly.
- Laetoli is very remote and very few visitors are likely to come and see the footprints if they were on open display or in a museum at Laetoli.
- The footprints in situ have a context and associated information, such as the animal prints, the volcano that deposited the ash and the surrounding natural landscape. This would be lost should the trackway be moved.
- The conservation of the trackway should be a viable solution that could be maintained by the existing authorities and people of Tanzania.
- Burial had proved effective preservation for the footprints for over 3 million years.

After considering these options, the best and most ethical solution was felt to be reburial since it would preserve the footprints in situ ensuring that they retained their context and could be investigated in future if necessary (Figure 1.8).

In 1995, Site G, the southern end of the trackway, which contained a 6.8-m-long stretch of the best (29) footprints, was re-excavated. Root damage from the acacia trees was fortunately limited to three of the footprints. The roots were carefully cut away and the friable tuff consolidated with an acrylic colloidal dispersion (Acrysol WS-24). The root voids were filled with Acrysol WS-24 and fumed silica. Any remaining root material was injected with a biocide and insecticide, both to kill off the root and remove any problem of potential infestation by termites. The footprints were recorded in great detail and fully resurveyed. They are no longer as clearly visible as they were originally, because of the exposure upon excavation and the use of Bedacryl (polybutyral methacrylate) which was applied to consolidate the surface of the footprints prior to making casts of the footprints in 1979. This polymer could not be easily removed without potentially damaging the footprints, so it was left in place.

To preserve the site, it was provided with a covering which consisted of:

- Sand from the Kakesio and Garusi rivers, in which the geotextile and biobarrier layers were seated. The sand was sieved so it contained no seeds or rocks and has similar chemical and physical properties to the volcanic rock so there should be no physical stress or chemical exchange between the rock and sand media.

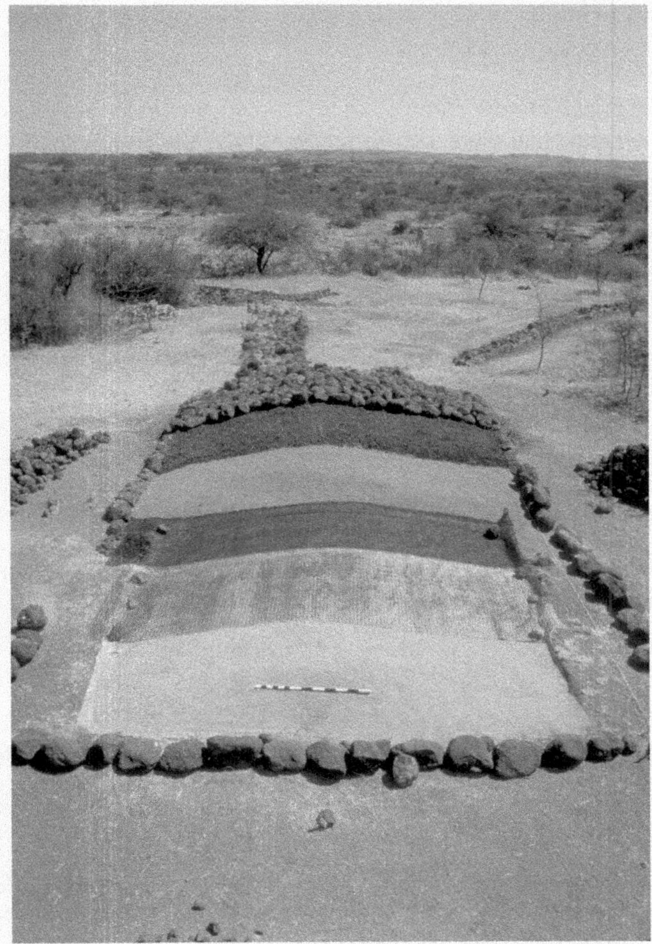

Figure 1.8 The trackway of 3.6-million-year-old human footprints, Laetoli, Tanzania, preserved beneath layers of sand, geotextile, biobarrier, Enkamat, local soil and rocks. © 1995 J. Paul Getty Trust (Photo: Neville Agnew).

- *Geotextile:* A water-permeable long-lasting polypropylene textile to deflect any future root growth. The geotextile marks the footprint horizon and protects the friable rock and sand beneath.
- *Biobarrier:* A polypropylene geotextile that has nodules that slowly release a long-acting root-growth inhibitor, 'Trifluralin', which will stop root growth but not kill off plants and is largely insoluble so it will not wash away (two layers).
- *'Enkamat':* A tough erosion-control matting to ensure that the sand was not lost.
- Local soil that was mounded up over the sand and geotextiles at an angle of 10–14 ° to deflect water away from the trackway.
- A substantial layer of lava boulders to provide physical protection from human and animal erosion.

These protection procedures were repeated in 1996 over the northern section of the hominid trackway. In addition:

- Banks of laval boulders were constructed to divert any rainwater run-off away from the site, so ensuring that there was no erosion of the site by running water.
- A committee of Tanzanian political representatives, national heritage officials and international experts was established to focus attention on the site and ensure that there is a mechanism for getting national and international assistance to the site if it is required.
- Locals were employed to maintain the site, both in terms of providing security and annually removing tree seedlings to limit any future damage to the site. Similar local-management agreements have become a feature of many of the successful arrangements for preserving sites throughout the world.
- The site was ceremonially adopted by the local Masai tribes as a sacred site. This raised its prominence and meaning to present day inhabitants of the area.

It is believed that this multi-pronged strategy, involving both technical measures and site management, will be the most likely chance of preserving the tracks for future generations. Conservation can be seen to be working at numerous different levels at this site.

Notes

1 Episodes are available for download as podcasts at https://www.bbc.co.uk/programmes/b00nrtd2/episodes/downloads. Accessed 5/28/2022.
2 Preservation can be defined as 'The protection of cultural property through activities that minimise chemical and physical deterioration and damage and that prevent loss of informational content. The primary goal of preservation is to prolong the existence of cultural property' (AIC (American Institute of Conservation) n.d.). As such it encompasses a wide range of activities, including, but not limited, to legislation, physical protection, and conservation.
3 For a fuller description of the biographies and changing values associated with the sarsens at Avebury from their use as sharpening stones prior to their erection to their deliberate burial in the medieval period; see Gillings and Pollard (1999).
4 This is a large topic with its own extensive body of literature covering topics such as building conservation (Jokileto 1999; Ashurst 2007) and burial environment monitoring (Corfield *et al.* 1998; Caple 2016) as well as long-term degradation studies (Fjaestad *et al.* 1998; High *et al.* 2016, 2018).
5 Exceptions to this include taking down, relocating, and re-erecting buildings. An early example of this practice was when the Gol stave church was dismantled and reconstructed in (1884–1885) in the open air museum of King Oscar II of Sweden and Norway on the peninsula of Bygdøy, west of Oslo (founded 1881). Many folk museums, open air museums and historical museums, such as St Fagan's National Museum of History in Wales and Historic Deerfield in the United States have adopted similar practices, to preserve not only the buildings but a sense of what the past was like. Individual buildings have also been relocated, such as Agecroft Hall, a Tudor manor relocated from Lancashire, UK, to Richmond, VA. Initially, the relocated house was used as a private home although it now serves as a historic house museum.
6 In a study on the impacts of weathering on archaeological sites, written in 1932, Herdman Cleland observed, 'When Delphi was excavated the archaeologists did a splendid piece of work, judged by their standards. They uncovered every column, every inscription, every carving and foundation stone that nature had so carefully preserved. Everything, in fact, is

exposed and the destructive work of the weather is at a maximum. The interesting notices in small Greek characters which tell of the freeing of the slaves, are on walls where they must inevitably rapidly become illegible … At Carthage not only are the mosaics exposed to the sun, but some of them are the stamping grounds for herds of goats' (Cleland 1932: 169–170).

7 Many rulers acquired and displayed collections to show their wealth, sophistication, erudition, aesthetic taste, and power. These royal collections formed the basis for some of the earliest museums.

2 The History of Conservation

Conservation's Prehistory

Keeping, safeguarding, and repairing objects are not a uniquely modern concern; however, what we now call 'conservation' is a product of the mid-to-late 19th century and the 20th century.[1] To understand how it has developed, it is necessary to look at why and how objects were preserved through history.[2]

Each civilisation collects and cares for the objects it values most highly. The necessities of life in the hunter-gatherer communities of our Palaeolithic and Mesolithic past required that everything had to be carried from one location to another to find and exploit food resources.[3] Function was valued and the few attempts to repair and restore things that have come down to us, such as the Montastruc spear thrower suggest that preserving function was important, although aesthetics or other factors may have played a secondary role (Ward *et al.* 2009). Bitumen repairs on stone and ceramic objects in the Neolithic and Bronze Age suggest similar motivations (Dooijes and Nieuwenhuyse 2009).

By the Greek and Roman Period, aesthetics played an important role in the retention and appreciation of objects, and we begin to see the names of makers (or artists) being associated with their works. Additionally, objects began to serve an educational component. Public displays of art showcased the wealth, authority and exceptional achievements of men who commissioned them. Greek sculpture was valued by the Romans and taken as booty to decorate monuments, serving also as testimonies to the military accomplishments of victorious Roman generals (Kousser 2015). In his *Natural History*, Pliny the Elder cites a reverence for objects of the past as the reason that 'restoration' was undertaken by the Romans on both objects and monuments (Sease 1996). There are also references by both Ancient Greek and Roman writers to the damaging effects of damp, light, and the threat posed by fire and insects (Strong 1973; Caple 2011: 2–5) indicating that the individuals collecting objects were aware of the need to care for them and had some understanding of what we might now term the agents of deterioration.

During the early medieval period, we see tantalising glimpses of preservation efforts tied to the curation of older items, for example, the signature of an Anglo-Saxon metalsmith on a reworked and restored brooch (Penn 2000). There are also continued efforts to combat decay mechanisms, such as the storage of manuscripts in satchels (Case Study 6B: Loch Glashan Satchel). However, functionality continues to be the focus and instances of preservation were balanced with instances of loss as many ancient buildings and structures were dismantled and used as quarries for pre-worked stone.

DOI: 10.4324/9781003009078-2

The Renaissance interest in the Classical world and its art meant that it became fashionable for elite individuals to collect classical statuary and architectural details recovered from excavations at Roman, Etruscan, and Greek sites and to display them in their gardens, private rooms, and public spaces. These pieces were rarely displayed as found, but instead were normally cleaned and often restored. Following the example of Cosimo de Medici in Florence, who employed Donatello to consult on the cleaning and acquisition of his antiquities (Sirèn 1914: 444), Cardinal Andrea della Valle (1463–1534) commissioned the sculptor Lorenzo di Ludovico to complete some of his broken classical marble statues, adding heads, arms, and legs as required. This appears to have set a trend for restoration, Vasari commented in 1550 'antiquities thus restored certainly possess more grace than those mutilated trunks, members without heads or figures in any other way maimed and defective' (Jokilehto 1999: 23). The sculptor Cellini regarded such work as the province of inferior artists, but did in fact undertake it himself, as he records chiselling off the earth and corrosion products covering classical bronze statues (Cellini 1878; Sease 1996). These restorations sought to repair the work and integrate the aesthetic values of the pieces. The sculptors did not know the exact form of the original and often used a certain amount of artistic license in reconstructing the piece, as evidenced by the various designs submitted to the contest to restore *The Laocoön.*

Not all works of art were restored. From the very first some statues, such as the Belvedere Torso of Hercules, were deliberately displayed in the broken state in which they were found (Jokilehto 1999: 24). Artists and sculptors such as Canova, refused to restore the figures carved by Phidias that Lord Elgin removed from the Parthenon, claiming it would be sacrilege to touch them (Podany 1994). This duality of approach, some objects restored, others preserved 'as found', continues to the present day.

The publication of Giorgio Vasari's *Lives of the Most Excellent Painters, Sculptors, and Architects* in 1550, helped to establish the scholarly tradition of art history and connoisseurship that has been considered a mark of education and refined taste in Western European society ever since. This book also introduced the notion that the works of dead artists should have more value than the work of living ones and established the cult of the 'old masters'. Despite an increasing veneration of 'old art' throughout the 18th century, restoration work could still be extensive, and artists of the ability of van Dyck and Sir Joshua Reynolds undertook restoration work (Kirby Talley 1998). The involvement of lesser artists in the process, and the high fees artists often commanded for this work, led to controversy, as did matters of aesthetics. The declaration by the art patron and tastemaker, Sir George Beaumont (1753–1827), that 'a good picture like a good fiddle should be brown' profoundly influenced taste to the extent that works were deliberately varnished with mixtures that would discolour and create a golden haze (Kirby Talley 1998). Artists like Hogarth, who lampooned it in his print *Time Smoking a Painting*, contested this aesthetic but it has remained a dominant one leading to cleaning controversies throughout the 19th Even in the late 20th century, the critique levelled at the conservation of the Sistine Ceiling echoed this idea (Beck and Daley 1996; Case Study 5A).

The 'Three-Legged Stool'

By the late 17th century, the taste for classical Greece and Rome had taken hold in Northern Europe and aristocratic young men were starting to make the Grand Tour to visit Rome and the lands of the Mediterranean, a practice that peaked in the 18th and early 19th centuries. Souvenirs of these travels included ancient statuary, ceramics, and coins as well as paintings. Over time, these objects began to coalesce (along with other more locally excavated objects) into national collections that highlighted both the national identities and learning of their host nations as well as their imperial aspirations. To serve these goals, objects needed to look complete, impressive, and well-maintained. By 1836, the British Museum was employing John Doubleday as a craftsman to clean and repair objects in its collections. Subsequent appointments of George Smith, Robert Sparrow, and W.H. Ready as craftsmen cleaners and repairers of objects in the British Museum were part of a continuing tradition of employing craftsmen-restorers to ensure that the collections were, as specified in the British Museum Act of 1753, 'preserved and maintained, not only for the Inspection and Entertainment of the learned and the curious, but for the general Use and Benefit of the Public' (Watkins 1997: 223). Similar craftsmen-restorer appointments were made at the Ashmolean Museum including G.A. Rowell and W.H. Young (Norman 2001; Schmisseur 2016). However, the names of many such individuals working in similar roles throughout Britain and the rest of the Europe remain unrecorded. The focus of their work was purely aesthetic, to transform dirty degraded fragments to complete objects which would engage the public: a continuity of the 'aesthetic integration' of the Renaissance. This is best exemplified by Doubleday's reassembly of the shattered fragments of the Portland Vase, smashed by a vandal in 1845 (see Case study 2A), which is a shining example of their skill. No recording, no analysis, no ethical discussion was requested of these skilful men by their appreciative museum directors. This 'age of craftsmen' is perhaps best summed up by the description of one of the last such individuals, Arthur Trotman. Appointed in 1936 as a 'boy learner' to assist in objects restoration work at the Museum of London, Sir Mortimer Wheeler said of Trotman 'most of his brains were in his hands' (Johnson 2001).

Throughout Europe, the enthusiasm for recovering archaeological remains, prompted by the discoveries at Herculaneum and Pompeii, led many antiquarians to attempt to clean and stabilise the fragile, decaying objects they recovered from the ground. Doubleday was mentioned, by Sir Henry Layard, as being particularly skilful in conserving the ivories from his Nineveh excavations. In Denmark, the collections of The National Museum in Copenhagen, founded in 1807, were classified and catalogued by C.J. Thomsen, who cleaned objects in the collection using vinegar and carborundum and paid others to wash clean the runestones in the collection (Brinch Madsen 1987). Thomsen was an archaeologist who, working with colleagues such as Christian Herbst, Japetus Stenstrup, and Christian Jorgansen, developed or utilised a number of techniques for conserving freshly excavated finds, including leaving soft freshly excavated prehistoric pots to stand and dry in order to harden and preserving fragile finds from the Hvidegard grave at Lyngby by coating them with shellac immediately after they were discovered. Thomsen also preserved waterlogged wood by boiling the wood twice in a solution of alum and coating it, about a month later, in purified linseed oil. This marked the start of the treatment of waterlogged archaeological materials although it has often received little recognition since it was published in Danish (Brinch Madsen 1987; Brinch Madsen et al. 2001). More widely read as it was published in English was advice by Flinders Petrie published in 1888 on 'the treatment of small finds' in the *Archaeological Journal,* while Albert Voss, the director of the Berlin Museums, published the German handbook *Merkbuch*

(Caldararo 1987; Seeley 1987). Throughout the 19th century, most advice and information, both to and from antiquarians regarding cleaning and care of their artefacts, comes in the form of discussions or private letters.

The difficult preservation problems posed by some archaeological objects and the instability of many salt-ridden objects excavated in Southern Europe and the Near East, once they were brought to Northern Europe, led to the involvement of chemists in the study of decay mechanisms and the pairing of scientific lines of inquiry with the crafts-based approaches of the past. The very delicate charred papyri uncovered in 1752 in the Villa of the Papyri at Herculaneum were some of the first finds to incite scientific investigation. They were a source of interest for many scholars and there was a desire to unroll them and access the contents. Work in the late 18th century by Antonio Piaggio, a Genoese monk and sub-librarian at the Vatican, led to the development of a technique for gradually unrolling and supporting these papyri scrolls by gluing them onto a thin backing of parchment (Seeley 1987). This technique was not always successful, but many of the less charred papyri were unrolled and translated. The British Prince Regent was fascinated by these discoveries and acquired copies of the translations. After he became King George IV in 1818, he instructed the President of the Royal Society, Sir Humphrey Davy, to study the remaining papyri. Davy, who had previously analysed classical wall paintings and vases, undertook a coherent body of research seeking to examine the condition of these papyri, looking for the cause of their decay, prior to devising a solution to the problem (Davy 1821). This is an approach that we would recognise as modern conservation research, a tradition of investigating the material and determining its process of decay. It was copied in 1826 by Sir Humphrey's brother Dr John Davy in his investigation of the corrosion on an ancient Greek copper alloy helmet (Davy 1826). Similar scientific exploration of the relationship between a material's composition, environment, and decay was shown by Sir David Brewster in his work on iridescence on glass (Brewster 1861) and James Fowler in his extensive work on the corrosion of glass (Fowler 1880). Throughout the mid-19th century, in addition to using craftsman-restorers, the British Museum consulted notable British scientists such as Faraday, William Brande, Professor Hoffmann, and Dr Frankland to advise on specific aspects of problems related to the corrosion of metals and the problem of salts in stone (Watkins 1997). Scientific investigation was not only limited to archaeological materials, in 1843 Michael Faraday undertook research on the decay of leather book bindings in the vicinity of gas-lamp burners (Faraday 1843), the phenomena we now know as 'red rot', which he demonstrated was caused by high levels of SO_2 (Caldararo 1987). The problem with gas burners continued to receive attention in later years (Woodward 1888) and marks an awareness about pollution and the environment that has continued to be important in conservation. Similarly, in 1888, two scientists, Dr W.J. Russell and Captain Abney, were enlisted to conduct a study of the fading of watercolours. They conducted extensive experiments on 39 pure colours and 34 mixtures, subjecting them to different light sources, wavelengths, intensities, exposure times, and environmental conditions to investigate their permanence (Lambert 2014).

In the mid- to late-19th century, the fashion for Gothic architecture swept through England, France, and other countries. Many churches were altered to remove original features and later additions and to recreate imagined gothic interiors and exteriors. In 1877, seeking to prevent further 'desecration', William Morris and other luminaries of the Arts and Crafts movement founded the Society for the Protection of Ancient

Buildings (SPAB). They aimed to stop further 'restoration' work and raise the value and appreciation of the original historic fabric. In the first report of this body, Morris wrote:

> Restoration of ancient buildings … a strange and most fatal idea – which by its very name implies that it is possible to strip from a building, this, that and the other part of history, of its life that is, and then to stay the hand at some arbitrary point and leave it still historical, still living and even as it once was … .
>
> (Morris 1996: 319)

Support for SPAB from academics, architects and the public grew, and schemes to renovate the tomb of Edward the Confessor in Westminster Abbey and the front of San Marco in Venice were halted through SPAB pressure (Chamberlin 1979). The idea that the original fabric of the object and its subsequent history were things that needed to be considered and respected became an important concept that spread from the preservation of buildings to all objects of the past. When paired with the existing tradition of craftsmanship and the emerging scientific practices of technical investigation, it formed part of what George Stout, the first president of the International Institute of Conservation, described as the 'three-legged stool' of conservation (Stoner 2015).

Conservation Emerges: 1888–1950

Perhaps the first instance of conservation as the discipline we know today, can be seen in the appointment of Friedrich Rathgen as the Director of the newly formed Chemical laboratory at the Royal Museums of Berlin in 1888. Rathgen, a young chemist was tasked with solving the problems of ancient Egyptian artefacts excavated in the 1830s by the German archaeologist Lepsius and transported to the Royal Museum in Berlin. They were showing signs of significant decay. Rathgen created a laboratory and developed many of the earliest conservation treatments, such as the desalination of stone, the baking of unfired clay tablets to preserve their inscriptions, and the use of synthetic polymers for adhesion and for coating artefacts. Rathgen collaborated with and built on the work of others. In 1889, Adolf Finkener developed electrolytic reduction to treat corroding bronze objects, while in 1892 Axel Krefting developed electrochemical reduction for cleaning corroding antiquities. Rathgen used and developed these methods and utilised the work of Marcellin Berthelot who, in regular papers to the French Academy of Sciences, had identified the role of chloride ions in causing high rates of decay in copper alloy objects. Crucially, Rathgen carefully diagnosed the nature of the decay of the artefacts and kept records monitoring progress. Thus, he was able to start building up a record of successful techniques, which could then be repeated. In 1898, Rathgen produced one of the first textbooks on conservation *Die Konservierung von Altumsfunden* (The Conservation of Antiquities), which was translated into English in 1905 (Gilberg 1987). In 1915, he revised, enlarged, and republished it adding materials about the conservation of ethnographic, folk art, and museum objects. The German loss of power and influence after World War I meant that few read Rathgen's later work, and the work of British and American authors on conservation became better known (Gilberg 1987).

Rathgen's appointment was followed, albeit slowly, by the formation of similar labs elsewhere. In 1890, Georg Rosenberg was appointed to the National Museum in Copenhagen. Trained as a sculptor, he taught himself the science he needed and established conservation laboratories and procedures in the Danish National Museum. He was also an early advocate of preventive conservation measures (Rosenberg 1917, 1933). After the discovery of severe mould, corrosion and soluble-salt damage affecting the British Museum's collections stored in the damp conditions of the London Underground system during World War I, Dr Alexander Scott of the British Government's Department of Science and Industrial Research was seconded to the British Museum to provide greater scientific input for the preservation of the collections (Plenderleith 1998). He published a number of reports in the 1920s under the general title *The Cleaning and Restoration of Museum Exhibits* and established laboratory facilities in the British Museum. The lab ran on a shoestring but was a vibrant place that was regularly visited by archaeologists such as Leonard Wooley, Howard Carter, Alfred Lucas, who brought samples and compared techniques for preserving artefacts (Plenderleith 1998). Lucas, a chemist who directed the conservation of the finds from Tutankhamen's tomb, subsequently wrote an influential book *Antiques: Their Restoration and Preservation* in 1924, based on his work on the objects from the tomb, followed in 1926 by *Ancient Egyptian Materials and Industries*, an examination of the technological approaches used to make Egyptian artefacts (Gilberg 1997). The excitement about Tutankhamun's tomb did much to promote the field of conservation; the public were interested in all things related to the find and Lucas gave numerous interviews about his work and his efforts to save the boy king's treasure, which reached audiences around the world and helped to catalyse the formation of other laboratories (Williams 2021). Many of these newly formed departments focused not just on the conservation of objects but also of paintings and other materials.

In 1928, Edward Waldo Forbes, the director of the Fogg Art Museum at Harvard, established a new Research Department, which was soon renamed the Department of Conservation and Technical Research. Forbes was interested in what would now be termed Technical Art History and taught a course on 'Methods and Processes of Paintings' at Harvard. In 1925, he invited Alan Burroughs, an early champion of the use of x-radiography in the analysis of paintings, to work at the Fogg (Hindin 2014: 8). In 1927, with the opening of a new building to house the Fogg collection, Forbes hired the artist George Stout, who had trained with a paintings restorer. In 1928, chemist Rutherford John Gettens joined the team. In 1932, the Fogg began publishing *Technical Studies in the Field of the Fine Arts*. It was the first journal dedicated to conservation and played an important role in sharing methodologies within the nascent field. Additionally, the Fogg conservation team undertook the training of many aspiring conservators and both staff and students went on to found additional conservation programs at museums throughout America (Bewer 2010; Hindin 2014) and to be influential of the formation of the field.

In 1930, the International Museums Office, a part of the League of Nations' International Institute of Intellectual Cooperation, convened an international conference in Rome on the 'Study of Scientific Methods Applied to the Examination and Conservation of Works of Art'. Nearly 125 delegates from at least 20 nations attended (Coremans 1969; Hindin 2014). Although the proceedings were not published in their entirety, Plenderleith and Stout published important articles based on their attendance in the *Museums Journal* (Plenderleith 1932) and the *Fogg Art Museum Notes* (Stout 1931) and additional papers were published in *Mouseion* (1931).

The 1930s saw the establishment of many conservation laboratories. In 1930 the Museum of Fine Arts in Boston founded a lab. In 1931, the British Museum laboratory was permanently established as the British Museum's Research Laboratory (Johnson 1993; Oddy 1997). It continued to be involved in training individuals, generating publications, and giving advice to numerous archaeologists and museums, shaping conservation in Britain for the rest of the century. In the same year, the Louvre, the Walters Art Museum, and the fledgling Colonial Williamsburg Foundation (Williams 2000) established conservation departments. In 1932, the Gabinetto di Restauro was established in Florence. 1934 saw the establishment of conservation at the Courtauld and the Brooklyn Museum of Art (under Sheldon Keck, a former Fogg tutee). Other labs established or formalised in the 1930s include those at the National Gallery of Art in London (under F.I.G. Rawlins) and at the Musées Royaux d'Art et d'Histoire in Brussels (under Paul Coremans).

The build up to war and the Second World War itself limited the establishment of new laboratories and impacted international exchange; however, communication between departments and conservators continued. Important exchanges about safeguarding art in times of conflict took place in both Britain and the United States (Brooks 2000; Lambert 2014; Hindin 2014) and Stout's work with the Monuments, Fine Arts and Archives Section or 'Monuments Men' brought him to Europe and permitted meetings with Rawlins, Plenderleith, and Coremans. Importantly, the notion of an association of conservators dedicated to training, establishing standards of practice and information sharing began to be discussed. The idea gained strength during the trial of Hans Van Meegeren, when many specialists including Plenderleith, Rawlins and Coremans were called to testify and during the Weaver Commission where experts including Stout and Coremans were brought to London to resolve issues of cleaning at the National Gallery (Brooks 2000). In 1950, the International Institute for Conservation, the field's first professional body, was formed. In 1952, IIC began to produce the journal *Studies in Conservation,* which remains an important publication within the conservation field. The organisation grew and spawned regional groups, some of which have since broken off to establish national conservation bodies such as the American Institute for Conservation and the United Kingdom Institute for Conservation (UKIC), which later merged with other UK conservation organisations to form ICON in 2005.

In 1959, UNESCO founded ICCROM (International Centre for the Study of the Preservation and Restoration of Cultural Property) in Rome, which in turn supported ICOM (International Committee of Museums) in an attempt to develop international standards in the care of cultural property and provide a forum for interchange of ideas on best practise in all aspects of curating cultural heritage. In 1965, International Council on Monuments and Sites (ICOMOS) 'a professional association that works for the conservation and protection of cultural heritage places around the world' was founded, following the conference which established the Venice Charter (1964). Along with IIC, these organisations have advised national governments and international agencies, provided intellectual leadership for the subject, spurred on the development of training programs, and fostered international communication between conservators, architects, archaeologists, curators, and others. They also help establish standards and extend best practice, which is achieved through publications, guidelines, charters, and encouraging the development of professional associations that have codes of ethics and practice.

Conservation Evolves: 1950–Present

Since the end of World War II, conservation has continued to evolve within a broader sphere of developments in the heritage sector and wider social change, which continue to shape the field. The damage caused by the Second World War, the urgent need for housing, and the increasing popularity of automobiles led to the redevelopment of many urban areas throughout Britain and Europe. Public concern about the loss of historic buildings and landscapes led to the formation of heritage advocacy groups and legislative change. In Britain this included the founding of the Victorian Society (established in 1958 to advocate for Victorian buildings) and the passage of the Town and Country Planning Act of 1968. The need to provide housing, infrastructure, and food for a rapidly increasing global population, which has grown from circa 2.5 billion in 1950 to 7.8 billion in 2020,[4] has resulted in threats to heritage in every country.

Economic factors, including post-war debt in European countries and financial booms in new global markets, meant that significant amounts of art moved from private ownership to public ownership. In England, for example, death taxes rose to 65% in the aftermath of the war and many landowning families found that they either had to sell possessions or give them to the government to pay off these taxes. By 1955, one country house was being demolished every five days while their contents were often sold to American buyers for export to the United States. In the 21st century, the economic power of many of the Gulf Oil states and of Asian economies has seen the migration of art to these areas. As art has become increasingly mobile, it has led not only to greater international collaboration between experts (curators and conservators) but also eventually to blockbuster travelling exhibitions, which has prompted conservators to develop new tools for documenting works of art and for keeping them safe as they travelled and were exhibited in new venues. As technological advancements altered traditional jobs and household chores, the public had more travel and leisure time, and heritage became increasingly important to locales as a way of attracting tourists and their money. Conservation was no longer located only in national museums and heritage bodies; a wider range of organisations, municipalities, local governments, and private foundations began to employ conservators and there was also increasing scope for conservators to go into private practice and to contract their services to smaller organisations (or private owners) who needed help but could not afford to retain a conservator full time.

By the late 1980s, it was increasingly apparent that there were large quantities of heritage and only finite resources (both fiscal and human) to take care of it. Increasing emphasis was placed on the development of preventive conservation approaches. The recognition that some environmental factors (light, humidity, pollutants, and pests, for example) cause damage and that certain actions can mitigate this damage has been present from the earliest days of collecting (Caple 2011; Staniforth 2013; Lambert 2014). However, it was not until 1978 and the publication of *The Museum Environment* by Gary Thompson that preventive conservation began to emerge from the shadow of interventive conservation. Work at the Canadian Conservation Institute structured approaches to the agents of deterioration within a risk management framework further emphasising the tactical role that preventive conservation can play in the care of large collections (Costain 1994; Michalski 1994). The rapid introduction of new analytical techniques and materials, particularly since the 1990s, has also altered the face of conservation, leading to the reevaluation of old techniques and the need to develop new ones as well as adding complexity to the training of conservators. There is a broader knowledge base for the practitioner to master. The global recession between 2007 and 2009 and the financial repercussions of the COVID-19 pandemic have both impacted the heritage sector, including layoffs and in some cases the permanent closure of heritage venues (ICOM 2021). While we cannot know the full impact of the pandemic on the field yet, it has already changed working patterns and opened digital possibilities such as the virtual couriering of museum loans and virtual conference attendance. Many of these themes are ones that we will return to throughout this book.

The Emergence of Formal Conservation Training

One of the questions that motivated the formation of IIC was how to train new conservators and share knowledge. Up until the 1950s, much of the training carried out was informal or on the job training. In Britain, the Institute of Archaeology had opened in 1937 and it offered some coursework in conservation as part of its degree program, but a dedicated conservation training course was not offered until much later. In 1944, the *Instituto Centrale per il Restauro* began training paintings conservators in Rome. It was not until 1961 that the first graduate-level program in conservation opened; the program at the Institute of Fine Arts at New York University was led by Sheldon Keck and brought many former members of the Fogg team, including Gettens and Stout, back together as instructors and advisors (Smyth 1989). Until this point conservation remained a discipline that most practitioners learned through apprenticeships and although knowledge was increasingly shared through publications, the transmission of practical knowledge was largely informal and still had elements of secrecy associated with it.

On November 4, 1966, an event occurred that stunned the world and changed the face of the field. After a week of heavy rain, the Arno burst its banks, flooding into Florence and bringing with it approximately 600,000 tons of mud, rubble, and sewage. An estimated 3–4 million books and manuscripts and 14,000 movable works of art were damaged. Art students, restorers, scientists, and budding conservators from around the world flocked to the city to help with salvage efforts. The opportunity to share ideas and methodologies proved very powerful. New treatments such as phased conservation and mass-deacidification were trialled and implemented. The entire city became 'an enormous restoration lab combining expertise, methods, and techniques from around the world' (Pintus 2009: 13). Discussions followed about how to continue such engagements and ensure that treatments were passed down. Formal education was seen as playing a role. This event contributed to the establishment of a number of training programs including Cooperstown (now SUNY-Buffalo-1970), the Royal Danish Academy of Fine Arts (1973), Winterthur/Delaware (1974), and Queens (1974). Simultaneously, the growth in archaeological and expansion within the University system led to the founding of courses specialising in archaeological conservation at Cardiff (1974) and Durham (1976) and the creation of archaeological science programs at other UK universities. Since the 1970s, conservation programs have continued to open around the world and there are now a diverse number of programs being offered at both the Bachelors and Masters levels in countries from China to South Africa.

Formalising the training that conservators receive as well as the creation of ethical codes of practice and the growing exploration of a discrete theoretical framework, which goes beyond the 'hows' of treatment and begins to consider its 'whys', have been important steps in the professionalism of the field. The creation of a series of textbooks in the early 2000s, including the initial volume of this book *Conservation Skills, Judgement and Decision-Making* (Caple 2000), as well at Liz Pye's *Caring for the Past* (2001), Miriam Clavir's *Preserving What Is Valued* (2002), and Salvador Muñoz Viñas' *Contemporary Theory of Conservation* (2005) spoke to this and were initial attempts at critically examining the field and the ways in which conservators work. They joined and have been augmented by many specialised publications that focus on individual materials.[5] However, as the knowledge base needed to practice competently has increased – Joyce Hill Stoner (2015) has commented that what was once a 'three-legged stool' is now a 'twelve-legged settee' – and conservation has increasingly moved out of museum environments and into the commercial/contract realm, conservators have struggled for visibility and recognition (Henderson 2001; Jones and Holden 2008). Although their contributions differ from many of their allied professions (such as archaeometry, technical art history and collections management), these differences are not always clearly visible to the public or to funding bodies who may be commissioning work, and concern is frequently voiced about this in professional circles. Responses to this have included engagement in professional outreach (Williams 2013) as well as the development of national accreditation and/or certification schemes, which seek formal demonstration of competence in key skills and on-going proof that these skills are being developed and maintained. Additionally, the growing number of conservators seeking PhDs signals the field's evolution away from its technical/crafts-based origins towards a more mature and well-rounded discipline.

2A Case Study: The Portland Vase (Smith 1992; Williams 1989)

This Roman glass vase, composed of white cameo-cut glass depicting a classical scene on a deep blue background, was probably created in the first century AD or BC. Clearly of the finest craftsmanship, it had always been a prized object and was disinterred in 1582 from a marble sarcophagus located beneath a huge burial mound south of Rome, believed to be that of Emperor Alexander Severus (222–235 AD). The vase passed through the hands of several owners before the Dowager Duchess of Portland acquired it in 1783. In 1810, The 4th Duke of Portland loaned the vase to the British Museum for display and safe keeping. In 1845, William Lloyd, a young man described as being 'in a state of nervous excitement after a week of drinking' used a heavy object to smash the museum case and shatter the Portland vase into hundreds of fragments. He could provide no reason for his vandalism and was sentenced to pay £3.00 or serve two months hard labour for the destruction of the museum case. He could not be prosecuted for the destruction of the vase as the Wilful Damage Act only applied to objects up to a value of £5.00. Subsequently, in response to this crime, Parliament passed The Protection of Works of Art and Scientific and Library Collections Act.

In 1845, the craftsman-restorer at the British Museum, John Doubleday, reassembled the vase, although 37 of the fragments could not be fitted into the restoration. The vase was displayed in this form until 1948 when, following its purchase by the British Museum, another restoration was conducted. The vase was 'taken down' and reassembled by the museum's chief restorer, J.H.W. Axtell but 34 fragments still could not be incorporated into the restored vase. By 1988, the adhesive used in Axtell's reassembly had begun to turn yellowish-brown in colour. Tapping the glass produced a dull knock, rather than a ringing sound, which indicated the presence of unadhered cracks in the restored vase, and areas of the 1945 gap filling had visibly shrunk. Therefore, Nigel Williams and Sandra Smith, senior conservators in the Glass and Ceramics section of the British Museum Conservation Department, undertook the re-conservation of this vessel.

There were no records from the 1845 and 1948 restorations of the vase, only a watercolour by T. Hasmer Sheperd immortalising the smashed fragments and the occasional image of the conserved vessel. The adhesive used in the 1948 restoration was unknown and when retired staff members were consulted, each gave a different answer. The gap fills were made of pigmented wax. Following the creation of temporary inner and outer moulds of blotting paper, the inner one stiffened with a thin wash of plaster of Paris, the vase was left in an atmosphere of water vapour and methylene chloride (1,1,1-trichloromethane) for three days, which softened the adhesive and allowed the glass fragments to be removed one by one. The fact that the adhesive was so degraded that it softened in the atmosphere, composed largely of water vapour, vindicated the judgement that re-conservation was needed due to the weakened state of the object. After mechanically removing the remaining adhesive from the edges of the sherds and cleaning the dirt and dust from the surface, through gentle washing in a solution of non-ionic detergent, 189 separate sherds were ready for reassembly. In reassembling the sherds, it was essential to choose a stable adhesive that would not discolour and would hold the vessel together effectively for many decades. It was also necessary to hold the glass fragments together in their exact registration so that there were no steps or gaps between the fragments. After testing, it was found that the most effective way to achieve these criteria was to use two adhesives: one, a slow curing (seven days) epoxy resin (Hxtal NYL) as the principal adhesive, the second a quick-setting UV cured acrylic resin applied in small patches just to hold the glass sherds together in the correct position while the epoxy resin gradually set. This necessitated the use of a strong UV source to ensure the acrylic set quickly. It proved difficult to line up the pieces of glass accurately while wearing protective gloves and goggles, essential when using the UV source (Smith 1992). The reassembly continued well up to the level of the shoulder; however, above this level around the neck of the vessel the sherds did not always fit together well. Closer examination revealed that, in a previous restoration, the pieces had been abraded with a file to make them fit, resulting in gaps between some of the sherds (Smith 1992). To achieve the correct shape of the vase, these missing areas were subsequently gap-filled. All but seventeen minuscule fragments were incorporated in the new reconstruction of the vase (Williams 1989). They all came from heavily damaged areas, where glass was missing due to the damage caused by the original breaking of the vase in 1845. The missing areas of glass were filled with epoxy resin tinted to resemble the glass. In creating the gap-fills, although the original shape of the blue background was clear, the details of the white cameo-cut figures were less certain. However, plaster casts and drawings of the vase made in the 16th century provided the information required to enable an exact copy of the original lines and decoration of the figures to be created. The whole vessel was subsequently given a coat of microcrystalline wax to restore the sheen to the surface of the glass (Smith 1992; Williams 1989) (Figure 2.1).

The decision to dismantle and reassemble the vessel was dictated by the fragility of the 1948 restoration and the clear risk to the vase's continued integrity. It was also apparent that building on developments in the restoration of glass and ceramic vessels, considerable improvement in the visual appearance of the object could be achieved using more stable modern materials. The conservators prioritised the need for good adhesion between the glass fragments over other considerations such as reversibility, and thus an irreversible epoxy resin adhesive was chosen. The gap fills and surface coating of wax restored its visual integrity (aesthetic quality) an important quality for its role as a display object. The 1988 conservation campaign revealed the deficiencies of the earlier restorers, both in terms of the lack of records and in terms of damaging the object. These practices were not unusual for the time, but they do demonstrate how conservation standards have evolved.

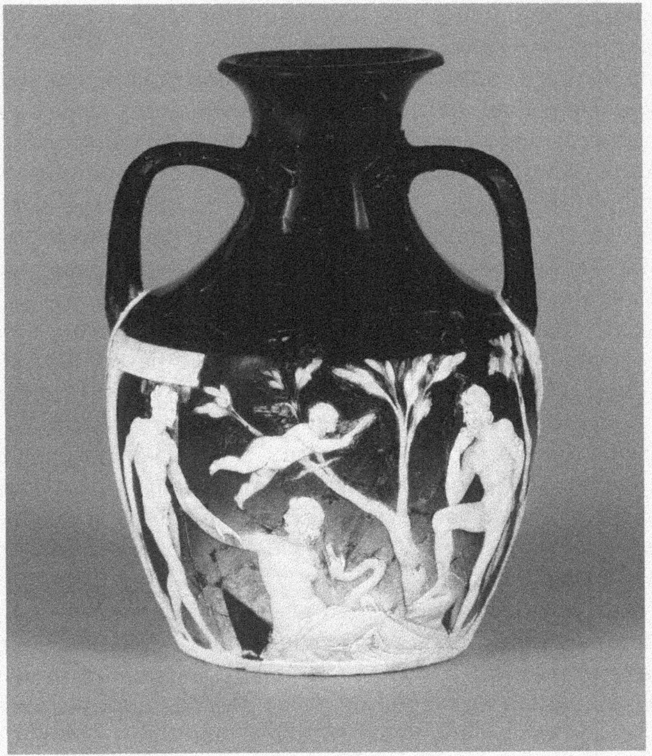

Figure 2.1 The Portland Vase, after conservation. ©Trustees of the British Museum.

2B Case Study: The Sutton Hoo Helmet (Maryon 1947; Williams 1992)

The Sutton Hoo helmet, discovered in the rich Saxon boat burial at Sutton Hoo in East Anglia, consisted of nearly 500 pieces of mineralised iron and gilded-bronze when found. Excavated hurriedly in 1939 on the eve of World War II (Bruce-Mitford 1978; Evans 1986) and stored throughout the war, subsequent analysis of the contents of the grave suggests that it belonged to Raedwald, the Anglo-Saxon king of East Anglia, who died around AD 625. Herbert Maryon initially undertook the conservation and reconstruction of the helmet in 1946 at the British Museum Research Laboratory (Maryon 1947). His initial reconstruction was subsequently taken down and reconstructed in 1968–1969 by Nigel Williams and the staff of the British Museum (Williams 1992).

X-radiographic examination and physical cleaning of the helmet fragments, together with some elemental analysis, revealed that the helmet was composed of iron plates decorated with thin tinned-bronze foils that were stamped with a series of complex figurative and decorative designs. Decorative gilded-bronze castings inlaid with silver wires, niello, and garnets formed a nosepiece with moustache and mouth, eyebrows, and crest terminals. The thin tinned and stamped bronze foils were affixed to the exterior of the iron plates using fluted bronze strips, which overlay the foils and were riveted to the helmet. The corrosion processes had fused the iron and thin bronze foils and strips together, forming a brown mineralised crust.

There were no photos or other records documenting the original positions of the pieces during excavation, thus the only guide was to try to piece together the helmet from the corroded iron pieces using actual joins between the pieces, the patterns of the decorative foils and the lines of fluted strip visible on the surface of many of the pieces. Comparison with the decorative and stylistic features of a series of similar helmets from Vendel culture graves in Sweden suggested the helmet was composed of a skullcap to which a face mask, neck guard, and ear flaps were attached.

Maryon's original restoration, which did not incorporate every piece, was heavily based on what little had been published about the Vendel helmets by 1946. After months of piecing together mineralised helmet fragments, he mounted them onto a preformed head made from plaster of Paris. Wire mesh and plaster backing were used for the earflaps. Any remaining gaps between the helmet fragments were filled with more plaster, which was coloured with brown umber to match the corroded iron. The principal lines of the fluted strip and decorative plates were incised into the plaster to give the viewer a clear impression of the helmet as a whole (Figure 2.2).

Subsequently, as additional information about Saxon and Vendel helmets became available, new excavations at the site revealed additional pieces of the helmet, and certain practical limitations to the reconstructed form became apparent, a new restoration was required. It was only because there was a first restoration that could be constructively criticised, that there was the impetus and greater knowledge needed for a second restoration.

It is unclear to what extent Maryon was conscious of using reversible materials when he made his first reconstruction. Removing heavily corroded iron pieces from a plaster backing is not a simple task; however, due to the difference in density between the corroded iron and plaster, the original reconstruction could be X-rayed, and the original helmet fragments and restorative plaster distinguished. Then the brittle nature of the plaster made it possible to remove the plaster from around the corroded iron leaving the pieces of the original helmet largely intact. Thus, the first reconstruction proved to be physically reversible, although it did require considerable effort.

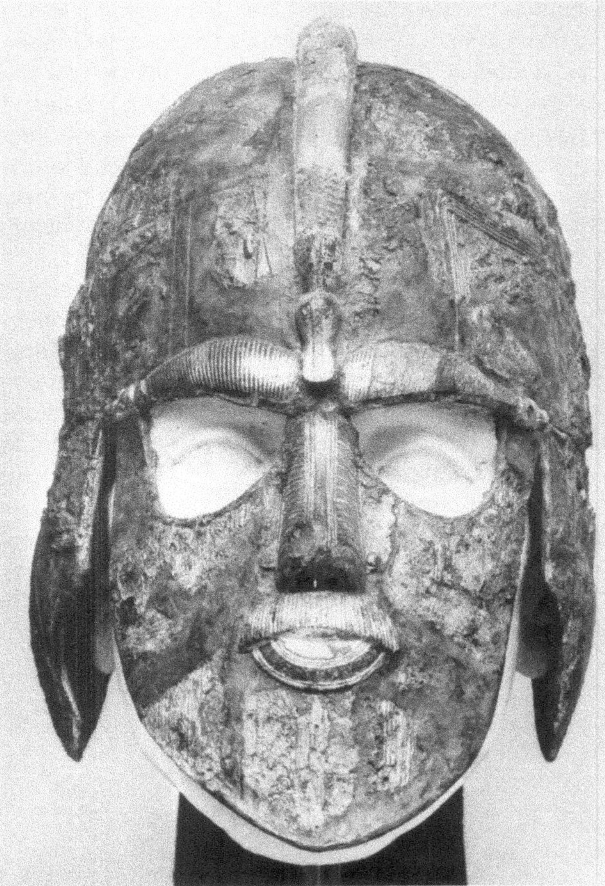

Figure 2.2 Sutton Hoo Helmet: the original 1946 reconstruction. ©Trustees of the British Museum.

The limited cleaning that the mineralised iron fragments received prior to the first restoration ensured that much evidence remained. There were variations in thickness and corrosion patterns on the inside of the helmet that may have related to internal leather padding and traces of gilding on the bronze strips near the helmet's crest. This information, together with a clearer understanding of the nature and arrangement of the tinned-bronze plaques on the helmet exterior, allowed the second restoration to place many more fragments in their original locations. After the position of as many of the fragments as possible had been determined, they were adhered together, and the missing areas infilled with a jute textile stiffened with adhesive, which was heat softened to form the curved shape of the missing areas and covered with pigmented plaster of Paris to recreate the full visual appearance of the helmet. This second restoration was larger than the original and gave greater protection to the head in the form of more effective earflaps and less room for sword thrusts at the neck and eyeholes. A clear pattern was established for the punched decorated bronze plaques and the location of all the cast dragon's-head terminals, including one which had not been incorporated in the original reconstruction, were found. This second restoration is widely accepted as more accurate than the first (Figure 2.3). The Tower of London armouries created a replica of the helmet that is currently displayed beside the original enabling museum visitors to appreciate how the helmet originally appeared (Figure 6.3).

Maryon's work, like the efforts of Renaissance sculptors as they approached classical statuary, was hindered by a lack of information as to how the helmet should look. However, in assessing Maryon's approach, it is important to remember that the iron fragments by themselves would have provided little interest to visitors or possibly even to scholars (after all museum stores are full of fragments of corroded iron). His efforts resulted in a recognisable object that could be appreciated and critiqued, and which could contribute to scholarly dialogue. The images and information generated both during his restoration and the later work by Williams indicate how new conservation interventions can add to historic ones. The restored helmet has been illustrated in almost every book on the Anglo-Saxon period produced since World War II and it is one of the British Museum's most iconic objects.

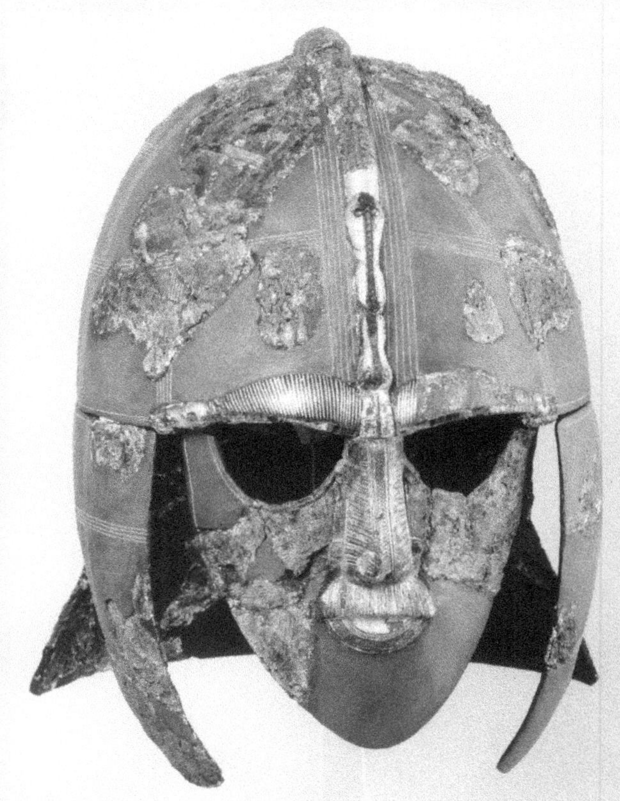

Figure 2.3 Sutton Hoo Helmet: the 1968/9 reconstruction. ©Trustees of the British Museum.

Notes

1 Conservation in Western Europe and North America tradition developed out of a desire for evidence, (a provable truth – creating not 'a past' but 'the past') a tradition stretching back to the Age of Enlightenment. However, other cultures do not necessarily place the same value on material evidence and may value other aspects more highly, such as tradition, intangible attributes or the form and decoration of the object. Replacing decayed parts to preserve the form or materials of the object or repainting the motifs on an object's surface may serve as desirable means of preserving both the tradition of making an object and its intangible attributes. These activities can also be understood as falling within the wider sphere of conservation.

2 What follows is a brief history of object conservation with some examples of sculpture and painting conservation to illustrate similarities or divergences. Each subdiscipline of conservation has its own history of repair, restoration, and evolution.

3 Surviving Palaeolithic art occurs as small carved and incised designs on bone/ivory or stone, such as the lion man sculpture from Stadel Cave in Germany, or as art on the walls of caves, such as Altamira (Cook 2013). This may be the result of differential preservation processes where only robust materials from caves survives or because of the peripatetic nature of the hunter gatherer community who needed to carry everything that they needed for life with them.

4 World population by year taken from www.worldometer.info/world-population/worl-population-by-year/, accessed May 28, 2022.

5 See for example architecture (Jokilheto 1999), textiles (Brooks and Eastop 2011), paintings (Conti 2007; Sitwell and Staniforth 1998), furniture (Rivers and Umney 2003; Wilmering 2004), glass and ceramics (Buys and Oakley 1993; Koob 2006), and wall paintings (Mora *et al.* 1984).

3 Conservation Aims and Ethics

Conservation: A Definition

In the previous chapter, we saw how historic skills-based approaches to cleaning and restoration merged with science-based inquiry and respect for the integrity of the object to form the basis for the modern practice of conservation. But what is conservation? Over the years, many authoritative conservation organisations and individuals have tried to define what conservation is and or what conservators do.

> The activity of the conservator-restorer[1] (conservation) consists of technical examination, preservation and conservation/restoration of cultural property.
>
> (ICOM-CC 1984)

> Conservation encompasses all those actions taken toward the long-term preservation of cultural heritage. Activities include examination, documentation, treatment, and preventive care, supported by research and education.
>
> (AIC 2020)

> The primary goal of conservation professionals, individuals with training and special expertise, is the preservation of cultural property. Cultural property … is material which has significance that may be artistic, historic, scientific, religious, or social … an invaluable and irreplaceable legacy that must be preserved for future generations.
>
> (AIC 1994: 1)

> Conservation is the action of safeguarding the objects and structures, which compose the material remains of the past, and it aims to ensure that these remains are available to use and enjoy today and in the future … Therefore it embraces a range of activities from protective legislation to laboratory treatments.
>
> (Pye 2001)

> The conservator-restorer is a professional who has the training, knowledge, skills, experience and understanding to act with the aim of preserving cultural heritage for the future … The fundamental role of the conservator-restorer is the preservation of cultural heritage for the benefit of present and future generations. The conservator-restorer contributes to the perception, appreciation and understanding of cultural heritage in respect of its environmental context and its significance and physical properties.
>
> (ECCO 2002)

DOI: 10.4324/9781003009078-3

What is clear in all these excerpts is that while preserving cultural heritage is a key component of what conservators do, the ways in which they do it are evolving and increasingly encompassing actions beyond treatment alone. Conservators are increasingly involved in advocating for artefacts, helping to develop legislation for the protection of cultural heritage, and working with curators to develop exhibits and catalogue raisonné.[2] They educate other conservators and allied professionals and conduct scientific analyses. They also work in a broad range of contexts from archaeological sites, libraries and museums to private labs, universities, auction houses, granting bodies, heritage organisations and even corporations. Conservation projects are often interdisciplinary, and conservators are increasingly involved in the design and management of these projects as well as the fundraising, marketing, and publicity needed to make them happen in the first place. Finally, conservators work on a wide range of objects ranging from collections of buildings to pixels and bytes of data, as well as an array of materials that can vary from highly ephemeral to very robust.

As can be imagined, with such a diversity of actives there are also a variety of perspectives on what the goals of the field are and how they should be achieved. Without concurrence, mutual understanding, and shared vocabularies, these divergent voices could become cacophonous. In this chapter, we will examine some of the mechanisms used to define conservation practice in greater detail.

Charters, Ethical Codes, and Guidelines for Practice

In Chapter 1, we discussed the importance of charters in articulating the role of values for cultural heritage management. International charters, such as the Athens Charter (1931), the Venice Charter (1964), the Burra Charter (1979), and the Nara Charter (1994), express a course or principle of action adopted or proposed by an organisation.[3] There are also many national charters and statements of principles such as *Principles for the Conservation of Heritage Sites in China* (China ICOMOS 2004). Due in part to the size and complexity of standing structures, many of the charters generated by the preservation field have focused on architectural monuments; however, it is important to note that the ideas in them are often applied to the conservation of moveable heritage as well. Preservation charters express consensus opinion of the members of the many different heritage organisations involved, though inevitably they cannot cover every aspect of heritage conservation practice. They require periodic adjustment and the creation of additional documents to refine them and guide practice. Sometimes this is through the creation of new charters or the revision of existing charters. For example, the Burra Charter refined and added to the Venice Charter. Additionally, the Burra Charter itself has been periodically revised and rewritten. It is a living document that is reworked as new understandings of heritage management and its implications for an Australian context have developed. In its most recent iteration (2013), it includes the addition of the Burra Charter Process, a mechanism for applying the concepts of values and significance contained in the charter to create and implement management plans.

Further guidance, beyond those contained in charters, is presented via codes of ethics and guidelines of practice. Ethics are defined as 'the principles of good or right conduct' and are predicated on 'a series of moral principles or values' (Edson 1997). Like charters, ethical codes are generally drawn up by consensus. Ethics or moral principles are a function of a society and as such vary from one society to another for example 'cannibalism is moral (and hence ethical) in a cannibal country' (Butler quoted in Child 1997). Ethical approaches may also alter over time. Laws represent the tools for achieving the ethical standards agreed by a country and transgressions are enforced through punishment. Ideas of right and wrong are determined by the society in which one lives and are designed to modify the behaviour of the individuals in that society for its benefit.

Like societies, most professions, including conservation, have developed specialised codes of ethics, which govern the behaviour of members and provide a basis for decision-making. Group members are expected to abide by these ethical codes and, in extreme cases, may be penalised with fines or expulsion for contravening them. There is always some uncertainty within any group as to how strictly the ethical codes of the group should be followed. Some groups and individuals treat such codes as absolute rules, which can lead to a regulatory environment that may stifle innovation (Ashley-Smith 2017), while others may regard them as guidelines to be consulted and/or challenged (Allington-Jones 2013). Such variations in approach can cause friction within the group and can be particularly confusing to new members of the group. Accreditation, certification, and licensing may be additional mechanisms that groups use to ensure compliance with ethical codes and to define the attributes that make a profession (and its practitioners) credible and respectable.

As conservation grew into a specialised profession, characterised by high-level training courses, conferences, and journals, conservators accepted a common series of aims or objectives and began to define acceptable and unacceptable behaviour for members of the field. The *Murray Pease Report*, which contained conservation's first code of ethics, was formally written and ratified between 1961 and 1963 by the American Group of IIC (now known as the American Institute for Conservation or AIC) and was published in *Studies in Conservation* in 1964 (Murray Pease Committee 1964). This document continues to be a living document that is periodically revised and reissued[4]). Many other national conservation organisations have created codes of ethics. In 1981, the United Kingdom Institute of Conservation (now the Institute of Conservation or ICON) developed an ethical code, which was revised and published in 1983, *Guidance for Conservation Practice* (UKIC 1983). The most recent iteration, ICON's *Ethical Guidance* was approved and published in 2020. The European Confederation of Conservator-Restorers' Organisations established in 1991, produced *Professional Guidelines* by 1993, which were revised in 2002 (ECCO 2002). Similarly, the Australian Institute for the Conservation of Cultural Material (AICCM) adopted and published a *Code of Ethics and Guidance for Conservation Practice* in 1986 (AICCM 1986), which was revised and reissued in 2002 (AICCM 2002). The New Zealand Conservators of Cultural Material (NZCCM) adopted their *Code of Ethics* in 1985 and revised it in 1995 and 2006 (NZCCM 2006) while the two primary Canadian conservation groups jointly issued a *Code of Ethics and Guidance for Practice* in 2000, which was a revision of one originally drafted in 1986. The fact that these codes have all been revisited and revised makes it clear that conservation ethics are both complex and evolving. Similarly, the fact that they are defined and developed at a national level rather than an international level (IIC and ICOM-CC), points to the important roles that a common cultural understanding, shared language, familiarity, and the local environment play in building the consensus needed to enact such codes.

In addition to the ethical codes that govern the conservation organisations of which they are a member, conservators may need to be aware of the ethical codes that govern allied professions. For archaeological conservators, this may involve familiarising oneself with archaeological codes of ethics, while for a conservator working within a museum context, familiarity with the International Council of Museum's code of ethics may be essential. There are also wider international conventions such as CITES (the Convention on International Trade in Endangered Species of Wild Fauna and Flora) whose regulations may affect the materials used by conservators.

Shared Themes and Evolving Concepts

The various conservation ethical codes form a series of coherent statements about the ethical basis for approaching conservation work. They share many similarities although there are also some key differences that speak to particular concerns within the communities that authored them. In each of the codes, there are clear statements about operating to the highest standards, the importance of documentation, recognising the limits of one's personal skill, the necessity of promoting the profession, the need to support education, professional conduct towards one's colleagues and the importance of the integrity of the object. Most contain specific statements regarding the need to use, or consider using, preventive conservation measures wherever possible. The codes of ethics are all accompanied by codes of practice, which invariably describe the nature of the relationship between the conservators, owners, curators, and fellow heritage professionals in greater detail. AIC goes further still and includes commentaries to its guidelines, which provide the rationale for each guideline and the minimum and recommended practice. The AICCM, NZCCM, and the Canadian include glossaries in their codes that spell out the definitions of key words to ensure that there are no doubts about meanings.

In the earliest codes of ethics, there was a conviction that the conservator's role was to reveal and preserve the 'true nature' of the object. However, by the 1990s attitudes were changing and increasingly museums and conservation organisations had dropped the concept of 'true nature' and were emphasising the conservator's responsibilities to the owners/custodians of cultural property and 'to the people or person who created it' (AICCM 2002). They emphasised the need for conservators to work with others to understand both the tangible and intangible attributes of the object prior to undertaking work. For some national groups a generic reference to 'stakeholders' is sufficient (ICON 2020), whereas other national conservation organisations are more explicit about whom to include and how. The *AICCM Code of Practice* notes that members

> should recognise the unique status of Aboriginal and Torres Strait Islander peoples as first peoples, and as key stakeholders in the conservation of their cultural heritage material. When undertaking conservation of Aboriginal and Torres Strait islander cultural property, the AICCM member should recognise that the objects and the information relevant to them are of equal importance, and that conservation practice must adapt to cultural requirements, particularly in respect of secret/sacred items.
>
> (AICCM 2002)

The idea of stewardship is deeply rooted in most conservation ethics. The term derives from the medieval period; when the lord or master of the house was away, his steward was responsible for the safekeeping of the house and its contents. When the master or his heirs returned, the steward was expected to hand the household back intact and as the master had left it (if not slightly improved). Museums and cultural heritage organisations have come to be seen as stewards of the nation's patrimony. They hold and safeguard materials for future generations and conservation plays an important role in this. Increasingly as the impacts of climate change are better understood, conservators are being called on to steward not only cultural heritage but also the natural environment. AICCM invites its members 'to undertake conservation treatments, or use materials, which have the lowest potential to pollute; unnecessarily waste resources; or otherwise damage the natural environment' (AICCM 2002) while ICON directs member to 'aim for the best quality and most sustainable action achievable with available resources' (ICON 2020). As sustainability initiatives increase throughout the field, it is likely that new language around the conservator's responsibility to the environment will be added to most codes of ethics.

Controversial and Enduring Concepts

True Nature

The concept of an object's 'true' or authentic nature has been at the root of many ethical dilemmas in conservation. The cleaning and often substantial restoration of classical objects undertaken by sculptors during the Renaissance aimed to reveal the 'true' beauty or nature of the object as the 15th/16th-century artist and his wealthy patron understood it. Aesthetic criteria were defined as the measures of an object's 'true nature'. Offended by the removal of later and post-medieval additions from medieval buildings, the Society for the Protection of Ancient Buildings (SPAB) proposed the notion that the true form of a building included all elements of its history, and that none should be more prized than others. The definition of true nature thus came to embrace historical value as well as aesthetic value. Early codes of ethics embraced the concept of true nature. The 1983 UKIC Guidance for Practice defines conservation as

> the means by which the true nature of an object is preserved. The true nature of an object includes evidence of its origins, its original construction, the materials of which it is composed and information as to the technology used in its manufacture.

Although perhaps originally intended to define a moment in the object's past before it decayed, this definition does not include evidence of use or of addition or alteration. It presumes the object is still as its creator intended it. However, no object exists solely for a single moment. Every object evolves through its use and interaction with the environment around it; any, and every, point along this trajectory can be described as its 'true nature'. A sword may eventually become a piece of scrap iron and both states represent the true nature of the object. Every object contains numerous truths, making it impossible to define any one point as the true nature of the object as opposed to any other. The purpose of this concept was undoubtedly to try to express the desire to remove later alterations and additions, which obscure the initial purpose of the object, and to remove decay and dirt from periods of burial or neglect. Problems defining any one precise state of an object as its true nature led to the demise in the use of this term and it vanished from the ethical codes of the 1990s. Contemporary codes of ethics mention the importance of respecting the 'physical, historic, aesthetic and cultural integrity of the object' (AICCM 2002).

The notion that objects have a 'true' nature persists, however, in discussions surrounding authenticity (Scott 2016) and the notion of 'truths' continues to inform discussions of meanings, significance, and value even if these are increasingly understood to be multiple, situational and to vary based on the viewer's perspective (Gao and Jones 2020). The idea of a true nature can be a useful concept expressing a desire to move towards revealing the truth(s) about an object and away from obscuring dirt, decay, or inaccurate and inappropriate restoration, but it is one that should be deployed cautiously.

Reversibility and Retreatability

By the mid-20th century, conservators were becoming aware not only of the impacts of past treatments but increasingly the impacts of their own approaches. Some late-19th- and early-20th-century approaches, such as filing down the edges of some sherds as a precursor to rejoining them (Case Study 2 A: The Portland Vase), had permanently altered objects and newer materials, such as soluble nylon and polyvinyl alcohol, were also beginning to show problems. The concept of reversibility – the ability to undo an action or remove a chemical added to an object – began to be espoused. Reversibility was enshrined in the earliest (1961) AIC Code of Ethics. It demonstrated the post-Second World War faith in the capability of science and technology to create desirable polymers (i.e. ones that were stable and readily removable). It also indicated that people had begun to lose their faith in the permanence of things. There was appreciation that although nothing stayed the same for very long, this did not matter provided you could undo what had previously been done.

The principal architects of the *Murray Pease Report*, where the term reversibility was used first, were paintings conservators (Applebaum 1987). They were no doubt thinking of processes such as inpainting, varnishing, and lining paintings. In this context, the public and the rest of the heritage profession could easily understand reversibility. It indicated that a more careful approach was being adopted by conservation and this created a distinction between conservators and the repairers and restorers of the past. The work of conservators was now intended as much for the future as for the present.

The terms 'soluble' or 'removable' were subsumed into the term reversible and applied to materials and processes alike (Applebaum 1987). As the use of the term grew during the 1970s, it became increasingly obvious that little the conservator did was in the strictest sense reversible (Jedrzejewska 1976). In reality, all cleaning actions, such as washing paper or textiles, were irreversible. Excavating archaeological objects caused irreversible chemical changes and analysis increasingly showed that any contact with a material left a few molecules present on the object. Horie's analysis of the consolidation of a modern earthenware ceramic with polymethyl methacrylate demonstrated the irreversibility of impregnation even with stable polymers (Horie 1983). Fifty per cent of the impregnating polymer was retained in the ceramic even after it had been refluxed with solvents in a Soxhlet extractor for eight hours (Horie 1983). In another example, the use of enzymes to treat stains on paper was shown to leave up to 2% of the enzyme in the paper even after extensive careful washing (Andrews *et al.* 1992).

There was additional concern that the term 'reversibility' could be potentially harmful since although conservators should have considered the aesthetic appropriateness or stability of the conservation material that they were using on an object

(Feller 1978), they might still rely on the impractical notion that they could remove any material that proved unsuitable in the long term (Applebaum 1987). The idea that nothing ought to be done that cannot be undone is an impossible goal, but it is one that remains desirable and something worth striving for. To this end, other terms such as removability (Charteris 1999), retreatability (Applebaum 1987) and minimum intervention have been proposed; however, none is without fault.

Retreatability, or the idea that a given treatment should not impede future conservation, is alluring but has its own risks. Objects are complex constructs, often combining multiple chemical makeups as well as various breakdown products and once we begin to add additional materials, it can be difficult to model what will happen and what the impacts will be over an extended period. When we factor in the combined impacts of environmental factors, it gets even harder. Additionally, practicalities such as size, cost, and feasibility may impact retreatability. For example, although polyethylene glycol treated wood is retreatable, is it realistic to assume that large, complex structures such as the *Vasa* or the *Mary Rose*, which took decades to treat initially, can be retreated? Do we in fact lull ourselves into a false sense of confidence about the future of such objects? Finally, to what standard should we hold retreatability? Claims have been made that wooden objects treated with alkoxysilanes are retreatable (Tejedor 2010), when in reality the properties of the alkoxysilane mean that only more alkoxysilanes can be applied in the future. While semantically, the wood can be retreated, will it be desirable to add the same material again if it is failing or no longer fulfilling its original purpose?

Despite all these issues, the ideal of reversibility remains at the heart of conservation practice. After a period where the term reversibility vanished from ethical codes, ICON's most recent ethical guidance stipulates that 'Actions should allow future re-treatment and remain as reversible as possible' (ICON 2020). Reversibility represents a laudable if unachievable perfection. It remains a useful concept when trying to explain the aims of conservation to a wider audience.

Minimum Intervention

Minimum intervention received prominence as an ethical approach to conservation in the 1980s when the term reversibility was declining in use. Minimum intervention has been defined or rephrased a number of times. Pye and Cronyn (1987) found it difficult to define minimum intervention and compared it with homeopathy, where reversibility was standard medicine. Corfield (1988b) considered that to practise minimum intervention 'the conservator is required to carefully weigh every process that is proposed for the object and decide whether or not it is really necessary … the less that is done the better'. Brooks (1998) defined it as 'doing the least possible consistent with the future safety of the object'. It was described as the 'minimalist principle' by Hanssen-Bauer (1996), who considered that together with the 'principle of reversibility' and the 'principle of stability' it formed the three principles to guide any intervention. Muñoz Viñas has pointed out that the term is illusory, that no treatment can be absolutely minimal and interventive – the two terms inherently contradict each other (Muñoz Viñas 2005).

The problem with minimum intervention is that it is an incomplete phrase – the minimum intervention needed to achieve what? Although we may take as a given that it is the minimum necessary to preserve the object, the question is dependent on context – for how long and in what conditions remain unstated. A minimally interventive approach to preserving an object sufficiently for it to stand outside exposed to the elements for ten years will necessarily be very different from the one taken to exhibit it for ten years in a controlled museum environment. Minimum intervention must therefore be defined for a given object over a given time in a given set of conditions. The alternative is not to use the phrase but rather to employ it as a question to assess each proposed conservation action (Corfield 1988b).

Implementing Ethics

Single ethical injunctions are easier to resolve than those instances where one or more ethic seem to be in conflict. For example, the notion of stewardship is central to most conservation codes of ethics (whether stated or unstated); however, the idea of protecting materials for future generations often conflicts with the idea of access and use in the present. If we prioritise one set of stakeholders (future generations) in our decision-making, we may exclude another set (those who could benefit today) (Henderson 2020). However, if we prioritise our contemporaries, we risk using up objects in the present. Discussion, negotiation, and context can inform decision-making. Conservators should not be making such decisions in a vacuum. Ethical codes seek to guide the conservator towards the considerations they should prioritise but in each case the conservator needs to listen, compromise, and consider how to balance other goals with those of the field.

Another impediment to implementing ethics lies in the allocation of resources. There is a rarely stated but ever-present truth that what can be achieved in terms of the conservation of any object is dictated by the resources available (Staniforth 1990; Ashley-Smith 1999; Unruh and Harbeck 2021). With limited time and budget, the conservator often selects the most suitable adhesive to hand, rather than testing every known adhesive to find the perfect solution. They use their knowledge and judgement to achieve the best possible result given the time, expertise, funding, and facilities available. When the constraints on resources impose limitations that are significant enough to potentially cause damage to the object, conservators should consider whether it is appropriate to continue. Lack of resources is not a justification for slipshod work or inadequate research.

It is important to consider what will realistically happen to the object if no conservation work is carried out. Sometimes the object can be protected in storage until resources are found; in other instances (especially within archaeological contexts), action may be the only way to record an object before it is lost. Balancing the risk imposed by the lack of resources with the potential for loss can be difficult and conservators must on occasion knowingly triage the care of objects. Good examples of this may be in the selection and treatment of better preserved or more unusual iron artefacts from historic sites rather than the treatment of all iron objects found at the site (Caple and Garlick 2018). Similarly, when considering both past and present conservation efforts, we should remain aware of the hidden impacts that resourcing, administrative edicts, history and even volume may have on decision-making and exercise understanding.

The ability to balance a wide range of ethical considerations is a key aspect of judgement. When exploring the case studies in this book it is possible to study how other conservators have balanced ethical considerations. While a minimally interventive approach was taken to the exterior of the Statue of Liberty (see Case Study 3A), inside the statue a far more pragmatic series of options associated with working objects was chosen. In the case of the Portland Vase (see Case Study 2A), the aesthetic properties of the vase outweighed the desirability for a reversible adhesive. There is little standardised information as to how ethical ideas should be considered or implemented and the individual circumstances of each object and each institution mean that what is ethical in one case may not be in another. Although Ashley-Smith (2017) and Wharton (2018) have suggested that institutions and sub-disciplines of conservation may need to develop their own bespoke codes of ethics, Applebaum (2013) has argued that the existing codes of ethics are flexible enough to extend to new circumstances and new media. Some institutions, such as the Conservation Department at the Victoria and Albert Museum, have developed checklists of ethical questions that every conservator should be asking themselves before engaging in any decision-making regarding an object to encourage the use of ethical actions in practice at every stage of the conservation process (Ashley-Smith Smith 1994; Richmond 2005); however, for many conservators the process remains an internalised one.

The problem posed by many of the guiding ethical ideas of conservation is the extent to which any of them can realistically be applied in a given situation. The extent to which any single ethical idea should be followed is difficult to judge when considered in isolation. For example, the desire to preserve all evidence following Oddy's stricture 'nothing should be done to an object which compromises any original part of it' (Oddy 1996) can leave a conservator too worried about removing evidence preserved in corrosion products to attempt any cleaning of a corroded iron object. The idea of preserving the past 'as found' untouched and with just the 'golden glow' of time is appealing to many (Eggert 2009); however, if taken to its logical extreme, we risk being surrounded like Miss Havisham[5] by piles of dust, fragments, and indecipherably corroded remnants (Lowenthal 1996). It is impossible to truly 'freeze time' and see the past. Entropy will win out; decay processes will continue and all structure and meaning will be obliterated. A more constructive method of approaching the ethical considerations inherent in conserving an object is to identify the desired balance between revelation, investigation, and preservation, and then explore the most ethical way of achieving it.

Revelation, Investigation, Preservation (RIP)

Before worrying whether the conservation treatment being undertaken is 'reversible' is 'minimally interventive' or 'does no harm', it is essential to establish what one is seeking to achieve through treatment. The aims and activities of conservation can be expressed in the form of three almost opposing goals: revelation, investigation, and preservation.

> *Revelation:* Revealing the object to a past form (either an original form or a transformed one) to make it more accessible. The visual form can be cleaned or restored to give the observer, typically a museum visitor, a clear visual impression of the original form or function of the object.

Investigation: All research and analysis which uncover information about the object, from visual observation and X-radiography to complete destructive analysis. This information informs the narrative which accompanies every object.

Preservation: Maintenance of the object in its present form, without any further deterioration. This will typically involve a full range of preventive conservation practices and the stabilisation processes of interventive conservation.

At the extremes, these activities are mutually exclusive; thus, to best preserve an archaeological object (and all the information preserved on it), it may not be excavated or even cleaned. Similarly, an object that is subjected to the fullest form of examination may be dissected, dismembered, or even destroyed to achieve as complete a file of information on the object as possible. Conservation can be seen as a balance of these three activities; in almost all cases, conservation involves all three of these activities and is rarely carried to any extreme. Thus, conservation activities can be characterised as lying in the space between these extremes (Figure 3.1). The individual activities practised by conservators – such as cleaning, gap filling, X-radiography, etc. – can be plotted in this RIP triangular space. It is useful in reminding the conservator of the balance and compromise they strike in undertaking conservation; for example, in cleaning (revealing) an object they will have less of the original object and its evidence to preserve. Some activities such as recording, though dependent upon investigation and used for education and revelation, are intended primarily as a means of preservation.

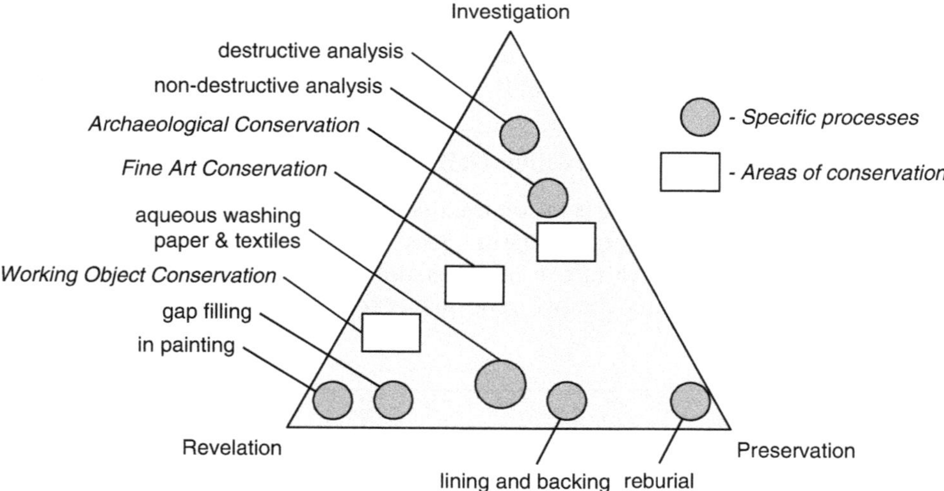

Figure 3.1 The aims of conservation: the RIP balance triangle. Chris Caple.

It is possible to describe both the entire conservation process as well as individual aspects of the conservation process within the RIP balance triangle. In cases of an entire conservation process the specific location derives from all the separate processes carried out as part of the conservation process; that is, the sum of all the different processes: cleaning, recording, analysis, the use of a reversible adhesive and storage with inert buffered materials. It should be emphasised that this is a relative measure with no numerical scales or absolute values. The relative ratios of the different processes may allow the suggestion that the balance differs for different types of objects. Archaeological objects may have higher ratios of investigation and preservation than revelation, whereas an object with considerable aesthetic properties, such as a work of art, may have a higher ratio of revelation to preservation or investigation (see Figure 3.1).

Processes such as cleaning do not serve a single purpose, the removal of dirt and corrosion products reveals the object, aids in investigation and will often help to preserve the object; for example, removing corrosion promoters such as chlorides from metal-corrosion crusts and removing acidic, hygroscopic dirt from the surfaces of textile, paper, glass, plastic, ceramic, and metals. The removal of such material will expose more of the original surface of the object, allowing closer, more accurate, and more detailed examination revealing information about the use and manufacture of the object. Thus, cleaning processes can occupy several points within the RIP balance triangle depending on the relative contribution the cleaning makes to the preservation and investigation of the object as well as the revelation.

Ethical concepts such as 'minimum intervention', 'reversibility', and 'do no harm' can be described as forces moving towards the extreme of preservation, whilst concepts such as 'true nature' can be seen as moving towards investigation and revelation. The RIP balance is drawn at a single moment in time; as further additional information is uncovered during the conservation process, the balance may be amended. When objects in museums are cleaned, re-assembled, and restored multiple times (Case Study 2B: Sutton Hoo Helmet), the conservation balance will be reassessed a number of times and a series of triangles may be created.

There is great value in exploring the relationship between the activities undertaken by conservators and the aims and objectives of conservation (Watson 2010). It ensures that the conservator questions what they are doing and why they are doing it, and avoids inappropriate and unnecessary activities, whilst keeping the values of the object to present day society and the future clearly in view.

The Conservation Process

For an object undergoing conservation a generalised sequence of actions and decisions can be envisaged (Figure 3.2). Not all the steps in the sequence must be enacted. At every step in this process the conservator is required to exercise judgement, no step is automatic.

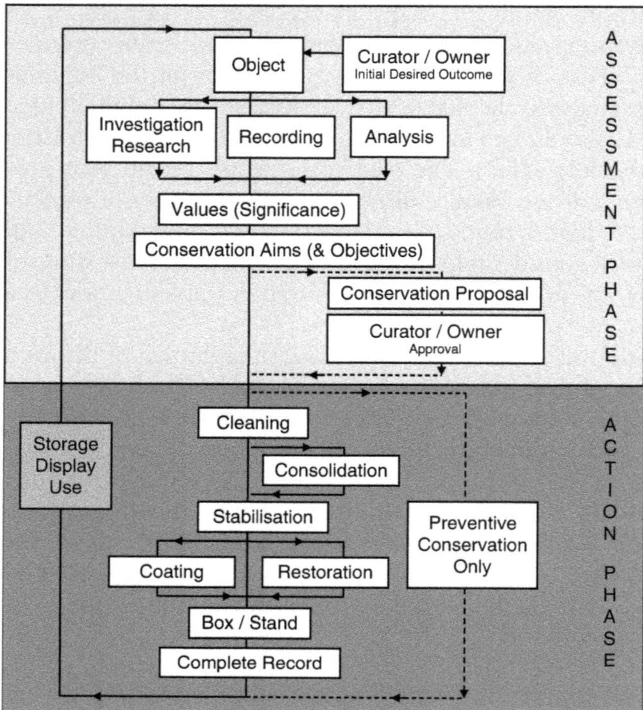

Figure 3.2 The conservation process – the sequence of actions and considerations undertaken to enact conservation. Chris Caple.

In almost all cases conservation starts with an *object*, which usually comes with a request, an 'initial desired outcome', from the *curator/owner* or archaeologist. This initiates assessment activity by the conservator, which may be relatively rapid for a small object with which they are familiar or time-consuming for a large or complex object, or one with which they are not familiar. The object is *recorded*, which normally includes a written description of the nature and extent of decay as well as photography but may include drawing, x-radiography etc. The object may also be *researched* to uncover information regarding dating, manufacturing techniques and maker (although sometimes this information is provided by the curator and merely needs checking). This may include considering any traces of its past life that are detectable and the context(s) from which it derives. *Analysis*, such as elemental analysis, is undertaken to identify how the object was made, what from and how it is decaying.

Considering the *values* the object has, and to whom, permits a clear understanding of its significance to be reached. Subsequently, the *aim(s)* of the conservation process can be formulated. These should meet the custodian's desires while respecting the physical nature of the object and its decay/stability issues and retain and enhance the tangible and intangible significance of the object (considering RIP here may help the conservator to reach a balanced decision). A series of optional *objectives* articulating specific details of the conservation work can be created. Where appropriate, a *conservation proposal* is created and sent to the curator/owner to ensure that they are aware of the work being done and that they formally approve that proposal. Proposals are particularly important for complex objects, where large teams of conservators and others are involved or for situations where the conservator has limited experience of this type of work, but they may not be necessary for experienced conservators undertaking familiar work for a client who has been engaged in the process or already approved similar work.

Subsequently, any interventive conservation work[6] agreed is undertaken. At any stage within the interventive conservation process, particularly during cleaning further analysis or recording may be undertaken. The information recovered is incorporated into the conservation record, which itself informs part of the narrative associated with the object. If after assessment, interventive conservation processes such as cleaning are not considered appropriate or cannot be resourced, then preventive conservation processes[7] alone may be undertaken. Both interventive and preventive measures may be carried out on the same object; for example, the removal of corrosion from an iron object and its subsequent packaging with silica gel to control the relative humidity and prevent further corrosion. The phrase *Box/Stand* acknowledges the need for specialised packaging, mounts and other preventive measures including handling and display instructions or specifications.

Factors Influencing Conservation

The subsequent chapters of this book will examine specific aspects of the conservation process such as documentation, cleaning, stabilisation, and restoration in greater detail and will consider some of the conservators' responsibilities as well. However, it is important to note several factors that must be considered at each point in the process.

The Initial Desired Outcome

Establishing the goals of conservation work is not undertaken by the conservator alone but also normally involves the curator or custodian of the object (Ramsay-Jolicoeur and Wainwright 1990). The reasons that have led the owner/curator to consider an object worthy of collection, study, preservation, and display (Chapter 1), also usually contribute to the desire to have it conserved. Numerous factors need to be considered, including the:

- Intended use of the object
- Context
- Conservation ethics
- Condition of the objects
- Object composition
- Evidence on and from the object
- Aesthetic appearance
- Informative activity
- Resources
- Conservator's competence
- Belief systems embodied in the object

- Artistry or living artist
- Stolen/looted objects

The intended use of the object is often the primary consideration. Factors such as the object's context and condition also weigh heavily in the balance. The range of factors and their weighting are different for every object, which is why every object, and its conservation, is unique.

In discussing the work with the client (owner/curator), the conservator needs to have a well-developed and clear understanding of the aims of and ethics of conservation as well as the technical possibilities and health and safety considerations for any proposed conservation work. This initial desired outcome needs to factor into the conservator's thinking; however, the conservator will normally undertake research/investigation before continuing the discussion with the client. Therefore, the initial request may be amended in light of new information (cost, practicality, date, etc.) provided by the conservator or that emerges during conservation. Throughout the process, as new information is revealed, it is important to consider any modifications to the treatment approach with the initial request in mind. Do the alterations meet the needs of both the object and the client?

Durham Cathedral Doors

An example of a decision-making process and how the RIP space was negotiated because of changing information and changing values is provided by the Durham Cathedral Doors Project. In 1991, as the 900th anniversary celebrations of the founding of Durham Cathedral approached, the cathedral authorities working with the cathedral's Fabric Advisory Committee and the cathedral architect sought to adapt the north doors of Durham Cathedral so they could be easily opened for processions and to improve their appearance with a new coat of black paint. A conservator was consulted and following research that suggested that the carpentry of the door's construction was early, a series of samples were taken for dendrochronology and radiocarbon dating. The north and south doors of the cathedral were dated to the 12th century using both C14 dating and dendrochronological analysis. They were thus shown to be the original doors and as old as the stonework surrounding them. They also had paint sequences on their exterior stretching back to the 17th century (Caple 1999; Caple 2006). This evidence of original fabric altered the shape of the project. The notion of repainting the doors was abandoned and an aged appearance was deemed appropriate for the original material of the doors. The new information generated changed the value of the doors and the narrative of the cathedral's construction. Although, initially the project was focused more towards revelation, the results of investigation led to a greater focus on preservation. This example illustrates the way in which approaches and decisions making can alter in mid-stream leading us to renegotiate the RIP balance.

The Envelope(s) of Possibility

All conservation activities occur within an envelope of available resources. As the discussion of values in Chapter 1 indicated, the overall value or significance of an object may determine the resources available. Where objects are large and internationally significant (Case Study 3A: Statue of Liberty) the resources that can be made available may be substantial; however, when the object is less broadly valued, such as a small scruffy piece of leather recovered from an underfunded excavation largely undertaken by volunteers (Case Study 6B: The Loch Glashen Satchel), the resources may be very limited. The resources available will often depend on where you are in the world, the size of the museum or excavation, even your own personal standing. Sometimes recording the object and its condition in the museum record or providing a protective housing made of stable storage materials may be the only interventions that resources will allow.

John Watson (2010) has created a useful conceptual model, which extends the RIP triangle to include economic practicalities (Figure 3.3). He charts these beside other conservation objectives – accessibility (revelation), integrity and durability (preservation) and against common conservation actions (investigation, intervention, prevention, and communication) – to show the range of possible outcomes paths open to a conservator.

		Actions			
Objectives		**Investigation**	**Intervention**	**Prevention**	**Communication**
	Accessibility making objects understandable	Read evidence through scientific examination	Restore	Facilitate limited access and use	Share results of investigation
	Durability Helping artefacts survive	Analyse forces of deterioration	Stabilise	Provide safe environments for objects	Advocate preservation
	Integrity Protecting historical evidence	Investigate historical evidence & treatment alternatives to preserve evidence	Minimise interventions and make them detectable	Focus preventive measures on culturally significant qualities	Maintain conservation records
	Practicality Economic and safety considerations	Limit investigation to fit time and financial constraints	Fit intervention to time and cost constraints	Balance cost and benefit in planning preventive measures	Make documentation affordable

Figure 3.3 Watson's elements of conservation (Watson 2010). John Watson.

Context

Typically, an object is part of a larger entity, such as a collection, a room in a historic house or even a landscape. Context is the relationship that an object has with other objects, places, and people which surround it, and with which it forms sets or groups. The object contributes to the group and critically it may derive its meaning from its context. Context is crucial when considering any conservation work (Eastop 1998). Brooks *et al.* (1996) and Jaeschke (1996) have noted that sometimes, identical objects that come from different contexts can receive different conservation approaches. In such cases, the balance of revelation, investigation, and preservation is clearly different for each object. For example, the Victorian (19th-century) upholstery on an antique Georgian (18th-century) chair may be preserved if the chair belonged to a famous Victorian person. However, if the chair were being conserved prior to an exhibit of Georgian furniture, a strong case might be made for removing the upholstery and restoring the chair to its original Georgian upholstered form. Similarly, the issue of context was an important consideration of the preservation in situ of the Laetoli footprints (Case Study 1B).

3A Case Study: The Statue of Liberty (Baboian *et al.* 1990)

The Statue of Liberty, a quintessential American icon, was conserved between 1982 and 1986. The work was covered by the international press and exposed the public to many conservation philosophies and practices for the first time. The statue was treated as part of its own centennial celebration. This object is important to Americans for the ideals it represents, although as the only statue of its size made in the period it also represents a major artistic and technical achievement.

Auguste Bartholdi, a French sculptor, initially sculpted the statue at reduced scale. France paid for the fabrication of the full-scale statue, which was created between 1874 and 1884 at the workshops of Monduit & Co. Composed of 300 2.5-mm-thick copper panels that were hammered into moulds to form the shape, the statue was riveted together over a wrought-iron armature. This thin bar iron was attached to an angle-iron frame, which was in turn attached to a central 'A' frame wrought-iron pylon composed of four substantial vertical girders. Gustav Eiffel probably designed the iron frame. This 'curtain wall' form of construction and the use of wrought iron for the armature allowed the statue to flex slightly in high winds and during thermal expansion and contraction without any weakening of the structure. To prevent galvanic corrosion, the iron armature was attached to the copper skin by a series of copper strips or saddles, which ran over the iron-bar armature and were riveted to the copper skin. A layer of asbestos soaked in shellac was inserted between the iron bar and the copper saddle and skin, separating the two metals so reducing the possible opportunities for galvanic corrosion.

The pieces of the statue arrived from France and were erected on a substantial hollow concrete plinth sheathed in polished granite blocks in the centre of Fort Wood on Bedloe's Island, subsequently renamed Liberty Island, in New York Harbour. The 151-ft-high (46-m) statue atop its five-storey plinth was officially inaugurated on October 28, 1886. Just prior to the opening, circular holes were cut through the skin of the torch and an electric light installed inside the torch, so that the statue radiated light and acted as a harbour light and a symbol of the freedoms of the New World (see Figure 3.4). The public could access the interior of the statue and the torch. The US Light House Board managed the statue until 1902, when it subsequently entered the care of the War Department from 1902 to 1933, before becoming one of the earliest national monuments in the care of the National Park Service.

Originally, the copper metal inside the statue was left bare. In 1911, it was covered in a coal-tar emulsion sealing compound, which was later covered with a total of 11 layers of paint: aluminium flake paint (1932), lead paint, enamel paint (1947), alkyd paint and in the 1970s, vinyl paints. In 1916, the flame had numerous holes cut in it and stained glass was inserted to create a brighter and more highly coloured appearance.

By 1982, many problems were evident with the statue:

- The asbestos layer had degraded and adsorbed salt-water spray creating very active galvanic corrosion cells and the iron armature was extensively corroded. The iron-corrosion products were pushing the copper skin and the retaining copper saddles outwards.
- In a few areas, where water collected, the copper skin was severely corroded.
- There were rust and paint stains on the exterior of the statue, where the internal iron corrosion and earlier paint coatings had seeped through cracks in the statue's skin.
- The torch was severely degraded. A lot of water had seeped in through the poorly joined glass panels inserted in 1916. The torch needed substantial repair and, to stop the problem reoccurring, the torch flame needed to be redesigned to make it waterproof.
- The paint in the statue's interior was peeling.
- The crown and spikes showed evidence of deterioration and required repair.
- Although the junction between the torch arm and the shoulder of the statue had been reinforced with steel plates in 1932, it required further strengthening.

A Centennial Commission was set up to oversee the conservation of the Statue of Liberty and of the neighbouring Ellis Island (the principal immigration point for the United States throughout much of the 19th and 20th centuries). The Commission worked with the existing Statue of Liberty – Ellis Island Foundation to fundraise and commission work. Over the four years of the project, the Foundation raised $66 million for the conservation work with further funds coming from the National Park Service. Private contractors overseen by the National Park Service principally carried out the conservation.

'Lady Liberty' is a national icon, a manifestation of ideals, so conservation had the potential to arouse strong feelings. The project team judged that the visual appearance of the statue was its most important aspect, and that major visual changes would be viewed negatively. They decided, therefore, to leave the external green patina of the statue intact. Although it would have been possible to strip the patina off and leave the statue 'penny bright', this appearance was not viable in the long term due to the corrosive coastal environment. Crucially the patina retarded the rate of corrosion; thus, the statue would last far longer by retaining its corrosion. The patina of the statue, which is principally composed of brochantite and antlerite (copper sulphate minerals) and atacamite (basic copper chloride), was simply washed with freshwater to remove dirt and accumulated salts. Paint and rust stains were mechanically removed. Inside the statue, the internal iron armature was corroding, and the continued pressure caused was damaging the external copper sheeting. After testing a number of metals, the whole iron armature was replaced with type 316 L stainless steel (UNS S31603), which was corrosion resistant, had similar physical properties to wrought iron (e.g. thermal expansion and strength) and could be cut to exactly the same size as the wrought iron that it replaced. The removal of the 1,800 pieces of the iron armature had to be carried out in full protective suits because of the health problems associated with asbestos dust. Each piece of stainless steel was individually shaped to match the wrought-iron piece it replaced and after shaping was annealed, cleaned, and passivated before being riveted into place with a layer of Teflon between the stainless steel and the copper skin and saddle to limit the electrochemical contact that could occur. A sample of the original wrought-iron armature, which was in good condition, was left in the right foot of the statue as a record of the original materials and structure used in the construction of the statue.

All the paint inside the statue, much of which was now failing as a protective coating, had to be removed from the inside of the statue to replace the iron bars. This removal could not involve any vigorous mechanical cleaning because of the potential damage to the copper metal skin and its outer patina. It was hazardous to use chemicals in the sealed confines of the statue because of the rapid build-up of toxic fumes. After experimentation, the outer layers of paint were removed by blasting them with liquid nitrogen (–196 °C), which made them brittle, so they flaked off easily. Traces of the initial coal-tar initial paint layer remained but could be abraded away using a stream of compressed air (60 psi) containing sodium-bicarbonate particles. This worked well, although if the sodium bicarbonate spilled through existing cracks onto the exterior it tended to turn the patina blue. Washing the exterior removed the sodium bicarbonate. Since paint had not originally been applied to the interior of the copper skin, it was decided to leave the skin unpainted. To stop water getting into the statue through the cracks between the copper plates, a silicon sealant was used. The central iron pylon and the rods connecting it to the armature were originally covered with red lead primer and six further coats of paint, much of which was flaking off. This was blasted clean with an air abrasive system using aluminium-oxide powder and an inorganic zinc dust and potassium-silicate coating was applied to the freshly exposed ironwork. This coating, developed by NASA, provided excellent corrosion protection and was subsequently sealed with three coats of 'Diamondite', a water-borne two-part epoxy-polyamide coating, which gave a very tough, irreversible, glossy, graffiti-resistant coating.

The torch was so degraded that most of it was replicated using the traditional methods and materials employed to create the original and replaced. Based on photographs and drawings, the torch's flame was recreated in the original completely solid form and gilded (as the original had been before 1905). When lit by spotlights on the ground and in the rim of the torch, it gives the effect of a glowing flame, the original intention. This created luminescence without the need for any holes in the skin that might admit water and promote corrosion within the monument. This was judged to be the best long-term solution for preserving the monument by the project conservators. It restored the artist's original intentions and the original form of the monument, while the original flame and upper part of the torch was cleaned and placed in a museum in the statue's plinth, preserving its evidence of manufacture as a document to the changing uses of the monument.

Additional stainless steel reinforcing bars were added to the statue's shoulder to provide better support for the torch arm. The possibility of remounting the arm into a slightly more secure position (possibly originally intended by Bartholdi) was considered but not undertaken because the visual transformation would be too great and would remove evidence of the original installation. The rays of the crown and their armature were made of brass, which originally appeared golden, rather than the pure 'tough pitch' copper used throughout the rest of the stature. They were extensively restored. Holes in the copper skin were repaired. Any new metal pieces and all the new rivets used in the replacement of the armature were patinated to blend in with the present exterior visual form of the statue.

In addition to the direct conservation and restoration of the statue, measures were taken to improve public access to the structure, to improve the visitor experience and to modify the interaction between the visitors (ca. 2.5 million annually) and the statue. A museum was created in the plinth to divert some visitors from ascending the statue and explain the monument and its conservation more. The spiral staircase that provides access to the crown level was strengthened and cleaned. Air conditioning was installed to cool the statue's interior, reducing the relative humidity fluctuation in the statue and making it more pleasant for visitors. New lighting, security and fire-protection systems were also installed. Where visitors could touch the copper skin at the crown level, it was protected with three coats of epoxy-polyamide paint on an acrylic-polymer base coat.

Conserving this statue required conservators make a series of careful judgements. Balance was needed between revealing the statue (replacing the torch, retaining the patina, and cleaning the unpainted internal surface of the copper skin), investigating it (studying the preservative effect of the patina and the form and construction of the replacement torch) and preserving it (retaining the original torch, sealing the cracks to stop water ingress, painting the iron support pylon, and adding air conditioning). The decisions made have meant that the statue in its present form is a restored compromise, with the patina of 100 years, the new flame in its original form and an open internal structure with modern air-conditioning, stainless-steel stairs, and glossy epoxy-painted ironwork. It has not been restored to an original state, nor thoroughly remade in a modern form, but instead gives (much of) the visual impact of the original while incorporating modern safety requirements essential for any public space and retaining the patina of age.

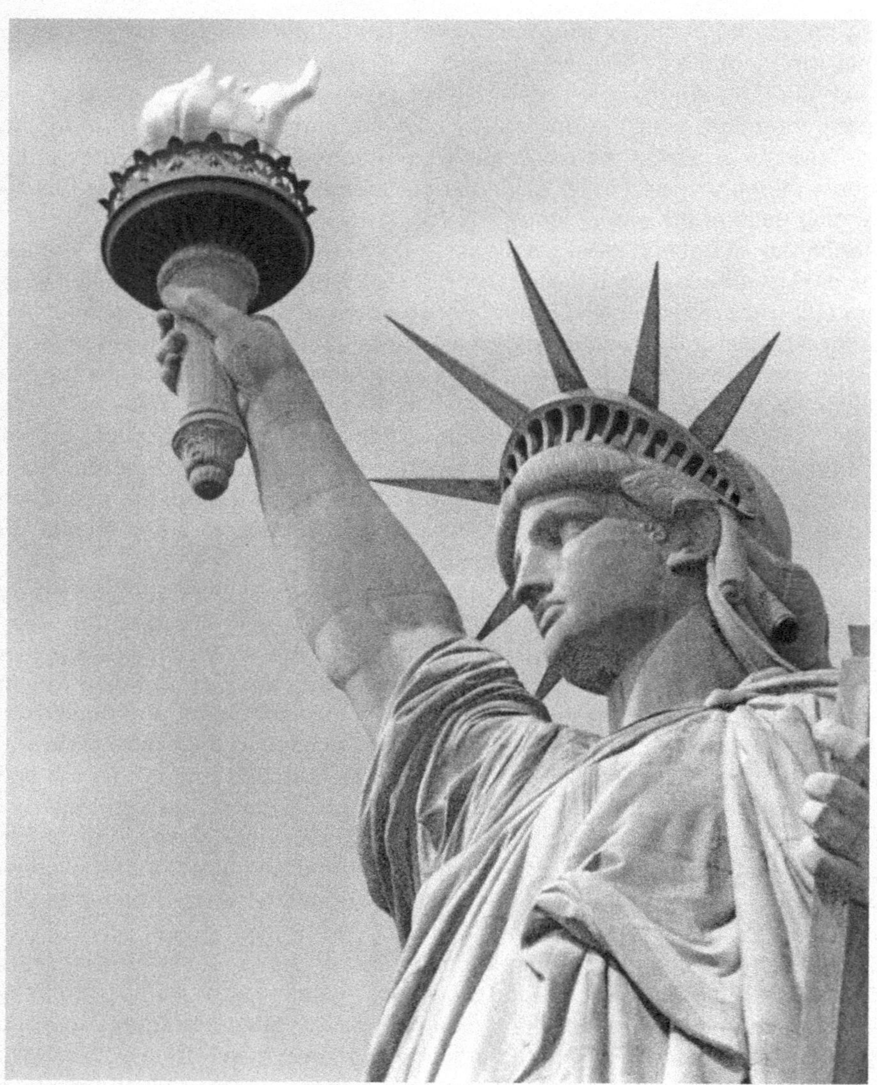

Figure 3.4 The Statue of Liberty. Robert Baboian.

3B Case Study: The *Mary Rose* (Jones 2003)

In July 1545, the fully equipped Tudor warship *Mary Rose* keeled over and sank in the Solent, as she was preparing to engage the French fleet. Almost all her crew drowned, they and her contents were trapped in the hull, which rested on its side on the seabed. Subsequently the tides slowly dragged away the timbers of her port side leaving the starboard half of the ship and its contents buried in the soft silt of the seabed. In the silt, oxygen-free (anoxic) conditions developed, which preserved much of the organic material. Rediscovered in 1971, by 1978 the decision had been made to excavate the site and recover the remains (Marsden 2003). Excavations between 1979 and 1982 removed the overlying silt, recovered over 19,000 artefacts, and exposed the hull. The internal decking, which was loose since all the iron nails had corroded away, was removed. Subsequently a steel frame was lowered into the water above the ship from which wires ran through the ship's structural framing to jack the half hull free of the seabed. The hull, suspended from the frame, was placed on a lower frame (cradle), which was bolted to the upper frame. The whole assembly was raised to the surface on live television. An estimated audience of 60 million people worldwide watched the ship emerge from the sea (Pearson and Schofield 2021).

The cradled hull of the *Mary Rose* was craned onto a barge and transferred to a dry dock in Portsmouth. Subsequently, still resting on its lower cradle, a temporary shelter was built over the dock permitting the hull to be cleaned and sprayed with chilled water (<5 °C) water to prevent microbial growth and prevent the timbers drying out and shrinking while allowing the marine salt to be washed out. Following detailed research, which showed that the wood of the hull had a microbial degraded outer layer and bacterially weakened internal structure, the hull was sprayed with a water-soluble wax (polyethylene glycol – PEG) solution to help preserve it. Initially (1994–2004) a low molecular weight PEG (PEG 200) was sprayed on the timbers, which helped stop the shrinkage of the cell walls of the wood. The concentration was incrementally increased to 40%. Subsequently (2004–2013) a heated solution of higher molecular weight PEG (PEG 2000) was sprayed on which helped fill the lumens and prevent cell collapse of the degraded wood cells on the outside of the ship's timbers. This solution was incrementally increased until it reached 60%. Since 2013, the ship has been slowly air-drying in a carefully controlled atmosphere (54% RH, 19 °C) to minimise the shrinkage and cracking of the wood. For the first few years, ducting was in place to distribute the conditioned air as evenly as possible and to prevent pockets of uneven drying or mould growth. The heterogeneous distribution of decay, PEG, and thus moisture content, within the wood has resulted in differential drying and thus slight movement of the hull (Lipkowitz *et al.* 2021).

While the hull was being treated, over 19,000 artefacts of different materials recovered from the ship were treated and in 2016, a new museum was opened in the dry dock, surrounding the ship, allowing all these finds to be seen alongside the ship. The conservation of the first artefacts retrieved from the

Mary Rose started in 1970 and has continued to evolve through to the present day. The initial challenge, as with all wrecks, was to conserve the very large numbers of waterlogged, salty, and vulnerable objects efficiently. Priorities needed to be set, a large team recruited and trained, and, in some cases, new treatment methods researched and developed. The materials the objects were made from, and the extent of their decay, guided the conservation treatment.

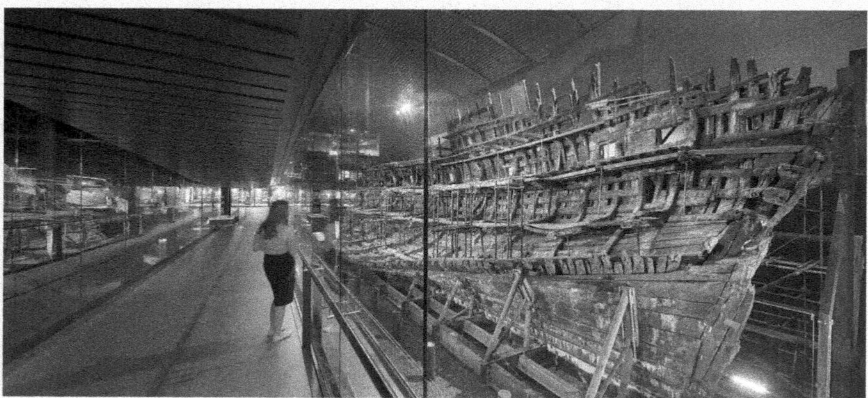

Figure 3.5 The starboard half of the *Mary Rose* hull, slowly drying out in the Mary Rose Museum, following PEG impregnation. Mary Rose Trust. © Hufton + Crow.

The decision to keep the ship intact (Figure 3.5) and to treat it in the configuration in which it was found has had a major impact on its treatment. While it might have been possible to dismantle the ship piece by piece and treat the timbers separately in large tanks and then air-dry them or to cut large beams into smaller pieces to fit in a freeze-dryer (as was done with the Dover Canoe and the Arles Rhone 3 ship), these approaches have downsides. Dismantling a ship, reduces its visibility, few people can see and understand it when it is a group of timbers in tanks, it can fall off the public's radar and interest can be lost. Cutting up timbers raises many ethical questions (Bernard-Maugiron and Courboulès, 2018). While these can be justified in certain cases, it is a hard decision to make. On the other hand, spray application of polyethylene glycol can lengthen treatment times, as it takes longer for the PEG to penetrate large pieces of wood.

An intact ship meant that members of the public, who already felt a connection to it after seeing it emerge from the harbour, could come and visit. Between 1982 and 2016, an estimated 7 million visitors saw conservation in action. They watched the timbers being cleaned and sprayed and air-dried and they generated valuable ticket revenues, which helped fund the ongoing work.

The *Mary Rose* Trust is a private charity (rather than a government funded project) so these funds were critical to the ongoing success of the project. The Trust has worked hard to generate a constant stream of media appearances, which focussed on research projects such as the ethnic origins of the sailors (DNA) or the medicines used by the ship's Apothecary, after the excitement of discovery and raising of the hull. Only such a high profile helps keep paying visitors coming and corporate sponsors and grant making bodies giving. If funding were to dry up, as it did for the Hasholme logboat, then the project risked being abandoned and only half-done.

Keeping the ship intact, also meant that the museum had to be built around the ship, necessitating even more careful and detailed planning than is typically needed for museum construction. Had the ship been being treated off site this might have been an easier process. Throughout the project, it has been essential to change both the organisational structure and focus from time to time. Different phases of the project from discovery and excavation to recovery and conservation to research and long-term conservation and display have required different skillsets and staffing configurations. The large initial team that focused on stabilisation has given way to a smaller team that is focused on maintenance and presentation. Such change is critical for the project to create a sustainable organisation that is capable of maintaining the hull and artefacts into the foreseeable future.

Ships are important part of the heritage for every major maritime nation, and many countries have now conserved ancient vessels (Sweden – the *Vasa*, Norway – the Oseberg ship, Denmark – the Roskilde ships, Germany – the Bremen Cog). Such ships provide a very detailed fragment of life at a specific moment (the day of the sinking) and are often prized as 'time capsules'. They have the capacity to captivate the public imagination as movies such as *Pirates of the Caribbean* attest. Although archaeologists focus on narratives of trade and shipboard life, rather than pirates and treasure, conserving such wrecks is a lengthy and hugely expensive business and only a small number of such projects can be sustained. Consequently, heritage authorities often prefer to preserve ships in situ, such as *Grace Dieu*, *Amsterdam*, and HMS *Hazardous* on the south coast of England (Oxley 1998). In England the Protection of Wrecks Act of 1973, legislation prompted by the risks faced by the *Mary Rose* whilst still a wreck site (Marsden 2003), now protects designated wreck sites. Excavation is only permitted if the site is under threat or there are sufficient funds guaranteed to see the project through to completion.

The research carried out on the materials from the *Mary Rose* has helped to shape our approaches to the conservation of archaeological objects from marine sites. Some of the initial conservation problems of dealing with wrecks have now largely been solved. However, new longer-term conservation issues have started to emerge:

- The stability of wood containing iron sulphides – the iron sulphides are slowly oxidising inside the wood making it acidic and causing it to lose strength. How can we address these problems without subjecting the ships to a costly and lengthy retreatment?

- Vessels that were designed to be supported by water are struggling to remain dimensionally stable on land and are slowly starting to slump. What are the best ways to support the ships and still make them accessible visually?
- Sustainability. Once the treatment is done, will visitors lose interest, or will we be able to continue generating the needed funds to support these materials? Since PEG treated wood has rather strict environmental conditions, how will we maintain these conditions as museums embrace the need for more environmentally sustainable solutions?

These are challenges for the 21st century.

Notes

1 The term conservator-restorer is often used in European definitions since in many European countries, especially those that speak the so-called 'Romance languages', variations on the term restorer are used to describe those who undertake conservation work.

2 A descriptive catalogue of works of art with explanations and scholarly comments.

3 For a full list of the charters relating to cultural heritage and links to their texts, please see https://www.getty.edu/conservation/publications_resources/research_resources/charters.html [Accessed 8/4/2020].

4 As of 2021, the Codes of Ethics are in the initial phase of another round of review.

5 Miss Havisham is a character in the novel *Great Expectations* by Charles Dickens (1861). She lives in a mouldering mansion forever accompanied by her past.

6 Interventive conservation – also sometimes called remedial conservation (Keene 1996) aims to prevent further decay and reveal information about the object through physical and/or chemical means. Interventive conservation activities typically include cleaning, consolidation, stabilisation, mending, and aesthetic reintegration. They are tailored to each object, depending on its composition and the extent and nature of the decay. Almost all early conservation textbooks (Rathgen 1898; Plenderleith and Werner 1971) focused on interventive conservation.

7 Preventive conservation – Aims to prevent further damage or decay from occurring. This involves mitigating threats to the object's safety by controlling the materials and environment around the object. Preventive conservation involves limiting access and handling of the object (e.g. through security, recording, packaging), physically supporting the object (e.g. appropriate packaging and mounts), and ensuring that environmental factors such as light, pollutants, relative humidity, and temperature do not promote decay. Many aspects of preventive conservation such as basic storage and simple cleaning (often defined as good housekeeping) can be undertaken by volunteers or staff not specifically trained in conservation. Other aspects, such as legal protection, risk assessment and environmental monitoring, are of a more specialised nature and are normally undertaken by heritage professionals.

4 Objects: Their Investigation and Recording

Objects and Society

Objects are products of larger cultures/societies, therefore examining objects carefully and understanding them not only allows scholars (and conservators) to learn something about the society that created an artefact but is fundamental to how we begin to recognise an object's values and significance. The complex relationship between people and objects as well as the ways in which modern Western society interprets past societies from their artefacts have been a matter of considerable study (cf. Miller *et al.* 1991; Pearce 1994; Hoskins 1998; Schiffer 1999; Caple 2006; Tilley *et al.* 2006; Hurcombe 2007; Robb 2009; Abousnnouga and Machin 2010; Gilchrist 2012; Hodder 2012) and the subject of a number of conceptual models that have explored the relationships between objects and people. In the 19th century, archaeologists interpreted objects as having a simple functional role, the form and construction of the object being directly related to the technological development of the society that made and used the object (Pitt Rivers 1875). The work of early 20th-century anthropologists, such as Malinowski and Radcliffe Brown, showed that complex social structure was invariably reflected within objects, while 20th-century archaeologists have shown that there is a complexity between social belief and the expression of form and decoration of an object. This has led to an awareness that all objects are culturally and contextually sensitive (Tilley 1994), and that even the materials of their construction have complex meaning and symbolism (McGhee 1994).[1] Thus, objects must be understood in terms of the culture and date from which they derive. Objects can also be seen as palimpsests, having an evolving series of meanings over time (Ames 1994; Williams 2020). Hodder (1987) has proposed that objects possess three forms of identity:

- As an object: raw materials shaped by technology to form an object, which performs a function within a given society.
- As part of a context: when associated with other objects, an item forms part of an assemblage that is codified and reinforced by the social order.
- As a signifier: embodying and signifying past experience, through its appearance it carries ideas (religious or ideological) of the past into the present.

Objects are physical manifestations of the thoughts and ideas of a culture. Everything which is created, as opposed to being found, is formed by the action of tools (including machines) upon raw materials. The tool is important but so too is the craft or expertise

DOI: 10.4324/9781003009078-4

to use the tool or operate the machine. Products emerge from this creative process. A carpenter's tools create a piece of furniture (product) from a block of wood (raw material). Equally, less tangible products can be produced; blowing air (the raw material) through a musical instrument (a complex tool) can with the ability of a skilled musician (expertise) create music (product). An author can produce a written document (product) using a pen (tool) and paper and ink (raw materials). The evidence of these processes is unevenly represented in the record of the past. A carpenter's tools and even his furniture may survive, but his expertise, his knowledge of joinery, does not survive directly. It must be deduced from the surviving tools and furniture. Where the product does not survive (e.g. music, or food), expertise may be impossible to deduce, although it may be partially preserved in the form of written description, recipes, musical notations, and/or descriptions of the artists or craftsmen at work. It is important to remember that a product can also serve as raw material for a subsequent process; for example, flour is both the product of a mill and a raw material for cooking, similarly a statue (product) may be melted down (raw material) to create another object.

Archaeologists, anthropologists, and curators have developed systems for exploring the wider cultural, technical, and social connections objects have. Such systems include:

- *Chaîne Opératoire:* A methodological approach that looks at the production steps needed to move from raw material to the creation of a desired object. Analysis of prehistoric flints in France revealed that visually similar flint tools had been formed using different sequences of flaking actions and that this occurred with consistency across a number of sites. Consequently, it was deduced that two groups or cultures were present; the sequence of events or chain of operations in a manufacturing process is often specific to (characterises) one culture (habituated activities reinforcing social organisation and beliefs) and distinguishes it from another (Soressi and Geneste 2011).
- *Object biography:* A life history of the object from its production (birth), through its use (life) to its discard (death). Proposed as an analytical technique by Igor Kopytoff (1986), object biography has been seized on to explore the relationships between objects and people and has been applied to both individual objects (Peers 1999; Seip 1999) and groups of objects (Rainbird 1999; Whitley 2002; Schamberger *et al.* 2012).
- *Object production and use sequence (OPUS):* This technique (Figure 4.1) builds on both chaîne opératoire and object biography to consider the object as a series of production and use sequences, which may include recycling and reuse, abandonment, loss, or rediscovery (Caple 2006).
- *Fragmentation and enchainment:* Artefact fragments have value as a means of invoking the whole object (enchainment). The part derived from and representing the whole is seen in Neolithic pottery fragments from the same vessel placed in separate postholes of a building (Chapman 2000; Chapman and Gaydarska 2007) to the fragments of the 'true cross' dispersed throughout Christendom. In such contexts, it may be inappropriate to unquestioningly re-join fragments as this may obscure their history as separate and valued objects.

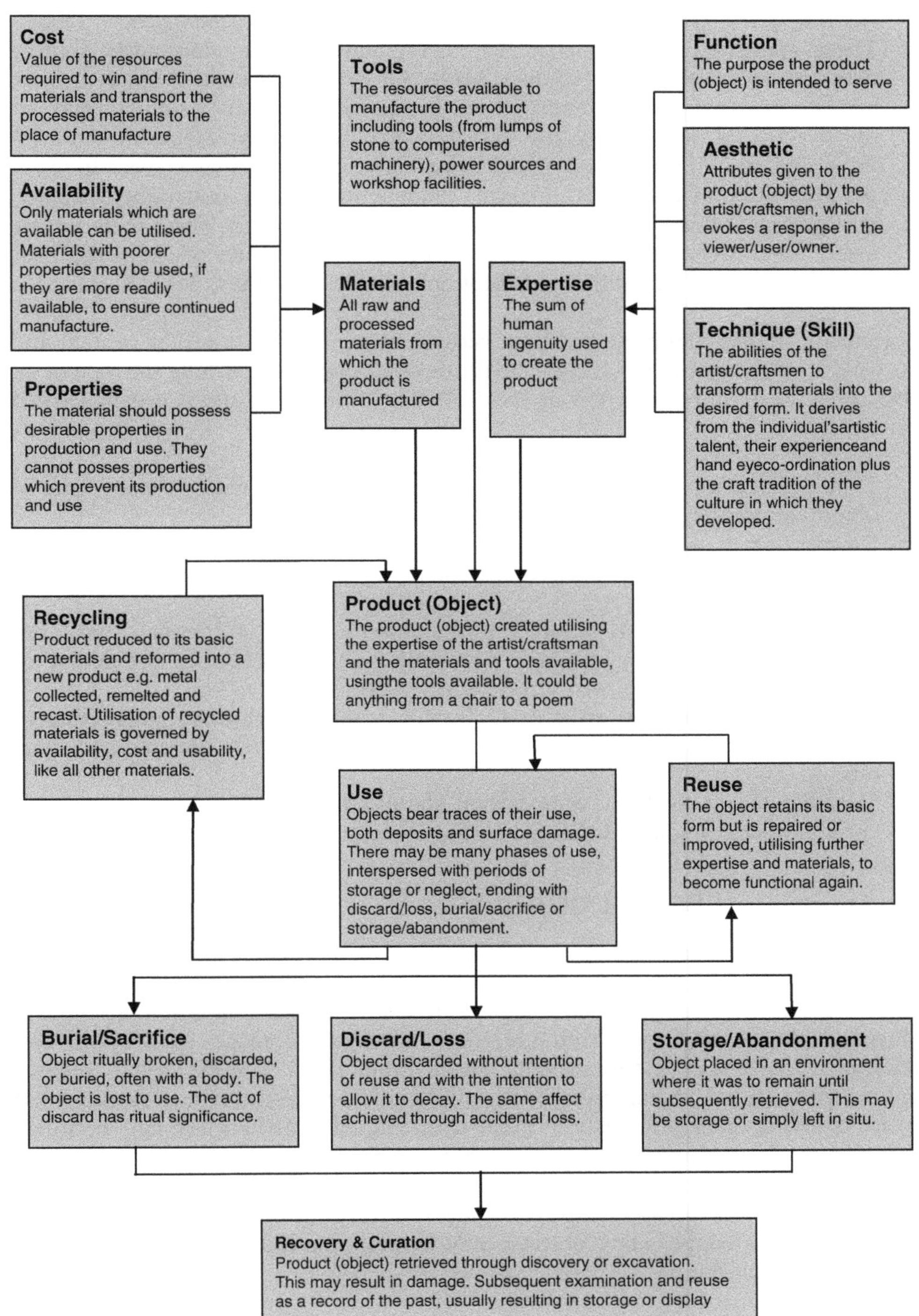

Figure 4.1 Object production and use sequence. Chris Caple.

- *Actor network theory (ANT), Symmetrical archaeology* and *entanglement* theory: These related approaches posit that everything exists in constantly shifting networks of relationships (Hodder 2012). All elements, humans, objects, ideas, and processes are equally important in creating social situations; humans may act on objects, but objects may also act on people shaping perceptions and world-views and on other objects. Symmetrical archaeology in particular seeks to avoid the imposition of essentialist dualisms (human/non-human; materiality/sociality; past/present) often present in our study of material culture. These methods are useful for conservation in terms of thinking about the agency of decay (Edensor 2011) and how it mediates our perceptions of objects and our world.

Objects are studied and preserved both because of the information they contain and for what they represent, which may change through time. Establishing the date of an object may be an important part of accessing this information and is usually carried out by:

- Typological comparison of the object's form or decoration with a known series of objects or artistic style or movement.
- Recovery from a known dated context.
- Identification of a material in the object that was introduced or abandoned after a given date.
- Identification of a historical record of the object in either written or visual form; for example, a specific mention in a will or its presence in a painting or photograph.
- Attribution to a known artist or craftsman, sometimes through a signature or maker's mark. In some cases, hallmarks may be used to date the gold and silver objects.
- Scientific means such as radiocarbon dating for organic materials, dendrochronology for wood and thermoluminescence for fired ceramic materials.

The Structure and Decay of Objects

Important information is present at the object's surface, which typically bears all the traces of decoration, signs of wear, manufacturing marks, and evidence of repair. This thin ephemeral layer (often only 1–2 mm thick) is also the one that endures constant damage and loss from use, the burial environment, excavation, and handling (Figure 4.2). Consequently, considerable effort is necessary to recover and preserve the valuable and fragile traces of evidence present at such surfaces and avoid removing them with hasty or excessive treatments. The surface may be soiled (Chapter 5), decayed, corroded, contain mineral preserved organics, or hold traces of gilding or paint, or accretions from use, such as cooking residues or DNA. Features of surface decay, such as craquelure (cracking on picture varnishes) or patinas on some copper alloy objects, may be desirable indicators of age, despite being products of decay.

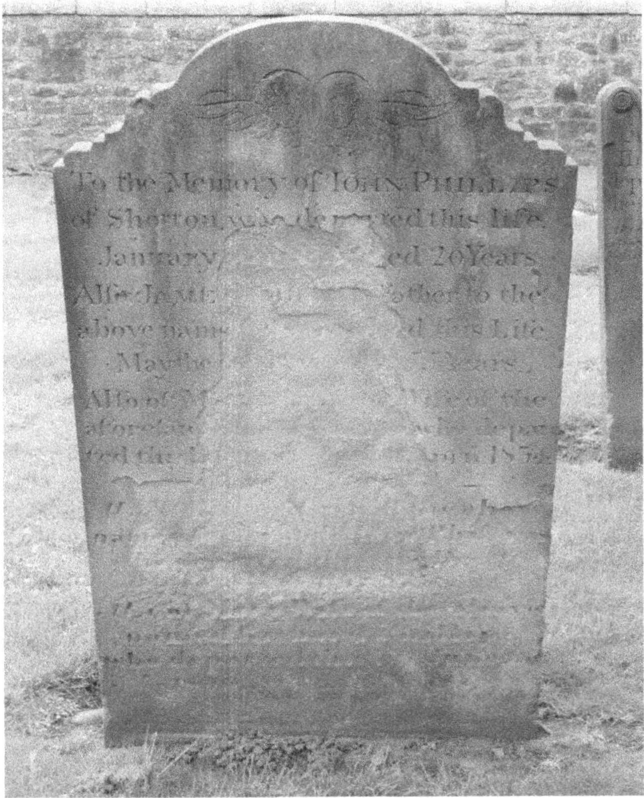

Figure 4.2 Gravestone in the churchyard at Staindrop, County Durham. The surface inscription is being lost due to weathering and decay. If this continues unchecked it will eventually be impossible to see for whom it was erected. Emily Williams.

Information is also present in the body or substrate of the piece – the main material(s) from which the object is composed, which may provide structural integrity to the object. The substrate's properties inform the nature of the object, for example, a ship with a wooden hull will behave differently from one with a metal hull. An underlying structure, such as a framework or armature, may support the substrate. In the case of a painting, the paint layer is the surface, the body of the painting may be canvas and the stretcher acts as the support (or framework) that holds the canvas taut. Similarly, bronze statues may have internal iron armatures that tie various, separately cast, elements together and support them (Case Study 3A: The Statue of Liberty). The role of the support may also be filled or augmented by fasteners, such as dowels, nails, and screws. Like the surface both the body and the supporting elements are subject to decay and this may endanger the object. For example, marble statues and architectural elements may be broken and stained by corroding iron supports, while the painted surfaces of Egyptian sarcophagi and statuettes can be endangered by fungal and termite attack to the wooden substrate (Davis and Chemello 2014).

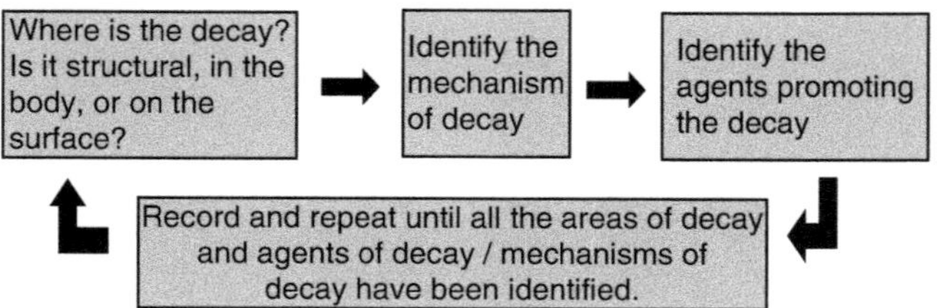

Figure 4.3 Decay detection sequence. Chris Caple.

Decay may be the result of physical, chemical, or biological decay processes. If the object is not stabilised, it may lose its surface and any associated information, and the decay may continue until the whole object is too fragile for handling or display and is eventually lost. It is not always easy to identify the primary mechanisms of decay and the agents that cause them (Cather 2003). The fact that multiple forms of decay may be present, one triggering or building on another (synergy), often complicates matters and results in a far more degraded artefact. To successfully conserved and stabilise an object, it is essential that the nature and extent of all the forms of decay forms are identified accurately (Figure 4.3). It is important that the most damaging issues, particularly those causing structural problems (such as the iron armature supporting the Statue of Liberty, Case Study 3A) are dealt with before the surface (cosmetic) issues are tackled.

Decay mechanisms are usually identified indirectly through observing their breakdown products, such as the frass from insect infestation, or their consequences, such as flaking paint or a loss in density. It is often appropriate to analyse and identify the cause of the decay either directly such as identifying the insect or fungi attacking the object or indirectly – identifying the breakdown mineral on a corroded metal object.

Investigation

The investigation of any object starts with a series of questions. These may include:

- What is the object's function? How does its shape or the materials that it was made from help or hinder this function and why?
- Why were the shape, colour, and decoration (including but not limited to writing, symbols, and figural motifs) chosen? What might they have signified to the user? And what knowledge or belief systems might others have needed to understand such symbols?
- Is there evidence of use, wear, or repair? What does it say about the changing uses of the object?
- What does the object's association with other places and things (its context) tell us about it?
- What can the object's deterioration tell us about its history?

The study of a complex object, or assemblage, with a complicated history may involve teams of curators, scientists, and conservators and be the subject of long-term research. However, individual conservators often find themselves needing to investigate discrete objects to begin formulating treatment approaches.

Careful examination and analysis enable the conservator to 'read' an object and understand how it was created, what materials were used, how they were assembled, as well as the nature of the decay processes that afflict those materials and whether subsequent repair or conservation work has been undertaken and how. To do this successfully, the conservator should take a holistic approach that avoids introducing pre-conceived notions of what should or should not be present, consult published information and where possible seek advice from experts. The process may consist of two steps:

1 *Examination:* A visual assessment of the object to determine what is present, how it was formed and whether it has altered. This is an ongoing process that does not stop with an initial assessment but continues to be carried out and revised throughout the conservator's engagement with the object.
2 *Analysis:* An exploration of the elemental, isotopic, molecular, and crystalline characteristics of specific material elements of the artefact using microscopic, instrumental, and chemical techniques. Analysis may help to determine specific attributes such as the cause of decay, date, or culture of the artefact. It may require sampling (testing a small amount) and be either non-destructive or destructive.

It is important to record both the observations and analysis so that they can inform not only the study of the object but also wider technical, social, and cultural studies.

Visual Examination

An initial visual examination can determine whether elements are missing from the object, as well as what parts are cracked, damaged, broken, and decayed. Cracks, folds, tears, corrosion, and losses should be photographed or diagrammed to record them. Many corrosion and decay products can be identified during this process through familiarity with the decay processes and visual observation of colour, texture, and form. The extent to which dirt, decay and loss obscures the surface is important to record, as so much of an object's informational content lies at its surface. This helps to determine the condition (stability or lack thereof) of the object and informs its treatment. Visual examination may also reveal features that are uniquely created by specific tools or manufacturing techniques, such as weave details on textiles, laid lines of paper, joining methods in wood and file marks in metal. These can be enhanced using raking (low angled) light which highlights small changes in surface texture. This information can help date the object and identify the culture that created it. Evidence of wear (smooth areas, loss of decoration, scratching) may point to the history and use of the piece.

Magnification (using stereo or binocular microscopy) extends visual examination making important features of manufacture and use more apparent. In the case of

Roman boxwood combs, magnification revealed the presence of nits and hair lice between their teeth (Fell 1996). This small find graphically revealed the problems of life in Roman Britain.

Visual examination can be augmented using portions of the electromagnetic spectrum. The most common of these examination techniques include:

- *X-radiography:* This technique reveals changes in the thickness and density of materials enabling the identification of iron objects buried in a mass of corrosion. Similarly, supports and internal armatures can be identified, as can earlier versions of compositions under paintings and discontinuities or flaws in materials (Gilardoni *et al.* 1994; Lang and Middleton 2005; O'Connor and Brooks 2007). Since the two-dimensional rendering of three-dimensional objects on the x-radiography may complicate interpretation (Figure 1.6) and there may be several possible explanations for the features seen, it is advisable to examine the object and x-radiograph together.
- *Infrared reflectography:* This technique relies on the differential reflectance or absorption of infrared radiation to reveal changes in composition. Infrared light is absorbed by charcoal revealing underdrawings that might otherwise be hidden by the paint surface and may reveal discrepancies between what the artist planned to do and what they ultimately painted (van Schoute and Verougstraete-Marcq 1986; Walmsley *et al.* 1992). It has also been used to make faint traces of ink more visible and allow early texts to be read. Examples include the waterlogged Roman writing tablets from Vindolanda (Bowman *et al.* 1974).
- *Ultraviolet-induced visible fluorescence:* This technique takes advantage of the fact that different minerals and resins are excited by exposure to UV radiation, causing them to emit characteristic visible fluorescence (Hickey-Friedman 2002). In contrast, areas that are not excited by ultraviolet radiation absorb it and appear dark. It can facilitate detection of modern restorations on a variety of surfaces and permits the separation of leaded glass from soda-lime glass (Measday 2017).

New imaging techniques including multispectral imaging (Case Study 4B: *Archimedes Palimpsest*), hyperspectral imaging, and reflectance transform imaging (RTI) are extending these capabilities further.

Basic knowledge needs to be combined with visual observation to identify things correctly. For example, many materials decay in characteristic ways, which can aid identification; for example, copper corrosion may be green or blue, iron corrosion is normally orange or red. Familiarity with a range of materials from different time periods, cultures, and burial or storage conditions can facilitate identification and may speed the process rendering it nearly intuitive.

Non-Visual Physical Properties

The visual qualities of a material are only one of many physical attributes that it possesses, including density (weight), smell, surface texture, hardness, elasticity, drape, magnetism, even taste. By comparing these with known specimens, conservators can often successfully identify the materials from which an object is composed. Examples include identifying plastics by the characteristic smells of their deterioration products or separating metallic iron from other white metals by using a magnet. The requirements placed on materials by functionality, as well as the limited range of materials cheaply available and normally used by any given society at a given date, may aid in the identification. Differences in properties can distinguish between likely materials; for example, melting point can be used to identify materials such as waxes, although mixtures can make this difficult.

Analysis

It might be imagined that conservators would want to analyse every bit of an object before they started conservation, so they could be certain about what they had, why it was decaying, and what had been done to it before. However, as noted above, there are often a limited number of possibilities and analytical techniques can be expensive, time consuming, and at times difficult to interpret. Therefore, in most cases, analysis may not be practical or even affordable. Prior to commissioning or undertaking analysis, a conservator should consider:

- Whether there is a sufficiently good justification for doing the analysis. Reasons that might justify the time and cost of analysis include the uniqueness of the object, the degree to which the answer can guide the treatment, and the accessibility of the analytical technique.
- Whether the analytical method selected can provide the information required. Although all analytical techniques provide information, it is important to formulate the questions carefully first to determine which technique can best answer them.
- The importance of qualitative information (the presence or absence of a particular element) and quantitative information (the amount of an element present). Quantitative information is more difficult and consequently expensive to obtain.
- Whether the conservator can understand and interpret the information produced. Interpretation usually requires detailed background knowledge and comparative samples or data against which to compare the unknown. Therefore, it may be as important to get comparative data or expert advice and interpretation as it is to get the initial analyses. Dauntingly, there may be several explanations for any analytical result.
- Whether the proposed treatment will render future analysis impossible. For example, some treatments can render later dating techniques invalid.
- Any reasons for not examining or analysing an object. These may include damage caused by taking samples from the object or ethical constraints (such as sampling sacred objects).

It is invariably appropriate to start with the simplest, cheapest analytical method capable of delivering a useful answer. Many materials, inorganic and organic, can be identified through microscopy, which reveals unique visual aspects of their microstructure, enabling their characterisation. Wood species (Hoadley 1991), leather (Haines 1985), textiles (Robertson *et al.* 2018), pollen (Moore *et al.* 1991), pigments (Feller 1978; Roy 1994), stone (Reedy 2008), paint cross-sections (Byrne and Cook 1976), dust (McCrone and Delly 1973), and metals (Scott 1991) can all be identified successfully by conservators with optical microscopy training. Where higher magnification is required, or additional analytical information required, scanning electron microscopy (SEM-EDS) is often used.

Simple chemical spot tests (Odegaard *et al.* 2005) can help identify many materials. In medieval British wall painting, common red pigments used were ochre (iron oxide), minium (lead oxide), and cinnabar (mercury sulphide). Chemical spot tests can identify them inexpensively but may require sampling and can be very time consuming if there are many samples to analyse. Using an elemental detection technique, such as portable X-ray fluorescence (pXRF) can eliminate the need for sampling, but the cost of the equipment may limit its availability. Information about which pigment was employed would be useful in the context of an archaeological report (cf. Caple 2007: 165–170) although treating the material to prevent flaking and pigment loss could potentially be done without knowing the answer. On the other hand, the treatment of the *Mary Rose* (Case Study 3B) could not have been carried out without a variety of forms of analyses, which have helped to determine the degree of sulphur contamination present and offered new treatment approaches (Chadwick *et al.* 2012).

Conservators should be familiar with the range of available scientific analytical techniques (Pollard *et al.* 2007) and their potential application to the analysis of historic, archaeological, and artistic works (Bromelle and Thomson 1982; Caple 2006; Stuart 2007; Artioli 2010; Shugar and Mass 2012). Since analytical techniques are ever evolving, detection limits are changing, sensitivity is increasing, and recommendations about sample size, handling, and storage can change, it is also important for conservators to update their knowledge regularly. Figure 4.4 shows some of the more commonly used techniques for the analysing inorganic and organic materials. Multiple techniques may be employed to provide accurate and complete answers. The more complicated the question, the more important it is for the conservator to work with a conservation scientist to define the optimal methodology and testing sequence necessary to provide the best answers and to utilise the fewest samples.

Every analytical system has strengths and weaknesses that must be understood. Repeated analysis of two corroded bronze statues from ancient Egypt took place at the Fogg Art Museum and subsequently the Harvard Art Museums between 1945 and the present day (Bewer *et al.* 2017). Various corrosion products were identified, and these identifications contributed to different interpretations of the cause of active decay and different interventions at different dates. However, the variety of instruments used – XRD, FTIR, and Raman – each with different sensitivities to various corrosion minerals may well account for the differing results (Bewer *et al.* 2017). Although the presence of a specific mineral was clearly demonstrated by the analytical system in each case, it was the assumptions made in relating the mineral to a specific decay mechanism and treating that as 'the' explanation of the object decay that was problematic.

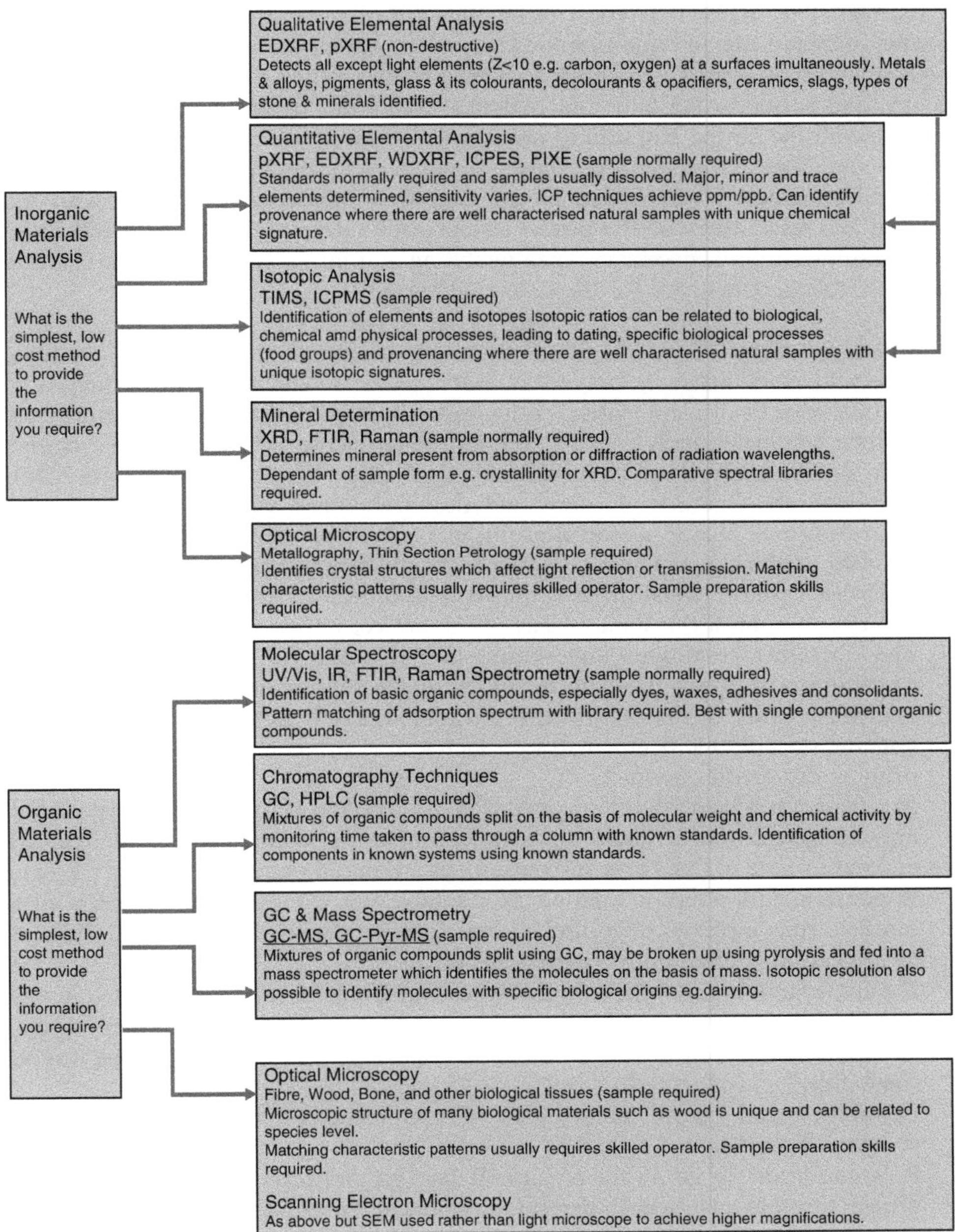

Figure 4.4 Common techniques used for the analysis of inorganic and organic materials in the opening decades of the 21st century. Chris Caple.[2]

Conservators should be cautious about the analytical data they obtain themselves or receive from others. Analytical techniques are often promoted as a 'black box' capable of answering any question; however, the answers are seldom so clear-cut. A single analysis of a surface without background knowledge of the culture, its technology, and period, using only one analytical technique, by an operator lacking experience with the device, can lead to meaningless, even potentially misleading results. Multiple analyses across the object using a range of techniques with standards and comparative material, interpreted by an analyst or conservator familiar with the material and technology of the period can provide information that is much more meaningful. Caution is necessary when analysing and interpreting data from historic and archaeological material for the following reasons:

- Corrosion and surface soiling on the exterior surfaces of archaeological artefacts, especially metal artefacts, may mean that the correspondence between the results and the object's original material is limited. Although portable X-ray fluorescence systems can increasingly provide non-destructive elemental analysis at reasonable cost, surface analysis can be misleading (Caple 2000: 86; Shugar and Mass 2012).
- The apparent accuracy of many analytical techniques, which quotes results to several decimal places, is often illusory. It is advisable where possible to analyse a certified analytical standard along with the unknown samples and compare the published results against the determined composition for this standard. It is good practice to publish this data as part of the project results.[3]
- The operating conditions and sensitivities of analytical instruments can vary enormously. It is important to be aware of the sensitivities and abilities of the analytical system in use and to know the minimum detectable limit of the element, mineral, or molecule being analysed. Such knowledge can prevent non-detection being interpreted as absence.
- An element can be present in many different forms (species). For example, copper may be detected in a liquid as; metal particles in suspension, as an oxidised mineral form (e.g. $CuCO_3$ in suspension), as a reduced mineral form (e.g. Cu_2O in suspension), dissolved in solution as a soluble ion Cu^{2+}, held in the form of a sequestered complex or deposited in some form on the sides of the vessel. Element identification is often only a partial answer.
- It is important to ensure that the analytical equipment is not contaminated in any way prior to carrying out the analysis, since this can lead to misleading results. Analysing a blank or a control sample of known composition first is one way to check this.
- Calibration and careful maintenance of equipment is important to ensure the veracity of results.
- It is important to be aware of natural background levels. Many elements are present in small quantities in the soil, groundwater, or atmospheric dust. The level detected must be significantly above background levels to be meaningful. Thus, the presence of traces of titanium in a pink paint (red and white pigments) may indicate an impurity in the iron oxide (red component) rather than that the white pigment was titanium dioxide.

- The surfaces of archaeological and historic objects are often aged, dirty, oxidised, and degraded. They consequently rarely provide simple clear analytical results. Analysts who normally analyse modern materials may consequently have difficulty interpreting the results in a meaningful way.

Sampling

Sometimes the only way of gaining meaningful data is to sample the object, i.e. to remove a small part to ascertain information about the whole. This may be because of the type of analysis to be undertaken, the location of the analytical technique, or the size of the object itself. In cases where the object is not homogeneous (due to natural variations in the manufacture or mixing of the component materials, construction, or decay) it may be necessary to sample in several locations. In the case of the Yarm helmet, four triangular pieces of iron sheet up to 18 mm × 8 mm were cut from separate bands and plates of the helmet and subjected to metallographic examination including SEM-EDS analysis of the slag particles. The samples were taken from areas that were already damaged and showed that the entire helmet was made of a low-temperature smelted phosphoric iron hammered from multiple blooms, typical of early medieval ironwork and very different to the homogeneous low carbon steel typical of the post-medieval period. The object, which lacked a secure archaeological context, was shown to be an original Viking helmet and not a 19th-century copy as had previously been hypothesised. The losses caused by sampling were subsequently filled. In this case, the damage caused by sampling was justified by the quality and certainty of the information recovered (Caple 2020a).

Despite the importance of samples for answering specific questions, it is important to remember that multiple sampling campaigns can inevitably eat away at the object and that future techniques may ultimately provide better answers. The long-term concern over the 'brown spots' on the walls of Tutankhamun's tomb and the worry that they were associated with visitation led to multiple sampling campaigns, resulting in significant loss (Wong *et al.* 2017). Eventually, improvements in scanning and imaging techniques permitted the careful comparison of historic images of the tomb with modern images and the realisation that the spots had neither multiplied nor changed since the tomb was opened initially.

Some analytical methods (destructive techniques) consume the samples, whereas others (non-destructive techniques) permit their retention. The owner's permission must be obtained before any sample is taken from an object; the risks and rewards associated with sampling should be clearly laid out to enable them to decide whether the information to be gained justifies the damage to the object. Where possible, it is important to retain the samples for future re-analysis. In some cases, such as metallographic samples, this may require special storage to ensure that the samples do not deteriorate over time. Samples should be catalogued in a way that clearly references the object they are taken from and allows them to be easily located. When removing a sample from an object, it is important to ensure that the removal process does not result in the contamination of the sample. This may require removing and storing the sample in very carefully controlled circumstances depending on the nature of the analysis.

Reporting Analytical Results

Any analytical work that is undertaken must be reported to the object's curator/owner. Details of the analytical system and its operating conditions should be given, so that any effects/biases of the system, such as non-detection, can be correctly interpreted. The report should:

- Describe the object and indicate where it was sampled.
- Describe the analytical method used. Indicate the accuracy, precision, minimum detectable levels, and operating conditions of the analytical system used. Any sample preparation techniques used should also be described as well as any data manipulation and standards used to obtain the analytical data.
- Present the data.
- Interpret the data with reference to comparative analyses.
- Present conclusions drawn from this analytical work.

Consideration should be given to making the information available to a wider audience such as publication or proving copies of the information to appropriate databases.

Purpose and Nature of Documentation

Documentation is a key component of ethical conservation practice, it is also a practice that is embedded in scientific method, so it is not surprising to find that Rathgen advised taking photographs prior to treatment to ensure information was retained in case the treatment failed or the object was lost (Rathgen 1905: 57). However, early conservation literature rarely referenced documentation (Moore 2001) and the standards of the documentation carried out varied widely (Aleppo 2003; Hindin 2014). Some early documentation was created for management purposes, to statistically demonstrate the types of work conservation studios carried out each year and how much of it they did (Aleppo 2003). The inclusion of specific guidelines on how to document treatments in the Murray Pease Report, the profession's first code of practice (Murray Pease Committee 1964), suggests that conservators viewed documentation as important and as something that set them apart from cleaners and 'restorers'.

Making a record of the object and its conservation serves many purposes:

- *Detailed examination:* Encourages conservators to examine objects in detail and ensures that they are fully aware of all aspects of the object's composition and decay and that the proposed cleaning and conservation work is appropriate. This sort of examination can take days or even weeks in the case of complex objects. Recording the process minimises the risk that details will be forgotten contributing to accidental damage or delay in the conservation process.
- *Information source:* All the information discovered about the object is assembled to form the record. This is an essential element in the investigation process, ensuring that all the information uncovered is available to others. The record pulls

together a wide variety of different types of information about the object: X-rays, photographs, analyses, observations, and published references. Findings made during examination and treatment can inform the work of allied professionals and speak to a broad range of topics ranging from the provenance of the object to its biography to the working techniques of the maker.
- *Preventive conservation practice:* A body of evidence is created that can be examined instead of the object itself. This may provide more information than the object and forms a preventive conservation measure limiting the need to handle and observe the object directly (e.g. the costume collection of Warwick Museum; Kavanagh 1990).
- *Collections management:* A visual and written record of the object at a given point in time is created in order that changes, such as corrosion, loss, or damage, that occur during conservation or during subsequent storing, handling and display, can be detected. Should the object's unique identifier (e.g. museum number or site code) be lost or deliberately removed, this record may facilitate identification.
- *Treatment evaluation:* A record of the conservation work and materials used on the object. Details of all chemicals, treatment times and coatings are recorded so that, in the future, the success of a particular conservation treatment or chemical can be established (Sully and Suenson-Taylor 1996; Williams 2004).
- *Treatment design:* A record of the information necessary to allow an object to be successfully re-conserved. It also provides health-and-safety information regarding the use of chemicals, biocides, and solvents and identifies any risk-posed objects or future conservators by the presence of hazardous materials. A valuable example for other conservators designing treatments for similar objects.

The creation of a conservation record recognises that treatment is not an end in itself, but rather part of a series of ongoing processes, which last for the object's entire life. It provides an important element of the object narrative and it acknowledges that others will come after the present conservator who will need information about the object and who may undertake further investigation, revelation, or preservation work. The record's importance is often recognised when it is consulted and found to contain valuable information such as evidence of the original appearance that subsequent deterioration has removed or details of a conservation treatment that was successfully/unsuccessfully applied. To be useful, the record must have three key attributes:

- *Permanence:* The record survives intact. It is no use if it is degraded/corrupt.
- *Accessibility:* It is useless if it survives but cannot be found when required. Computerised records with searchable terms fit the accessibility criteria.
- *Valuable content:* Images and information that are useful. It is not useful when it is found intact but was poorly compiled and does not contain the required information.

Digital records hold tremendous promise in terms of accessibility, but permanence can be an issue, since the lifespan of some hardware used to store digital media can be as low as five years (Beck 2013). Paper records and print photographs may last a

100 years or more but can be harder to access unless robust tracking systems are in place. While the conservator undertaking work on the object is responsible for the initial record, it is important to identify who has responsibility for maintaining the conservation record (from carrying out periodic migrations of digital records to ensuring that paper records are accessible and kept in appropriate archival conditions).

The Conservation Record

Whilst the need for a conservation record is unquestionable, its nature and extent are a matter of judgement. Consequently, the type of information and level of detail noted in a conservation record can vary enormously (Bradley 1983; Corfield 1983; Corfield 1992; Dollery and Henderson 1996; Keene 1996; Applebaum 2007: 395–417; Watson 2010: 171–179). No single recording system is universally applied due to both the variations in the type and nature of objects treated and the fact that the conservation record is often part of a larger sequence of records maintained by a heritage institution (Aleppo 2003). The individual facts recorded in the conservation record provide information relevant to one or more of the functions mentioned above.

Information is often grouped into two forms:

- *Conservation proposal:* A proposal of the work to be undertaken. This may be created for a client (curator/owner) to approve or as roadmap for a group of conservators working together on a complex project to help ensure that roles, sequences, and approaches are clear.
    - Typically, it will include information from sections A, B1, and C.
- *Treatment report:* A report of the treatment work undertaken. Typically, these are individual records tailored to each object although occasionally they may also be batch records, reporting on the identical treatment of a group of artefacts. The level of detail included is a matter of professional judgement depending on the complexity and 'value' of the object. The potential benefit from the record is balanced against the time (cost) taken to create the record.
    - Typically, it includes information from sections A, B2, and C.

The following list indicates information that is frequently recorded, although not all treatment reports contain every field:

A – Object Data

Client's name: This may be a curator in the heritage institution where the conservator works, or it may be the owner (an individual or another institution) who is commissioning the work. The client is the entity that will approve the work and to whom reports should be sent.

Object number: Every object should have a unique identifier (typically an alphanumeric sequence but occasionally, as in the case of a painting, a title) and which usually relates to the museum or collection where the object is housed or the place from where it was excavated or recovered. Some objects have several numbers, all of which should be included in the conservation record.

Name: This may include the common/short name and if known the full or correct name. Wherever possible reference should be made to standardised terminology (Thesauri) and definitions where they exist (MDA 1997; Szrajber 1997).

Laboratory number: In some institutions this may be the object number, in others every object coming into the laboratory is given a unique number. The object or laboratory number ensures that information, unique to each object, is associated with the correct object.

Photograph/digital image: Every object should be photographed to capture the detail of its appearance (Dorrell 1989; Warda 2011). The image should contain a scale, colour card, and object or laboratory number. A 'before' image is normally taken to record the condition prior to treatment, and an 'after' image is taken once conservation is complete. For three-dimensional objects a full record requires that all sides of the object are imaged. Additional 'during photos' may be taken to record new information revealed or steps in the treatment. These may be in the form of details or overall images.

Drawing: Annotated sketches or drawings are a particularly effective way of providing information about an object. They can be very quick sketches or full technical drawings (Adkins and Adkins 1989; Griffiths *et al.* 1990). The act of drawing an object can help a conservator to better understand how component elements integrate and why it is in the condition it is in.

References to further information: This may include the numbers and location of photographic negatives or positives, past treatment records, digital images, IR reflectograms, UV images, X-ray plates, technical analysis.

Technical information: Trade names, maker's marks or numbers associated with the object should be recorded. Bear in mind these may only become visible once treatment has been initiated.

Provenance: Where is the object from? If known, who was the artist/manufacturer? If known, when does it date to?[4] Some of this information may be provided by the curator or client.

Dimensions: Maximum dimensions of the object expressed as length, height, width, breadth, depth, or thickness. Weight is also sometimes recorded. Measurements should be in SI (metric) units: millimetres and metres, grammes, and kilogrammes.

Materials: The principal materials used in the construction and decoration together with the method of identification.

Detailed description: A full description of the object ensuring that details, such as the method of fabrication and decoration, the presence of paint or other coatings, the colour of various pieces and wear or use, is noted. Colour(s) may be described using a standardised colour recording system such as L*a*b* (Minolta 1988) especially areas of original colour or where the object has dyes or pigments that are fading/likely to fade.

History: It is not necessary to recreate existing curatorial records, but any previous repairs or conservation work should be noted. Recent history that may contribute to condition is also worth noting.

Values/statement of significance: Why is this object valuable to people in the present day? What elements are important, to whom and why? Tangible and intangible values should be considered. This may be recorded separately (Cutajar *et al.* 2016) or may, more commonly, be part of the object description.

Condition: The state the object is in. It should include, but is not limited to, the extent and nature of dirt, damage, corrosion, fading, loss, and how fragmentary or fragile the object. The source of the dirt, damage, or decay should be determined and noted.

Aims: What will be achieved through the proposed conservation work? This should take account of the significance/value of the object and its condition – the threats it faces.

B1 – Treatment Proposal

Proposed conservation treatment: Proposed conservation treatments, these should be justified – explaining how they achieve the stated aims of the work and preserve or enhance the stated values.

Authorisation: Box for the signature of the owner/curator/archaeologist/senior conservator to authorise and approve the treatment proposal and date.

B2 – Treatment

Conservation treatment: All aspects of the conservation treatment should be recorded. Details of the tools and/or chemicals used, their concentration and any specific temperatures or pressures used should be recorded. Any additional information about the object that comes to light during the cleaning and conservation process should be noted. Any deviations from the conservation proposal and the reasons for them should be recorded. This information should be filled in as the conservator goes through the conservation process, so details are not lost or forgotten.

Name of the conservator(s) undertaking the treatment.
Dates on which the work was carried out.

C – Future Care

Storage and recommendations: The conditions in which the object should be stored or displayed should be recorded together with details about any support or housing created for the object and any restrictions to the object's handling or use.

For management purposes additional information, such as the time taken, or cost is sometimes recorded. Ideally, all conservation activities should be recorded, even simple ones such as washing ceramics or building a new storage box for an object. The length of the conservation record may be short where involvement with the object is limited or considerably longer when major work is undertaken. Other forms of conservation records that may be generated include condition surveys.

In the 21st century, conservation records are typically generated in digital form. There is a lot of variation in the records produced from simple 'Word' documents to bespoke relational databases that integrate the curatorial and conservation records. It is important to migrate and update digital information, so it remains available and useful. Rapid software and hardware evolution can leave data stranded on obsolete systems; frighteningly, by 1975, the computerised data from the 1960 US Federal Census could only be read by two computers, one of which was already a museum exhibit (Westheimer 1994). Unfortunately, the longevity of digital media has not improved. Three factors impact the longevity of digital media: the storage medium itself, the hardware, and the interpretive software (Beck 2013). It is the conservator's responsibility to guarantee the permanence of their records. In larger institutions, information technology (IT) teams may be responsible for backing up the data and migrating it to new servers but in smaller labs the conservator should familiarise themselves with these procedures (Warda 2011). At a minimum, a second digital (back up) copy and a physical hard copy (paper) record are important to ensure that conservation records are not lost (Applebaum 2007: 413). Physical copies of records should, if possible, be stored according to archival standards (i.e. BS 4971:2017). Older records (1880s–1990s) will often be in paper form. Images are often on film (slides, negatives, prints), which may be unstable (Townsend and Tennent 1993). The desirability of digitising these records, to increase the accessibility of their information is widely recognised; however, such projects can be daunting for small institutions.

Frequently, conservators are the individuals who study objects most closely. They are often the only person to examine an object under a microscope or sees an artefact when it is disassembled so it is important for them to record any details, such as wear, construction, or alteration. It is important that these details and any discoveries made during conservation are shared with the curator, owner, or archaeologist responsible for the object. A copy of the conservation record is normally retained by the laboratory treating an object and a second copy of the record normally accompanies the object, especially when the treatment is a private commission.

The importance of records within conservation means that it is essential that time is made in the working day to ensure that they are completed. The conservator exercises considerable judgement regarding the extent to which any object is recorded. It is possible to waste considerable time illustrating and describing the most inconsequential details of an object, information which will never be required. Equally it is possible to ignore information that is crucial to the understanding of the object and neglect to record information that is subsequently lost when the object is cleaned. It remains particularly difficult to judge what information will be considered essential by a future generation of conservators. Inadequacies in past records, particularly regarding the use of pesticides, mean that conservators working with ethnographic and natural history collections struggle to determine how safe it is to handle some older collections (Odegaard and Sadongei 2005). Finding the perfect balance between efficiency and utility is difficult but should be a goal for all conservators.

4A Case Study: Bradwell Box (Keepax and Robson 1978)

During the excavation of the Bradwell Roman villa a corroded mass of iron fragments was discovered. The archaeologists and conservators on the excavation judged that that there was considerable potential for gaining further information from this concreted mass and decided to carefully lift and excavate it back in the laboratory in order to facilitate slower and more careful micro-excavation in controlled conditions. The corroded iron mass was carefully isolated from the surrounding soil, covered in aluminium foil and after a wooden crate had been inverted over this, the gap between the foil covered mass and the crate was filled with expanding polyurethane foam. The object was detached from the soil beneath and taken, safely held in its wooden crate, to the conservation laboratory. It was X-rayed and identified as the fittings of a chest or box dating to the 2nd century AD. Painstaking excavation followed. No traces of the wood from which the box had originally been composed were recovered. Only the iron nails, corner clamps, straps, and hinges remained.

As iron corrodes, it releases ferrous ions into solution. These subsequently oxidise to form ferric-oxyhydroxide minerals (rust). If iron corrodes quickly in association with organic material, the iron minerals can be deposited:

- Around the organic material forming a 'cast'. Eventually the organic material will degrade leaving an impression of the decayed organic material and its structure.
- Inside the organic material replacing it as it degrades. This forms an exact copy or 'pseudomorph' of the organic material.
- In both 'cast' and 'pseudomorph' forms.

Such deposits are known as mineral-replaced organics or mineral-preserved organics, and they can reproduce the microscopic features of the organic material (Keepax 1975). This process occurred on all the iron fittings of the Bradwell Box.

By noting the mineral-replaced organics present on the fittings, information about the type of wood and the construction of the box could be deduced. Microscopic examination of the microstructure of the mineral preserved wood permitted its identification as oak (genus Quercus). Observing the depth of the wood grain on the nails and the length of the nail shank before the points were bent over clarified that the base board of the box was 22 mm thick, whilst the sides were 25 mm thick, as was the lid. Evidence remained that the boards were made from sawn planks.[5] The direction of the wood grain on the corner clamps made it possible to deduce that the four pieces of wood forming the sides of the box were held together with dovetail joints, which conformed well in size and shape to modern carpentry practice. These traces indicate the high level of expertise of the craftsman who constructed this object. The dovetail joints were only used for joining the lower half of the sides of the box; the upper half used mitred joints. Iron straps that ran from the front of the box all the way to the top of the box's back appeared to have been hinges running under the lid of the box. Their spacing was preserved by the careful lifting allowing the height and depth of the box to be determined, whilst the positions of the corner clamps that had also been preserved allowed the approximate width of the box to be established.

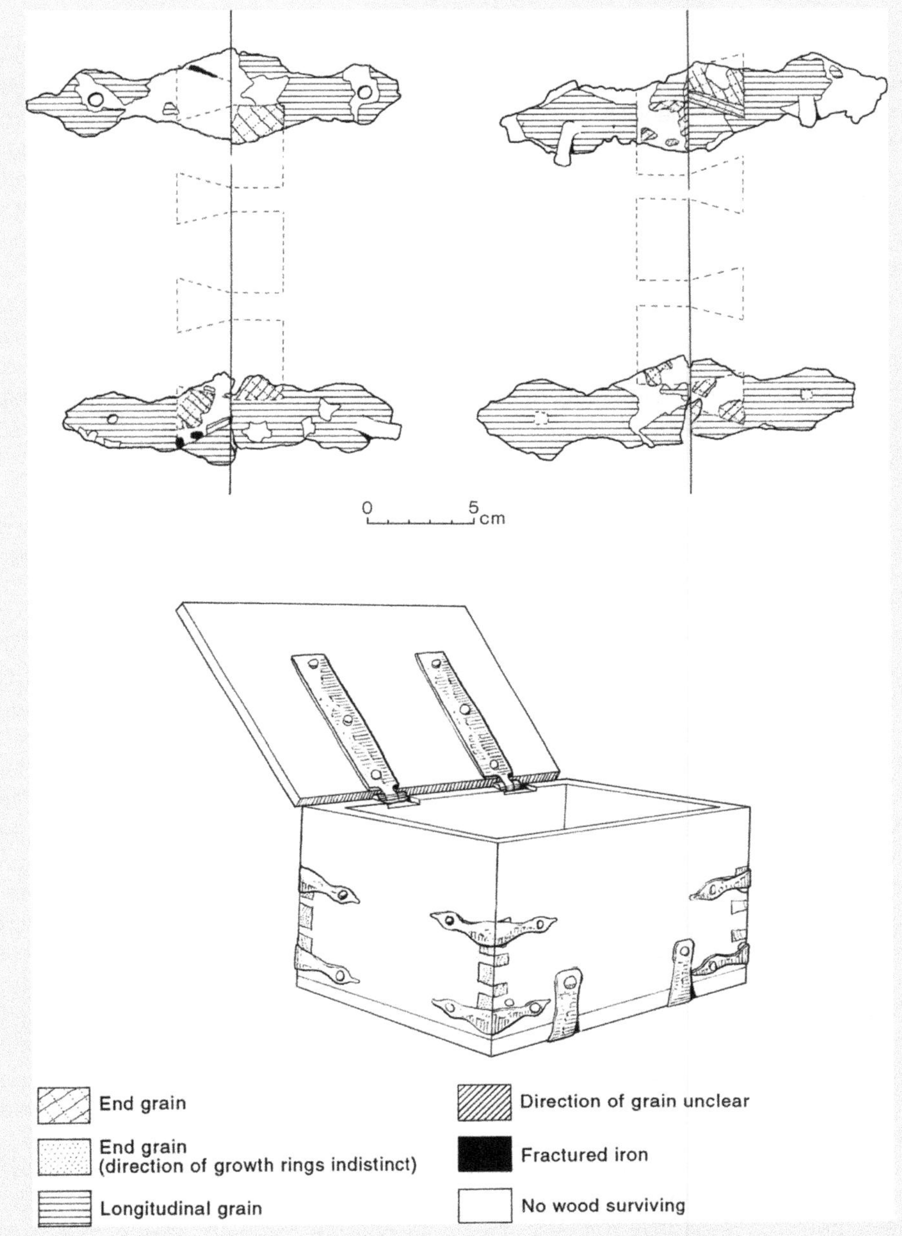

Figure 4.5 The Bradwell Box. The direction of the grain of the mineral-replaced wood permitted the original nature of the joints of the box to be deduced and the accurate reconstruction of the box. Redrawn by Yvonne Beadnell from Keepax and Robson (1978).

Crucially, the on-site recognition of the object's potential to reveal information, the use of X-radiography and microscopy to examine and identify the mineralised fragments, and the decision not to clean off the evidence permitted the carpentry techniques involved to be revealed. A thorough examination allowed the traces left by the mineral-preserved organics to be deciphered and permitted an accurate reconstruction of the original box to be created (see Figure 4.5). The careful documentation of this object added to our knowledge of Roman furnishings and forms a useful reference point for approaches to similarly corroded fastenings. It is important to note that at many points along the way crucial information could have been lost. Had the excavators chosen to recover the iron lumps individually, had the corroded iron been cleaned quickly or without an understanding of the information it contained, had measurements not been taken and documentation not been maintained, the significance of the object could not have been appreciated.

4B Case Study: The *Archimedes Palimpsest* (Griffiths *et al.* 1990; Down *et al.* 2002; Quant 2002; Netz *et al.* 2011a, 2011b)

The *Archimedes Palimpsest*, a manuscript written in Greek in the early 10th century, is the earliest surviving compilation of works by the 3rd century BC Greek philosopher, scientist, and mathematician Archimedes. Likely produced in Constantinople, the manuscript is a large (188 page) book that contains what are the only surviving copies of Archimedes' *The Method of Mechanical Theorem* (which uses mathematical examples that prefigure calculus), *On Floating Bodies* (about the displacement of water) and the *Stomachion* (a mathematical puzzle). The manuscript also contains four other Archimedean treatises, which have survived in less complete versions in later manuscripts, as well as several other texts. Two hundred years later, the bound manuscript was taken apart and the parchment was recycled. To realise this, the surface of the parchment was treated with weak organic acids and then scraped with pumice to try to remove traces of the ink (the term palimpsest derives from the Greek word for scraping 'palimpsestos'). Traces of the text would still have been visible, so the scribe rotated the sheets 90 ° before making an Euchologion (a liturgical text) and decorating it with large coloured initials and decorative borders along the top.

The Euchologion may have spent part of its life in a Greek Orthodox monastery in Palestine, where it would have been used in services and may have been damaged by fire and water, as well as rebound. In the mid-19th century, the palimpsest returned to Constantinople where a visiting German scholar identified it as a palimpsest and removed a single leaf (a single sheet consisting of two pages), which was later sold to Cambridge University. In 1899, the palimpsest was catalogued by a Greek scholar. In 1906, it was photographed by the Danish philologist and expert on Archimedes, Johan Heiberg, who published a series of articles about it on his return to

Copenhagen. The next few years of the palimpsest's life are mysterious but by 1930 it was in the hands of a collector, Marie Louis Sirieix. Either during this period or after Sirieix acquired it, several leaves were vandalised or lost, mould growth occurred and 'medieval'-style Evangelists' portraits were painted on four pages, possibly to raise the sale value of the manuscript. Following a legal battle over ownership, it was sold by Sirieix's daughter at Christies auction house in 1998. The buyer, a wealthy American, partnered with the Walters Art Museum to disband the manuscript, conserve, image, transcribe, and ultimately exhibit the palimpsest.

The palimpsest was very fragile, the mould had broken down the protein of the parchment in many places causing holes and losses, additionally there were tears, folds, and wax deposits from use and reuse over time. Before it could be studied, it had to be stabilised, the binding had to be removed, the wax deposits needed to be removed to make imaging more successful, repairs needed to be made to the tears and fragile areas supported. Additionally, the parchment was humidified and relaxed to help flatten sheets that had become cockled, and the leaves were encased in a double-sided frame. The decision not to rebind the book, meant that each leaf could be more easily studied and that portions of the Archimedean text that were in the gutter of the binding would no longer be hidden.

Although Heiberg had published much of the Archimedean text, he was hampered by the binding of the manuscript and by areas where the text was difficult to discern because of the overwriting. Additionally, he had not paid attention to diagrams that had been copied into the text. Multispectral imaging (numerous photos taken at different wavelengths of visible, infrared and UV light) was carried out as well as raking light images. Algorithms were then applied to the digital images to bring out particular characteristics of the ink and to permit the Archimedean text to be separated from the Euchologion, false colour was added to separate them further and make the palimpsest easier to read (Figure 4.6). Further computer processing was used to help predict the shape of letters in areas where the scraping had been too successful. Each letter and line were checked by a team of scholars who transcribed and translated the text (Netz *et al*. 2011a, 2011b), including the non-Archimedean parts of the palimpsest that Heiberg had not translated, and which turned out to include unknown speeches by an important Athenian orator, Hypereides. In 2005, X-rays produced by synchrotron radiation were used to scan the pages covered with gold leaf – allowing the words hidden beneath to be imaged and transcribed.

Over the seven-year duration of the scanning, the technology used changed dramatically. Initially, each leaf was imaged at 600dpi in 10 sections using three spectral bands. However, by 2007 a new system allowed each leaf to be scanned once using 12 spectral bands and captured at 800dpi.

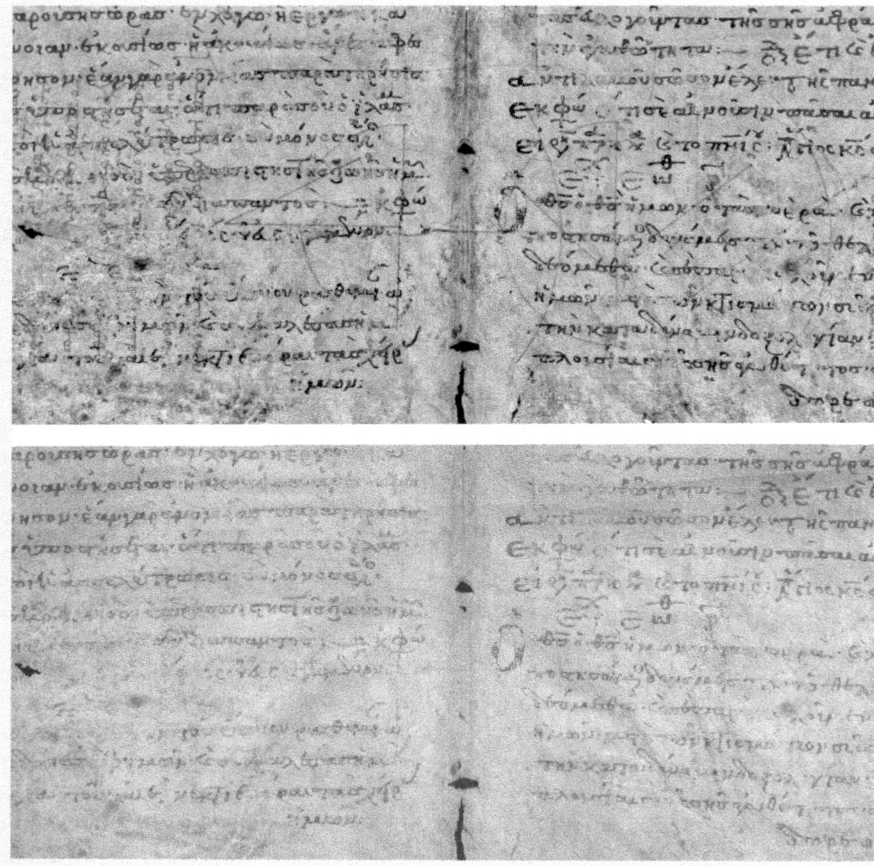

Figure 4.6 The *Archimedes Palimpsest* (Eucologion 17r–16v). Lower – page as seen in normal white light, Upper – multispectral image, combined red, green, and blue under UV (365nm illumination), leaving the palimpsest drawings and text clearly visible.© Owner of the Archimedes Palimpsest.

The *Archimedes Palimpsest* has a complex biography, which speaks to how different forms of knowledge were valued at different periods. Although Heiberg translated much of it, the new analysis added considerably to our understanding of the text and pushed the development of new imaging techniques. The careful work taken to document and preserve the manuscript will allow its continued study as new analytical tools become available.[6]

Notes

1 McGhee (1994) has argued that the people of the pre-Inuit, Thule Culture in northern Canada, made harpoons and ice knives primarily from ivory (seal or walrus) whilst their arrowheads were made from caribou antler. These materials were selected partially for their magical sympathy with their intended use. This belief system, which correlated sea-mammal ivory with winter, women, and the sea and antler with men, the land and the summer, also carried on into the verbal traditions of the later Inuit peoples (McGhee 1994).

2 Acronyms of major analytical techniques:

EDXRF = Energy Dispersive X-Ray Fluorescence
pXRF = Portable (energy) Dispersive X-Ray Fluorescence
WDXRF = Wavelength Dispersive X-Ray Fluorescence
ICPES = Induction Coupled Plasma Emission Spectrometry
PIXE = Particle (or Proton) Induced X-Ray Emission Spectrometry
TIMS = Thermal Ionisation Mass Spectrometry
ICPMS = Induction Coupled Plasma Mass Spectrometry
XRD = X-Ray Diffraction
UV/Vis = Ultra-Violet & Visible Light Adsorption Spectrometry
IR = Infrared Adsorption Spectrometry
FTIR = Fourier Transform Infrared Adsorption Spectrometry
GC = Gas Chromatography
HPLC = High-Performance Liquid Chromatography
GC-MS = Gas Chromatography & Mass Spectrometry
GC-Pyr-MS = Gas Chromatography – Pyrolysis – Mass Spectrometry
TG = Thermogravimetric
DSC = Differential Scanning Calorimetry
Also
OES = Optical Emission Spectroscopy
AAS = Atomic Adsorption Spectroscopy

3 Accuracy of a Bruker Tracer 5i pXRF system; using 'GeoExploration' software for quantitative analysis of geological materials, run at 50 kV for 90 seconds in an air path with a collimator giving an 8 mm x 100 mm beam spot area, analysing a 13-mm diameter, 5 mm thick, disc of compressed powdered homogenised material. Geological standard NBS 99a 'Soda Feldspar' Related to published mortar analyses (Caple 2020c).

Sample	*NBS 99a – Soda Feldspar Sample Analysis 1*	*NBS 99a – Soda Feldspar Sample Analysis 2*	*Publish analysis NBS 99a – Soda Feldspar*
Al_2O_3	19.56	20.05	20.64
SiO_2	73.85	73.39	65.64
CaO	1.40	1.38	2.15
Fe_2O_3	0.05	0.06	0.07
MnO	nd	0.02	0.00
MgO	nd	nd	0.02
K_2O	5.12	5.07	5.24
S_2O_3	0.03	0.03	0.00
P_2O_5	nd	nd	0.00
TiO	nd	nd	0.00
Na2O	nd	nd	6.24
Total	100	100	99.99

4 This may be a culture (e.g. Roman or Ancient Egypt) rather than a specific date. The culture that made the object may be different from the one that used and deposited it.

5 Sawn planks are a characteristic product of Roman carpentry that replaced the radially split planks used in prehistoric Britain. Sawing produced planks more efficiently and at less cost and maximised the number of planks that could be cut from a single tree; however, the quality was not equal to the earlier split planks.

6 The palimpsest's owner has made all the images and findings publicly available. Additional information about the palimpsest is available at http://www.archimedespalimpsest.org/

5 Cleaning

Cleaning

In a conservation context, the term 'surface cleaning' can encompass a variety of activities including brushing dust and insect debris off objects, washing, soaking, and mechanically removing dirt particles and corrosion products from the surface of an object or chemically removing stains, salts, and other encrustations. It can also include the removal of discoloured varnishes, aged adhesives and overpaint. Surface cleaning is normally undertaken to make the surface of the object more legible, improve its appearance, and remove the threat that dirt may represent to the stability of an object. It can be carried out either as an independent treatment or as a treatment step prior to other steps, for example, cleaning the edges of a ceramic vessel prior to mending them together.

The impulse to clean, to remove the dirt and dust that obscures an object, stems from the idea that cleanliness is an exalted state. This notion, dating back to the Babylonians, has deep roots in many world religions, which often include elaborate purification rituals involving both physical and metaphorical cleaning. In the early 18th century, the cleric John Wesley coined the phrase 'cleanliness is next to godliness'. In the past, the concept of cleanliness also held class implications, denoting those who had people to clean for them and those that did not, a connection that was further reinforced in the 19th century as disease was linked to dirt and squalor. In the museum context, a coating of dust is frequently seen by visitors as a sign of neglect, whereas a clean object demonstrates that the owner values and cares for it.

Soiling

Soiling in the form of dirt from burial, caked-on mud, grease, oil, dirt, sweat or even blood from use, and dust from storage is often deposited on the surface of objects and can damage them. The sharp edges of soil particles can scratch metallic surfaces and abrade the surfaces of fibres. On organic objects, soiling acts as a food and moisture source for microorganisms. Microbial activity centres on the soiled area, resulting in subsequent attack of the substrate by microorganisms such as moulds and pests. Soil

DOI: 10.4324/9781003009078-5

particles and microbial growths adsorb water and retain it in close contact with the substrate, acting as a source for metal corrosion and the hydrolysis of organic materials. Soiling is usually acidic; the corrosion and hydrolysis reaction rates increase as the pH decreases. Soluble materials drawn into the object cause staining and discolouration.

Dirt and dust can obscure the surface of the object, making it appear duller and darker than it actually is and hiding decorative details and other features. Soiling may be present on the surface of the object in several forms:

- Solid matter deposited during burial or storage. In the case of storage, this is sometimes referred to as 'museum dust'.
- Solid matter deposited during use (Oddy 1994). Also sometimes referred to as 'use dirt' or, historically, as ethnographic dirt (Greene 2006).
- Decay products: the layer of material produced from the reaction between an object's primary or secondary materials and water, light, oxygen, or biological organisms. This may include corrosion products on metals or yellowed varnishes.

Under these layers, secondary materials (layers of materials added to the object through its working life, for example, paint layers) and primary materials (the substance of the original object) may be present. Although conceptualised as distinct, soiling and decay products frequently form a single layer. It may be almost impossible to identify and deal with these layers as separate deposits. The extent to which the conservator removes soiling and decay products is a matter of careful judgement, balancing the loss of information that these materials can contain against the benefit of improving the stability of the object and revealing more of its original visual form.

Removing Soiling

Museum dust is often removed with little concern due to its obscuring and uninformative nature. An argument can be made that this too is part of the object's biography and that, 'an object never ceases to accumulate history' (Jaeschke 1996) but it is not necessarily a revealing part when compared with the interpretive histories an object may accrete during its time in a museum. Conservators have studied both the make-up and deposition of museum dust (Lloyd *et al.* 2002; Wurst *et al.* 2005; Uring *et al.* 2020) and used the results to create mitigation strategies. In general, the potential damage dust can cause is felt to necessitate its removal and museums, historic sites, and other heritage organizations carefully undertake periodic cleaning programs wherever possible to reduce dust levels.

Many archaeological objects have corroded, discoloured, and are covered in earth because of their long burial in the ground. It is often appropriate to remove adhering soil and corrosion (Figure 5.1) from the object's surface; however, it is important to determine whether the soil and corrosion products contain valuable information (such as mineral preserved organics or gilding) prior to removing them.

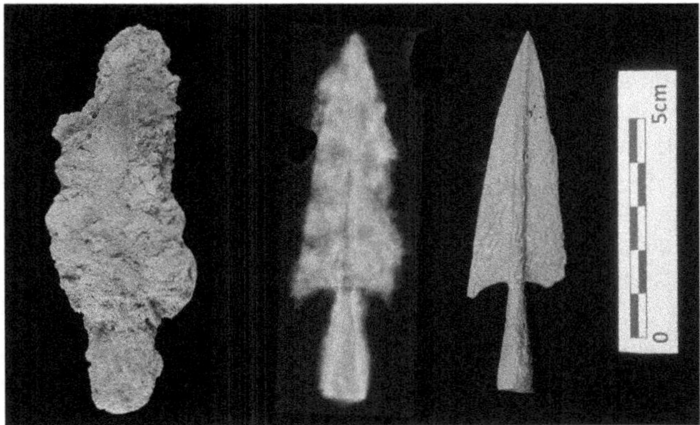

Figure 5.1 12th-century arrowhead from Nevern Castle. Left – as found, centre - X-radiograph, right – after cleaning using air abrasion. Removing the soil and concretion has revealed the form of the object permitting study. Martha Infray & Chris Caple.

An object's interpretation may determine what is retained and what is sacrificed during cleaning, while the object's artistic merit, as well as the date and pervading ethical climate when the decision to clean was made may impact the degree of cleaning. During the Renaissance, whatever obscured the beauty of classical statuary was removed – cleaned, ground, or chipped away (Cellini 1878). This urge to clean off the dirt and decay that comes between the viewer and the artist's vision has in the past been justified as revealing the 'true nature' of the object. However, because it is difficult to define any single point as the true nature of the object, cleaning can just as easily remove aspects of an object's 'true nature'. The Vix crater, regarded as the most important example of Greek metalwork imported into North-West Europe in the Iron Age, was buried around 500BC. It is the largest known metal vessel from classical antiquity and demonstrates both the wealth of the Celts and their contact with the classical world. When it was excavated in the 1950s, traces of soil and degraded leather, which surrounded this object when found, were cleaned off as it was perceived that 'they harmed the beauty of the object' (France-Lanord 1996). The aesthetic nature of the crater and the classical scenes depicted in the metalwork, outweighed the evidence that it had been wrapped in a piece of leather for burial. In the case of the Bradwell Box (see Case Study 4A), a more utilitarian object, the importance of the evidence held in the mineral preserved organics was privileged over cleaning the iron hinges and straps, items that are well-represented in other collections. In the case of archaeological objects where considerable cleaning is considered appropriate, an area may be left deliberately uncleaned to preserve evidence of the extent and nature of the corrosion, as in the case of the Lincoln Hanging Bowl (Hunter and Foley 1984: 18).

Where soiling relates to the use of the object, there is a more difficult balance to be struck between preservation of the object and preservation of the information about its use. Accepting accelerated decay due to the retention of dirt, dust, staining, body fluids, etc. may be judged worthwhile if the information is crucial to the understanding of the object. This retention of soiling can become a matter of subtle judgement. In the case of a biker's leather jacket from the 1950s, the textile conservator at the York Castle Museum judged that the jacket was deliberately kept and used by its owner in a stained and soiled state as part of the antisocial rebellious creed of the biker subculture. While the jacket undoubtedly had points within its history when it was clean, there was additional information and a message in its dirty state (Eastop and Brooks 1996). Similarly, the hood worn by Robert Merrick, known as 'the Elephant Man', was not wet cleaned; it was felt that future analytical techniques might be able to recover information from the body staining of this cloth, which could not be obtained at present (Eastop and Brooks 1996). Even simple surface cleaning, such as vacuuming, can remove evidence of a garment's use that we might wish to retain; for example, the turn-ups on an agricultural worker's trousers might contain wheat seeds and husks, which can provide evidence for the wearer's occupation (Eastop and Brooks 1996). In some cases, deliberate attempts have been made to keep crucial evidence. At the Australian War Memorial Museum, the uniform of a WWI soldier who had served at the Somme in France was consolidated to retain the mud of the battlefield, which was viewed as a key element of this object's significance (Brooks and Eastop 2006). The nuanced awareness of the significance of soiling that is apparent in some areas of conservation, such as textile conservation, is not always routinely present in other areas of conservation, such as the conservation of historic vehicles. It remains challenging for conservators to distinguish between use dirt and the dirt acquired during storage or burial or accretions added to the object during its use and those added by museums or collectors after it was acquired (O'Hern *et al.* 2016). Particle size may be a differentiating factor but often there is little physical or visual difference.

In the case of fine and modern art, the artist's intent when creating the work is a guiding principle that influences the way in which it is cleaned. Where the piece is by a contemporary artist or creator, it is not only possible but also desirable to discuss the cleaning and restoration of the work with them. In some cases, the artist may be interested in how the work decays and does not want it to be altered or cleaned but in other cases they may be interested in maintaining a pristine quality to the work and regular cleaning is essential. The older the work of art, the less likely that the artist's real intent can be known and the more that artist's intent becomes a matter of curatorial judgement. For example, overpaint may be valued as part of an object's history or cleaned away as being detrimental to appreciating the artist's intent. Once the object has become established in a particular condition, it can be difficult to argue for it to be cleaned to its original look – as seen in the case of the Statue of Liberty (Case Study 3A). In the case of archaeological objects, the degree of transformation that an object may have experienced in the burial environment and the potential for that transformation to tell us about the use life of the object (i.e. the presence of mineral preserved organics on the surface) mean that objects may not be fully cleaned or returned to their original appearance. Thus, although cleaning is often presented as a simple binary opposition (clean or not clean), we see that different factors ranging from aesthetics to ideology to scholarly interest may inform how clean the object really is.

Original Surface: A Concern When Cleaning

The original surface of an object contains valuable evidence about how the object was manufactured and used; therefore, retaining this information is a logical goal in cleaning. However, both its identification and nature pose problems for conservators since the surface is also the interface between the object and the environment and therefore a site of alteration. Organic materials preserved in waterlogged contexts, such as wooden timbers, have delicate surfaces on their exteriors, which often preserve tools marks but can be so soft that excavators can put finger marks into them when lifting the object from the ground. Other surfaces that we think of as robust, such as glass, can be transformed and flake away, while in metals corrosion can hide the surface.

The Danish conservator Gustav Rosenberg was the first to put forward the concept that the original surface could be retained in the corrosion products found on metals (1917). However, he offered little guidance for retaining these surfaces, in part because many of the techniques used for treating metals were electrochemical and resulted in the stripping of the corrosion products from the metal. Although these techniques stabilized the object and halted further decay, in removing all the corrosion layers they also removed valuable surface evidence (Norman 1988). In the 1960s, the idea that the original surface could be preserved in the corrosion layers was revived again and began to be conceptualized prior to being defined and fully embraced in the late 1980s (Bertholon 2004). More recently, Regis Bertholon has noted that even though the morphology of the surface may be preserved by the corrosion, the 'original surface' is no longer truly extant because it has been altered through corrosion. He proposed employing the term 'limitos' to talk about the limit between what makes up the original surface of the object (be it metal, mineral, or organic) and the environment at the time the object was abandoned (Bertholon 2002, 2004). When cleaning very corroded archaeological metal objects, we are seeking a non-material entity (the limitos) that can only be identified by carefully reading the material clues above it (the inclusion of sand and pebbles in the concretion), those corresponding to it (the way in which corrosion layers cleave apart, the presence of secondary metal coatings or inlays) and those below it (changes in corrosion products, voids, and bare metal). This means that the choice of how far to clean remains a subjective one, subject to the conservator's eye and recognition of the layers, and it also remains dependent on cultural ideas of what should or should not be removed (Case Study 3A: The Statue of Liberty).

As stone decays, it can form a crust above a fragile powdery layer. This crust can blacken and be visually disfiguring. Durham Cathedral is built of a beautiful honey-coloured sandstone, which, by the 18th century, had become blackened with soot and degraded by weathering. The cathedral architect, John Wooler, had stonemasons chisel 'a couple of inches' of stone off the whole of the outside of the cathedral (Roberts 1994) to restore the beauty of the building. This changed all the exterior architectural details; the windows were circa 100-mm wider, while the pillars and all other decorative motifs were circa 100-mm thinner altering the proportions of the stonework. Today we would not dream of taking such a drastic approach to the treatment of stone, but it is not uncommon to use lasers to remove a microns-thick layer of blackened crust and return stone to its original appearance.

Overpaint

Original surfaces can also be buried beneath layers of later applied material. Artists often chose to overpaint their own work. Sometimes these overpainted areas were small areas, the movement of a hand or the repositioning of background elements but occasionally entire images were overpainted with alternate subject matter. Such reworking can reflect the recyclying of canvases or speak to broader world events. In 1589, Adrian Vanson painted Sir John Maitland over Vanson's own earlier portrait of Mary Queen of Scots. Mary had been executed two years earlier and owning her image might have endangered the artist/owner (Kennedy 2017). When it comes to conservation decisions about removing the overpaint, the later image is usually retained because it preserves both the original image (even if unseen) and the subsequent one, because it reflects the artist's intention or because the image below may never have been completed, as is the case in the Vanson painting. In some instances where the overpainting is applied later, the decision-making is more nuanced. The later overpaint may hide damage, meaning its removal would require the application of new overpaint by the conservator to reintegrate the work and might not add to our knowledge of the image. In such a case, the overpaint might be removed if it were poorly done or had aged differently from the original painting. Less frequently, paintings were partially overpainted at later stages in their life to update them and make them more fashionable. The painting *Henry Prince of Wales on Horseback* by Robert Peake the Elder was painted circa 1610–12. The original image is of the young prince seated on a medieval warhorse, surrounded by the iconography of courtly love and jousting. At a later point (most likely between about 1690 and 1730), the background was overpainted, and the horse remodelled so that the prince was now shown on a dashing white horse in front of an arboreal Arcadian landscape (McClure 1992). At the time, the complex iconography of the original painting would have seemed obscure and old-fashioned and the overpaint was designed to bring the picture in line with contemporary fashion and taste. After consulting with the owner and art historians, the conservation team documented the overpainting and removed it. In this case, the original painting represented the artist's complete vision and perhaps his most impressive work, whereas the later alterations simply indicated the fashions of a later age. Undertaking such a radical transformation of a work can be daunting, and the conservator should have both the confidence and experience to make such decisions.

Varnishes, Lacquers, and Painting Cleaning

Historically, varnishes, waxes, and lacquers have been applied to decorative surfaces for a variety of reasons. Tinted varnishes were sometimes deliberately used to make cheap materials appear richer and warmer or to tone down overly bright and raw surfaces allowing them to meld with other materials. Furniture was polished, metal surfaces were coated to retard corrosion and oil paintings were varnished to protect their surfaces (Beeton 1859). Such coatings worked in three ways. They formed a protective film over the surface, saturating the surface, reducing light scattering, and making colours appearing deeper and more intense rather than cloudy and dull and made painted surfaces more robust, reducing flaking, powdering and loss of surface pigment. Initially transparent, if not clear, many coatings yellow or darken over time and can shrink and/or crack slightly. They can hold dirt and dust on their surface, especially at higher RH and temperatures.[1]

Traditionally, many coatings were removed (either mechanically in the case of furniture waxes or with solvents, in the case of painting varnishes) and new ones reapplied. Often as it was the outer surface of the varnish that held dust and had yellowed, most of the varnish was removed. The newly applied coating covered the object surface sealing and protecting the very base of the original varnish with the object. This process was well understood by the craftsmen traditionally involved in such work and there are references to painters cleaning and revarnishing the works of their predecessors (Kirby Talley 1998). Modern conservators continue the tradition of removing old varnish and replacing it with new, more stable but ultimately replaceable varnishes.

The noticeable visual alteration of pictures, when they have had their yellowed varnish and the dirt and grime of decades removed, is shocking to some. Photo-oxidation affects almost all organic materials and induces a noticeable yellowing in traditional picture varnishes over time. Dauma and Henchman (1997) studied the distorting effect of yellowing varnish on the chromatic diversity of varnished oil paintings. Using colour measurement, such as the CIE or L*a*b* system, the chromatic variation experienced by a viewer looking at an aged, varnished picture was shown to be limited to a narrow variation in the yellow-brown part of the spectrum. The only method of seeing something close to the original colours and the original intention of the artist is to reduce or remove the varnish layer. Walden (1985) critiqued the 'complete cleaning' of oil paintings as practised principally in Britain and North America as over-cleaning and saw the 'partial' or 'selective cleaning' practised in continental Europe as preferable[2]; however, Hedley (1986, 1990) noted that no objective evidence has yet been provided showing the loss of original paint during complete cleaning. Walden (2006) drew a correlation between the clarity and brightness of completely cleaned pictures and the art, advertising, television, and photography of the late 20th century. This, she suggested, was the distinctive visual style of the late 20th century to which modern-day conservators unconsciously transformed the pictures upon which they worked. Walden (1985, 2006), Gombrich (1962), Beck and Daley (1993), and others believed that the darkened pictures of the past possess greater subtlety and harmony. This may, however, be largely attributed to the tonal harmony induced by the yellowing varnish (Hedley 1986, 1990). A preference for looking old can be just as subjective as a preference for looking bright and new. As noted by Hedley (1986, 1990), the image presented by any picture in the present day is not quite the one intended by the artist; the pigments have differentially aged and have reacted with the binder and covering varnish to permanently alter the chromatic and tonal balance of the picture. This means that no matter how a picture is cleaned, it is impossible to fully recover the artist's intentions and a new 'relativity' between the artist and the viewer must be established. However, the removal and replacement of varnish can bring the picture closer to the original intended by the artist.

The chromatographic effects of aging varnishes and their impact have been most enthusiastically explored in the painting conservation literature, but these effects are not uniquely experienced by paintings. Objects that have varnished or lacquered surfaces also experience chromatographic shifts. Because original coatings contain important information about the object's history, it is important to understand whether any discolouration is linked to a coating applied when the object was manufactured or to one applied at a subsequent point. For example, a yellowed lacquer on a wooden funerary object from the Egyptian New Kingdom excavated in the 1920s could be either Pistacia resin applied when the object was made to give it a yellow appearance that was considered more divine and more suitable for the afterlife (Serpico and White 2001), or a shellac coating applied when the object was excavated to consolidate flaking paint, or a later application of a cellulose nitrate-based consolidant (Gleeson 2014). Before removing the coating, it is critical to understand what it was and why it was applied.

Cleaning Processes

When cleaning is required, it is important to select the most appropriate method and materials. Cleaning techniques can be divided into two categories:

- Mechanical cleaning – these are methods in which a material or force (such as an abrasive powder, dry ice, or sound waves in the case of ultrasonic cleaning) or a tool (such as a scalpel, porcupine quill, or brush) mechanically breaks the bonds between the dirt and the object. Some cleaning methods such as laser cleaning and ultrasonic cleaning utilize physical forces to effect a mechanical cleaning action. In ultrasonic cleaning, high-frequency sound waves cause the formation of bubbles in a solution which implode with such force against the surface of an object that they dislodge dirt and other contaminants. Laser cleaning utilizes thermal expansion and steam generation.
- Chemical cleaning – methods which use chemical means to break either the primary or secondary bonds between the dirt and the object's surface. Temperature and pressure can be varied to increase the efficiency of chemical methods (Drews *et al.* 2013). Chemical methods can also be paired with mechanical methods; for example, silver polishes that combine abrasives and sequestering agents.

A single cleaning method can involve both techniques (for example, agitating an object in a detergent solution) or several cleaning methods involving different techniques may be paired together (for example, mechanically cleaning a ceramic by dry brushing to remove most of the dirt and then soaking it to remove the remaining dirt).

The choice of which cleaning method is most appropriate depends on the object's materials and condition, the nature of the soiling, the surface topography, the size and construction of the object, health, and safety considerations, and to a lesser extent the expertise of the conservator and the availability of the technique. Cleaning methods may be tested on surrogate materials although, due to the many variables involved in the creation, soiling, and biography of an object, these are not guaranteed to perfectly simulate either the object's surface or the effect of cleaning. When testing on the object itself, cleaning methods should always be tested on as inconspicuous a part of the object as possible to ensure that if there is an unexpected side effect, it will leave the least trace. When testing any cleaning method, it is important to carefully note all the parameters of the test (concentration, dwell time i.e. the amount of time the material was left on the surface, number of applications, and any removal method), and to record the results of all methods (both successful and unsuccessful). Numerical scores and comments are often used to rate efficiency and ease of application. It is important to be as consistent as possible when using these so that they can be easily assessed after the fact.

The nature and extent of cleaning will depend on the agreed aims of the conservation. Mechanical cleaning with hand tools can be highly controlled but it is slow, painstaking, time-consuming work. Chemical cleaning is much faster but often means trading some control for speed. For finds such as coin hoards where large numbers of almost identical artefacts are recovered from the same archaeological context, conservators, working in conjunction with numismatists, may clean some coins by hand, but may clean the remainder in small batches using chemical methods to identify all the coins within a reasonable time.[3]

Greater analytical capability has permitted the accurate identification and monitoring of both the object and the cleaning agent during the conservation process, which in turn has permitted greater control of the process. Early attempts at electrolysis utilised rapid hydrogen evolution at the object's metal surface to strip away the corrosion layers resulting in information loss while objects without a coherent metal core often fell apart. Better understanding of the roles chlorides play in iron corrosion and their chemical removal has made the process more controllable and yielded better results (Hamilton 2010) while monitoring and control of the current has enhanced consolidative reduction (Carradice and Campbell 1994). Improved understanding of scientific principles and material reactions has facilitated the appropriation of new cleaning methods, such as laser cleaning, from other industries. The development of Q switched Nd:YAG lasers[4] in the 1990s led to their adoption for conservation work (Cooper 1998; Nimmrichter *et al.* 2006). More recently Er:YAG lasers have been introduced (Teppo 2020). Initially used primarily for cleaning stonework, lasers are now used for a wider range of materials; their use being largely limited by the initial cost. The development of tuneable lasers is making the removal of different types of soiling far more precise.

As it has become easier to study the impact of chemicals on objects, it has also become easier to study their impact on conservators. Concerns over health and safety have led to reductions in the volumes of chemicals used and in the toxicity of chemicals chosen. Green approaches have been introduced (Sousa *et al.* 2007) and the use of solvent gels, especially for painted surfaces, has reduced the volume of solvents used, increased control over the cleaning, and improved the safety for the conservator (Anglove *et al.* 2017). As sustainable approaches to conservation practice continue to develop, this is an area that is likely to see continued growth.

As many studies have shown, no cleaning method is entirely without risk to the object. Even cleaning methods that appear to be benign on a macro level can cause residual damage on a micro-level (Goodburn-Brown 1996; Gessler and McEnroe 2019). Decisions about which cleaning method to use may at times be question of choosing the least aggressive method, or the one that will result in the least potential damage or choosing not to clean at all.

Risk/Benefit Analysis

Just because it is possible to clean an object does not mean that it *should* be cleaned. A conscious decision is required as to what the conserved state of the object should be, and the reasoning should be explicitly stated. Cleaning is an irreversible process, and it is important to be aware that any cleaning activity can unintentionally remove evidence of the object's past or alter the object. This is balanced against the harm that the dirt and corrosion layer may inflict on the object if left. Furthermore, cleaning has the potential to damage some objects. Bleaching paper may remove staining and improve the aesthetic appearance of paper but must be set against the potential damage that bleaching may do to the paper fibres. For a badly stained print that is going on display, the balance given may lie with the 'cleaning' action due to the desire to see the subject matter. For a historic document in an archive, the balance may lie with preservation and against bleaching.

Cleaning an object should stop when the risk of damage outweighs the benefit of the desired result. Leaving dust in place obscures the object and acts as a potential centre for corrosion; however, removing dust simply by wiping it off can drag hard gritty particles across an object microscopically scratching the surface. Almost all mechanical polishing processes are mildly abrasive and mechanical removal with scalpels, wire wool, jeweller's rouge, or air abrasive can potentially damage the layers beneath the dirt or corrosion. In the hands of a skilled conservator, the risk of such damage is minimized. The decision to clean should be taken only when the risk of damage to the object is acknowledged and judged acceptable.

More aggressive and potentially damaging cleaning methods may work faster, while gentler ones may take a longer time. A balance must be struck between minimising damage to the object and completing the cleaning in a reasonable time. There is a cost-benefit element to cleaning; if the conservator spends a long time carefully cleaning one object, then other objects may not be treated.

Examples of over-cleaning are rarely published meaning that emerging conservators are often overly concerned that they will be the first to clean too far. All conservators, even experienced ones, have, at one time or another, found themselves unintentionally over-cleaning objects (Smith 1990). Difficult and embarrassing as it is to admit, this is where the question of an ethical approach becomes crucial. It is not ethical to damage an object intentionally; therefore, once a problem is noted, continuing in the same vein is not an option. The conservator's willingness to stop cleaning, record the damage they have unintentionally done and modify their cleaning method, demonstrates their commitment to ethical practice. Upon discovering that an object has been over-cleaned there may be an urge to 'cover up' the mistake. Concealing the damage to restore the visual integrity of the object may even be appropriate. Such an action should be seen as restoration and like other restoration actions should be recorded and reversible restoration techniques and materials should be used where possible (Chapter 6).

The more that our ability to target cleaning approaches improves and the more enhanced our ability to extract meaningful information from the tiniest samples becomes, the more that objects once regarded as 'clean' now appear to have been 'over-cleaned'. When assessing past cleaning actions, we must be careful not to project present-day ethical and environmental standards into the past. The British Museum has been critiqued for over-cleaning the Elgin marbles, resulting in the loss of paint from the surface. While it is true that many of the methods used would be considered overly aggressive today (Oddy 2002), many were a response to pollution levels that were much higher than those currently experienced and were undertaken using the tools available at the time. However, our present understanding of the past develops slowly and imperfectly when evidence is stripped away.

Although criticism is often levelled at over-cleaning, it is rarely levelled equally at under-cleaning. Indeed, the narrative of discovery that is key to the scientific understanding of objects celebrates the under-cleaned objects that permit later analysis to be carried out and to reveal new information about a known item (Case Study 2B: The Sutton Hoo Helmet). While much research focuses on optimizing cleaning techniques, what is rarely discussed or assessed is what losses (in terms of accessibility, and potentially accelerated deterioration) may have been caused by under-cleaning. Doing nothing and leaving objects 'as found' leaves the public admiring piles of dust only able to see a dirty, dusty, damaged past, devoid of the colour, beauty, and energy of the ancient world. Neither over-cleaning nor under-cleaning is justifiable, and thus we must judge the evidence carefully as we clean, cautiously revealing every aspect that is original while removing the obvious later soil and dust. This approach relies on the discretionary judgement of conservators and other experts and can lead to the sorts of inconsistencies inherent when comparing the work of any group of professionals who may assess values and risks differently.

The Goldilocks Principle[5]

In the museum setting, the public, confronted with replicas and reproductions, may not believe that a clean, seemingly flawless object is authentic. Their perception, based on relentless marketing campaigns that promote the purchase of 'new' consumer goods, is that old things should look dirty and damaged. In the limited time that many members of the public interact with an object, museums want them to read the object correctly and understand that it is authentic. Therefore, some soiling giving an 'aged' appearance may be appropriate. This leads to the concept of a 'Goldilocks point', not too clean (so it is seen as 'real') and not too dirty (so it does not appear uncared for). For some objects this is not difficult to achieve; for example, it can be hard to remove all the ingrained dirt from porous ceramic or stone surfaces without damaging the object, so some soiling invariably remains after conservation. For other objects, it is more challenging. It is not suggested that anything should be added to make it 'look' old. The Goldilocks point, varies with artefact type; dirt is expected on archaeological objects, but not on fine art. It is also culturally contexted; it varies with public perception (Lithgow *et al.* 2018). It changes over time and is different in different parts of the world. Conservators should collaborate with curators, owners, or other heritage professionals to define the extent to which objects should be cleaned, 'since the significance of many museum objects depends (partly) on their being old, cleaning involves achieving a balance between clarification of surface features and retention of the signs of age' (Pye 2001: 134).

Silver cleaning exemplifies the Goldilocks principle well. Silver is a bright reflective metal that naturally tarnishes forming a thin layer of black silver sulphide when it is exposed to hydrogen sulphide (a common gaseous pollutant). Silver objects were often decorated with raised and sunken decoration. In flickering candlelight or low-light environments, the raised areas would have thrown light back and the shadowed sunken areas would have given a sense of depth, making the decoration more legible. In today's museum environments, with bright even lighting conditions, if we polish the silver too much, we lose much of that contrast, the surface becomes uniformly bright and the decorative detail less clear. Retaining small amounts of tarnish in the crevices allows the relief decoration to stand out more and ensures that the decorative scheme is readable. Therefore, conservators often attempt to polish the silver only to a 'historic' level (one that is not too bright and that may retain some depth). Defining exactly where this point is, is a matter of judgement, personal preference, and negotiation with stakeholders.

Another place where we can see the Goldilocks principle in action is in the approach to historic interiors. Historic houses often contain furniture and decorative elements from numerous styles and periods. Occasionally, a room is conceived as a single coherent element and survives through time in that state (this is often the case in 'state rooms' in English country homes) but more frequently, items from many different periods cohabit in one room. In many cases, such spaces are retained in their present form and cleaning may become a delicate balance between removing dust and maintaining an integrated appearance. These spaces may contain a variety of surfaces that no longer have their original characteristics; for example, the silvering on a mirror may have tarnished or puckered and may no longer possess its original finish, the varnish on an oil painting may have yellowed, and the dyes on textiles may have been soiled by years of handling. Within such an environment, cleaning one element too much, for example, polishing metal surfaces too highly, can create a visual imbalance that visitors find difficult to resolve; one component of the room (the metal) looks more cared for, and consequently more valued, while other elements of the space look less cared for and less valued.

Cleaning: Concluding Thoughts

After careful consideration of the nature of the object, its condition, and its intended use (display, study, or storage), the conservator and curator/owner should reach a decision regarding the nature of the conservation work required. Though cleaning may then commence, conservation is an iterative process, and further evidence is often recovered during the conservation process. The original judgement often needs re-evaluation due to this new information. Berducou (1996) has described this as a 'dialectical relationship' between studying the object and realizing its cleaning. In some cases, this may mean cleaning further than originally intended and in others, it may mean being less aggressive as the nature of the dirt and decay deposits are better understood. When viewed in these terms the final cleaned, conserved form of the object can be described as 'the concrete expression of a critical judgement' (Berducou 1996).

Cleaning imposes a vision upon the object, a conscious decision is taken to remove some things and not others; thus, cleaning is not an interpretively neutral treatment (Orlofsky and Trupin 1993; Eastop and Brooks 1996). The conservator has a responsibility to decide what aspects of the object are important and reveal them through cleaning so that they can be displayed. Such decisions can be difficult, and it is important to remember that:

- The present surface of an object is an arbitrary effect resulting from its interactions with humans and nature. A dusty, damaged, rusted, dirty surface may have occurred due to neglect by previous owners, the attentions, and deprivations of servants in centuries past, the variable effects of burial in the soil or the impatient cleaning of an archaeologist. It is frequently not a deliberate or meaningful surface. Research and investigation can generate a clearer picture of the object and its history, and a more meaningful surface can be identified and recovered.
- Conservators are in a unique position to make decisions regarding cleaning. They have unparalleled access to the object's surfaces and understand their significance and fragilities better than most. Consequently, they have the greatest chance of successfully revealing the desired result. It may be appropriate to recommend that

an object not be cleaned based on the information at hand. However, it is also important to weigh the possibility that in that case, and particularly if the decision is controversial, other less well-informed and less-skilled individuals may be asked to do the work. The conservator's approach to recording and treatment will not be used. The conservator should be cognizant of the potential consequences of their inactions as much as of their actions.

- If a decision is made not to clean, the reasons for not cleaning should be clearly stated in order to inform subsequent conservators. Objects that are not cleaned because of a desire to preserve the soiling and information associated with the object should be distinguished from those objects where cleaning with the present facilities, expertise or methods presents an unacceptable risk of damage to the object.
- Every effort should be made to minimise risk to the object. The deeper the cleaning the greater the risk.
- Cleaning takes time and resources, consequently it is sensible to consider cleaning options in cost/benefit terms (Caple 2000: 170–174). The conservator must make decisions throughout the cleaning process to minimize risk to the object and to any evidentiary value present in the soiling. These decisions may include the decision not to clean, the decision to clean but to remove samples of soiling for future analysis, or the decision to partially clean an object. Careful documentation is an element in minimising risk.
- Cleaning should not be undertaken simply because similar objects have previously been cleaned, or are always cleaned, in a particular manner. A case needs to be made for each object as a separate entity and, even if a process is repeated on one object after another, it is because it can be justified in each separate case.
- It is important to remember that all the aspects of an object's past are important. A conscious decision regarding the balance of revelation, investigation and preservation should be made for each object. This decision should balance the loss of information upon cleaning against the information revealed.
- Cleaning is not an end in itself. The future use of the object should be considered and where possible consideration given to avoiding future cleaning or prolonging the intervals between cleanings. This may include considering the benefits and pitfalls of applying coatings, minimizing handling or use, or designing storage and display environments that incorporate protective coverings and scavenging materials. Cleaning may lead to the need for other decisions, such as how to present an area of loss or whether to apply a protective coating to an object.

Although there are risks inherent in cleaning, it is important that a conservator not over-value the object to the point that they are afraid to touch it. Emerging conservators may lack confidence when they first start to clean artefacts. Developing confidence takes time and practice and the experience of seeing a variety of different surfaces and how they respond to different cleaning methods. Confidence without ability is dangerous and can result in damage. Good judgement and good conservation skills are required to balance the risks of damage to the object against the benefits of gaining information and transmitting it through display.

5A Case study: The Sistine Chapel (Brandt 1987; Ekserdjian 1987; Colalucci 1991, 2017; Mancinelli 1991, 1992; Beck and Daley 1993)

The Sistine Chapel was built by Pope Sixtus IV in 1477–1480. Between 1481 and 1483, Tuscan and Umbrian artists, including Sandro Boticelli, decorated the walls with frescoes. These were primarily executed in the true or *buon* fresco technique in which finely ground inorganic pigments were painted on to fresh lime-based plaster. In 1508, Pope Julius II commissioned Michelangelo to replace the original ceiling scheme of a starry firmament, with nine scenes from the book of Genesis flanked by figures of youths, prophets, and sibyls. Michelangelo also undertook the decoration of the lunettes above the windows with depictions of the ancestors of Christ. Subsequently in 1536–1542, Michelangelo painted *The Last Judgement* on the altar wall replacing an earlier damaged fresco by Perugino.

As early as 1543, the office of 'mundator' (cleaner) was created to keep the frescoes of the Sistine Chapel clean from dust and lamp smoke. Accessible areas were likely cleaned annually. There are sixteenth-century written references to the blackening of the ceiling by the smoke of candles and to the presence of salts and cracking. A substantial cleaning operation is recorded in 1625; Simane Lagi cleaned the wall and possibly the ceiling frescoes, initially dusting them with a linen cloth then scrubbing them with slices of coarse bread, occasionally moistened with water. In 1710–1712, Annibale Mazzuoli cleaned the frescoes with Greek wine and sponges. While many artists and writers still found the frescos visible and exciting works of art well into the 19th century, others commented on their obscured darkened and blackened form.

More substantial 'restoration' work was also carried out. Between 1565 and 1572, Matteo da Lecce and Hendrick van der Broeck repainted the frescoes on the entrance wall following subsidence damage sustained in the early 16th century. In the late 16th century, Domenico Carnevali restored the ceiling, reworking several of the scenes and figures. Where these additions and restorations sought to match the colour of the earlier Michelangelo frescos the artists used much darker colours since the original frescoes were discoloured with soot. The fact that cleaning and restoration work started in the 16th century indicates that there was extensive soiling and some damage to the original frescoes early in their lives and consequently what was seen by the mid-20th century was not what the artist had originally intended.

In 1904, Seitz sealed and consolidated the plaster and conducted limited cleaning tests. In the 1920s and 1930s, Biagetti also undertook consolidation work. Between 1964 and 1974, the frescoes on the side walls were cleaned to remove the accumulation of surface soiling. Following work in 1975 to prevent rainwater reaching and damaging the ceiling, the van der Broeck and da Lecce frescoes on the entrance wall were cleaned in 1979. These frescoes had been subject to numerous previous cleanings and restorations, and after the 1979 removal of the surface dirt, these later restorations created a patchy image. The Vatican conservators argued that a more unified and thorough cleaning and restoration programme was needed to give visual integrity to the chapel and to address structural problems.

The conservation work of the 1930s and the 1970s indicated the presence of a thick even layer of glue over much of the surface of the ceiling frescoes, which was impacting the chromatic range of the fresco colours (Dauma and Henchman 1997). In places there were several layers of glue with deposits of dust and soot present between them and on the surface. The glue, attributed to Mazzuoli's 18th-century restoration, was causing some flaking of the paint; therefore, the Vatican restorers decided to remove it. It is important to note that there is no mention in the historic records of any cleaner or restorer putting glue or varnish onto the ceiling, although clearly, they did. Other unrecorded work included the over-painting of details on *The Last Judgement* in 1762 and the regilding around some the ceiling figures in 1814. In a building that is otherwise regarded as having a well-documented history, the poverty of the historical record regarding cleaning and restoration speaks to the regard in which these activities were historically held and the difficulties of researching past interventions.

Conservation of the ceiling frescoes commenced in 1975. First, the vault above the frescoes was waterproofed to stop the ingress of water, which had caused problems of salt efflorescence and cracking and delaminating of the intonaco (the thin surface layer of plaster containing the pigment). The cleaning and conservation was undertaken in three phases: the images of the Popes and the lunettes 1980–1984, the ceiling 1985–1989, and *The Last Judgement* 1990–1993. The work, sponsored by Nippon TV (who in return, gained the visual rights to the Sistine Chapel images for the period of the restoration plus three years), was completed by April 1994. Visitor access to the Sistine Chapel was maintained throughout the conservation work and many tens of thousands of people consequently saw the conservation process in action.

The cleaning of the ceiling was principally undertaken using AB57, a solution of ammonium bicarbonate, sodium bicarbonate, and Desogen (a fungicide, bactericide, and mild sequestering agent) in a paste of carboxymethyl cellulose. It was applied for three minutes and removed with a repeat application 24 hours later followed by thorough washing in distilled water. This cleaning agent solubilised the glue and dirt layers, and acted on the calcium sulphate crusts, which can form on the very outer skin of marble, limestone, lime plaster, and mortar surfaces, holding dirt at the surface. The limited application time and gel formulation restricted the penetration of this agent into the plaster ensuring it only had a surface effect. Any areas of *a secco* work (pigment held in a binder added to the dry plaster wall, often used to add details and apply fugitive pigments to *buon* fresco images) that were identified were consolidated with Paraloid B72 (an acrylic copolymer) while cleaning occurred around them. They were then separately treated with appropriate organic solvents. Substantial areas of the intonaco were found to be delaminating from the underlying arriccio (the substantial plaster backing of the wall), due to the infiltration of rainwater over the centuries. This necessitated re-adhesion of the intonaco using Vinnapas (a polymer-based dispersion) and, where necessary, grouting the voids with La Farge desalinated hydraulic mortars. The overall effect of removing the dirt and darkened glue was a dramatic heightening of the colours of the ceiling frescoes (Figure 5.2).

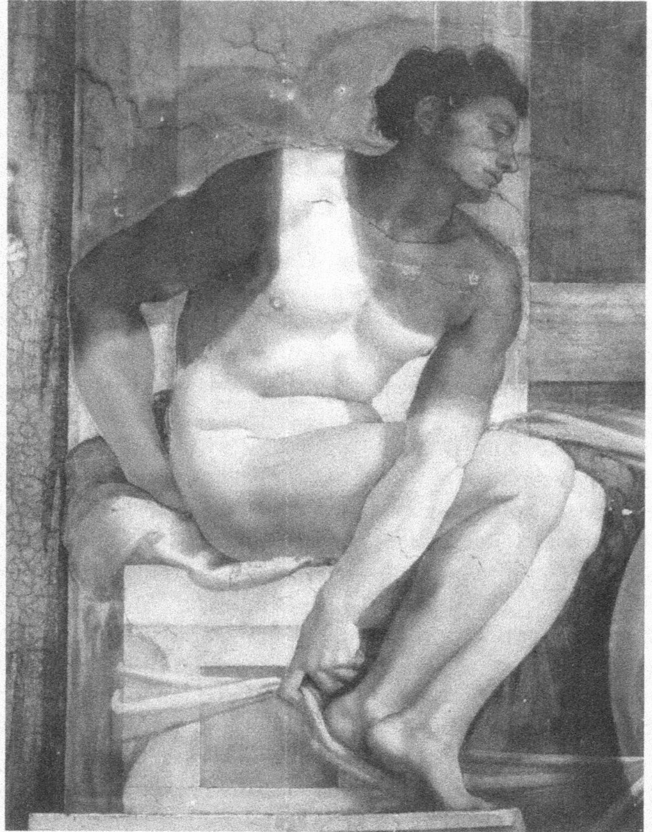

Figure 5.2 Partially cleaned fresco from the Sistine Chapel Ceiling. © Governorate of the Vatican City State Directorate of the Vatican Museums.

The cleaning of *The Last Judgement* was achieved using a slightly different approach. Michelangelo completed substantial areas of this fresco *a secco* using Naples yellow and lake pigments, which must be applied in a binding medium because applying them directly to the alkaline plaster degrades the pigments and their colour. *The Last Judgement* was initially washed with distilled water then treated with an ammonium carbonate solution and nitro thinner. A second application 24 hours later used the same solution applied through Japanese paper and then washed off with distilled water. Weak and powdering areas were consolidated with Paraloid B72 or Primal (an acrylic colloidal dispersion). The few damaged or missing areas on the fresco were gap-filled with lime and marble dust and then coloured using watercolours in a cross-hatching technique to give visual continuity to the image, while allowing the restored areas to be readily identified upon close inspection.

When *The Last Judgement* was unveiled in 1541, initial reaction was mixed. Many clerics were troubled by the nudity displayed and the positions of some of the figures. One year after Michelangelo's death, Daniele da Volterra was hired to repaint two of the figures (Saints Catherine and Blaise) and to cover some of the other naked figures, following an order by the Council of Trent in 1564. Additional coverings were painted onto figures in the 18th and 19th centuries. During the conservation work, the draperies that post-dated 1600 were removed where possible, while those dating to the 16th century were retained as they were judged to be of 'significant historical importance' (Colalucci 2017: 93, 98). This decision to honour one set of alterations but to remove another speaks to the complex balance of decisions at play in any conservation. Since da Volterra had chiselled away the surface of the fresco to repaint the two saints, restoring Michelangelo's intent in that area would have been difficult.

In addition to the interventive cleaning work, preventive conservation work was undertaken. Following the study of the chapel's microclimate, a new cold-lighting system was introduced, and an anti-dust carpet was laid on the steps to the chapel to reduce dust levels. The windows were sealed to prevent the polluted Roman air entering the building and air conditioning was installed to help maintain stable temperature and humidity despite the large numbers of visitors to the chapel.

The art historian James Beck, a vocal critic of the Sistine Chapel fresco cleaning, has questioned whether the glue layer was, at least in part, the *a secco* work of Michelangelo and thus part of the original fresco. Based on analysis carried out during the cleaning the Vatican conservators have indicated that there is virtually no *a secco* work by Michelangelo on the ceiling. Beck and others claim that it is extensive based on their reading of other artist's statements about Michelangelo's style. Paint cross-sections show slight dirt layers beneath the glue and a part of the original fresco covered by the 1560–1570s restoration does not exhibit a glue covering. Additionally, Michelangelo consistently used earth pigments in his work on the ceiling frescoes, pigments which survive well in *buon* fresco, rather than the less stable pigments that are associated with *a secco* work. This evidence supports the suggestion that the ceiling was completed almost entirely in pure fresco techniques.

It appears likely that the initial application of glue, which stabilised the plaster also obscured the salts that were forming and increased the depth of colour of the frescos. It was applied at a date well after the frescos had been completed. There were a number of subsequent applications of glue producing a complex indivisible sequence. Traces of black outlines and shadows present within this glue layer are seen as the work of later restorers either enhancing the outlines of Michelangelo's figures, which were becoming indistinct as a result of the accumulating glue and dirt layers, or creating additional modelling and shading (chiaroscuro). The exact dates and creators of these effects are unknown, wherever possible they were deduced from traces of stratigraphy within the glue layer by the conservators working on the image.

Despite concerns raised by Beck regarding the loss of shading, there remains considerable evidence of shading and modelling on the images. Differences, particularly in the extent of shadows and shading, have been observed between the photographs taken prior to the restoration and those taken after it. Brandt (1987) has suggested that photographic evidence is a poor guide to the visual improvements in the frescoes. The pre-cleaning photographic images minimised the effect of the dirt layer because of the penetrating depth of the photographic lights and some of the post-treatment images appear flat and thin since the rougher surface of the fresco now deflects a large amount of the strong photographic light (Brandt 1987). Statements by writers, art historians, and others from the Renaissance to the present day regarding Michelangelo's use of shading, modelling, and colour are entirely subjective and unreliable in determining the truth of this matter. The cleaned images with their heightened colour appear similar to other Renaissance frescoes, and Michelangelo's use of pigment and technique is consistent with the Tuscan tradition of fresco painting.

Beck's criticism of the work pitted his connoisseur's eye and expertise against the scientific underpinnings of conservation – a tactic that he is not alone in adopting (Scott 2016).[6] Cleaning can bring about dramatic change and for those whose professional life is bound up in the study of an artist or a period this change can be threatening. Conservators, and those who employ them, need to be aware of the responsibility to bring public opinion with them, especially when cleaning well-known and much-loved works of art. In Italy, decisions regarding the release of information on conservation projects are made by the art historians, scientists, and owners/curators of the object, who are in overall charge of the project (Cather, personal communication). In this case, the hierarchical structure of Italian wall painting conservation projects and the natural reserve of the Vatican initially led to a slow and limited response to the criticisms by Beck and others over the cleaning of the Sistine Chapel frescoes. This allowed the criticism to take hold in the media, which embraced the controversy (Lister 1991) and struggled to convey the science; thus, opinions about the cleaning, voiced principally by art historians, initially overshadowed the cleaned images and technical information emerging from this conservation project.

Now that the 'shock of the new' has died away a wider public has become comfortable with the bright colours of Michelangelo's frescos, which are now understood to be typical of Medieval and Renaissance fresco work. Scholars have begun to re-appraise Michelangelo's work in its cleaned form with the new information on technique, approach, symbolism, and meaning that it conveys (Colalucci 2017). Slowly the old appearance of the ceiling has faded from memory and with it the ideas of an older generation of art historians. The subjective response has changed; initially weighted to the 'I loved it when it was dirty' (Pollini quoted in Colalucci 2018: 173) side of the argument, new authors have responded positively to the cleaned image (Trutty-Coohill 2005). It is in the nature of academic debate for experts to disagree; such controversy can stimulate research, scholarship and even release funding. Such disagreement can be beneficial, even to those whose work is being attacked. Colalucci wrote that 'it obliged me to verify the validity or otherwise of whatever argument was brought against the restoration' (2018: 172). The controversy over the Sistine Chapel work was not the last of its kind. The conservation of other frescos, including Leonardo da Vinci's extensively damaged *The Last Supper* (Barcilon 2001), has subsequently attracted critical attention. It is unlikely that these will be the last such controversies and conservators will need to continue to document their actions carefully and communicate their processes and decision-making to the public to counter the strong pull that the familiar and known (if sometimes fictive) image can exert.

Notes

1 Different varnish mixtures have different glass transition temperatures (Tg) or points where the polymer transitions from hard to pliable. Above this Tg, particles slowly adsorb into the surface (Horie 2010).

2 Criticism of the degree to which paintings have been cleaned has been a recurrent theme in the history of conservation – a point satirised in Hogarth's painting *Time Smoking a Picture*. Controversies erupted at the National Gallery in London in the mid-19th century, the 1930s and 1940s (Kirby Talley 1998; Modestini 2005) and in Italy in the 1980s (Case Study 5A).

3 A single coin hoard may contain hundreds or even thousands of coins. Ascertaining what the earliest and latest coins are, whether forgeries are present and where the coins come from (mintmarks) is important to interpreting the hoard correctly (Goodburn-Brown and Jones 1998).

4 Nd = Neodymium, Er = Erbium, YAG = yttrium aluminium garnet.

5 The Goldilocks Principle is recognized in other fields, including developmental psychology, biology, astronomy, engineering, and economics. It is derived from the children's story Goldilocks and the three Bears in which a young girl tastes three different bowls of porridge. She prefers the bowl that is not too hot and not too cold but rather 'just right'.

6 Another common trope that Beck employs is the idea that conservation actions are determined by a secretive cabal who carefully guards its knowledge (Beck and Daley 1993; Rodgers 2004). This notion, which has roots in the secretive practices of 18th- and 19th-century restorers, has little connection to the transparent approaches of modern practitioners but has traction since the scientific underpinnings of the field can seem inaccessible and because conservation literature has traditionally been sequestered in its own journals and publications.

6 Restoration

Restoration

Restoration encompasses the various treatment steps needed to return an object to an earlier and/or more understandable state. These steps may include reassembly, re-shaping, loss compensation (the addition of new materials to replace missing elements of the piece), and aesthetic reintegration (inpainting or toning designed to make the new elements harmonise with the original material).

Restoration is an important part of the process of the meaning-making that takes place in museums and other heritage institutions. It makes objects visually accessible (Figure 6.1) and augments the written interpretation that the curator or specialist produces (Doumas 2010). It may also add value to an object (Case Study 2B: the Sutton Hoo helmet). Restoration implies the use of original material, often a substantial amount, and a resulting visual form that is very close to the original. Actions taken during restoration should satisfy the desire for aesthetic harmony and legibility but not at the expense of authenticity. They should be evidence-based and stop at the point when imagination begins. 'Restoration must aim to re-establish the potential unity of the work of art, as long as this is possible without producing an artistic or historical forgery and without erasing every trace of the passage of time left on the work of art' (Brandi 1996).

Given the important role that restoration plays in making objects legible and 'explain(ing) how things work' (Mann 1994), it is imperative that areas of restoration are detectable, so that the additions can be identified under close inspection and the veracity of the object revealed. Definitions of what constitutes conservation acceptable restoration have varied, often depending on the date, culture, and history of the object and the experience of the conservator-restorer.

Definition of terms

Different terms are used to describe activities that are similar to restoration but which can differ subtly. Sometimes, particularly in the popular press, these terms are used incorrectly. Similarly, dictionary definitions are frequently too broad and self-referencing to provide useful distinctions between the terms. The definitions offered below focus on the most common agreed usages, allowing a wide range of subtle and specific meanings to be conveyed.[1]

DOI: 10.4324/9781003009078-6

- Reconstruction – Bringing the object to a form very similar to the whole original, where there is evidence or material from the original. Thus, historic buildings may be reconstructed from existing foundations, surviving fragments, and documentary evidence.
- Recreation – Like reconstruction but starting with nothing of the original. It is undertaken using new materials and may involve a certain amount of imagination. A recreation was made of the Sutton Hoo helmet in its 'as new' state.
- Renovation – Return to working order usually using some parts of the original object. It implies subsequent use of the item and is generally more complete than a repair. 'Action of renewing an object without necessarily respecting its material or significance' (BS EN 15898:2019).
- Rehabilitation – The process of returning a property to a useable state through repair or alteration, enabling an effective contemporary use, while preserving those portions and features of the property that are significant to its historic, architectural, and cultural values (Brand 1994). Although initially used for buildings the term may also be applied to objects.
- Refurbishment – As for rehabilitation, implies bringing back into use or improved use, but is used to refer to equipment and other objects as well as buildings.
- Replacement – Constructing new parts or an entire object to perform the function of an original. Usually used in conjunction with the creation of a part in a new material to take the place of an old, damaged, or worn part. Damaged or exhausted parts of machines are replaced to keep them running.
- Repair – Make good and return to working order. When repaired, a watch will work again.
- Reuse – Brought back into use, previously dormant and unused it again performs a function. As with reused timber, it does not have to perform its original function, though it often does. 'Adaptive reuse' is often used to refer to the reuse of a building for a function it was not originally designed or intended for.
- Revived – Brought back into use after a period of dormancy and neglect; the item performs its original function. Life, worth, and vigour are implied.
- Renewed – Made functional or valid again.
- Replication – Manufacture using new materials to exactly resemble an original visual form. Often a specific object is faithfully copied.
- Reproduction – Manufacture using new materials to resemble an original visual form. It usually implies a generic style from the past (e.g. reproduction furniture) rather than a specific copy of an object.
- Repristination – made appear new or pristine again.
- Reassembly – putting fragments or pieces back together.
- Reintegration – additions of substance and colour to infill areas, which are missing to achieve a more complete form or appearance.

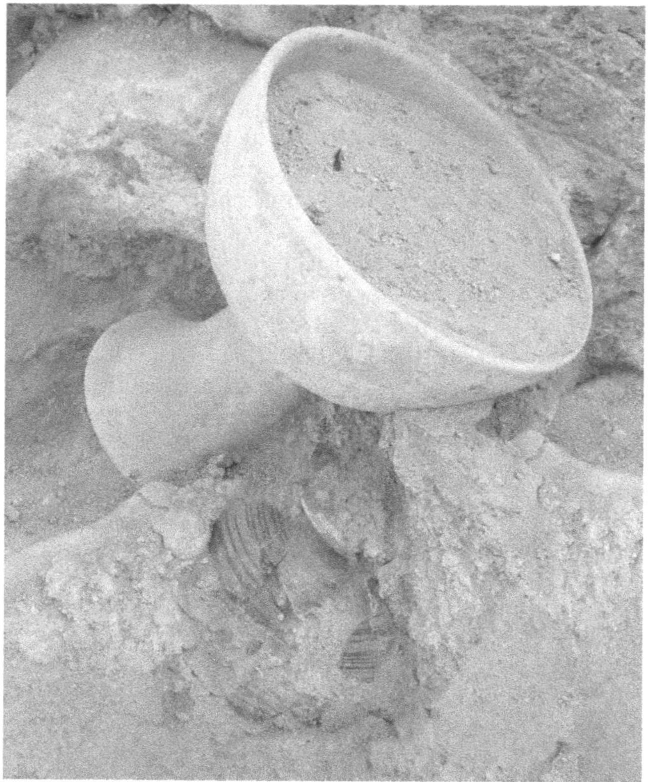

Figure 6.1 Pottery exposed during archaeological excavation. While the form of the chalice is immediately recognizable the small vessel beneath it is heavily fragmented and its form can only be understood through reconstruction. Emily Williams.

The Development of Restoration

Restoration is in many ways the most visible aspect of conservation and its history is tied closely to the history of conservation. Due to the close connection between restorative approaches and the way we see and experience art, it has also engendered controversy, especially over the last 200 years. As discussed in Chapter 2, numerous instances of restoration and repair have been recovered from the archaeological record. These include the repair of a 13,000-year-old Magdalenian spear thrower (Ward *et al.* 2009), bitumen fills, and repairs on ceramics from the Near East (Dooijes and Niewenhuyse 2007), lashings on prehistoric canoes and ceramics from Denmark (Brinch-Madsen 2009) and metal repairs to many materials including ceramics, metals, stone, glass, and even organics (Brinch Madsen 2009; Cobb and Evans 2009; Balogh and Grayson 2019; Williams 2021). What is unclear in some of these examples is whether the goal was merely to retain the function of the item or to restore its visual and aesthetic aspects or whether those undertaking such actions distinguished the meanings from each other. King Nabonidus of Babylon (ca. 620–539 BCE) undertook one of the earliest recorded examples of restoration after discovering a statue of King

Sargon that was missing part of its head (Grayson 1973). Nabonidus brought in expert craftsmen and had the head and face restored. He is also credited with excavating, recording, and restoring the temple at Ebbabar founded by Hammurabi (Berducou 1996). Nabonidus' approach to these objects reflected his reverence for the earlier Babylonian kings and was commemorated on cuneiform tablets.

The repristination of ancient statues in the Renaissance period was also rooted in an appreciation of the past (Giusti 1994). It took many different forms but could include either cutting or abrading decayed, discoloured material from the exterior, adding new pieces of marble (often heads, arms, and legs) to the stumps of an antique torso to return the object to its pristine 'as new' state or marrying parts from several statues together to create a pastiche. This placed the aesthetic beauty of the object and its fitness for display above all other things. It was felt that the damage evident on classical statues was an act of barbarism and that restoration removed evidence of that barbarity (Yourcenar 1996). These practices continued into the 18th century, however increasingly they drew criticism. By the early 19th century, there was a movement away from such interventive restorations to classical sculpture. This has been attributed in part to Canova's refusal to restore the Parthenon sculptures (Podany 2003) as well as to the development of classical archaeology and the Romantic notion of the purity of the 'fragment' (Pinelli 2003; Risser and Saunders 2013). In 1818, a royal decree prohibited the integrative restoration of all classes of ancient objects including ceramics and wallpaintings found in Pompeii, Herculaneum, and their surrounds (Milanese 2013). The decree noted that restorations were an obstacle to the interpretation of objects because it was difficult to tell the original features from the additions. However, Andrea Milanese (2013) notes that another reason for the decree may have been that it was becoming increasingly difficult to tell forgeries from restored antiquities.[2]

Unfortunately, a recurring historical theme is that appreciation of items from the past can be distorted by current fashions and too often enthusiasm for one period leads to damage and to neglect of other periods. The fashion for Gothic architecture in the late 18th and 19th century led to the removal of substantial amounts of 15th- to 18th-century architectural features and the incorporation of many 'Gothic' features into restored buildings for which there was no evidence. In the mid-19th century, art was also 'restored' for moral purposes, which manifested itself as the additions of fig leaves and loincloths to cover genitalia. Cleopatra's leg, amorously draped over Anthony, was cut from a Brussels tapestry owned by the Worshipful Company of Goldsmiths and the gap woven in red to replicate part of Anthony's cloak (Brooks *et al.* 1994). The differential fading of dyes has now resulted in a bright orange leg-shaped patch on the cloak. Conservators in the 1990s were uncomfortable restoring the leg since they knew nothing about the detail of 18th-century original and so the distracting orange patch remained as a very visible reminder of 19th-century moral sensitivities (Brooks *et al.* 1994).

As early as 1846, Alfred Bonnardot produced a book on the restoration of paper in which he warned other practitioners against the removal of historical evidence as part of the restoration process (Kosek 1994). The Italian painter/restorer Secco-Suardo who, in 1866, advocated avoiding excessive retouching, and using tempera or watercolour for retouching since they do not darken upon ageing (Bomford 1994), also evinces a similar sensitivity to the restoration of works of art. The formation of the Society for the Protection of Ancient Buildings engendered a wider spread of sympathy for the value of original work and the value of objects, such as buildings, as historic documents (Chapter 2).

As conservation developed into a discreet profession, it sought to separate its methodologies from those of other practitioners. As a result, the term 'restoration' was often problematised, and a bright line was drawn between its practices and those of conservation. Restorers were painted as having little interest in the object and lacking skill and intemperate analogies to religious or medical divisions were sometimes drawn (Philippot 1996).[3] In reality, restoration is an inseparable part of the conservation process. Like cleaning, it increases the accessibility of an object and moves it towards a more informative state, adding material to the object rather than removing it.

The 1960s saw the concept of 'de-restoration' emerge. The Glyptothek in Munich removed restored elements from pedimental sculptures of the Temple of Aphaia in Aegina. The fragmentary sculptures were excavated in 1811 and then heavily restored by the sculptor Bertel Thorvaldsen between 1816 and 1818. Subsequent excavation at Aegina in 1901 had shown that his interpretations were fanciful at best and frequently very mistaken. Between 1962 and 1965, Thorvaldsen's additions were removed and when the museum reopened in 1972, metal supports were visible in the place of the former interventions. The decision to de-restore may have been due to many factors, including a desire to remove reminders of the Nazi affection for the sculptures (Diebold 1995), but it also spoke to the increased emphasis on authenticity following events like the van Meegeren trial (Godley 2015) and the changing influences that modern art brought to aesthetics. Other museums undertook similar de-restoration campaigns.

Objects and paintings were increasingly valued not only for their aesthetics but also as rich sources of information about themselves. In this environment, it was understood that damage may be of equal value to understanding the work and its history (Te Marvelde 2011). Additionally, there were demands from some art historians to distinguish the original material in paintings from subsequent restoration campaigns, leading to developments such as visible in-painting (Bomford 1994). This could be achieved at numerous different levels, from using a neutral monotone in the infilled area, to copying the colours and shapes exactly as in the painting but not imitating the natural craquelure of an aged paint film. The Instituto Centrale del Restauro in Rome developed perhaps the best-known technique of 'visible' inpainting (Idelson and Severini 2018). Known as *tratteggio*, this technique uses discrete vertical brush strokes in the colours of the missing elements of the picture, which allow the original colours in the missing area to be reproduced when seen at distance, but the vertical strokes remain visible, and thus the in-painting is obvious, upon careful inspection. The *tratteggio* technique has been used to good effect on many wall-painting restorations (Mora et al. 1996), although the main use of this technique has been for infilled areas in oil paintings. The success of *tratteggio*, and related techniques such as *rigatoni*, can be variable, depending on the nature of the painting and the skill of the practitioner as it is not easy to achieve the required chromatic balances (Vaccaro 1996).

Although many de-restorations were carried out with fanfare (Diebold 1995), since the late 1980s museums have increasingly chosen to re-restore statues. For example, in 1991 the Getty chose to re-restore the Lansdowne Hercules, a statue that had been de-restored less than 20 years earlier (Podany 1994). The reasons for re-restoration vary from institution to institution but generally centre around questions of legibility. Fragmentary objects are harder for the public to read and appreciate and often the losses dominate perception, drawing attention away from what remains. The desire to easily remove and insert restorations has led to the exploration of new treatment methods. Examples include detachable fills (Koob 2006), non-intrusive approaches to upholstery conservation (Graves and Howlett 1997; Eastop and Gill 2001; Graves 2015; Spicer 2013), the use of 3D scanning for virtual reconstructions (Stanco *et al.* 2011), and digital restoration of old photographs (Ctein 2010). There is also a growing interest within the conservation field in the history of restoration and earlier restorations as well as restorer's practices are increasingly being studied (Te Marvelde 1999; Risser and Saunders 2013).

Restoration in Practice

Since humans recognise objects, or parts of objects, by comparing them with existing images from their memories (Chapter 10), the gaps, losses and disconnects between the viewed object and the remembered object are automatically highlighted in the mind. For example, a jug without a handle is troubling because we are conditioned to expect the handle to be there. Such losses stand out. Eye movement studies indicate that perception is achieved through initially seeing the outline and key elements of an object, thus the outline of losses shows up quickly and prominently in perception (Schutz *et al.* 2011). Particularly in two-dimensional works, such as paintings, the losses can become so prominent that what we perceive are patterns of voids instead of the paint surface itself. The image cannot be viewed without first seeing the loss (Vaccaro 1996). In a three-dimensional work, because of differences in the planes and angles of an object, we are initially better able to visually compensate for smaller losses (such as chips); however, larger losses can make it difficult to understand the form and function of an object. Thus, to see and experience the object, especially a decorative object, and not focus on the damage, the loss or break needs to be visually integrated into the whole.

The object, the information available, the time and materials available, the expertise of the conservator/restorer, and what is appropriate for each individual loss will dictate the level of integration chosen. Different levels of integration may even be appropriate on the same object depending on how much is known about the loss (Case study 6 A). The ethical position on restoration, or loss compensation, has become more consistent in recent years. The AIC *Guidelines for Practice* regards compensation for loss as acceptable, provided:

- It is fully recorded.
- It is reversible.
- It is detectable by common examination methods.
- It does not falsify the aesthetic, conceptual, or physical characteristics of the object.
- It does not remove or obscure original material (respect for the traces of time).

Restoration comprises:

- Reassembly of the broken pieces of an object. This is undertaken to achieve the most complete form of the object possible. Wherever possible all fragments of the original object are included. The resultant object should be stable, and the pieces should be in their correct, original positions.[4] Reassembly is widely practised. Examples include, but are not limited to, putting together fragments of stone forming parts of a building (*anastylosis*), mending ceramic or glass sherds to form a vessel or assembling the pieces of metal in a clockwork mechanism. Depending on the complexity of the object, re-assembly is a time-consuming and potentially costly business. It can result in unstable and incomplete objects. Particularly in the case of archaeological materials, losses and deterioration during burial may result in fragile, fragmentary objects that require additional support (Baldwin 2017; Unruh and Harbeck 2021). In some cases, such as a bag of ceramic sherds, it is important to remember that their current form may be more stable (although less legible) than the reconstructed (but potentially partial and unbalanced) vessel and to weigh the necessity of reassembly. If determining the typology of the vessel or the decorative schema on the surface will help to date the site or context or provenance of the piece, reassembly may be required; if the type is already recognisable and well-understood it may be better not to reassemble the vessel unless it is required for display or illustration. Where the breakage was deliberate (such as when an object is ritually 'killed') or when the fragments were subsequently used as objects in their own right (Chapman 2000) it may not be appropriate to reassemble them. Adhesives used in reassembling objects should be weaker than the object so that if failure occurs it is the adhesive that fails (breaks) rather than the object. Similarly, they should not shrink and pull on the object or deteriorate in a manner that will cause further damage to the object.
- Reshaping. Materials, especially organic materials, are often distorted by their own weight, by objects placed on them or by the pressure of surrounding soil during burial, and may require reshaping. In reshaping an object, the conservator is imposing their idea of the 'correct' shape on the object. This shape may relate to the original shape of the object, the shape acquired during use or a shape that is closer to these but mediated by the damage the object has incurred. In theory, the distortions caused by neglect, burial, etc. are removed and those associated with use are normally retained; however, unless an object is very well understood it can be difficult to differentiate these. Reshaping is an interpretive act, and it can be controversial as in the case of the Bush Barrow gold (Case Study 10 A). Metal objects are reshaped using heat and pressure and must be ductile enough to permit this approach. In the past, bent archaeological metal artefacts were often reshaped to recover their original form. This is now undertaken less frequently as the deliberate folding and breaking of metal objects is appreciated as a final act in their working lives (Needham *et al.* 2006; Greaves *et al.* 2019).[5] Cellulosic materials (such as paper, textiles, wood, cotton, and linen) and proteinaceous materials (such as leather, wool, and silk) are often reshaped through humidification and weighting or clamping. Supports may be needed to maintain the new shape or to combat the object's 'memory' of its old shape.

- Reintegration. Reintegration can be further broken down into two activities.
  - Loss Compensation, also sometimes called gap-filling or infilling, refers to the filling of a loss and may be used in reference to filling a surface finish, a substrate or the decorative elements of an object. Replacing the missing leg of a chair, reapplying the missing ground layer in a painting loss, or reworking a hole in a tapestry, are all examples of loss compensation. Fills may provide structural support for the object, or they may re-establish the aesthetic or functional attributes of an object. For example, filling the gap in a mosaic with new tesserae ensures that the original tesserae adjoin the lost edge do not work free and become lost, further damaging the piece. Similarly, replacing a missing leg on a chair or chest of drawers prevents the furniture from overbalancing and being damaged. Depending on the object, different levels of gap-filling may be carried out. On archaeological ceramics, gap filling is often limited because archaeologists are interested in seeing the degree of damage and loss and accessing the broken edges of the ceramic, which may reveal information about the vessel's fabric type, provenance, and manufacture. Line chips (the small chips along break lines) and other small losses are rarely filled. On the other hand, break lines and line chips on decorative ceramics are almost always filled as leaving them would detract from the aesthetic nature of the piece. The decision to fill should consider the nature and type of the artefact, its intended use (i.e. handling, storage, display) as well as whether the damage has historical or cultural significance.
  - Aesthetic Reintegration. Also sometimes called inpainting or retouching, aesthetic reintegration aims to make the loss and any resulting fill blend into the original object. Again, different approaches may be taken, a background colour may be applied, making the fill less visible, but not emulating the existing decorative scheme (Figure 6.2). This approach is the most appropriate when the exact nature of the decoration is unknown but can be unconvincing and distracting if poorly executed. Mottled colour schemes, like camouflage, may be more natural and less visually intrusive than large fields of a single colour. Alternatively, the filled area may be restored to its 'original' appearance and all elements of the design included (Case study 6 A: *The Ambassadors*). Inpainting is time-consuming and costly, and the approach taken may depend on the nature of the object, the size of the fill and intended use of the object. The larger the loss, the greater the conjecture and skill needed to emulate the decoration. When inpainting a fill it is important to consider any variations in lighting between the studio/laboratory and the place where the object will be displayed as these can change the appearance of the inpainting. It is important to consider how the materials will age, as variations in ageing characteristics between old and new materials can make initially discreet fills highly visible within a short time. Simple guidelines, such as '6 foot 6 inches' suggesting that inpainting be undetectable from a distance but visible on closer inspection, provide a memorable articulation of the desire to maintain the visual continuity of objects while allowing restoration to be detectable (Hodges 1975; Buys and Oakley 1993). In practice, much closer inspection with UV light, raking light, microscopy, or x-radiography is often necessary to detect very skilful inpainting.

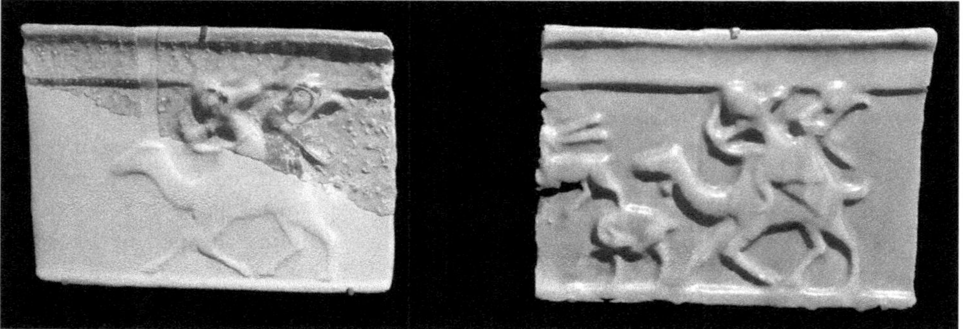

Figure 6.2 A restored polychrome tile (left) exhibited next to a complete monochrome original (right). The added elements are toned with a neutral colour and enough of the missing elements of the scene are indicated to make the tile legible, but other (unknowable) elements are omitted. Emily Williams.

The choice of restoration materials can present challenges. Unconsidered use of modern materials in the past, such as Portland cement (Burden *et al.* 2004; Ballard 2004), AJK or BJK dough (Koob, 1998; Fulcher 2014), and soluble nylon (Sease 1981), has led to visually intrusive and damaging restorations. The reaction in some cases has been a return to the use of traditional materials and in others to develop more sympathetic and long-term stable conservation materials. Traditional manufacturing materials are often well suited to restoration as their properties are closely related to those of the object itself.[6] However, they can be difficult to distinguish from the original materials. On the other hand, traditional stewards and caretakers may see modern conservation materials as problematic. Ethical restoration involves careful consideration of all the materials used, their short-term benefits and their long-term advantages and shortcomings as well as consultation with all stakeholders to determine the best course of action.

Where an object is too fragile for restoration, increasingly digital options are available. Damage or alteration of the object to facilitate its restoration is generally considered unacceptable (Brooks 1998); however, in a limited number of cases, damage may be accepted as a regrettable necessity. Examples include sculpture and furniture conservation where conservators assembling heavy, structural elements may need to secure a broken piece by drilling into the object and inserting a pin or dowel (Case Study 11B: Tullio Lombardo's *Adam*),[7] or removing and remaking an element that is too weak or damaged to provide structural support any longer. It is important to reduce the amount of loss associated with such activities and the risks inherent in them (Podany *et al.* 2009). For example, drilling may release stresses in an object leading to cracking and breaks and improperly chosen dowels can cause additional stresses to the object. If poorly done, the damage incurred may outweigh the gains. Similarly, while reversible adhesives are generally sought, stronger more irreversible ones, such as epoxies, may be required when the object is heavy or lacks purchase (Case Study 2 A: the Portland Vase). Being cognisant of the risks and working to minimise them will generate a better outcome.

Current ethical guidance regarding restoration demands that restoration only be carried out when there is clear evidence for the final form. Thus, symmetrical vessels can readily be restored, and objects with repeating decoration easily be inpainted. However, what constitutes 'clear' evidence may vary depending on the object, the owners, and the specialism of the conservator and need not be limited to the evidence on the object itself. Paintings' conservators frequently study related works by the same artist to see how they handled certain elements and look to prints and other paintings to better understand the fashions of the time to determine how best to inpaint areas. Similarly, an object conservator treating a jug that is missing its handle might look to other period examples to determine what handle type is most likely to have been present. In instances where there is no information, vague generalised shapes may be used to convey the impression of the work and avoid visual disharmony, such as the use of featureless faces for the unidentified saints depicted in the reconstruction of the 13th-century glass mosaic from the Baptistery of Florence (Giusti 1994).

Challenges Presented in the Purpose, Acceptability, and Extent of Restoration

Differing approaches to restoration can stem from dissimilar aesthetic and evidentiary (historic) values. Factors such as age, original function, and rarity may also play a role. In practice, the nature of ownership also often affects the choices regarding the extent and nature of restoration. Objects that are in personal collections are often more extensively restored than items, which are held in public collections (Edge 1994). This relates both to the way privately held objects are displayed and how they are acquired and traded. Private collectors often live with their collections around them and to achieve visual balance, it is easiest to raise everything to a pristine condition. Evidence of age, history of use and original features may take second place to the owner's view about how the object should look. Additionally, because of the often-competitive nature of collecting and the machismo that can be associated with large, showy purchases, auction houses and dealers may extensively restore items to an idealised condition prior to sale, knowing that such conditions will command higher prices. This was the case when the heavily restored Crosby Garrett Roman parade helmet sold for 2.3 million pounds in 2010 (Breeze and Bishop 2013; Barnes 2010). Such sales and the associated publicity and advertising normalise expectations about the condition of these types of objects and can result in calls for publicly owned objects of this type to be restored to a similar standard (Case Study 6 A: *The Ambassadors*). These commercial considerations, often transmitted through television shows, such as *The Repair Shop*, *Art Detectives* and *American Restoration*, and via newspaper headlines, influence how restoration work is perceived by the public and how they value objects from the past (Chapter 1). Consequently, restoration (or perhaps more accurately renovation or refurbishment) for aesthetic purposes and functionality often has greater importance in the eyes of the public, than in the eyes of the heritage professionals, such as conservators.

If condition is associated with value in the private sphere, in the case of religious art there can be associations between condition and veneration. Fresh coats of paint or fanciful restorations may be seen to signal devotion and may or may not be guided by what previously existed (Molina and Pincemin 1994; Williams 2002: 464). This can present a challenge for conservation since both the intangible, in this case the religious practices of the community, and the tangible, the materiality of the object, must be balanced. In 2012, parishioner Cecilia Giménez attempted to restore the 80-year-old fresco *Ecce Homo* (Behold the Man) in the Sanctuary of Mercy church in Borja, Spain. Her work, motivated by fear that the water-damaged figure might otherwise be lost, resulted in a figure with a pasty and bloated face, and led to condemnation and ridicule. However, once it was understood who had undertaken the work and why, there was no prosecution and little local criticism. Due to the media and internet coverage the painting became an unexpected tourist attraction (Jones 2018). In four months, more than 40,000 people visited the church. Although the visitor numbers later fell, sales of merchandise and visits have provided funds for a local charity and employment for townspeople (Jones 2018). Not all such cases have ended so fortuitously and there are many instances where similar actions have led to additional work and expenditure or loss; however, it is important to consider what the restorer seeks to maintain – the shape or the substance. In the case of *Ecce Homo*, the devotional substance was preserved, but the shape was lost.

Building material that is weathered away or worn down by visitors, such as steps, may be routinely replaced to provide safe access and to preserve the historic form of the structure. Weathered stone and wood siding is routinely replaced on historic buildings, paint and gilding renewed on exterior surfaces. Although we often think of these actions as 'maintenance' or 'preservation', such restorations help to retain the historic form of the monument and thus the power and emotion it arouses. Like objects that are repeatedly restored over time such buildings pose problems. At what point does object identity triumph over material authenticity (Lowenthal 1992)? Does a thing remain the same after many or all its parts are replaced? Plutarch famously posed the problem of Theseus' ship.[8] Saved by the Athenians, the boards were slowly replaced until no original boards remained (Plutarch 1914: 47). At what point does the ship cease to be Theseus' ship? The answer depends on whether you consider the term 'Theseus' Ship' to be the 'title' and idea of the object or whether you consider it to relate to the materials composing the object. An interesting corollary for the art world is whether there is a point at which a damaged painting or work of art should cease to be attributed to the artist and instead be attributed to the last restorer? This question was tested in Ascalon vs. Department of Parks and Recreation *et al.* (Grant 2010). The artist David Ascalon successfully sued the Harrisburg, Pennsylvania, Department of Parks and Recreation after his work was heavily restored and his name removed from it. Although the restoration had not been carried out in a particularly ethical way, Ascalon's win reinforced the importance of working with living artists when preparing to restore their works.

Many modern artists have exploited the impermanence of art materials to explore issues such as impermanence, ownership, obsolescence, and transience. Frequently, the intentions of the artist and the owner may vary. Some artists wish their artwork to continue to decay, others wish to replace (restore) the decaying material in order that the visual impact of the initial work survives. Owners, who may have invested heavily in the art, often want the work to be sustained. This provides a variety of challenges to the conservator (Heuman 1995; Skowranek 2007; Marçal 2019). When working with such artworks, the conservator must work with the artist (if living) or their representatives as well as with the owner/curator to establish their desires for the future of the artwork.[9] There should be no *a priori* assumption that the work is intended to be physically preserved and restored.

Although restoration seeks to restore an object to its former appearance or an earlier form, we should remain aware that in the process we are altering the object that we seek to restore. We are creating something that it never was. If we think about a ceramic vessel where losses have been filled, the object may now consist of ceramic, plaster, acrylic paints, and a conservation-grade adhesive. It is changed by the additions (even if they are reversible) and will react differently to the environments it encounters. Similarly, if we have chosen not to fill the cracks and line chips it may also present an altered appearance (complete but broken) that it did not present before. Although the vessel is more legible, it is also no longer what it once was. Muñoz-Viñas (2020) argues that acknowledging this alteration can make us both more prudent (because we are less likely to uncritically accept routine processes) and more decisive (because we are less constrained by the fear of altering the object). Sweetnam and Henderson (2021) take this concept further advocating the use of 'disruptive conservation' as a way of centring the role of interpretation in conservation and confronting what they see as damaging narratives in conservation and museum practice.

In presenting the past, we project, often unconsciously, our present ideas into it, selecting the facts we consider relevant and important and shaping history to the form that we currently think it ought to have. In restoring objects, we unconsciously mould the physical form of objects to fit our perception of the past. Thus, restoration says as much about the present day as it does about the past. The colour and texture of the materials used, the examples copied, the knowledge exhibited and the extent and nature of the restoration, all betray the age and aesthetic tradition to which the restoration belongs. No matter how much guidance the object may offer about its original appearance and nature, restoration work is always an interpretive act and as such it is not neutral. We (as a society) choose which objects are 'worthy' of conservation and restoration and how the work should be carried out (Genbrugge 2017). As conservators, we make both large and small decisions about how much damage can be tolerated, what evidence is present and how to interpret and utilise it, which values it is significant to preserve and how best to do that with the resources at our disposal. It is important to be as conscious as possible about these decisions, examining our biases and documenting the decision-making process and the factors that influenced it (Bomford 2003; Unruh and Harbeck 2021).

Alternative Approaches

For some cultures, the original material of the object is less essential than what the object symbolises and what it embodies (Yagihashi 1988). Within Japanese culture the tradition of *kintsugi* ('patch with gold') and *kintsukuroi* ('repair with gold') seeks to transform a broken or flawed object through the intentional inclusion of the damage. In this tradition, the damage becomes a 'central element of the metamorphosis of the damaged ceramic into an object imbued with new characteristics and an appearance that exerts a completely different approach' (Iten 2008: 19). Objects repaired in this way are often valued more highly than when they were whole and are seen as expressions of two Japanese philosophies *mottaini* (remorse over wasted or misused resources) and *wabi-sabi* (seeking peace with the natural progression of life by accepting the beauty of change) (Iten 2008). The repair thus becomes a tangible expression of intangible concepts.

In societies that have a tradition of building in stone, decay is often associated with loss and destruction whereas societies that have extensive traditions of using organic materials often develop an acceptance of decay and renewal as an integral part of their culture. For these latter groups, the act of copying or renewing the object may be considered more significant than attempting to preserve the original material (Kitamura 1988; Clavir 2002). Within cultures where artefacts may be viewed as ancestors, the process of restoration should be considered as extending not only to the physical form of the artefact itself but also to the networks of relationships within which the ancestor is a part (Sully and Cardoso 2014; Pouliot *et al.* 2017; Johns 2018).

In some instances, because of the fragility of the object, or the tangible values it is invested with, it may not be possible to restore the object itself. In such cases, replication may offer alternative approaches.

Replication

Replicas can be created as exact copies of the object in its current form, or they can be a recreation of the object in its original form. Replicas are useful didactic tools because they reveal the original form of an object that may have subsequently changed. In the 19th century, plaster of Paris replicas of famous sculptures and important works of art, allowed working men and women to access cultural icons in their own towns. Cast galleries were established in many museums. Today, the ease of travel allows people to see the 'real thing' so replicas may play a supporting role in displays or stand in for objects that have perished or are highly degraded. For example, the recreation of the Sutton Hoo helmet's as new appearance gives us a different sense of the helmet than we might have when we view it in its corroded state (Figure 6.3). Other powerful reasons for making replicas include:

- Experimentation: Replicas also allow us to investigate ancient technologies and understand how objects were used in the past. The replica of the Sea Stallion from Glendalough, a replica of the Skuldelev 2 vessel found in Roskilde Fjord (Bill 2007) is touted as the largest and most authentic Viking longboat. The replica allows us to better understand the skill needed to build such a ship, the amount of time it might take a skilled boatbuilding team to create such a vessel and how the ship performs when it is on the water. It has the added benefit that we can test it to destruction if desired, whereas even if the original vessel were seaworthy, we might not test it in the same way.
- Recording: Replicas can help us to preserve an accurate record of what is currently present but may not survive due to environmental factors or the instability of the materials from which it is made. Analyses of 19th-century plaster cast taken from marbles at the Parthenon, which were not removed by Lord Elgin, provide a graphic example of how both pollutants and tourists have changed the sculptures in the intervening years (Payne 2019).
- Replacement: Replicated elements have been used to replace damaged or missing components of objects, particularly working objects (Chapter 9). Similarly, historic houses often use both replica and reproduction textiles to 'dress' furniture, such as beds, or historic rooms (Nylander 1990).
- Access: Replicas are frequently used to enable visitors to understand what an object may have looked like in its original context after the object itself has been moved into a museum for safekeeping. Replicas also permit people, especially children, the blind and the partially sighted, to interact with objects through touch and minimise the risks to original objects from handling (Pye 2008; Wilson *et al.* 2017).

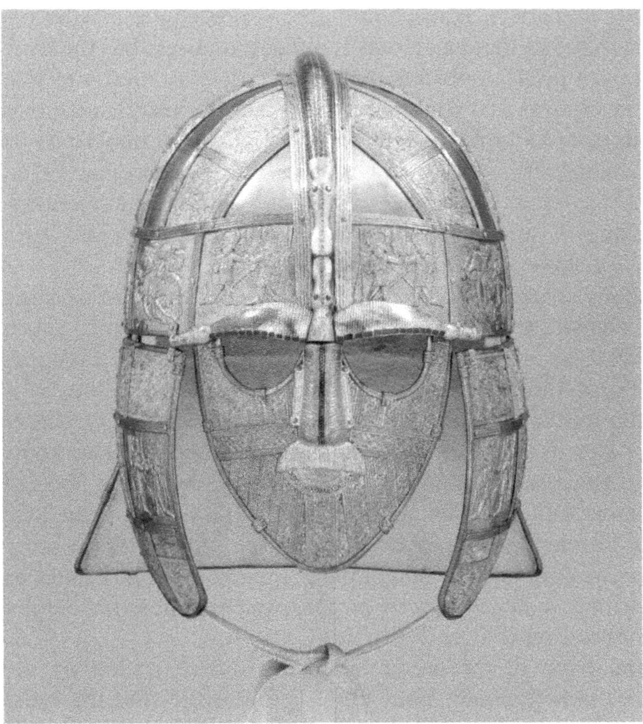

Figure 6.3 Recreation/replica of the Sutton Hoo helmet in its 'as new' condition. © Trustees of the British Museum.

Most replicas fulfil several roles. The original cave at Lascaux was closed to the public in 1963 due to the damage caused by the increases in temperature, relative humidity and microorganisms resulting from the rising number of visitors (Mauriac 2011; Geneste and Mauriac 2014). In 1983, a replica (Lascaux II) opened near the site.[10] In 2016, an improved replica (Lascaux IV) opened which replicated more of the cave and incorporated interactive galleries to improve the visitor's experience (James 2017).[11] Over 10 million people have visited Lascaux II and IV. The replicas help preserve the original by giving visitors a way to approximate the experience of visiting the cave and learning about the paintings. They take the pressure to provide access to the original off of the authorities, while at the same time providing a revenue stream that helps with additional preservation efforts.[12]

Replication brings with it risks and ethical issues. There are risks of damage to the original object when creating a mould. Silicone rubber and other moulding materials can in rare circumstances stain the surface of the original and they can exert pressure, pulling at the surface, causing very small amounts of the surface material to be lost. These risks are reduced when using non-contact techniques such as 3D Scanning and Photogrammetry scanning to create a 3D model that can then be printed in metal, ceramic, or a polymer using rapid prototyping (RP) technology such as 3D printing (Coon *et al.* 2016). The costs associated with such equipment are becoming increasingly affordable but as with all technology the more accurate the need the more costly the product will be. The polymers used in RP technologies change rapidly. New products are continually introduced, and many contain additives including stabilisers, flame retardants, antioxidants, plasticisers, and colourants. The long-term stability of these materials is difficult to assess but there are indications that the heat used in the printing process may initiate deterioration and that some of the materials emit solvent vapours that could result in changes in historic materials (Cimino *et al.* 2018). The need to store multiple versions of an object, which may be made for different purposes, poses sustainability issues for many museums (Coon *et al.* 2016). The ability to cut stable materials to exact copies of objects using computer numerically controlled (CNC) milling machines is a potential alternative (Baumeister *et al.* 2020) although it permits less freedom of shape and can be more expensive.

With more traditional moulding materials there can be issues of accuracy; cheaper moulding compounds, such as alginate moulding compounds, do not pick up as much detail as more expensive materials such as silicon rubber. Mould materials, such as rubber latex, are not always chemically or dimensionally stable over long periods, thus it is advisable to make casts soon after moulding using materials such as epoxy resin or plaster of Paris, which are more stable. In selecting the right technique, it is important to know how the replica will be used, how accurate the mould must be, and how much loss of detail can be tolerated. For example, some loss of detail may be tolerated in a replica created for children to handle but might not be tolerable in a research application. Many 19th-century casts were 'improved'; missing areas were filled although the accuracy of the fills could be poor. As a result, the cast was neither an accurate copy of what was present at the date of the moulding nor an accurate restoration (Payne 2019).

Many 20th-century artworks have discoloured, distorted, and degraded as the polymers from which they were made decayed. They no longer convey what the artist intended. In some cases, museums and galleries have removed them from display and created 'authentic replicas' with the approval of the artist (if still living) or their estate. For example, Naum Gabo's *Construction in Space (Crystal)* of 1937–1939 was replicated by the Tate Gallery in 2015 (Lawson and Cane 2016). Such objects are designated 'authentic replicas' to distinguish them from other replicas and fakes. Although there is little or no physical difference between such replicas, they have an added (intangible) value as an approved copy that is guaranteed to continue conveying the artist's vision. This can be important since not only the lack of 3D colour printing standards can create challenges for faithful replication (Coons *et al.* 2016) but changes in material availability can also result in slight compromises in appearance.

Foster and Jones (2019) have argued that replicas are not just copies but things in their own that acquire their own cultural biographies. These biographies are distinct and different from those of their source object and can engage visitors and build emotional responses and connections that are separate from those formed by the 'real' object. As a result, conservators are increasingly engaged in analyzing and conserving replicas (Foster and Jones 2020; Turner 2020; Risdonne *et al.* 2021).

6A Case Study: Hans Holbein's painting *The Ambassadors* (Wyld 1998)

Many objects, particularly paintings, have long histories in which they change ownership and are restored many times. This history does not end once they reach a museum as the case study of *The Ambassadors* by Hans Holbein shows. Painted on an oak panel in

1533, the picture is a full-length double portrait depicting Jean de Dinteville, French Ambassador to England, and Georges de Selve, Bishop of Lavaur, standing on an intricately inlaid marble floor, with a rich green patterned curtain in the background. Between the two men is a table covered with a carpet on which scientific instruments (including two globes, a quadrant, and a polyhedral sundial) as well as a lute and hymn book sit. In the foreground is an anamorphic depiction of a skull, an image depicted as if seen through a distorting lens or at an extreme angle (Figure 8.3).

The picture, regarded as one of Holbein's finest, was passed through the de Dinteville family and there are records of it being taken to Paris, to the South of France and then back to Paris. During this period, it is possible that the painting was divided into two and displayed in two different locations, since the half depicting Jean de Dinteville shows signs of having been exposed to a different environment (including much higher humidity and possibly a flood) than the other half. There is also evidence that the damage caused by the humidity necessitated restoration work. One clue that suggests a date prior to 1787 for some of the restoration is that the medal de Dinteville wears was accurately retouched despite belonging to the Ordre de Saint-Michel, a French chivalric order. In 1787 *The Ambassadors* was auctioned, and by 1792 it had been sold again and had made its way to England. In 1808–1809 it was purchased by the Earl of Radnor, who hung it in Longford Castle. At some point, possibly to make it more attractive for one of its sales, the green curtain was heavily overpainted, and its colour changed from a light green to a dark green. In 1890, the painting was sold to the National Gallery. Public excitement over the purchase meant that it was hurriedly displayed, despite evident structural issues.

In 1891, the painting was restored. William Morrill worked on the wooden panel, and William Dyer worked on the painted surface. The panel, formed from a series of planks, was planed down from the back to a thickness of 5 mm and then subjected to heavy pressure to flatten them and a mahogany 'cradle' (two-layered lattice of vertical and horizontal batons) attached to the back to provide a more stable backing. Although this sounds extreme, it was designed to counteract the concave warping across their width, which had created gaps that had necessitated 'cement' fills in prior restorations. Dyer removed and replaced the worst of the earlier restorations revealing some details, such as a silver crucifix and the original curtain colour, which had not previously been visible. He also replaced the discoloured varnish.

Despite the structural work carried out on the panel, it continued to be unstable. And splits and blistering paint were noted and addressed in 1892, 1895, 1929, 1939, 1940, and 1952. The impact of changes in Relative humidity was not well understood and rather than making the panel more stable thinning it made it more reactive to environmental changes. It was only when air-conditioning was installed in the gallery in 1952 that both the relative humidity and the panel stabilised.

By the early 1990s, the varnish had darkened and was foggy in areas due to exposure to high light and UV levels between the 1890s and 1950s, which hastened the discolouration of the mastic and walnut oil mixture that Dyer had used. As the 500th anniversary of Holbein's birth was approaching, conservators at the National Gallery were asked to restore the painting as the centrepiece of an exhibit entitled *Making and Meaning: Holbein's Ambassadors.* Within this context, a heavy emphasis was placed on the use of extensive analytical investigation to guide the restoration efforts. Dendrochronological analysis of the oak planks determined that the last growth ring dated to 1515 and that the oak originated in the Baltic-Polish region. Gas-chromatography mass-spectroscopy (GC-MS) was used to analyse the binders in the paint and cross sections of minute amounts of paint in test-cleaned and adjacent uncleaned areas were used to ensure that the solvents that were chosen to remove the varnish and the overpaint did not have a negative impact on the original paint. These cross-sections also provided information about Holbein's working techniques, which was paired with Infrared reflectance imaging and careful examination of other Holbein paintings. X-radiographs of the painting were consulted to determine where losses and areas of overpaint lay. If the earlier retouchings did not cover areas of original paint, were of a similar texture as the original surface and the fill below them was firmly attached, they were left in place.

The removal of the 1890s' varnish and of some earlier restorations revealed even more of the Holbein original than had been expected. Details of the original form of the dagger hilt, the original notes and words of the hymn score and aspects of Jean de Dinteville's clothing were revealed. The extent of Holbein's original work was fully recorded, and new information gleaned about both the making of the painting and its history. The National Gallery's policy is that its public should enjoy an image without the interruptions caused by damage, loss, panel joins, etc. As a result, it usually chooses to retouch paintings, restoring them to their original image, while recognising the need to balance legibility and authenticity. Images are only restored where there is a clear indication of the colour and form of the original image. In most cases, the losses on *The Ambassadors* were so small that the missing areas could be clearly extrapolated from the colour and form of the surrounding areas. In some areas, such as the floor and carpet, the symmetry of the image clearly indicated what was missing. In one or two areas, though the general nature of what was missing was apparent, the exact nature of the original could not be determined. In these areas, difficult decisions had to be made balancing the need to achieve the true aesthetic experience of the picture and avoid falsehood. In each case, the range of possible outcomes was discussed between the conservators and curators and the approach that best achieved the desired aims selected. In one example, the folds of the drapery suggested that the figure of Jean de Dinteville originally wore a codpiece; however, insufficient information existed to indicate the form or extent of such a garment and so the existing dark folds of the garment, seen in earlier restorations, were replaced. Similarly, restored areas on the globe were retouched according to information from existing globes of the period. Outlines of continents were added but lettering and any other specific information were omitted. The skull posed a particular quandary, large losses in the jaw and the nasal area distorted the anamorphic depiction; however, each skull differs slightly from another, and the conservators did not have access to Holbein's original skull. Discussion centred around whether the right transformation of perspective could be achieved and if not, whether viewers would accept an unfinished or generalised approach to such a key area. Ultimately, extensive research using digital imaging enabled the distorted form of the anamorphic depiction of a skull to be accurately reproduced allowing the conservators to feel more confident that the principal components of the skull could be accurately restored (Figure 6.4).

Once the inpainting was complete, the picture was varnished with a dammar resin, which, although it yellows slightly on ageing, was found after testing to be preferable to modern varnish alternatives that required a heavier less period-appropriate coating to saturate the colours of the picture properly. A new frame, suitable to the period was made and the picture displayed.

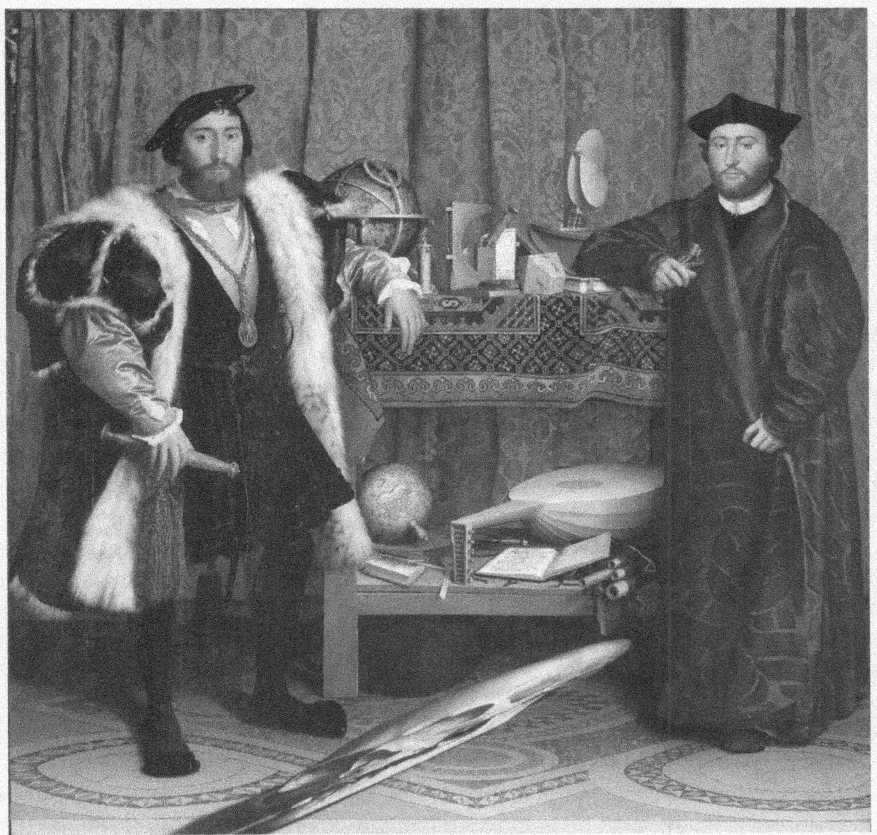

Figure 6.4 Hans Holbein painting: the ambassadors, following restoration. © The National Gallery.

Information panels, publications, and television programmes explained the process of conservation to the public as well as the judgements that the conservators had made. Earlier restoration work created issues for this conservation project, but not all past restorations needed to be removed. Close examination, analysis, and historical perspective all provided important information to guide the decision-making process. The reaction both to the restored image and to the careful conservation work was very positive.

6B Case Study: The Loch Glashan Satchel (Lewis 2005a, Lewis 2005b)

In 1960, an artificial island (known as a crannog) formed of earth, timber, and stone and set within a ring of timber piling was hastily excavated at Loch Glashan in Scotland. Conducted over three-and-a-half weeks, the excavation took place in advance of the construction of a dam that would submerge the site. Dating to the early medieval period (late 6th to 9th century AD), the crannog was waterlogged. Pottery, stone, and wood artefacts were recovered from it as well as 90 pieces of leather, including fragments that were interpreted by the excavator, Jack Scott, as a jerkin. This interpretation stuck and after conservation the jerkin was partially re-assembled and mounted on a mannequin for display whilst the unattached fragments were stored. It was subsequently pictured in books describing early medieval Scotland (Alcock 2003). Scott died in 1999 and the site was not written up and published until 2005 (Crone and Campbell 2005). A re-examination of the finds, prompted by the archaeologist/curator Colleen Batey, revealed that the re-assembled jerkin did not make a convincing garment. Problems included the fact that the seams did not meet, there was a questionably narrow waist, similarly narrow cuffs, an implausibly high neckline, and the garment had creases in places that did not correspond with normal human wear. Although the initial conservation in 1960 had preserved the leather, the fragments were now stiff, dark, brittle, and glossy and there were clumpy deposits of wax on the surface. Consequently, the object was removed from the mannequin, re-evaluated, and re-conserved; a process complicated by the absence of the original conservation records.

Solvent tests indicated a wax was used in the initial conservation. A mercury II chloride test suggested the wax was polyethylene glycol (PEG) (Hoffman 1983) and thus water soluble, although the molecular weight was unknown. All the fragments were recorded on sheets of Melinex®, detailing creases, tears, and cuts. Based on the drawings and careful study, it could be determined that:

- A fragment of a thong woven through a line of slits in the leather indicated how the leather was fastened together.
- The presence of two lines of identical slits with a crease mark between showed that the flat leather had been thonged together to create a 90 ° turn (Figure 6.5).
- A number of pieces of leather had identical sequences of irregularly spaced lines of slits – indicating that they had been cut and thonged together to join pieces of leather.
- When the pieces of leather were reassembled using this information, the object formed by these pieces of leather was not a jerkin but a book satchel.
- The cockling and creasing of the leather corresponded with that normally seen on a satchel. Damage, loss, and additional slits corresponded with the point a carrying strap would have been attached to the sides.
- The cut end of the thong and worn state of the leather showed that at the end of its life the object had been disassembled and was being used as scrap leather for repairs (recycled).

Subsequently the leather was re-conserved; removing as much PEG as possible through repeated soaking in water until PEG could no longer be detected. It was then treated with 20% glycerol in water and freeze-dried. After re-humidification, the pieces regained their natural shape, colour, and texture. They were stored as separate pieces and an illustration of the restored form of the object was created to avoid the unnecessary strain reassembly would have placed on the leather.

Books were very valuable in the early medieval period; they were viewed as containing the word of God and took thousands of hours to create using rare and precious materials. There were very few of them and they were vulnerable, especially to moisture. Books were protected in satchels, such as the one from Loch Glashan, which could be hung from projections on the walls of monastic cells for safety. Only three other satchels are known, all from Ireland, but all are of 12th–15th-century date, making the Loch Glashan example by far the oldest. At 370 × 370 × 15 – 120 mm it is the correct size to hold a gospel book, such as the *Book of Kells* (Meehan 2005). The satchel is also one of the earliest objects from Britain associated with care and preservation of an historic and artistic work.

The initial function posited for the leather unintentionally biased the subsequent observations and reconstruction. It stayed with the fragments until they were fully reconsidered and re-conserved. Securing appropriate resources to fully research and conserve dirty wet archaeological fragments retrieved from a brief excavation with very limited stratigraphy can be challenging; however, the effort put into securing resources for the conservation work enabled the leather to survive. The initial conservation treatment was reversible, allowing the object to be reconsidered. This study highlights the importance of careful investigation prior to the reconstruction of any object and the need for good communication between the archaeologist and the conservator. It also speaks to an increasingly prominent element of the conservator's workload, the revisiting and rethinking of past interventions.

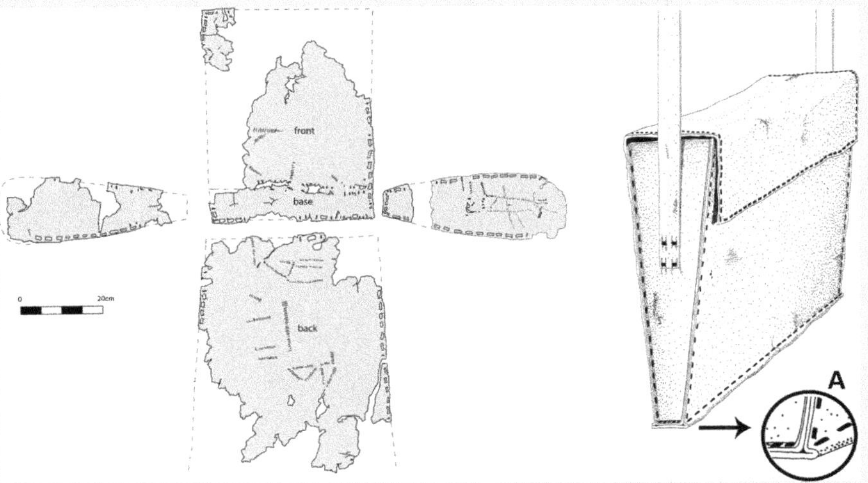

Figure 6.5 The surviving Loch Glashan leather fragments and the reconstruction as a satchel. Redrawn by Chris Caple from Lewis 2005b.

Notes

1. The European Committee for Standardisation has developed and published *Conservation of cultural property – main general terms and definitions* BS EN 15898:2019. These drew in part on definitions given in the first edition of this book (Caple 2000).
2. When restoration began again in 1821, strict rules were in place to better demarcate the two (Milanesi 2013).
3. Terms such as 'back-alley restorer' were sometimes used to distinguish between those with the knowledge and equipment to do the job properly (conservators) and those who did not.
4. 'Floating sherds' – sherds whose position could be guessed but that had no physical join to the reassembled vessel used to be located in their approximate position within the fill. This practice is carried out less frequently now.
5. The exception is where the value of the information recovered is seen to outweigh the value of the metal in its final use state, such as in the case of Roman curse tablets and window leads. The potential to extract inscriptions and dates from these objects means that they are frequently unrolled and opened (Dove 1981; Cunliffe 1988; Egan 2012).
6. For example, hide glue may be used to both make and repair a chair.
7. Substantial repair elements (such as a new leg on a chair) are often marked or dated to help future conservators identify original materials, early repairs, and later restoration work.
8. Similar questions have been posed by others using alternate objects. For example, Chris Caple approached the question by considering how the changes to his grandfather's axe might alter it over time (2000: 132). The issue of scale may mean that some objects are impacted by multiple phases of restoration more rapidly than others. In a small object such as an axe it may take considerably fewer modifications to alter the piece than it does in a larger object such as a ship.
9. Such consultative practices honour the 'artist's intent', which is protected by the Berne Convention and in many countries by copyright law.
10. https://archeologie.culture.fr/lascaux/en/lascaux-ii-and-iii.
11. Lascaux III is a travelling exhibit that has toured the world and includes replicas of key panels from the cave.
12. This is not an unusual role for replicas to play. The creation and sale of numerous replicas and recreations of both smaller objects and scaled-down versions of larger objects provides a source of income, identity, and awareness for many museums. Costs ranging from inexpensive to very expensive relate to the accuracy of the replica and the materials and manufacturing techniques used to make it.

7 Stabilisation

The Nature of Survival and Stability

Survival

The surviving remnants of the past represent the difference between everything that has ever been created and everything that has subsequently decayed or been destroyed. They have survived through two mechanisms:

- Accidental (unconscious) preservation: this occurs when the artefact (object, image, building) is protected from destructive forces such as people or weather. Although it reacts with the surrounding environment, the reactions occur slowly; low decay rates can lead to the preservation of objects in their historic context. Tutankhamun's tomb and the artefacts in it were preserved through a fortuitous accident. The debris and worker's huts from later Ramesside tombs covered the entry to the boy king's tomb allowing it to pass out of memory and saving it from the depredations of tomb robbers. Inside the tomb the dry environment and low oxygen levels led to the preservation of a wide variety of organic materials as well as metal, stone, and ceramic items.
- Deliberate (conscious) preservation: the artefact is deliberately preserved by human action. Resources, including skilled and knowledgeable practitioners as well as time, energy, and effort, are poured into shielding the artefact from potential threats such as human beings, insects, wind, oxygen, and water. Such efforts are normally made only to protect valuable or significant parts of the past. The efforts expended are intended to make the object 'stable' in perpetuity.

Stability

One of the primary goals of conservation is to make materials stable where possible. Stability is not an absolute state. An object is only stable relative to the environment in which it is situated and over the period being considered.

- Environment: If a buried object has survived for hundreds or thousands of years, it has reached (near) equilibrium with its surrounding burial environment. A waterlogged boat may remain stable inside the saturated waterlogged soil for centuries, bodies may be preserved intact for millennia in frozen ground or glaciers. However, after excavation rapid changes in the environment surrounding

DOI: 10.4324/9781003009078-7

the object can place this equilibrium in peril. Waterlogged wood will dry out, warp, crack, and start to break apart within hours. In museum conditions, a frozen body will quickly warm and decay. To ensure an object's stability, it must be at equilibrium with its new environment. Typically, the greater the difference between the original environment and the new environment, the less stable an object is likely to be and the more interventive stabilisation is likely to be. In general, treatments seek to stabilise objects in typical museum display conditions.[1] Many historically utilised materials have survived well in environments that were often less benign than museum environments. In the 20th century we have increasingly begun to utilise materials that are unstable. These include newspapers, plastics, polymers, pigments, dyes, and even metals such as aluminium (Quye and Williamson 1999; Shashoua 2008; Chemello *et al.* 2019).

- Time: Rapid decay, such as the drying out, cracking, and warping of waterlogged wood, prompts a quick conservation response. Slow, long-term degradation, such as the fading of coloured textiles, can often go unnoticed and unaddressed over decades. As human being we are focused on change over short time intervals. We notice changes that happen over the period of a few hours or a few days easily but are poorer at noticing changes that occur over years. As museums and their collections are designed to survive for centuries, conservators should consider object survival over longer time frames; however, many economic decisions are shaped by short-term fluctuations.

As we seek to make objects stable (for research, investigation, or public display) we can either make the object stable with regard to the museum environment or adjust the museum environment to support the object's stability. Making the object stable to the museum environment is typically referred to as interventive or remedial conservation, adjusting the environment is referred to as preventive conservation (Chapter 8). Interventive and preventive conservation can be seen as parts of a continuum; it is possible to utilise one or the other or both to achieve the goal of a stable object.

Interventive conservation approaches have traditionally been used to make archaeological, historical, and art objects stable. Recently greater use has been made of targeted preservative environments for archaeological and historic artefacts such as the low humidity storage of archaeological iron, the use of oxygen-free (anoxic) conditions for the display of the US Declaration of Independence, Constitution and Bill of Rights or the refrigerated storage of Őtzi (a Bronze Age man preserved in an alpine glacier). The high costs associated with maintaining non-standard museum environments to stabilise objects, especially for display, continue to limit the extent of these approaches.

Objects that are stored or displayed outdoors are subject to more extreme chemical, physical, and biological conditions than those in museums. Conservators frequently respond by seeking to put more substantial protection in place for the object. Interventive approaches may include the deliberate creation of protective patinas, the removal of plants and biological growth, and the use of coatings. Preventive conservation measures include the construction of shelters. Since most shelters and applied coatings break down after a few years, maintenance programs, such as regular repainting, will be required to maintain stability. In some cases, such as that of the Statue of Liberty (Case study 3 A), natural, partially protective patinas may be formed naturally or created and maintained artificially.

Change

In the case of an object buried in the soil, the rate of decay will initially be quite fast, although it usually slows with time as it comes to equilibrium with its environment (Dowman 1970). This is due to the build-up of the decay or corrosion layer at the interface which slows the rate at which active chemical, biological agents diffuse through this buffering layer. If the object does not reach equilibrium with its environment, it will continue to decay at an accelerated rate and will ultimately be lost. When the object is disturbed (e.g. through excavation), the rate of decay will suddenly increase until it eventually slows as it comes to equilibrium with its new storage environment (Figure 7.1). Again, if it fails to reach equilibrium with its new environment, decay will continue until the object is lost.

For objects that are in continual use, the process is slightly different. The object will initially be stable but as time passes use wear will result in degradation including loss of hardened or protective surface material or increased pressure as forces act on smaller areas. Consequently, as reliability engineering has shown, the rate of degradation will increase as small-scale damage is enlarged until there is either a catastrophic failure (Strlič *et al.* 2013: 83), or the object is conserved, and the rates of decay return to low levels to again climb slowly with time (Figure 7.1). Similar decay curves have been suggested for the decay of buildings. Brand (1994: 112) showed that reduced decay and lower costs were achieved with regular maintenance, occasional maintenance led to higher decay rates and higher costs, whilst no maintenance led to extremely high decay rates and the high costs of total refurbishment. This is because buildings are not initially stable structures and are under constant attack from the weather, which is an aggressive continual-use environment. Eventually buildings become ruins slowly reaching equilibrium with the environment.

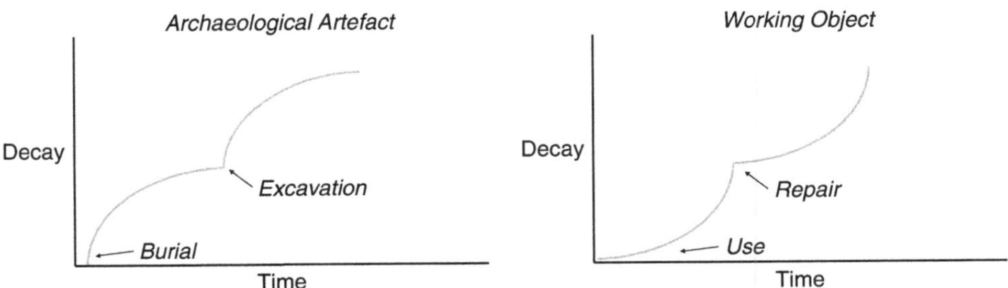

Figure 7.1 Decay rates for an excavated archaeological object (from Dowman 1970) and a repaired continually working object, such as a clockwork mechanism. Chris Caple.

The Nature of Stabilisation

The cessation of decay processes (or more frequently their slowing to a minimal rate) results in stabilisation. It requires that the cause(s) of decay and its mitigation be identified. Any stabilisation, whether interventive or preventive, normally seeks to retain the object's present visual form so maintaining its historic, aesthetic, and cultural values. Decay and stabilisation processes occur in three categories: biological, chemical, and physical (Figure 7.2).

Category	Measure
Biological	Immobilise organisms – reduce oxygen, water, light, temperature
	Create barriers to organisms or reaction agents
	Kill organisms – biocide, eliminate oxygen, water, impose extreme temperatures, introduce predatory organism.
Chemical	Remove reaction agents – water, light, oxygen, light, catalysts etc
	Create barrier to reaction agents
	Add agents to deactivate further decay
Physical	Eliminate reaction agents – force, water, oxygen
	Create barriers to reaction agents
	Consolidate and support

Figure 7.2 Sources of decay and their mitigation. Chris Caple.

In the laboratory, the decay of individual materials can be accurately predicted through dose-response relationships; however, in real-life multiple agents are involved, creating a synergistic system where one decay process enhances another, leading to accelerated rates of decay, which are difficult to model and predict (Pollard et al. 2004, 2006). Thus, the decay of waterlogged wood occurs through chemical decay, hydrolysis of cellulose, and consumption of cellulose by micro-organisms (fungi or bacteria depending on the environment) leading to a weakened structure, which is then supported by water. The loss of the water (drying) causes physical damage in the form of cell collapse and shrinkage of the cell walls (Cronyn 1990).

Biological

Stabilisation of biological decay processes can be achieved through the denial of reaction agents essential for sustaining biological organisms. This includes placing an insect-infested object in a freezer to deny the insects heat, which will kill them (Blyth and Hillyer 1993; Carrlee 2003) or placing the object in an oxygen-free environment, such as fumigating with nitrogen (Gilberg 1991), to deny the insects oxygen. In modern-day conservation treatments, these denial mechanisms are preferred to using fumigants, insecticides, and biocides,both because they are less interventive ways to stabilise an object and because of health and safety concerns (for both conservators and the public). Barriers, such as biobarrier materials to prevent root growth (Case Study 1B: the Laetoli Footprints), may be effective over the short term, but as with all barriers, given the risk of failure, checking and maintenance are advisable.

Chemical

Chemical decay, such as the corrosion of metals, can be stifled by removing one or more of the agents of decay such as oxygen, water, or salts. Storing archaeological metalwork with a desiccating agent, such as silica gel, denies water vapour to the corrosion reaction, though reconditioning the silica gel is often required. In other instances, metals may be given coatings, such as paints, to reduce or slow down the ingress of moisture. Light can initiate chemical changes in textiles, paper, and other organic materials. Storage in the dark blocks the damaging effect of light (see Figure 7.3). Plastics and rubber degrade via oxidation and may be stored in oxygen-free environments to slow deterioration (Dyer *et al.* 2011; Shashoua 2008: 2014). Almost all chemical reactions can be stifled by removing heat. As all chemical reactions virtually halve their rate of reaction with every drop of 10 °C simply lowering the temperature will considerably slow reactions.

Chemically unstable materials, or materials that catalyse decay processes, such as soluble salts or acids, can in some cases be removed from objects. A variety of techniques have been developed to remove chlorides from corroding archaeological iron (Watkinson 1996; Mardikian 2013; Watkinson and Rimmer 2014). Although eliminating the materials that promote or catalyse decay is desirable, it can be hard to fully achieve in practice; however, in most cases their reduction can improve object

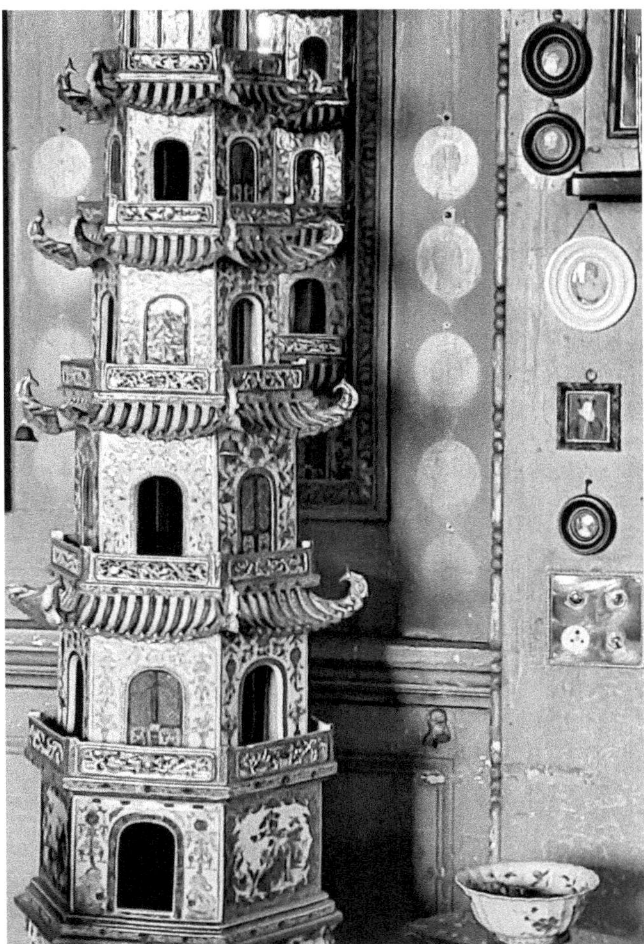

Figure 7.3 Light damage: the varnished wood has darkened through interaction with light, except where it was shielded by decorative oval plaques. Emily Williams.

stability. An alternate approach is to add chemical agents to the object to stop the reaction. These agents often react with or block the most chemically active sites on the object. Examples include adding antioxidants to organic consolidant systems to soak up radicals and prevent their reaction (Bilz *et al.* 1993), the use of alkaline-buffering agents to stop the acidic hydrolysis of the cellulose in paper (Smith 1987), using benzotriazole to curb the copper-corrosion process (Brostoff 1995), and employing DTPA to neutralise iron/sulfur salt formation in waterlogged wood (Pearson *et al.* 2018). The development of nanoparticles has added a new method of delivering chemical agents to suppress chemical reactions (Baglioni *et al.* 2015).

Physical

Physical forces apply pressure to an object. Soluble salts present in porous materials, such as ceramics, stone, or bone, may exert enormous pressure as they crystallise, breaking up the structure of the material. Removing the soluble salts or controlling factors, such as the temperature and humidity, so the soluble salts do not repeatedly recrystallise can prevent damage. For a standing structure, a barrier, such as a damp course, can prevent the access of soluble salts. The formation of ice crystals can also damage porous materials. Background heating can prevent the freezing and ice formation of some building stones. Physical damage may occur when objects are moved. Creating a suitable box or container around an object can prevent impact and vibrational damage, while physical supports can prevent the distortion of fragile objects by gravitational forces. Such supports may include linings for oil paintings, support cloths sewn to fragile textiles, mounting fragile paper prints on to a new paper backing or armatures for heavy and unwieldy objects.

Fragile porous artefacts may also be strengthened physically by impregnating them with a consolidant. Consolidants, normally liquids, permeate an object and solidify providing cohesion and support. Whether they solidify by cooling (wax or solder), or solvent evaporation (polymer solvent or aqueous systems), consolidants are difficult to reverse; those which solidify through chemical reactions (epoxy resins or silanes) may be impossible to reverse. Consequently, any consolidant used should be stable over the long term, so that it will not degrade and harm the object later. The use of soluble nylon in conservation serves as a useful cautionary tale with regards to consolidants. First mentioned in the conservation literature in 1958, soluble nylon was rapidly adopted and used on a wide range of materials, however, what was not initially understood was that despite many other excellent properties, it cross-linked over time resulting in darkened, obscured objects. In less than 23 years, conservators were making the case against using it (Sease 1981) and it has now been abandoned, although many museum objects remain irreversibly marked by it.

Treatments

To successfully treat an object, it is important to understand exactly what is degrading it, the mechanism by which the degradation operates and the agents that cause the process to continue. The more you know, the more options you have to stop the decay without damaging the object or reducing its values. Many early conservation treatments focused on the symptoms rather than a cure. They did not halt decay, they merely delayed it for a while; eventually making the situation worse (see for example

Case study 5 A: the Sistine Chapel ceiling or 6 A: *The Ambassadors*). Once decay mechanisms were better understood, stabilisation techniques evolved. Today our awareness of decay mechanisms suggests that more holistic approaches are required. Where multiple agents create a complex synergistic effect, treatment can be challenging. It can be beneficial to combine several different stabilisation techniques; for example, treating a copper alloy object with benzotriazole to chemically deactivate the corrosion process, then coating the surface with 'Incralac', an acrylic copolymer that reduces the rate of ingress of water and oxygen, and storing the object with silica-gel to reduce water-vapour levels. While this may not represent a minimally interventive approach, it ensures the object's continued stability even if, despite one's best efforts, the surrounding environment changes and becomes less benign.

Stabilisation treatments can sometimes alter the visual form of an object; for example, consolidation can darken a surface or make it overly glossy. It is important to strike a balance between gaining a physically stable, robust object and the change in visual appearance. Where the goal is to preserve the object unaltered because of its importance as an historic document or the subtlety of its colouring, then consolidation may not be appropriate, although the object remains at greater risk of physical damage. Where the greater need is to preserve the whole form of the object for informational or aesthetic purposes then it may be appropriate to consolidate. Knowing which features or traits of the object are significant is important. It allows judgement to be exercised and if necessary, permits less important features to be sacrificed to ensure the survival of more important ones. Equally importantly, defining the significant features can guide experimentation and the search for new stabilisation methods that respect all the object's values.

In searching for appropriate stabilisation treatments, be wary of making such substantial interventive changes that you end up altering the very thing that you were trying to save (Sanchez and Allen 1990). Equally if the object's stability must be maintained in a bespoke environment, there will be little benefit unless the object can be accessed, displayed, and analysed when necessary. The balance between stabilisation and access presents challenges to objects that are to be stabilised and preserved in situ.

Stability of Conservation Materials

Up to the 1970s conservation used a wide variety of commercially available polymers as adhesives, coatings, and consolidants. However, as problems became apparent with materials such as soluble nylon (Sease 1981; Bockhoff *et al.* 1984) it was clear that long-term polymer degradation and cross-linking had not been fully appreciated. There was an increasing awareness that the plastics industry's concept of stable referred to a working life of a few years, and not the decades to centuries that conservation requires. In 1978, Robert Feller categorised common conservation polymers by a system of stability to light degradation based on the ISO R105 and BS 1006:1971 'Blue Wool' standards. He used a simplified classification system to define their stability (Feller 1978):

- Class A: Excellent stability with a stable working life of more than 100 years (e.g. Paraloid B72) (Al > 500 years, A2 > 100 years).

- Class B: Intermediate stability with a stable working life of 20–100 years (e.g. Elvacite 2044).
- Class C: Unstable or fugitive with a stable working life of less than 20 years.
- Class T: Materials which should only be in temporary contact with an object having a stable working life of less than 6 months.

The breakdown of a material is not a single event, but a gradual one. Polymers have numerous different breakdown stages; an epoxy resin may yellow with age, although it may still adhere strongly. Thus, the critical factor may not be the onset of change. As ageing progresses, the polymer normally breaks down rendering it inadequate for the function for which it was intended. Protective coatings may begin to fail, rendering objects more susceptible to corrosion and other forms of damage while adhesive failure may potentially cause physical damage as fragments detach and fall. A final point that some polymers may reach is the point where their breakdown products begin to promote degradation in the object itself. Hanssen-Bauer (1996) has emphasised the need to be more aware of these stages. Some materials are better as conservation materials since their failure does not harm the object, whilst other materials, initially resistant to breakdown, have damaging breakdown products, such as the hydrochloric acid gas given off by degrading PVC. Thus, a profile of the breakdown pathways and resulting products is ideally needed to accurately judge the appropriateness of any conservation material for use.

Although many adhesives, varnishes, and consolidants have been tested for use in conservation (Down 2015), barriers remain to both the testing of materials and the development of new materials appropriate to conservation needs:

- There is no well-funded central agency to undertake testing.
- Tests carried out in different labs and with different setups may produce different results, making interpretation difficult (Green and Thickett 1993; Green and Thickett 1995; Korenberg *et al.* 2018).
- The range of parameters for which stability could be tested is enormous.
- The commercial nature of many products means that manufacturers can (and do) vary the exact formulation of products. They also contain additives such as detergents and plasticisers which make potentially stable products unstable.
- As an industry conservation remains small and it can be difficult to support the creation of new materials suited to its need. Testing is expensive and there is no funding for such work.
- There are problems with accelerated ageing, the traditionally used method of testing for shorter times at higher temperatures. Both Down (1995) and Bilz and Grattan (1996) found problems using the Arrhenius equation to extrapolate back from higher temperature experiments to normal storage and display temperatures.

The need for stable materials in conservation is not limited to adhesives, coatings, and varnishes but also extends to display and storage materials as well. Rapid tarnishing of silver by materials releasing sulphurous gasses and the corrosion of lead by materials that gave off volatile organic compounds (VOCs), led Andrew Oddy of the British Museum to develop a simple test for materials intended for use in museum displays and storage (Oddy 1973; 1975). These 'Oddy Tests' have been subsequently developed, refined, and expanded (Blackshaw and Daniels 1979; Green 1991; Green and Thickett

1993; Lee and Thickett 1996 Korenberg *et al.* 2018). Additional tests can be used to augment the Oddy test and provide a more comprehensive series of tests for material stability (Lee and Thickett 1996).[2] Though many products have been tested, there are always new ones to be assessed and the frequent reformulation of products by commercial companies demands constant retesting of 'safe' materials.

Conservators have an ethical responsibility to ensure that materials used in conservation, as well as for the display and storage of objects, are stable and will not cause harm to objects over time (Ganiaris and Sully 1998). Larger museums may have staff who are dedicated to materials testing, however many smaller museums do not and are reliant on past experience and reports of successful tests from other institutions.[3] This situation is not necessarily problematic if staff at these museums understand the limitations of the tests and how to interpret them. Museum exhibits have become shorter in length due to concerns about light exposure and the desire to attract and retain visitors. This compression places burdens on staff and can lead to shorter planning cycles as well as pressure to reduce exhibit costs. In this environment, the lead time needed to test materials is often consumed[4] and institutions may rely on previously used materials or opt to take risks and use less stable materials for short-term exhibits. This type of calculation may work well until circumstances, such as unexpected postponements, staff changes, global pandemics, or insufficient funding, mean that rotations are delayed. It remains important to record what materials are used in the conservation and storage of objects so that unstable materials/products can be identified and their use stopped and encourage research as well publication of material tests.

Assessing Stabilisation Effectiveness

Analysing conservation records and conducting condition assessments of treated and untreated artefacts allow the effectiveness of treatments to be established (Ganiaris *et al.* 1982; Paterakis and Hickey-Friedman 2011). In practice, few treatments or storage conditions have yet been described in terms of their statistical 'likelihood of achieving stability' (Keene and Orton 1985; Keene 1994; Rimmer *et al.* 2013). This is partly due to missing or incomplete conservation records and frequent gaps in the environmental data for storage, which often results in insufficient data on which to form an accurate assessment. Gaps highlight the need to create and retain accurate, detailed conservation records and records of storage conditions,[5] and to consider stability with reference to the specified timescale. As reversing past treatments and re-conserving objects is becoming an increasingly large part of the conservator's workload (Pye 2001, 135; Caple and Garlick 2020) the need for assessing the efficacy of stabilisation efforts over the long term is rising.

Conservators are becoming increasingly aware of the full costs of conservation processes and are seeking to achieve stable artefacts in a more sustainable manner. Although the term sustainability is increasingly being associated with environmental practices such as reducing energy consumption, managing waste and how we procure materials it is fundamentally a cost-benefit equation.

- What is needed to keep the object stable?
- What is the cost?
- Is that cost something society is prepared to pay?

To ensure the stability of objects and collections over a period of 100 years or more, the timeframe Feller suggested conservators should think in, requires ecologically sustainable approaches that incorporate long-term funding solutions, decision-making processes that focus on the big picture rather than short-term objectives and work practices that can be maintained. Achieving this will include:

- Using a balance of interventive conservation stabilising treatment and the preventive conservation conditions to create the most long-term sustainable situation for each object.
- Looking critically at the lives of objects to determine where, when, and why stability has (or has not) been achieved and using these factors as a basis for improving care. This process can prove challenging because many factors may be at play (synergy) and there should be a commitment to engage with the process holistically rather than to simply find the easy answer. It is simple to say that an object has become unstable because of a change in RH but it is only when all the root causes for that change are examined that a sustainable solution can be identified.
- Establishing the actual cost of keeping objects stable over decades and critically assessing this against the value(s) society places on them. Extending this further and considering how these costs may impact the potential to achieve sustainable solutions for other objects adds a level of complexity to the equation. However, it is important to also factor in the potential for the values associated with the object to change over time.

When Stabilisation Is Not Possible

There are circumstances where it can be difficult to stabilise the object either by interventive or preventive means. These include:

- Those situations where the objects or monuments are exposed to the weather and/or it is not possible to move it.
- Those instances where the object and the materials from which it is made are inherently unstable. Examples include some 20th-century plastics such as cellulose nitrate film.
- Where there is insufficient money to fund stabilisation or environmental control e.g. for large complex collections, large objects, buildings, machines, or even landscapes as well as for some archaeological materials.
- Where a religious or cultural object is in active use and that use is causing damage.
- Situations where the object is threatened by conflict.

In some cases, decay can be minimised by providing some form of shelter as at the neolithic site at Çatalhöyük (Atalay *et al.* 2010), or a regular cleaning and maintenance regime as at the Forth Road Bridge (Case Study 9 A) or reburial for monuments preserved in situ, as in the case of the palaeolithic footprints at Laetoli (Case Study 1B). In other cases, it is simply not possible to preserve the object for the long term. It may therefore be most appropriate to carefully record the object and to make a replica of it (Chapter 6). An example where this approach was taken is the stone pillar at Eliseg[6] (Watkinson 1982).

7A Case Study: Lindow Man[7] (Stead *et al.* 1986; Turner and Scaife 1995; Omar *et al.* 1989; Joy and Farley 2019; Daniel 2019)

Lindow Moss is a 30-hectare (74 acre) peat deposit located near Wilmslow in Cheshire. In August 1984, two men working on the peat-processing machinery discovered a severed human foot. Excavation by the Cheshire County archaeologist in the area where the peat had been cut, several months earlier, revealed additional human remains belonging to a single individual (initially referred to as Lindow II and later as Lindow Man). They were removed on a block of peat and sent to Macclesfield District Hospital. Following the removal of samples for radiocarbon dating and further careful excavation and packing, the peat block was placed in the hospital mortuary cold store.

Following confirmation from the radiocarbon dates that the remains probably came from the late Iron Age/early Roman period, they were sent to the British Museum for excavation and investigation. The body was stored at 4 °C to prevent microbial growth. It was X-rayed to aid the excavation, which commenced using water jets, brushes, plastic, and wood tools to gently remove the peat from the body; no sharp or hard implements were used that could damage the fragile skin. Regularly sprayed with distilled water to keep it damp, the body temperature was monitored and every time it rose to 10–12 °C excavation was stopped and the body re-cooled. To minimise the temperature, the number of people around the excavation was kept to a minimum and 'cold lights' were used for filming the process. The body, which had originally been found in a slumped face-down position, had been packed with peat and turned on its back during the lifting process. Consequently, the front was now visible and was fully exposed and cleaned.

An exact mould was made of the front using cling film followed by a layer of water-activated fibreglass tape and layers of fibreglass and resin. These layers set hard enabling the body to be turned and the back cleaned. Subsequently a mould of the back was made using fibreglass and, with the two pieces of rigid mould bolted together, the remains could be safely moved for further investigation. Conventional X-radiography, computer aided tomography, and nuclear magnetic resonance imaging were used to image the internal features of the body. The body also underwent endoscopic examination and samples were removed for analysis.

The excavation and analysis revealed that:

- Due to the damage from the peat cutting, only the upper half of the body was present together with the left foot. There was considerable damage to the hands and lower arms.
- The body was naked apart from a small band of fox fur on the upper arm.
- The body was that of a strong, well-built man around 25 years old and 5′6″ tall. His beard and moustache had been carefully trimmed with shears (indicated by the stepped pattern on the cuts) and the smooth ends of his fingernails suggested that he did not undertake manual labour, implying that he was a member of a religious or secular elite.

- The stomach contents indicated a last meal of unleavened bread, such as a griddle cake, containing heather-charcoal fragments from the cooking. He drank water with traces of 'sphagnum' suggesting that his last meal was prepared and eaten near a bog or moss, such as the one in which he was sacrificed. The presence of small amounts of mistletoe pollen, the sacred plant of Druids, may suggest some religious rite associated with the last meal.
- He had several wounds:
  - Two blows from a blunt axe on the crown of the head probably administered when the victim was in the kneeling position. These would have rendered him unconscious.
  - A blow from a blunt instrument to the occipital region of the skull.
  - A broken rib consistent with a blow to the chest.
  - A sharp deep cut to the throat, which severed the jugular vein.
  - A short two-strand ligature was found around his neck. The ligature, made of animal sinew, was knotted at both ends and had an overhand knot securing it tightly around the victim's neck. Although the ends of the ligature were quite short and thus would have been difficult to use to strangle the victim, they could have acted as a garrotte where the ligature was tightened with a stick, constricting the windpipe, and breaking the neck. Damage to the third and fourth cervical vertebrae were consistent with this form of execution. From this evidence, it appears likely that blows were delivered to the victim's head to render him unconscious, then he was garrotted (breaking his neck and probably a rib in the effort), and finally his jugular vein was cut to induce a spurt or stream of blood.

- From the excavation, it is clear that after being killed, the individual was dumped into the pool of boggy water in the middle of Lindow Moss.
- Radiocarbon dating of parts of the body by different laboratories gave dates between 2 BC and 119 AD. The practice of depositing bodies in bogs appears to have been most prevalent in North-West Europe circa 800 BC to 200 AD. The fact that a number of bodies have similar strangulation and stab wounds suggests that many were ritually killed.

The body was preserved by being quickly buried in the anoxic (oxygen-free) waterlogged deposits of the bog. Chemicals such as sphagnan (5-keto-D-mannuronic acid) present in the sphagnum moss of the bog have a variety of preservative, antiseptic, collagen-stabilising actions (Painter 1995).

When bog bodies or any waterlogged skin or leather is allowed to dry out naturally, they harden, shrink, crack, lose all strength, and often fall apart. Consequently, it is necessary to stabilise such materials if they are to be retained for future research and display. Prior to the recovery of Lindow Man, no bog bodies had been recently conserved, though bog bodies recovered earlier in the century had received a variety of treatments:

- Grauballe Man (Denmark) discovered in 1952 (Glob 1969) was conserved by tanning through soaking in a slurry of oak bark which was refreshed three times during the 18-month submersion. This was followed by immersion in Turkey red oil and gradual drying and impregnation with a mixture of glycerol, lanolin, and cod liver oil. Some areas were additionally consolidated using cellulose nitrate dissolved in ethanol and diethyl ether.
- Tollund Man (Denmark) discovered in 1950 (Glob 1969) was soaked in a solution of formaldehyde and acetic acid for six months, then in a solution of 30% ethanol followed by 99% pure ethanol with toluene, pure toluene, and then toluene containing increasingly high concentrations of wax.

To conserve Lindow Man, experiments were undertaken using freeze-drying, a conservation technique that is used for preserving waterlogged archaeological leather and wood. Conservators practised on pieces of pigskin, which had been packed in peat for several months. The best results were obtained by pretreating the pigskin in a solution of polyethylene glycol 400 (PEG 400) and then freeze-drying. Accordingly, Lindow Man was attached to a Perspex support, immersed in 15% PEG 400 for 10 weeks, then frozen to −28 °C and freeze-dried. After slow acclimatisation to room temperature and humidity, it was clear that Lindow Man had been successfully conserved with only slight shrinkage (1.4–4.5%). The skin had lightened and stiffened slightly, although it remained flexible. The body was otherwise quite stable with no hardening, cracking, or odour. To increase the long-term stability of Lindow Man's remains, they were placed in an air-conditioned showcase to ensure a stable temperature and relative humidity (53–58% was achieved). It was recommended that the body be displayed at reduced light levels (<100 lux). Subsequently, where slight cracking was observed, surface applications of a PEG 400 solution were employed, increasing flexibility, and removing the cracking (Daniel 2019: 60).

The body has been on permanent exhibit in the British Museum since 1986 except for three loans to the Manchester Museum (the closest major museum to the find site) in 1987, 1991, and 2008–2009. Over time the body has become noticeably lighter. Light monitoring, in March 1990, showed occasional readings of up to 1200 lux due to light spillage from nearby skylights and spotlights. Repositioning the case, using a canopy, and covering the case with a cloth when not on public display reduced light levels to average weekly levels of 40–129 lux. Since 1997, a new case facing into a corner has further reduced average weekly light levels to 30–50 lux. Experiments have shown that some of the lightening of the skin is likely due to photochemical damage, however, the loss of PEG from the surface and changes in the surface texture are also significant factors (Daniel 2019: 65).

It is now clear that at least three individuals were ritually killed and deposited in Lindow Moss in the late Iron Age/early Roman period. In 1983, a woman's head (Lindow I) was found. In 1987, 70 pieces of a male body (Lindow III) were uncovered from Lindow Moss. In 1988, the buttocks and left leg of a male were retrieved, very close to the site where Lindow Man was recovered and are believed to belong to Lindow Man.[8] These deposits appear to be part of a long-lived cult of human sacrifice in watery places; only those deposited in the preservative environment of bogs have survived.

The treatment of human remains reflects the cultural norms of a society. In Northwest Europe, prior to 1950 bog bodies were normally reburied in Christian cemeteries, reflecting the dominant cultural beliefs and practices of the era. By the 1950s, when Tollund Man was unearthed, the significance of the antiquity of these bodies was becoming appreciated, as was the value of scientific investigation, and an archaeologist and not the local priest was contacted to deal with these remains. Subsequently many bog bodies have been conserved and put on display in the museums of Northwest Europe.

Human remains are frequently popular displays for the public; Lindow Man's body has remained one of the most visited exhibits in the Iron Age galleries (visitor numbers and enquiries) over the last 30 years (Joy and Farley 2019). However, the display of human bodies remains a subject of debate within the academic and museum professions (Giesen 2013), and human remains are increasingly located in spaces where visitors must make a conscious decision to see them, often behind offset entry points that highlight what the visitor will see if they choose to enter the space.

Discussions of the treatment of human remain often centre around questions of respect (Cassmann *et al.* 2007; Balachandran 2009; Antoine and Taylor 2014; Science Museum Group 2018). However, respect is socially constructed and contingent on many factors. What may be respectful at one time or in one culture may not be in another. If we impose a single approach to all such remains, are we in fact disrespectful to some? Thus, decisions to rebury human remains and bog bodies in Christian burial grounds in the 19th and early 20th century might have been deemed respectful by those who were doing the burying but, if it had been possible to consult them, might have been viewed as very disrespectful by those being buried, particularly if they did not share a Christian worldview. In Ireland where, active peat cutting continues, recent bog body finds have prompted the establishment of the National Museum of Ireland's Bog Body Tissue Samples Bank, formalising the basis on which such specimens are stored, investigated, and held (Mullhall 2020). Similarly, there is an Ancient Egyptian Mummy Tissue Bank at the Manchester Museum (Lambert-Zazulak 2000; David 2008). Such tissue banks speak to the importance our society places on scientific research. While the banks are run according to strict protocols aimed at incorporating respectful treatment, there is a growing discussion about the ethics of sampling and the violence inherent in such an approach. Such discussion stems in part from past colonial engagements with human remains which aimed to prove racialised theory using techniques such as craniometrics and physiognomy. Even the use of terminology is being questioned. The term mummy, most frequently applied to Ancient Egyptian remains but also frequently used in the context of bog bodies (Ogilvie 2020), has been critiqued for its objectification of the deceased individual (Abd al Gawad *et al.* 2020; Parent 2021; Artifact lab 2021).

The importance of stabilisation remains a key tenet of these discussions but approaches to stabilising and presenting human remains will continue to be shaped not simply by what is chemically feasible but also by the social engagement with this topic.

7B Case Study: The *H.L. Hunley* (Mardikian 2004; Smith 2016; Rivera and Scafuri 2017)

In 1863, the submarine *H.L. Hunley* was constructed in Mobile, Alabama. A tube made of 3/8″ (10 mm) thick steel plates riveted onto a steel frame and pinched shut at either end, the submarine was just 39′5″ (12 m) long, 4′3″ (1.3 m) tall, and 4′6″ (1.37 m) wide. It had two short conning towers of cast iron with glass portholes for observation, each had a hatch that closed on a rubber gasket forming a watertight seal. A simple rudder and bow planes allowed the vessel to be steered by the captain who stood looking out of the forward conning tower. A hand crank turned by seven seated crew members drove a screw propeller, achieving speeds of up to 4 knots. Iron weights beneath the keel, attached with screws, helped keep the vessel submerged. Ballast tanks, filled with water or air, controlled buoyancy. Attached to the submarine's base was a 22 ft (6.7 m) long spar at the end of which was a copper canister (torpedo) containing 135 lbs of gunpowder, which could be pushed against the hull of a ship where it would explode on contact or be detonated from the submarine.

After sinking twice during trials, killing members of the crew, the *Hunley* slipped quietly away from a quayside on Sullivan's Island, South Carolina on February 17, 1864, to attack the USS *Housatonic*, part of the Union blockade of Charleston Harbour (Hicks and Kropf 2002). The charge detonated and sank the *Housatonic*, but the *Hunley* was not seen again. In 1995, the wreck was located by the National Underwater Maritime Agency (NUMA) funded by author Clive Cussler. In the following years the ownership of the submarine, and which Federal or State agency should oversee the recovery and display of its remains, was disputed. Eventually a joint arrangement was reached; title to the wreck lay with the Federal government while the State of South Carolina would control the *Hunley*'s recovery and interpretation (under the aegis of the *Hunley* Commission). Work to excavate the submarine was undertaken by the National Park Service (Underwater Archaeology Branch) and South Carolina Institute of Archaeology and Anthropology (SCIAA) culminating with the submarine's raising on August 8, 2000.

The hull was largely filled with silt, within which were believed to be the remains of the crew as well as associated artefacts. Therefore, the decision was made to recover the submarine intact from the seabed and undertake controlled excavation in the laboratory. As the *Hunley* was slowly exposed from the surrounding silt, slings suspended from a steel framework (truss) were run beneath the *vessel* to retain its 45 ° list. When totally free of the seabed, the submarine secure in its truss was craned onto a barge that transported it to the *Warren Lasch Conservation Centre,* at the former Charleston Harbour Naval yard, where it was placed in a 90,000-gallon filled with water. Throughout the journey the submarine was sprayed with water to keep it wet and prevent the marine corrosion crust from drying out and cracking off, which would accelerate the corrosion process.

The conservation, currently being undertaken by Clemson University, supported by funds raised by the Hunley Commission and the Friends of the Hunley, has three phases: excavation of the contents, removal of the bulky external corrosion products, and desalination to remove the harmful chloride minerals that catalyse iron corrosion. Once this work is completed, the submarine will be dried out and placed on permanent display. Limiting corrosion during the first two phases was paramount. So that the *Hunley* did not continue to corrode in the tank of water, an impressed current cathodic protection system was used. The object served as the cathode and long anodes connected to an external power supply, ran alongside it to suppress corrosion. The impressed current system also protected the steel truss in which the wreck remained suspended. Further safeguards to reduce decay included chilling the water in the tank to 10 °C and passing it through filters so that it did not support microbial life and remained clear so visitors could see the *Hunley*.

The excavation of the submarine's interior commenced in February 2001. Three plates were removed from the top of the hull, providing entry for archaeologists and enabling the sediment to be safely removed. Removing the plates required drilling out several hundred rivets, but it was the only way to gain safe access. Later a fourth plate was removed so the whole vessel could be cleared. Archaeologists and conservators working together slowly excavated the remains of the eight sailors who manned the vessel and following analysis of their remains, they were reburied with full military honours. Over 1500 artefacts were recovered from the vessel's interior. The excavation process involved block lifting areas of sediment (49 in total) to recover the remains of the sailors' clothing. As the excavation proceeded the positions of all the artefacts and bones were measured in 3D prior to their removal, in the hope that their distribution would shed light on the fate of the *Hunley* and its crew. Many specialists were involved in the conservation and analysis work. To prevent active corrosion, the corroded metal crust surface was kept wet through the long days of excavation and the cathodically protected vessel was covered in water each night.

After excavation, the hull was laser-scanned to create a virtual 3D model that was employed to assess its strength using finite element analysis (Blouin *et al.* 2010). With 11 tons of sediment and the keel ballast blocks removed, it was deemed safe to rotate the hull in its slings slowly over the course of three days. In 2014, removal of the outer corrosion crust, which was over an inch (25 mm) thick in places, began. Pneumatic chisels and hand tools were used to reveal the original iron plates beneath. Throughout this process, the marine crust was wetted so it did not uncontrollably crack and restart the corrosion. Initially, the crust along the seam lines was removed to facilitate study of the construction techniques. Removal of both the interior and exterior crusts took many months to complete (Figure 7.4).

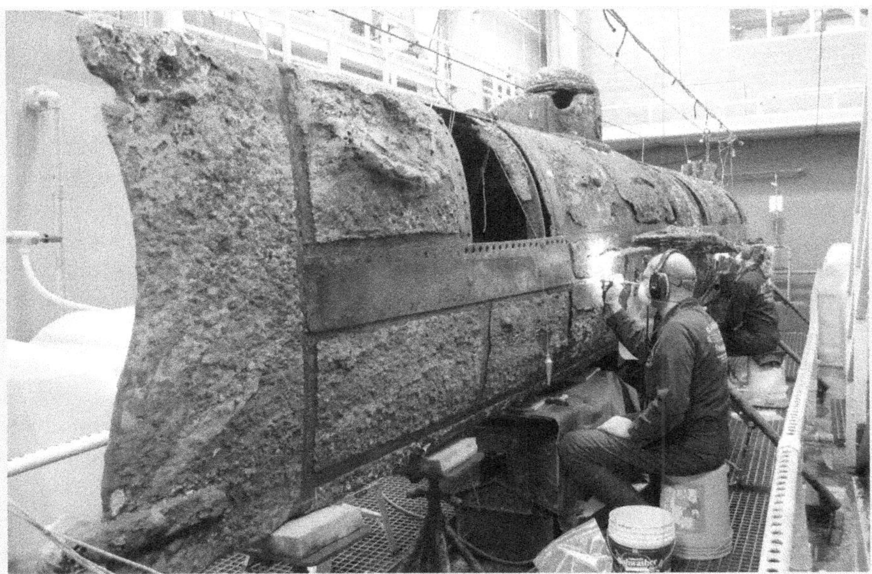

Figure 7.4 The Hunley during the de-concretion process. Friends of the Hunley.

Perhaps the greatest challenge facing the conservation team was how to stabilise the iron of the submarine after its 135-year soak in the chloride-rich environment of Charleston Harbor. Iron attracts chlorides when it is buried, and these chlorides contribute to and accelerate corrosion processes. The impressed current was not a long-term solution for stabilising the *Hunley*. Chloride removal was necessary and to this end the team investigated the efficacy of traditional desalination techniques (Mardikian *et al.* 2010) and developed new methods such as the use of sub-critical fluids[9] (Drews *et al.* 2013; Näsänen *et al.* 2013). In addition to the stabilisation of the submarine itself the variety of materials recovered from its interior required the use of unusual conservation methods, such as freeze-drying highly degraded textiles from ice blocks (Peacock 2005) and employing supercritical fluids to stabilise waterlogged cork (Drews *et al.* 2010).

To desalinate the metal, the fresh water and cathodic protection system has been replaced and the tank filled with a bath of sodium hydroxide. Testing showed that soaking in this solution was the most effective and feasible way to safely lower the chloride levels, diffusing them into the sodium hydroxide solution (Mardikian *et al.* 2009). Although the use of sub-critical fluids was extremely promising, it could not be scaled up to treat something the size of a submarine economically. It will take years of soaking and many solution changes to reduce the chloride levels, but it is not realistic to presume that they can be completely eliminated. Although plans for the final display of the submarine are still being developed it will most likely be displayed in a very low RH environment to minimise the risk of corrosion resuming. The already conserved contents also require very stable conditions for storage, prompting the creation of dedicated, air-conditioned, steel-walled storage units, one for metals (20%RH), the other for organics (45%RH ±5%) (Rivera 2017) inside the *Warren Lasch Conservation Centre*.

The care taken with the conservation of the *H.L. Hunley* contrasts with earlier, less successful experiences conserving iron vessels.

- In 1956, *USS Cairo,* the first of the 'City' class ironclad gunboats which secured the Mississippi and Ohio rivers for the Union in the American Civil War, was found in the mud of the Yazoo River. Beginning in 1960, numerous well-preserved artefacts were recovered from the ship, including the pilothouse, and an 8-inch cannon. In 1964 the state authorities attempted to raise the hull of the vessel. Without an accurate appreciation of its fragility or the stress of the lifting process, the steel lifting cables sliced into the hull spilling the contents of the vessel into the river. She was subsequently cut into three sections and efforts were made to preserve and store her iron and timber elements. Corrosion, weather, and vandalism took a toll on the remains, which have now been incorporated into a part replica/part restoration in the Vicksburg National Military Park, which is under shelter but not enclosed (Bearss 1980).
- *Holland I*, the first Royal Navy submarine entered service in 1901 and sank in the English Channel in 1913 whilst being towed to the breakers yard. Located in 1981 it was raised by commercial salvage contractors and Royal Navy divers without any significant conservation input. The vessel was treated as a working object (Chapter 9) by engineers who made it look like an old working submarine. The hull was cut into three sections to facilitate its transport to the Royal Navy Submarine Museum, Gosport where it was 'restored'. The three pieces were welded back together, some corroded parts were discarded, parts from other submarines were added, and replica pieces were made. No records were made or kept. The hull and internal machinery were painted, a doorway was cut into the side of the vessel to allow the public to enter, and it was displayed outside. The failure to stabilise the iron vessel meant that it quickly re-corroded and by 1995 analysis showed that; the sheet metal had thinned, the rivet heads had largely corroded away, there was deep crevice corrosion and overall, it was in a fragile state, too weak to be moved. Consequently, to conserve it, a tank was constructed around it, and it was immersed in an aqueous sodium carbonate solution to stabilise the corroding iron. The solution was replaced five times. In 1999, the chloride levels were generally found to be below 40 ppm, and the next phase of the project began. The sodium carbonate treatment was removed, the vessel was dried and cleaned and most of the interior was painted white as it would have been in use, the exterior was given a wax sealant coating and a building constructed around it. A dehumidification system maintains approximately 30% RH in the building (Patterson *et al.* 2002; Mealings 2009).

What has been important to the success of the Hunley outcome has been the focus on stabilisation throughout and the recognition that stability is not a single point. It alters throughout the course of an object's recovery, treatment and eventual display and requires continual assessment. For some objects, it is more easily achieved, while for others, such as the *Hunley* or the *Mary Rose* (Case Study 4B), the pursuit of stability is complicated by the size, economic factors, aspects, and the factors, such as chlorides, that are causing deterioration in the first place.

Notes

1 Typical museum conditions are often understood to be 18–22 °C, 40–60% RH, 50–1000 lux, and 20% oxygen (MGC 1998a).
2 Examples include the Azide (Daniel and Ward 1982), Beilstein (Williams 1986), Iodide-Iodate (Zhang *et al.* 1994), Chromotropic (Zhang *et al.* 1994), Surface and Aqueous Extract pH tests (BS 2924: 1983), as well as chromatographic techniques (Stephens *et al.* 2018).
3 Results of Oddy testing can be found at: https://www.conservation-wiki.com/wiki/Materials_Testing_Results
4 An Oddy test takes 28 days to complete and if the material fails, additional time is needed to identify a new material and test it.
5 The move from paper to digital records over the last 30 years has resulted in the need to digitise and transfer paper conservation records onto interrogatable digital databases. This has still to happen or be completed for many institutions. The closure of conservation laboratories and museums makes access to their conservation records even more difficult.
6 Believed to be the shaft of a 9th-century cross, the pillar was inscribed in Latin with the pedigree of the Kings of Powys, a Welsh kingdom, and set on a Bronze Age barrow. The pillar was broken up in the English Civil War and then reerected in 1779. Due to the extent of weathering, the importance of the pillar's placement relative to the barrow, and the near illegibility of the inscription, a mould was made, and a replica cast as a record. The pillar itself was left in situ.
7 We recognise that viewing human remains is troubling for some and accordingly we have chosen not to include an image of Lindow man. If you are unfamiliar with him and would look to seek out an image, they can be found in any of the publications cited for this case study or on the internet.
8 Were this a marble statue, such elements would probably be rejoined. This is not seen as necessary or appropriate in this instance.
9 Fluids where the application pressure and temperature are elevated significantly to optimise their performance.

8 Preventive Conservation and Storage

Preventive Conservation[1]

Preventive conservation encompasses 'all measures and actions aimed at avoiding and minimising future deterioration or loss … These measures and actions are indirect – they do not interfere with the materials and structures of the items. They do not modify their appearance' (ICOM-CC 2009). Preventive conservation actions include environmental management (light, humidity, pollution, and pest control), risk management (emergency planning, staff training, security, developing museum procedures for registering, handling, packing, and transporting objects), and legal protection of sites or collections.

The human need to surround oneself with objects and to interact with them poses risks for the objects and considerable research has centred around the resultant need to define 'safe' parameters for storage and display conditions that support low rates of decay (Thomson 1978; Knell 1994; Roy and Smith 1994; Caple 2011a; Staniforth 2013). Historical examples of object care can be found in the treasuries built to store historic objects in ancient Greece and Japan and protect them from earthquake, fire, and weather (Caple 2011) and in the elaborate housekeeping procedures that developed to protect objects housed in castles and country estates during the early modern period. As scientific investigation turned to the analysis of artefacts in the late 18th and early 19th centuries, studies focused on mitigating the effects of light and pollution (Lambert 2014). Museums began to adopt the use of air-conditioning as early as 1908 when a system was installed in the Museum of Fine Art in Boston to maintain a range of 55–60% relative humidity. The Cleveland Museum of Art installed heating and humidification in 1915 with the aim of maintaining 50–55% RH. Attempts to protect national collections during the two world wars confirmed the importance of considering relative humidity when safeguarding collections. During World War I, many items from the British Museum collection were stored in Holborn's underground railway tunnels. The end of the war revealed that mould damage and corrosion had resulted from the high relative humidity and poor airflow in the tunnels. Preparations to safeguard collections during World War II placed greater emphasis on relative humidity. The British Museum collections were moved to the Bath stone quarry at Westwood, where many months of preparation including sealing the porous limestone walls and installing a refrigerant dehumidification system had achieved a stable RH. Similarly, the National Gallery stored their collections in specially constructed buildings within the huge caverns of the Manod slate quarry in North Wales. Heating the air in the buildings to 63 °F (17 °C) enabled a near constant RH of 58% to

DOI: 10.4324/9781003009078-8

be achieved. An epidemic of blistering paint and other forms of instability when collections were returned to their less environmentally stable museums placed tremendous focus on the importance of RH control in collections care in the years following World War II and created a desire for clear environmental standards to minimise damage (Davies and Rawlins 1946; Haynes 1993; Lambert 2014) (Case study 8 A: Neil Armstrong's spacesuit).

The publication of Gary Thomson's influential book *The Museum Environment* in 1978 was an attempt to define such standards in scientific terms and to bring them together into a coherent form. Thomson articulated the case for establishing appropriate environmental conditions based on the museum's climate zone, identifying bands within which artefacts might be safely stored and monitoring environments to ensure that the desired conditions were attained. His recommendations were rapidly adopted and were widely implemented throughout the museum world. Monitoring environmental conditions, a process greatly aided by the increasing availability and affordability of computers and digital monitoring devices from the 1990s on, became a commonplace museum task.

Unfortunately, although the notion of environmental standards gained acceptance, in seeking to demonstrate their level of care and concern for their objects, museums began to specify increasingly narrow levels of light, RH and temperature for the loan of their objects. These new 'ideal' standards were problematic for a number of reasons. Frequently they could not be accurately monitored, let alone achieved (Ashley-Smith *et al.* 1994). Although national museums often specified very tight parameters for loaning collections to other museums, few of the national collections could reliably and consistently meet such standards themselves and increasingly environmental standards became viewed as an exclusionary control mechanism rather than a preservation tool. The conditions frequently promulgated – 50% RH ± 5% and 20–22 °C (70 ° F ± 2 °) – were only attainable for portions of the year in a small temperate band (largely restricted to Northern Europe) or through the extensive use of climate control (HVAC-heating ventilation and air conditioning) and for collections acclimatised to drier or more tropical conditions they could prove damaging (Agrawal 1981). Additionally, maintaining non-fluctuating year-round temperatures and humidities was increasingly shown to be impractical given the varieties of buildings that collections are housed in, the budgetary constraints of museums and the variable numbers of visitors who frequent museums. As the realities of climate change and the demand for sustainable solutions for storage and display have become more pressing, conservators have increasingly embraced the need to reexamine and reformulate such standards (Rhyl-Svendsen *et al.* 2010; ICOM-CC 2014).

Ideal Museum Standards

Reflective of a mid-20th century belief that science could provide hard and fast answers and technology could provide solutions, the conventional late 20th-century approach to museum environmental conditions has been to set single 'ideal' standards and if these cannot be achieved specify 'compromised' or 'relaxed' conditions (generally understood as 40–60% RH). The further the actual conditions diverged from the 'ideal' standards the greater the resultant damage was held to be (Michalski 2007).

Establishing 'ideal' standards, hard and fast values, makes life easier for all those involved with protecting collections – curators, registrars, architects, engineers, and conservators. Such standards give us single points against which we can measure our successes and generate the metrics that administrators and funders often require and value. They also provide shared reference points that facilitate the quick indoctrination of new members of the profession; it is much easier to learn a single formula than to wrestle with all the contingent factors that might be at play. Frequently to make such standards work we must overlook outliers and adopt an approach that puts the needs of the many over the needs of the few. For example, although it is well documented that archaeological iron is vulnerable to corrosion at relative humidity above 12% (Turgoose 1982; Watkinson and Lewis 2005; Watkinson *et al.* 2019), the choices for many museums are to display such objects at ambient or potentially ideal museum conditions (40–60% RH), segregate them from the rest of the collections both in storage and on display (potentially limiting their interpretive value) or integrate them with other collections but display them in expensive and often visually intrusive microclimates. The latter choice while safest can be hard to justify given the aesthetic and monetary values associated with corroded iron, and many museums adopt the former path, accepting the need for repeated interventions (treatments) to address outbreaks of active corrosion, while implementing preventive approaches elsewhere.

Every conservator must judge how close to the ideal they can/should achieve. How stable (and costly) should conditions be? The stability of archaeological metals is determined by the reactivity of the most unstable mineral in the corrosion crust. In practice and depending on the site from which they are retrieved, archaeological metals may contain greater or fewer unstable mineral species. Additionally, the unstable mineral may be locked in a dense corrosion crust, often with limited permeable to water vapour. Thus, in practice, corroded archaeological objects may survive well over shorter timescales at relative humidities above the ideal levels (Watkinson *et al.* 2019). The balance of how low an RH the museum can achieve and maintain against cost and time remains a matter of judgement for the conservator (Thunberg *et al.* 2021). Experiments achieving stability for archaeological metals using anoxic environments have proved promising (Mathias *et al.* 2004) although issues such as the permeability of the polymers and seals to oxygen and the capacity of oxygen absorbers to achieve 0% have not been fully tested (Dyer *et al.* 2011). It remains difficult to measure low values of oxygen and testing over long periods of time have not reported results.

Risk Management

Work carried out in the early 1990s at the Canadian Conservation Institute (CCI) and at the Smithsonian Institution tested some of assumptions underlying the establishment of tight RH parameters. The work demonstrated that RH cycling in the midrange (40–60% RH) does not damage most objects (Michalski 1993; Erhardt and Mecklenburg 1994); however, extremely high, or low RH may lead to direct damage, especially in the case of stressed, jointed, or composite objects. Costain (1994), Michalski (1994), Waller (1995), and others also found that museums were becoming concerned about RH and were spending limited resources on increasingly accurate ways to monitor RH rather than ensuring they had adequate fire alarms and smoke detectors. Consequently, these researchers advocated a more holistic approach to threats to collections based on the principle of risk assessment. Risk assessment promotes an objective evaluation of risk in which risks are identified, their potential consequences and the probability of occurrence are weighed, and ways to mitigate or reduce probability are identified and implemented.

The ten risks to collections were identified as:

- **Physical forces** – these range from earthquake damage to dropping an object.
- **Criminal activity** – including object theft of objects and vandalism.
- **Fire** – damage may occur from direct combustion or the effects of smoke.
- **Water** – including floods but also rising damp and sprays from fighting fires.
- **Pests** – insects such as wood boring beetles and cloths moths, also moulds, fungi, and rodents.
- **Pollutants** – gases and dust, from degrading display and storage materials or from the wider environment i.e. road pollution and industrial waste.
- **Light** – damage, such as fading and embrittlement, may occur due to both UV and visible light.
- **Incorrect Temperature** – heat can cause thermal expansion and softening even melting of waxes and polymers. Cold can lead to condensation, shrinkage, cracking, and the embrittlement of polymers. It is important to note that the greatest risk caused by temperature lies in its relationship to relative humidity.
- **Incorrect RH (Relative Humidity)** – high RH leads to biological activity such as mould growth, encourages insects and exacerbates metal corrosion. Low RH can lead to shrinkage and cracking of organic materials.
- **Custodial neglect** – including the loss of objects or records.

All the environmental factors mentioned above will lead to the loss of objects when extended over long periods of time e.g. 100 years, although some factors (such as fire) may result in more immediate loss. We can therefore see that loss may be associated with three types of events:

- Catastrophic events (rare), such as fire and flood, these are combatted by reducing risk and being prepared for such occasions – emergency (disaster) plans.
- Severe events (occasional) – such as insect infestation and dropping an object, these are combatted through developing good collections management.
- Gradual change (continual) – such as light damage, pollution, and RH fluctuations, these are combatted by monitoring and control.

It is essential to compile factual evidence about actual damage and loss to gain an accurate picture of the greatest threats to the collection and the most appropriate mitigation strategies. For example, a study by Peek (2011) examining theft in Dutch museums found that the theft of Old Master paintings was low (despite the enthusiasm with which the press highlighted each case) and that the potential of recovery was high, whereas the theft of books and manuscripts was much higher and the potential of recovery low. In Peek's study, the risk of internal theft was shown to be higher than that of external theft, suggesting that organisational controls such as staff training, collections registration, staff screening, controlled access, and bag checks may all be important to implement especially in collections with small, portable objects that are not well recorded.

Some risks can be mitigated with simple, no-cost approaches, whereas others may require much more expensive approaches (such as the installation of sprinkler systems for fire suppression). The severity of the threat may vary greatly depending on whether objects are on display, in storage or in transit. Additionally, it is important to remember that threats do not act in isolation, one or more may combine and this may magnify their impact. Collecting and sharing data allows museums to assess the potential of the risk, the nature of the threats, and the most appropriate responses to them. This process allows every museum, from a small volunteer-run institution to a large national museum to identify how it can best enhance its procedures and focus its resources to reduce the risk of harm to its collections.

Risk assessments can be carried out quite simply, such as assessing the impact and likelihood (1–5 scales) for the risks associated with different agents of deterioration and comparing them to a series of possible mitigation options (including doing nothing) or RAG ratings[2] allow clear visual representations of the risks to be created. Such approaches can provide clear visual information and serve as justifications for action (Garside *et al.* 2018). Alternatively, risk assessments can be very detailed (Ashley-Smith 1999; Waller 2003) and may become specific even to the level of individual objects and audiences (Pretzel 2000, Michalski 1997). Such assessments may require considerable teamwork to accomplish successfully. Administrative buy-in, staff support from multiple departments (conservation, curatorial, maintenance, security), and on-going financial commitment are all necessary. Very few museums have the analytical and/or staff resources to engage in a full and detailed risk assessment but any organisation can undertake a basic risk assessment.

Risks change with time, sometimes creating opportunities and sometimes exposing new threats. Risk assessment is a cyclical process rather than a one-off one. Monitoring risk has contributed to changes in collections care in many areas, including the following:

- Thinking about balancing light exposure and access has led to new practices. Greater appreciation of the difficulty that older visitors have in perceiving object details at low light levels (Michalski 1997) has led to a move away from simple maxima light levels to the use of annual exposure limits of 100,000 lux hours (for the most sensitive materials) or 450,000 lux hours (for moderately sensitive materials). Such limits permit the planning of shorter displays at higher light levels but may mean that a greater number of objects receive light exposure on an annual basis. New technological advances have reduced risk. For example, Thomson's initial limit for UV radiation – 75 microwatts per lumen (Thomson 1978) – was set in response to the capabilities of incandescent lights available in the 1970s. However, the current availability and use of LED lights and UV filters means that much lower levels of <10 microwatts per lumen can now be achieved (Bickersteth 2014).
- Concerns about chemical use have led to a reduction in the use of fumigants and insecticides. Insect pests are now normally monitored and managed through housekeeping regimes, quarantines, and integrated pest management rather than periodic mass extermination. Such approaches reduce the risks to the collection and the risk, through fumigant and insecticide toxicity, to the conservator and others (Child and Pinniger 1994) but may not be as lethal for the pests themselves, allowing pest populations to flourish. Additionally, monitoring and housekeeping routines are vulnerable to staff change, economic cuts, and institutional mission creep.

- Warming temperatures have meant that pests are now being found in places that they were not previously found (Xavier-Rowe *et al.* 2018).
- The increasing dependence on blockbuster exhibits and the constant movement of objects between museums around the world for exhibitions poses risks. Examining the shock experienced at each point in the transportation process using triaxial accelerometers has shown how vulnerable objects are to damage during transport. Preventive measures from careful handling to using air ride suspension vehicles and trollies have reduced shock levels (Kamba *et al.* 2008) as has the development and widespread use of impact-resistant packing cases that can be climate controlled (Mecklenburg and Merrill 1997; Marcon 2011).
- Vibration during building work has been recognised as a potential collection threat resulting in increased monitoring (Johnson *et al.* 2013). Mitigation measures include removing the most vibration susceptible objects (those with old adhesive joints) and agreeing protocols with construction companies for actions, such as cessation of activity, when specific trigger levels are measured. Vibrations greater than 13 mm/sec are responsible for cracking plaster (Johnson *et al.* 2013) therefore a threshold level of 3 mm/sec was used for the cessation of activity during construction at Liverpool Museums in 2011 (Wei *et al.* 2018).
- Dust threatens many objects. Dust levels are often related to visitor activity (Lloyd *et al.* 2002) and are an inevitable consequence of display, especially open display Air filtration has often been considered necessary to make significant reductions in dust particle levels. Such filtration is often present as part of HVAC systems; systems which may be an unjustifiable and unsustainable cost for most historic houses and smaller museums. However, active monitoring of relative dust levels can identify dust sources (which can be removed) and identify the dustiest locations (where the nature of floor coverings and cleaning schedules can be adjusted to minimise dust levels).
- The role of gaseous pollutants in the degradation of objects is better understood and has expanded from concerns about the high concentrations of sulphurous gases to a broader understanding of the impact of nitrogen oxides (from cars) and volatile organic compounds (from case materials, paints, adhesives, and furnishings) and improvements have been made in detecting and reducing individual gases in museum environments (Tetreault 2003; Thickett 2018; Smendemark *et al.* 2020). Where additional work remains to be done is on understanding the synergistic impacts of pollutants (Thickett 2018).
- Longitudinal studies of how climate change has altered rainfall patterns and placed more historic properties at jeopardy of flooding have led the National Trust and English Heritage to subtly alter historic buildings by changing roofing specifications and installing larger capacity gutters and downspouts (Street 2008; Watson 2008).

Disaster Planning and Response

Loss often triggers improvements in collections care. A series of high-profile and costly disasters in the late 1980s and early 1990s including the Hampton Court fire (1986), Uppark House fire (1989), Hurricane Hugo (1989), the Loma Prieta Earthquake (1989), and Winsor Castle fire (1992) prompted efforts to ensure that all museums, galleries, and historic houses had disaster plans and disaster response teams.

Disaster plans detail the procedures to be followed in the event of a disaster together with appropriate building plans, information, suppliers' addresses, etc. Disaster response teams comprise trained individuals who enact both disaster mitigation measures aimed at preventing emergency situations from escalating[3] and response measures once the disaster has occurred (Keene 1996). Disaster response teams may be formed at the institutional level or at an organisational level (such as The National Parks Service Incident Management Teams), or regional and national level (such as the Alliance for Response initiative in the United States and the American Institute for Conservation's National Heritage Responders program). Despite concerted international efforts to ensure that museums draft disaster plans many small and volunteer-run museums still do not have them. A survey of American institutions found that while 85% of large and medium museums had disaster plans only 45% of smaller institutions did and only 24% of all museums have both a plan and staff trained to carry it out (IMLS 2019). These numbers are not unique to America and many museums continue to have work to do in this area as the risk of collections damage from severe weather and climate change continues to increase.

Storage

As part of museum collections, objects have both financial and cultural value which depend on many factors including rarity, informational content, source, artist, and relevance to a community or place (Cane 2009). The purpose of storage is to retain objects as a source of information without diminishing their value for education and display. To do this, we seek to minimise change and to preserve them as near as possible to their present condition. At its simplest, putting a chair in an attic may store it for the future ensuring that it is both preserved and readily retrievable. However, storage is not static. Eventually the attic roof may leak or pests may find harbourage and a useful food source there. It is, therefore, helpful to think of storage as a continuum – a series of measures taken to increase protection. A series of increasingly protective and useful levels of storage can be defined, which may be considered in three levels each of which consists of one or more steps (Figure 8.1):

BASIC Storage

- Initially objects are gathered together (collected) in a safe place, normally a room or building, to prevent their loss, deliberate damage, or disposal.

Basic storage can be improved when

- Every object is given a unique identifier (**catalogued**) and a written record of information about the object is made. The more information that is captured and the more widely it is communicated (through a database, publication, or website) the more accessible the object will be enabling a wide range of people to be aware of it.

GOOD (Standard)

- The collections are **categorised** by type or location and stored together to aid object and information recovery.

- The collections are **housed** providing some protection against physical and environmental damage. Large objects may be covered while smaller objects are boxed. Such measures reduce handling and physical damage to objects, insulate the object against changes in temperature and humidity and reduce accessibility for insect pests. Objects are placed on shelves or on pallets to lift them above the floor surface and the risk of flood damage. Security measures such as locked doors reduce the risk of theft.

BEST (Superior)

- The collections are in environmentally controlled storage which is monitored and maintained. Objects are stored in specialised conditions with regard to their material composition e.g. archaeological ironwork is stored at low humidities to prevent further corrosion or photograph negatives are stored at low temperatures. Archival/inert storage materials are used. Many objects, especially fragile ones, will have specially made supports that provide high levels of physical support and protection. Objects are stored in specific locations that are numbered (building, room, aisle, bay, shelf, box) and marked on the museum object record.

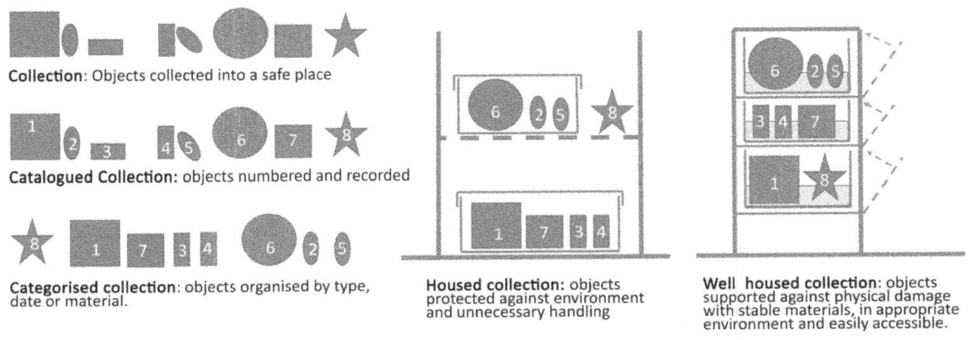

Figure 8.1 Levels of storage. Chris Caple.

This incremental approach of moving from 'Basic' to 'Best Practice' corresponds with the desires of museum staff to improve the care of their collections. Similar approaches have been advocated by the Museum and Galleries Commission (1998b), Re:source (2002) and the Collections Trust (2018) to guide and encourage improvements in museum storage. Many countries have also established standards to promote collections care. In the UK, one of the first national standards was for archives. BS 5454 *Recommendations for the storage and exhibition of archival documents* was first issued in 1977 and revised in 1989 and 2000. In 2012 it was replaced by BSI (British Standards Institute), PD 5454:2012 *Guide for the Storage and Exhibition of Archival*

Materials. Subsequently the BSI has issued over 40 (in 2020) British and European standards on specific topics associated with 'conservation of cultural heritage', many of which relate to preventive conservation, such as BS EN 16893:2018 *Conservation of Cultural Heritage – Specifications for location, construction and modification of buildings or rooms intended for the storage or use of heritage collections*. The frequent revision of these standards indicates that this is a subject where rapid development and change is occurring. To achieve these preventive conservation measures, museums require trained staff to monitor and enact mitigation measures.

Condition Surveys

Recognising that the stability of the object is a function of its materials and its surrounding environment, it is appropriate to survey museum storage and the objects therein to assess how stable the objects are, how well the museum's store is functioning, and what improvements (if any) are needed (Walker and Bacon 1987; Keene 1991, Keene 2002). Collection surveys are typically based on the premise that the condition of the collection can be ascertained by taking a representative sample and recording data on the objects' conditions and the nature of the storage. Using a series of standardised categories allows for statistical analysis and these can be maximised when specific criteria are assessed numerically (Sully and Suenson-Taylor 1996; Wellman 2010). The resulting data facilitates decision-making regarding which actions may need to be taken to maintain or improve the storage and how best to deploy limited resources to ensure the greatest positive result.

Effective collection surveys are designed around key questions and careful selection of the questions posed and the categories of information collected allow the information produced to be maximised. Questions may be as simple as 'have the conditions in storage materially changed in the last ten years' or they may be more complex such as 'given the conditions in storage, should a small number of objects be stored well or a larger number of objects be stored at a more basic level?' In 1994, faced with the large amounts of archaeological iron and the eternal question of which to treat first, the National Museum of Wales paired a condition assessment and curatorial assessment (grading the object in terms of its research importance and display potential) to determine the priority for conservation and storage resources (Dollery 1994). This approach ensured that objects that were likely to degrade but had high archaeological value were given conservation treatment first, while stable objects of little archaeological value were treated later.

Although condition surveys have been critiqued as lacking objectivity (Taylor 2013; Taylor 2017), these limitations can be minimised. Standardising and defining terms, ensuring that a limited number of trained assessors carry out the process and that all assessors are initially trained or 'calibrated' on a control group of objects so that they all record the same in the condition issues the same way helps to minimise 'surveyor bias'.

Effective condition surveys, particularly in large collections, take time to carry out and require a serious allocation of resources. Time spent in assessing the results of past surveys and in the careful set-up of the new survey can help to ensure that the data produced is optimised and that there is broad institutional buy-in. Although surveys can produce very valuable information, caution should be exercised about over-interpreting results, especially between surveys. Financial resources frequently limit the extent to which all the findings of a survey can be carried out; however, the greater the time since the survey, the more potential for change within the collection there is and the greater possibility that what was once a viable solution may no longer be sufficient. Ideally, surveys should be repeated on a periodic basis, but careful thought must be given to how much time should elapse between each survey given the resource-intensive nature of carrying out surveys.

Although a survey allows one to understand the problems facing a collection, a number of subsequent stages are needed in order to effect change. These include:

- Determining a solution – in some cases the solution may be obvious, such as the need to replace non-archival storage materials, but in other cases it may be more complicated and may require working with engineers and others to figure out.
- Gaining resources – this may include reallocation of existing budget lines if the solution is relatively cost-effective, recruiting volunteers, or even lengthy grant writing.
- Implementing the solution
- Monitoring the solution to ensure it is working – this may require a new or follow-up survey. In such a case it is important to consider whether the survey needs to revisit all the objects surveyed initially or just a sub sample.
- Ensure the solution is maintained – this step, while seemingly the easiest, can be one of the hardest to ensure as priorities shift, and new problems are identified elsewhere in the collection.

In practice, storage conditions (and solutions) are greatly influenced by the limitations on the museum's resources; the need to have easy access to objects at minimal costs often means retaining the existing storage systems even when that means potentially maintaining sub-optimal storage. A survey of the storage conditions for archaeological ironwork in the museums in the northeast of England in 2006–2007, revealed that more than 50% had no environmental control (Harder 2007).

Sustainable Storage

Bringing objects into a museum collection, cataloguing them, and providing storage materials and facilities is costly. Storage costs include:

- Building and Environment: rent, rates (local taxes), services, security, maintenance, heating, cleaning, environmental monitoring, and control.[4]
- Materials: storage boxes, acid-free tissue, shelving, purpose-made supports, computers, or cards for recording.
- Time: curator to catalogue; museum assistant, volunteer, or conservator to store; curator or museum assistant to retrieve object when required.

The costs of collecting and storage are appreciable (Lord *et al.* 1989), the higher the object's value the greater the extent to which the benefits of storage outweigh the costs.

Storage costs are easily justified for valuable objects such as 'old-master' paintings; however, in the case of lower value or less aesthetically pleasing objects, collections managers may need to work harder to secure funds. Archaeological collections can be particularly problematic as finds are constantly being deposited by commercial archaeology companies (CRM) resulting from work done in advance of development. The large number of objects found on sites can put enormous pressure on collecting institutions and repositories (Swain 2010). Increasingly, repositories have instituted 'box fees' to offset the cost of storage. The downside of such approaches is that they promote no-collection policies and can result in only a limited selection of 'special' finds being deposited rather than the whole assemblage, impacting our ability to go back and reinterrogate the site. The high cost of storage has also led to the exploration of reburial or in-situ preservation schemes (Case study 1B: the Laetoli Trackway) and the recording of objects (Means 2017), especially larger ones, rather than collecting. While these alternatives may have lower initial costs there are issues of long-term sustainability to consider. Reburial initiatives require careful thought and work to ensure that they are not merely object dumps. They also need long term-measures to ensure that the area is protected, and the site is monitored. Recording also incurs costs. Physical records need storage, while digital records must be stored and periodically migrated to ensure that they remain accessible. As recording techniques have become increasingly sensitive the size of the files that they produce has increased as have the costs of storing those digital files.

Museums are becoming more aware of the full costs of storage and are seeking to stabilise artefacts in more sustainable ways. It is increasingly clear that to balance appropriate storage and display environments with economical sustainability means:

- Adopting broad RH and temperature limits and allowing seasonal fluctuations.
- Maintaining only a small number of objects in tighter but more costly environmental conditions.
- Conducting effective, accurate, detailed monitoring over the long term and evaluating its results.

For museums and archives in urban areas achieving this balance may also mean increasing the distance between storage and display or accepting limitations in access. DeepStore, located in a former salt mine in Cheshire, and Iron Mountain's 'Underground' facility (situated in a limestone mine) offer long-term storage solutions that take advantage of the stable environmental conditions at such sites although ease of access is sacrificed.[5]

8A Case Study: Neil Armstrong's Spacesuit (Baker and McManus 1992; Savage 2019; Young and Avino 2013; Young and Young 2001)

Spacesuits seem like they should be indestructible. They are made of the highest-tech modern materials and are built to withstand the harshest environments, including temperatures ranging from −150 °C to 120 °C. They are modern marvels of engineering designed to keep their wearer safe for a single mission; built up from over 20 layers of synthetic polymers and natural rubbers they contain complex internal structures that permitted the astronauts to breathe oxygen, eat drink, void waste, and regulated their body temperature as well. What they were not designed for was long-term preservation in a museum environment. As early as the manufacturer's testing and design phases, oxidisation of the neoprene and natural rubber blends that make up parts of the suits was noted. Because of the time pressures imposed by America's race for space, stop gap measures were introduced which were designed to extend the life of these materials beyond the planned usage time (typically reckoned to be six months).

In March 1967, an agreement between the National Aeronautics and Space Administration (NASA) and the Smithsonian's National Air and Space Museum (NASM) gave the museum first refusal on items retired from service in the space agency. In the years that followed, spacesuits sporadically entered the museum's collections, along with other space-related hardware and equipment. Divided into two categories, 'flown' suits (those which had been used on a mission) and 'training' suits (those used in training and simulations), the spacesuits were initially loaned and displayed without much thought to their long-term preservation. The newness of the materials and the suits themselves meant that little experience of the ways in which they might deteriorate had been built up and in the absence of this experience it was difficult to build an effective preventive conservation strategy.

As early as 1978 damage was noted in the spacesuit collection, during a museum-wide inventory. At this point, loans of the most significant and iconic spacesuits began to be limited and a refrigerated 'Bally Box' storage unit was commissioned at NASM. The unit was designed to maintain a storage environment of 45% RH and 41 °F (5 °C) and represented a 'best guess' at appropriate storage based on existing information about the ageing of rubber. In the period between 1980 and 2000, the suits in this storage continued to show signs of deterioration as did those on display and it became apparent that other factors were at work. In particular, it was noted that the Polyvinyl chloride (PVC) tubing used for the life support hoses showed signs of advanced deterioration including stickiness and it had changed from clear to dark brown. Additionally, it was causing staining to neighbouring materials. Rubber components were seen to be brittle and flaking or oozing and distorted while the aluminised fabric of the Mercury program spacesuits was changing colours. Other issues that were noted were distortions resulting from inadequate support, patchy discolouration due to uneven light when on display and in several cases (including Neil Armstrong's suit) potential damage from alkaline cement dust that was used to create a 'lunar landscape' in two display cases that exhibited materials from the Apollo 11 and Apollo 17 missions. The cement dust had penetrated the weave of the fabric and was suspected of contributing to the flaking of the outer layers of the material.

In March 2000, NASM initiated a major research project, with support from the Save America's Treasures grant program, designed to document the current condition of all the spacesuits, undertake research into the causes and mechanisms of deterioration of the suits, design and test storage systems and produce guidelines and standards for the handling, storage, and display of spacesuits both at NASM and at those institutions to which it loaned items. The project revisited the question of refrigerated storage but also considered issues relating to the size of physical storage, the types of cabinets used, the support of the suits, and the nature of pollutants to which they were exposed. The recommendations produced stipulated that spacesuits should be maintained at temperatures between 63 and 65 °F (17–18.5 °C). This very tight window is necessary because below 60 °F (15.5 °C) rubber may begin to crystallise while over 68 °F (20 °C) there was a greater likely that mould spores and fungal colonies could grow on the suits. It was recommended that the RH be maintained at or below 35%. Light levels should be limited to 100 lux and UV exposure should be minimal. It was recommended that handling be kept to a minimum as it has a high potential to cause damage due to the weight and awkwardness of the suits as well as the presence of lunar dust on the lunar suits. The dust, which consists of sharp, angular pieces of silica and other minerals, is highly abrasive and can tear and cut the fabric of the cloth. Finally, pollutants such as sulphur dioxide, nitrogen dioxide, carbon dioxide, and ozone should be monitored and removed. The Bally box was altered to meet these new specifications and filtration systems were put in place to remove pollutants and the suits were supported on purpose-built trays that allowed them to be moved without manipulating the suit itself.

The decision to put Neil Armstrong's suit on display both for the 2019 commemoration of the lunar landing and in the Destination Moon exhibit planned as part of NASM's multi-year transformation, posed many issues for conservators. As perhaps, the most iconic space-related item the suit has tremendous emotional value to visitors. It was on continuous display between 1973 and 2001, when the difficult decision to take it off view was made to ensure its preservation. How could it be best presented to the public without causing further damage to it? NASM launched a $500,000 Kickstarter campaign entitled 'Reboot the Suit'[6] designed to study this problem and raise awareness about the preservation issues that modern materials and spacesuits in particular face. Headed by Lisa Young, who had led the earlier Save America's Treasure grant-funded research and had continued to work with the space collection in the intervening years, the project aimed to conserve, digitise, and display the suit. Scanning the suit using 3D scanning, CT scans, and other visualisation techniques allowed the conservators to better understand aspects of the suit, document all the stitch holes, repairs and coatings, and tailor solutions to the suit's unique measurements. The scans also serve as a reference point against which further change and deterioration can be measured and created a resource that the Smithsonian has made available worldwide for use in classrooms and other educational facilities.

Designing the support system for the suit was a major challenge. The suit, which weighs 45lbs (20.4 kg), was made to Armstrong's measurements although it has shrunk slightly as the materials have aged. Given the deterioration of the PVC and other materials that has already occurred, it was important that the mannequin push the suit out gently enough to provide support but not push it out hard enough to cause additional damage. Additionally, unlike clothing that can be draped over a mannequin, the mannequin used for the space suit would have to be assembled inside the spacesuit using the limited access provided at the arms, feet, and neck. A lightweight aluminium structure that could be clicked together and could rotate at key points was designed using a Computer Aided Design (CAD) program and then 3D printed. This skeleton was then padded to the exact specifications needed at each point in the suit using an inert polyethylene foam covered with an archival textile to keep the foam from catching on the interior. Since attaching the boots, gloves, and helmets to their original attachment fittings creates a closed environment that allows the degradation products of the various plastics and acids to build up inside the suit and accelerate damage, new mounts needed to be created that allowed air movement. To further promote airflow through the suit, external air hoses connect to the suit and pump fresh, filtered air into the suit allowing the air inside to exchange with that in the case every three days. The case was equipped with mechanical systems that maintain the tight temperature and RH standards achieved in storage and permit the air to be scrubbed and all pollutants removed.

The careful accretion of knowledge about how best to store and display these complex and highly vulnerable objects will hopefully ensure the preservation of the spacesuits for many decades yet to come and allow NASM to continue to share these inspirational objects. Although the engineering involved in both their manufacture and preservation remains a key element of their presentation, it was important to the conservators and curators that they convey the humanity of the individuals wearing the suits. Therefore, in building the mannequin and support structure emphasis was given to creating 'movement' and a sense of Armstrong taking his 'giant leap for mankind' rather than a static display. The project was further humanised by the hundreds of press interviews and appearances that Lisa Young has given over the last 20 years and the enthusiastic way in which she has conveyed the importance of preventive approaches for this material. These public engagements have highlighted not only the marvellous engineering of this American icon but also its fragility and the research and care needed to ensure that it continues to inspire future generations (Figure 8.2).

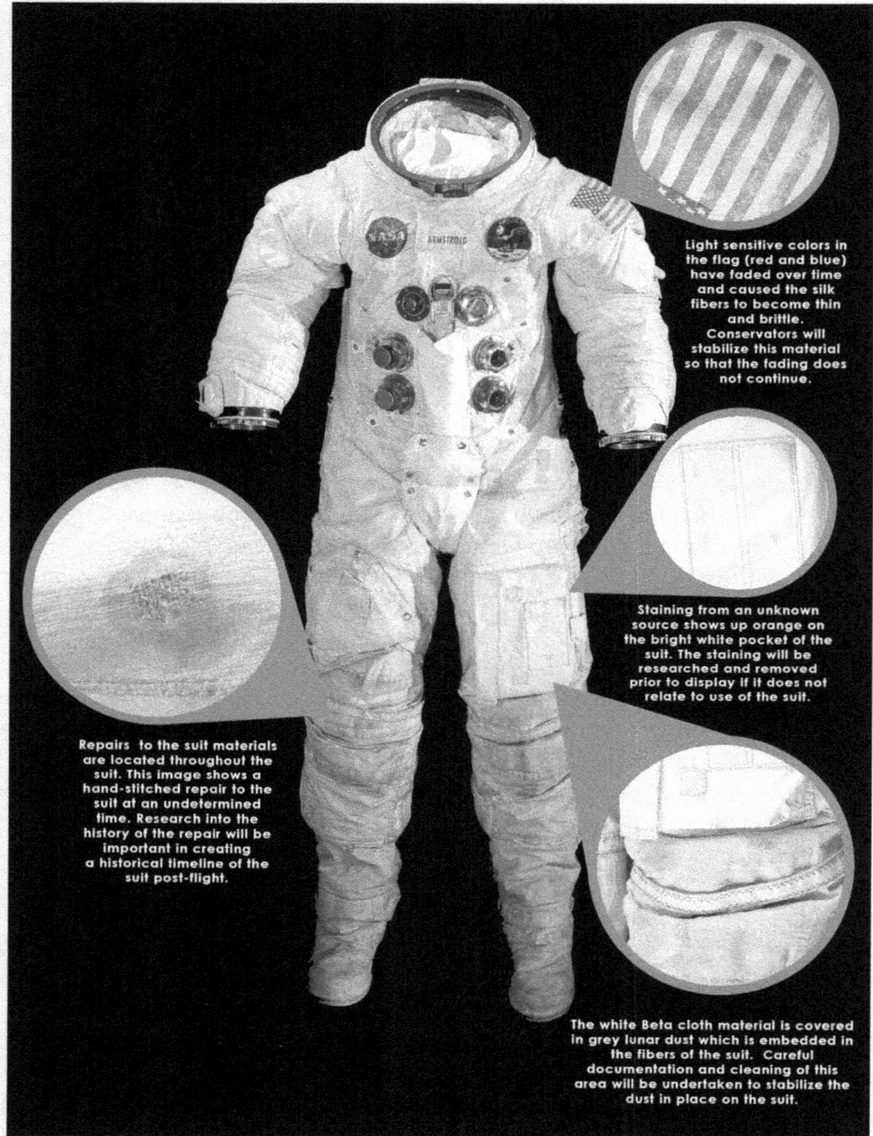

Figure 8.2 Image created by the National Air and Space Museum to raise awareness and support for the conservation of Neil Armstrong's Apollo 11 spacesuit. National Air and Space Museum of the Smithsonian Institution.

8B Case Study: Brodsworth Hall (Allfrey 1999; Allfrey and Xavier Rowe 2012)

Between 1976 and 1979, the National Trust for Historic Preservation[7] commissioned studies of one of their newly acquired properties, Drayton Hall, to help them determine how best to preserve it. The house, recognised as one of the finest Southern plantation houses was built between 1738 and 1742, had survived hurricanes, earthquakes, and the American Civil War and had entered the 20th century largely unmodified although economic downturns meant that some architectural features and the house's contents had been removed (Drayton Hall Preservation Trust 2018). At the end of these studies the decision was made to stabilise the property 'as found' without restoring or altering it. Highly controversial at the time (George 1984) this decision has gone on to influence the preservation of other houses, including, in the UK, Calke Abbey (1985), Brodsworth Hall (1990), Mr. Straw's House (1990), and Tyntesfield (2002), and Rouse Hill House in Australia (1999).[8] These 'time capsule' houses, complete with their contents, recorded not only the decorative schemes of the period of their construction, but also their role as homes and the decline these properties suffered during the 20th century. The decision to preserve the buildings and contents and display them unrestored, recognised that up to this point almost all historic houses had been restored to a particular period; invariably the principal period of the decorative scheme of the house and that consequently the story of the decline of the English Country house and the 'lived-in' quality of such houses had not been told[9] (Figure 8.3).

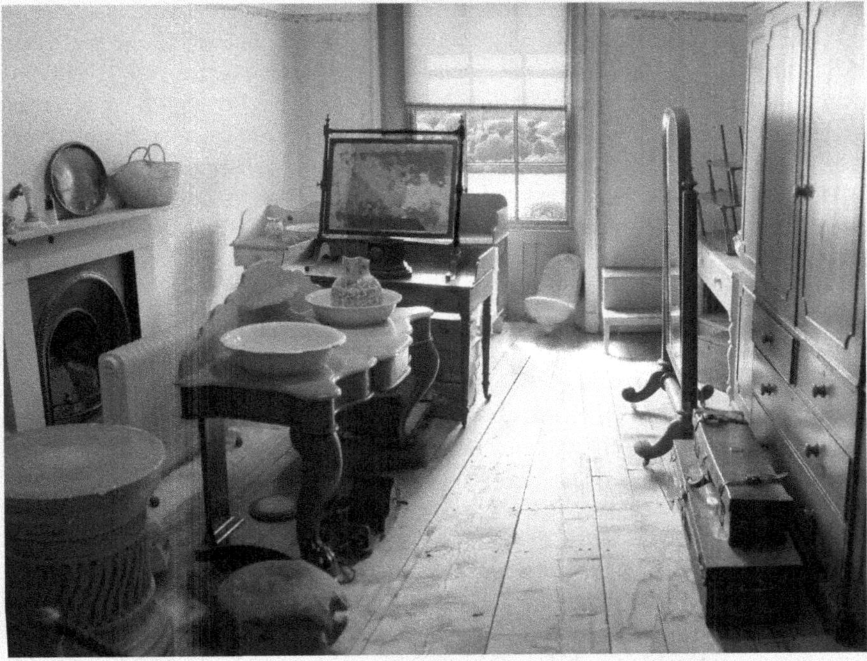

Figure 8.3 Unused furniture and other items stored in an upstairs servant's room in Brodsworth Hall (English Heritage). Chris Caple.

Brodsworth Hall is a country house with nearly 60 rooms located in South Yorkshire. It was constructed, decorated, and initially furnished in 1861–1863. It is a typical Victorian English historic house, but after World War I its owners lacked the income from the dwindling estate to pay for the large staff required to run the house.[10] Consequently, they shut up rooms and failed to fully maintain the rest (Carr-Whitworth 2009). Crucially the family stopped redecorating and remodelling rooms in the latest fashion, as their predecessors had. This meant that what they inherited survived largely intact, decaying gently with just a few modern conveniences such as electric lights and heaters added to make the rooms in which they lived habitable. When acquired by English Heritage in 1990 Brodsworth was described as 'the most complete surviving example of a Victorian country house in England'. For curators working on the project the opportunity to 'stop the clock' was exciting and it was felt that the Tupperware in the kitchen was as important to the story of the place as the old master paintings in the dining room.

The decision to conserve a building 'as found' and the logistics of doing it are not the same. At Brodsworth Hall, the building was suffering from subsidence, water was coming in from the roof, there was rising damp from blocked drains and rotting timbers. There were active pest infestations, mould was rife, and many fragile objects were falling apart under their own weight or from the pressure of other object heaped upon them. Paint was flaking off walls and objects, and light-damaged textiles were turning to dust. On the back stairs, the pink Sienna marbled paintwork appeared dull orange-brown due to aged, discoloured varnish. Following an extensive recording process, all the contents (over 17,000 objects) were removed while major structural repairs were undertaken, and a new roof put on the building. Meanwhile the objects were cleaned and conserved. Throughout this work care was taken to maintain the 'as found' appearance. Preventive conservation steps included freezing (down to –30 °C) to kill larvae as well as insects, although where necessary (upholstered furniture) some fumigation was used (Berkouwer and Church 1993). Because it is not advisable to leave dust on objects,[11] damaging moulds, dirt, and dust were removed from all objects. The heating system (radiators) was repaired and was supplemented with electric heaters to create a conservation heating system (RH).[12] An integrated pest management system (IPM) was put in place.

Active treatment included supporting and consolidating fragile elements where required. However, the objects were not restored. Flaking paint was consolidated, but missing areas were not retouched (Babbington and Hughes 1992). Most metal objects were left with their patina in place and not polished. However, interestingly, repairs made during the later occupation of the house, such as self-adhesive tape, which can cause damage, or crude overpainted losses which obscured the original surface finishes were removed, filled, and consolidated to blend with the present appearance. After five years, the objects were carefully returned to the house. In some of the principal rooms that had been maintained in a reasonable state, meaning they appeared almost as they did in their heyday of the 1860s, the 'as found' appearance of the house did not vary much from what visitors expected to see in a stately home. Other rooms, such as the bedrooms in the servant quarters, were filled with the discarded debris from 130 years of inhabitation. Further rooms appeared cluttered and 'lived in' and exhibited subtle signs of age such as water damage or peeling wallpaper.

Historic houses encourage visitors to learn through context without the visual intrusion of notices. At Brodsworth, room stewards ensure security and provide information to visitors through a friendly chat. Guidebooks are available for purchase for those interested in specific facts as well as ambience, but there are not normally notices or labels. Though English Heritage hoped to convey a 'well-worn and gently dilapidated air', to get across a message that the 'as found' state of some of the rooms was deliberate, in practice they found some initial visitor instruction was required so that they did not feel that parts of the house were simply neglected (Allfrey 1999). The 'conserved as found' appearance of some historic houses has drawn criticism from those who found the piles of 'rubbish' meaningless, the impression of neglect overpowering any appreciation of the period its art, achievement, and beauty. Simon Jenkins labelled Calke Abbey 'not a time warp just a house in need of a visit from the dustman' and pilloried the fact that 'every tonic bottle, every matchbox' was taken out catalogued, stabilised, and replaced as it was (Jenkins 2003). Visitor numbers suggest that there is appeal to this approach with 407,000 visiting Calke Abbey in 2021 (ALVA 2021). For some the attraction may lay in a sort of prurient fascination in the 'warts and all' lives of other people but for others it is the way in which these houses humanise the experience of living in a big house, removing some of the glamour and reducing the experience to the common headaches of replacing roofs and keeping up with the cleaning.

Maintaining a fully consistent 'conserved as found' approach is not entirely possible. Modern health and safety legislation and accessibility regulations require adaptations to historic buildings that are open to the public. For example, original electrical wiring must be replaced with new and additional lighting, fire detection and alarm systems must be installed, although this is done as unobtrusively as possible. Reflecting on the results of a comprehensive risk assessment, conducted nearly 20 years after Brodsworth opened, Allfrey and Xavier-Rowe (2012) also questioned whether it was a sustainable approach. They noted that concessions had had to be made. Inappropriate light levels meant that UV filtering film had to be placed on windows and curtains purchased for some rooms that had not previously had them. The fragility of the house's surviving carpets and floor surfaces meant that they needed to be covered with druggets (coarse durable floor coverings) or matting along the visitor access paths. Despite attempts to match colour schemes to the faded appearance of the floor these coverings often remain monochromatic and visually intrusive (Allfrey and Xavier-Rowe 2012). As historic houses have increasingly embraced more free-form visitation and less confined access ways, houses like these can come under pressure to remove stanchions and permit greater access. Finally in properties such as Brodsworth there are frequently divides between the 'conserved as found' building interiors and other portions of the property such as the gardens which are cleared of overgrowth and replanted replicating the original planting schemes – effectively restored, these spaces can create cognitive dissonances for visitors that make it harder for them to see past the unkempt interior.

In 2017, major renovations were undertaken at Brodsworth. The roof was repaired. The existing heating and electrical systems were once again updated and new environmental monitors were installed. Despite this, maintaining an

RH low enough to ensure object stability is challenging in some spaces (Figure 8.4). Major repairs were also made to the roller shutters, one of the house's original protections against light. The renovations offered a chance to check collections and to find out more about the visitor's perception of the site and the conservation approach taken at it (Chitty 2018), which was overwhelmingly positive.

Preserving buildings and their contents in a 'conserved as found' state minimises the amount of restoration and replication work required. However, the objects cannot be simply left as they are, they need to be conserved, a realistic appraisal of their likely rate of decay should be made and steps are taken to minimise that decay. Thus, this approach is best understood as a philosophy and a visual style to which objects are conserved, cleaned, and restored like any other period in the object's life. It requires resources (staff and finances) and commitment to succeed and must be re-evaluated periodically to ensure that it is accomplishing its goals. Such 'as found' properties permit not only reflection on the lives of the houses' inhabitants but also the resources needed to care for 18th- and 19th-century houses in the 20th and 21st centuries.

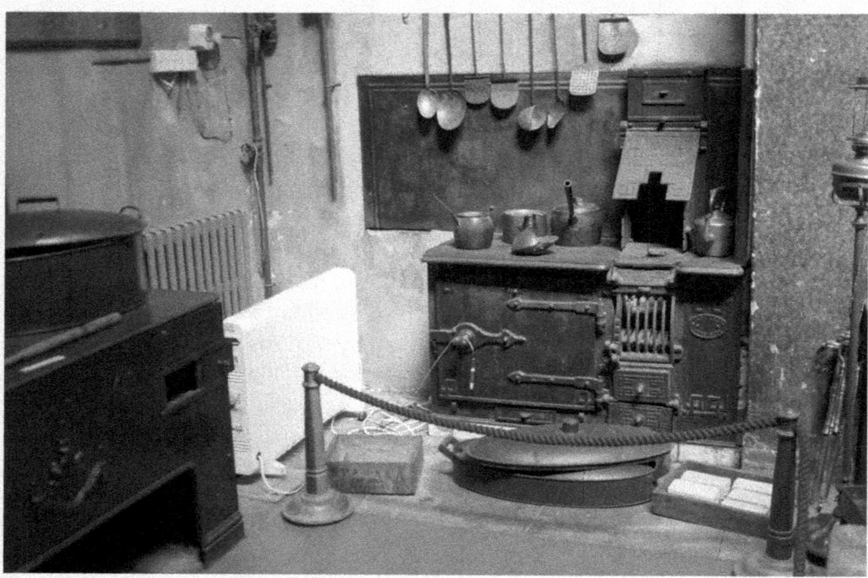

Figure 8.4 The kitchen at Brodsworth Hall. Note the juxtaposition between the aged interior and the RH monitoring equipment and heater used to control the RH levels. Chris Caple.

Notes

1 Also referred to as preventive care (Pye 2001) and care of collections (Knell 1994), however, preventive conservation has become the most widely used term (Roy and Smith 1994, Caple 2011, Staniforth 2013). Staniforth (2013, xiii) defines preventive conservation as 'procedures that generally act on a group of objects or a collection by adjusting the condition in which these objects are kept'.
2 RAG (Red-Amber (or Yellow)-Green) ratings, also known as 'traffic lighting', are used to summarise indicator values, where green denotes a 'favourable' value, red an 'unfavourable' value, and amber a 'neutral' value.
3 Such measures may include moving collections away from windows, battening down hatches, and putting out sandbags in advance of severe weather, such as hurricanes or floods, or it may include protecting collections in times of conflict. Examples of the latter include the work done to protect the mosaics in the Ma'arrat al Nu'man Museum during the Syrian Civil War (Al Quntar *et al.* 2015).
4 Rising energy costs have prompted many museums to place a greater focus on improving building envelopes, buffering, insulation, and slow seasonal variations (Cassar 1995) to reduce their reliance on air conditioning.
5 Such solutions may be seen as being somewhat akin to Preservation in Situ solutions. They prioritise the preservation of the object for future generations over access in the present.
6 Although the campaign was designed to raise \$500,000, it was so successful that it ultimately raised \$720,000. This is an indication not only of the public affection for this object but also of the effectiveness of the educational efforts run in conjunction with the campaign.
7 This American preservation organisation is not to be confused with the English National Trust, although it is in part modelled on it.
8 English Heritage also adopted a similar approach to Wigmore Castle (Coppack 1999).
9 Properties such as Mr Straws' House and Hardman House and Studio (National Trust) told the story of the lives of the middle class and professional people (English).
10 They abandoned many traditional housekeeping practices such as regular dusting and cleaning regimes, leaving curtains drawn, blinds down and shutters closed, this led to increased dust, insects and light damaging the objects and interiors.
11 Dust stains and promotes corrosion and when the RH is over 80% can start to adhere to objects (Brimblecombe *et al.* 2009).
12 Known as 'conservation heating' such systems go into operation when the humidity reaches a particular set point at which time the heating raises the temperature to a few degrees above ambient temperatures thus bringing the humidity down due to the inverse relationship between heat and relative humidity. This serves to protect the interiors from the damaging effects of relative humidity, such as mould growth and metal corrosion.

9 Preserving Intangible Heritage: Working and Socially Active Objects

While the preceding chapters of this book have focused on mechanisms that preserve the physical material of an object, it is important to note that the intangible characteristics of the object can be equally important to consider when designing treatments. In the late 1980s, the importance of intangible heritage was formally introduced into discussions about the preservation of cultural heritage, beginning with the 1989 UNESCO *Recommendation on the Safeguarding of Traditional Culture and Folklore*. This document was followed by the 2001 UNESCO *Universal Declaration on Cultural Diversity* and the 2002 Istanbul Declaration and in 2003 UNESCO adopted the *Convention for the Safeguarding of the Intangible Cultural Heritage* which formally identified, defined, and created lists to aid in the protection of intangible heritage. These documents acknowledge the importance of intangible cultural heritage as a 'mainspring of cultural diversity' (UNESCO 2003) and define intangible heritage as 'the practices, representations, expressions, knowledge skills as well as instruments, objects, artefacts, cultural spaces associated therewith, that communities, groups and individuals recognize as part of cultural heritage' (UNESCO 2003). UNESCO's definition of intangible heritage focuses on the nonphysical intellectual wealth (folklore, customs, beliefs, traditions, knowledge, and language) that is expressed through oral traditions, performing arts (music, dance, plays, etc.), social practices and festive events (food preparation, celebrations, etc.), knowledge and practices concerning nature and the universe, as well as traditional craftsmanship.

Nonphysical qualities are often both dependent on and vested in tangible objects. For example, falconry has been recognised as part of the intangible heritage of many countries. The knowledge needed to rear and train the birds are intangible aspects while tangible manifestations of the practice include the hoods used to calm the birds, the jesses they wear and the falconer's gauntlets. How we preserve certain material objects is therefore informed and altered by the intangible characteristics that are rooted in the object. These may include the sounds, smells, motions, tastes, and emotions produced by or associated with the object but may also incorporate the beliefs and traditions employed to make or use the object. These characteristics are often part of the values that the object has for people and communities (Chapter 1). In the case of working/dynamic objects

DOI: 10.4324/9781003009078-9

and socially active objects these intangible qualities play important roles in conservation decision-making.

Working/Dynamic Objects

All objects initially performed a function (worked), however the term working objects is typically used for objects that contain moving parts where the motive power is provided either by the human body (a bicycle) or coiled springs and descending weights (clocks), water (mills), wind (organs), steam (engines), electricity (machines), or some other power source (Pye 2016). Objects that do not exhibit physical movement, but which emit light and sound, such as radios, computers, and televisions, are often also considered to be working objects. The movement of the object as well as the noises, smells, and traditions associated with its use may be as important as its aesthetic and tangible characteristics. In some instances, such as the Gamelan[1] (Jacobsen *et al.* 1975; Jones-Amin *et al.* 2006), tradition and belief may add an additional layer of cultural significance that requires consideration.

There are many types of working or dynamic objects. The most common are vehicles (from carts to spacecraft), various forms of manufacturing machinery (from spinning wheels, early washing machines to conveyor belts), clocks, and musical instruments. Given their size and complexity, dynamic objects are frequently challenging to care for and to maintain in working conditions (MGC 1994; Dollery and Henderson 1997; Newey 2000; Thorrowgood and Hallam 2004; Child 2006; ABTEM 2018). There are advantages and disadvantages to keeping working objects in running order and periodically using them.

Advantages include:

- Enhancing the use of the object as a visitor attraction and educational exhibit. Objects, such as mills and clocks, are understood better when seen in motion.
- Using an object can prevent damage that might otherwise occur from static display and lack of use. The higher RH (relative humidity) generated by periodically playing wooden musical instruments prevents them from drying out and cracking. Similarly, engines and other mechanisms benefit from lubrication during use and regular movement adjusts the loads in a structure, preventing distortion of stressed or loaded components such as wheels and tensioning wires. Brief periods of use are sometimes considered better at preventing deterioration than simple static storage (Thorrowgood and Hallam 2004).
- Sound, smell, taste, and touch are highly evocative senses and add to the intensity and apparent 'reality' of any experience. Viewing a steam train is a far more immersive encounter when one smells it, hears it, and feels it thundering past (Figure 9.1).

- Museum visitors are drawn to movement, light, and sound – they are attracted to working objects and enjoy seeing them work. The engaging experiences of movement, sound (particularly music), and smell move the visitor from the here and now into 'the' past[2].

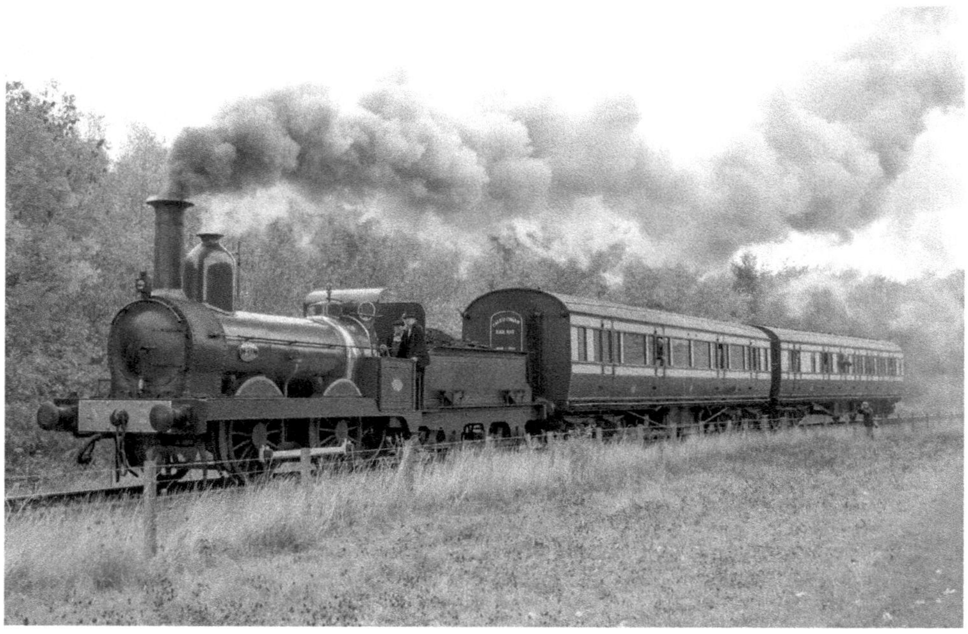

Figure 9.1 Furness railway steam locomotive No. 20 (built in 1863 by Sharp, Stewart & Co. for the Furness Railway, Britain's oldest standard-gauge operational steam locomotive) hauling two vintage Caledonian Railway carriages at the Bo'ness & Kinneil Railway. © Greg Fitchett (cc-by-sa/2.0).

Disadvantages include:

- The potential for component failure (Wain 2017: 82). Components are stressed during use (e.g. the strings of musical instruments), leading to an increased risk of failure (such as a broken string). The loss of the last airworthy de Havilland DH 98 Mosquito T3 (G-ASKH, ex-RAF serial RR299), which crashed one mile west of Manchester Barton Airport (EGCB) during an air show on July 21, 1996, illustrates the risk of catastrophic loss inherent in using some working objects.
- Use may alter the object. Working objects must meet modern safety standards and it is difficult to achieve this without making significant additions or modifications to the objects; for example, installing guard rails, adding covers to hide exposed machinery, installing cut-out switches, even replacing old boilers with new, safe, and certified ones. Such measures can create false impressions of

the past and damage the object as a historic document preserving evidence of the past. However, it is also worth noting that a desire to remove later modifications and to return a working object to a 'purer' original state can also be problematic. In the case of the de Havilland Mosquito, investigation of the crash suggested that lack of later understanding regarding modifications to the carburettors (made to prevent failure under negative g-forces during use in the 1940s) contributed to the loss of the plane (AAIB 2014).

- The wear and heat generated during running degrades the condition of the object, even if it occurs at barely perceptible levels such as the increased oxidation and eventual breakdown of the polymer sheathing on electrical wiring. Similarly running a gearbox or similar mechanical device, even with an oil-filled sump to keep it lubricated, will still lead to wear on the teeth on the gear cogs. No historic working object can operate without wear. The wear and tear of use requires that a maintenance regime be established to replace worn parts.
- Keeping working objects running is expensive, which is why so many are static (Wain 2017: 86–87). Costs include:
    - Operators and maintenance staff must be properly certified (e.g. have a current driving licence or pilot's licence).
    - Training and retaining skilled staff.
    - Regular safety checks and inspections – this is particularly true for vehicles that take passengers such as members of the public.
    - Fuel costs in some cases.
    - The regular replacement of consumable components.
    - Space in which to manoeuvre the object. Many working objects are large and sometimes unwieldy and require significantly more space than a static object does, which has associated costs.
- Restoring an object to working order often requires that damaged and worn parts are replaced rather than repaired. Original material may be lost raising questions of authenticity. How long will a working object retain its original materials if the worn and damaged parts are replaced? Some restored cars have little more than the original chassis number remaining in some instances. Working objects challenge our perceptions of originality. Does original mean the material that was present when it was first made? Is it a reflection of the designer's intent or does it encompass the materials accumulated over the different periods in which the object was active? (Wain 2011) Although these questions are relevant for all objects, the regular replacement of components and improvement of some working objects make them more pressing in these cases.[3]
- Smaller working objects, such as musical instruments or watches, are susceptible to wear and damage due to their portability, frequent movement, extensive handling, and the adjustments (and repairs) needed to improve their functionality. It is unusual to find musical instruments that still have all their original elements. Typically, elements such as reeds, strings, and skins that are under stress (from pressure, load, or impact) are replaced frequently.
- Larger working objects are frequently housed outside. Maintaining external structures, especially ironwork, against the effects of weather is an expensive, but

essential, process (Case Study 9A: Forth Railway Bridge). These processes begin shortly after the object is commissioned and must be maintained throughout its life, including display.
- Can an object be kept working in perpetuity? Do the resources exist, and is the device capable of such sustained use?

It is possible to overcome many of these disadvantages. Working objects can be operated at lower temperatures and pressures to reduce the risk of dramatic failure; for example, running steam engines on compressed air rather than steam (as at Bradford Industrial Museum),[4] running vehicles on private roads without other users, limiting the number of users and the length of run times.[5] Similarly using gradual warm-up procedures, suspending operation when trained personnel who know that particular object well are not available, performing regular maintenance and developing disaster response procedures can mitigate the risk of damage and loss. In addition to the normal museum and conservation records, working objects require operating manuals in which all aspects of safely operating the object (e.g. warm-up times, fuel, lubricants, operating temperatures and pressures) are outlined, as well as an operation log that records each use. These records help ensure safe operation, limit the risk of catastrophic failure, and ensure that minor faults are reported and checked.

Working Objects in Museum Contexts

Working objects can be present in a variety of museums but are often found in large numbers in the following types of collections:

- Science-and-technology museums – originating in the late 19th century these institutions seek to make the public aware of scientific and technical principles and achievements, which working objects are often uniquely able to demonstrate.
- Folk and industrial museums – these large often open-air museums emerged in the late 19th century to preserve traditional lifeways threatened by industrialisation (Kavanagh 1990). Rural activities, such as milling and threshing, were demonstrated as well as traditional crafts. As early forms of technology also began to become obsolete or were replaced, industrial museums often grew up around them. Examples include the Albany Whaling Museum (Western Australia), Iron Bridge Gorge (England), and the Rahmi M. Koç Museum (Istanbul).
- Transportation museums – collections of vehicles, objects, and memorabilia associated with those vehicles. In some cases, the museum collects a single type of vehicle (i.e. trains), and in other cases, they may collect multiple types (i.e. planes, trains, and automobiles).
- Military museums – since the advent of the atlatl and bow and arrow, warfare has been dominated by working objects. The regular obsolescence of military hardware means there is a constant stream of weaponry for heritage displays. Many military museums, from regimental museums to mothballed aircraft carriers and submarines (USS *Intrepid*, HMS *Belfast*, HMAS *Ovens*), preserve and present these devices.

- Local and regional museums – many collect machines and other working objects that are important to local industries or daily life in their towns or regions.
- Specialist museums such as clock museums and musical instrument museums.

Some working objects, such as vehicles, are readily understood out of context because of their form or their similarity to other examples,[6] but many working objects, such as the diesel-powered generator in the Wustermark railway shunting yard near Berlin, only make real sense when seen in situ, connected to other equipment such as a rotary current generator, transformers, wiring, and junction boxes, delivering electric current to all parts of the marshalling yard (Dempwolf 2006). Initially preserved by accident or neglect – they are often too large and difficult to break up for scrap value; sited in unvalued old industrial locations, such machines (steelworks, mines, and other large factories) rarely survive unless some key elements have sufficient value to be deliberately preserved (Khatchadourian 2019).

As they pass from industrial use into museum collections, working objects go through a series of identifiable phases (Figure 9.2). The value of the object's functionality declines, its educational role increases and eventually the value of the original material becomes so high that the object's value as a record (evidence) of the past (or the work of an original creator) becomes paramount. While a few (rare) working objects, such as the Antikythera mechanism (Jones 2019), are clearly at the end of this process, most working objects are nearer the start. Mann (1994) highlighted this in the regret he expressed that the original fragments of Stephenson's *Rocket* were not treated like valued archaeological objects but instead had been incorporated into various reconstructions.

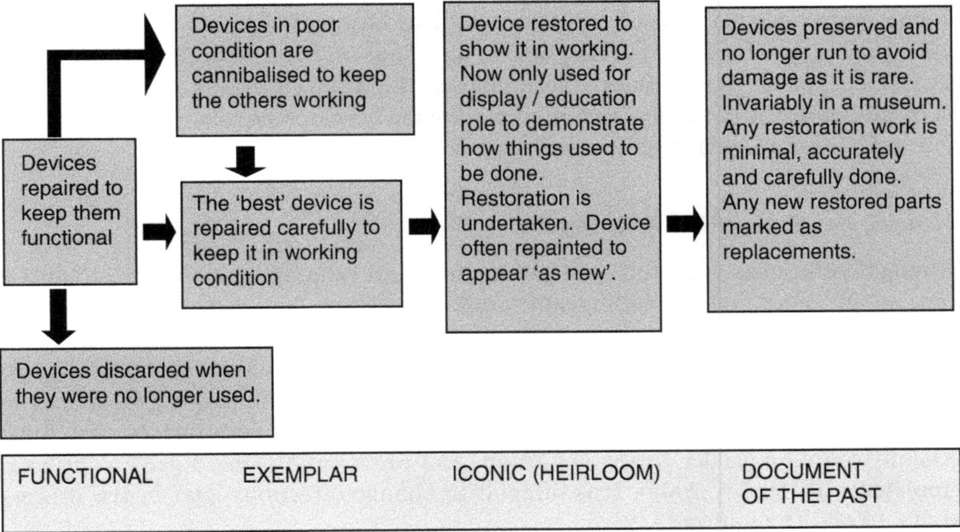

Figure 9.2 The movement from functioning object to preserved remains via repair and restoration. Chris Caple.

Individuals from the industries that made, maintained, and used working objects are often involved in their initial care. When an industry shuts down, or a mechanism (such as a vehicle) reaches obsolescence, there is often a brief window where former operators and manufacturers voluntarily sustain and restore the material remains of the industry/vehicle. Such individuals bring unique and detailed knowledge to the process but may prioritise the restoration of the object over the retention of evidence. An unconscious perception that an 'as new'/showroom ready look is correct can run deep. The role of the commercial product and the historic object can become confused, leading objects to be 'ruthlessly glamorised'[7] a state seen as desirable by many owners of historic vehicles. On the other hand, conservators who may be more attuned to the preservation needs of the object and more adept at balancing its historic nature with its modern appearance, often lack the specialist knowledge needed to restore the function of the item. In a plea for interdisciplinarity between organ builders and conservators, theorist and instruments conservator John Watson noted, 'the one who knows how to reconstruct a traditional feeder bellows is not the same person who can employ spectrographic examination methods to reveal evidence of the long-lost original' (2010: 10). Increasingly, museums, such as the National Air and Space Museum (Washington, DC) and the National Railway Museum (York, England), that curate large numbers of complex and highly specialised dynamic objects are building and maintaining multidisciplinary teams to care for and restore these objects. Within such teams, cross-disciplinary training, and respect for the expertise that each member brings are important commodities and can help to balance the potential for loss (either of material or functionality). Given the size of many working objects and the scale of conservation projects on them, large numbers of volunteers are often essential. If the community of volunteers do not enjoy the working environment, like each other's company, learn things, and have a project in which they can take pride, they will not come. Conserving industrial heritage requires enthusiasm, leadership, organisation, and funding and it can be difficult to draw all these elements together. While the first challenge of preserving large working objects may be as obvious as protecting them from the elements, the long-term issues of sustaining working objects in perpetuity are the real test of the conservator's ability and often require the development and nurturing of soft skills in addition to 'hands-on' conservation competencies.

Balancing the Roles of Working Objects

Although enthusiasts often focus on getting an object running, in a museum context a wider range of options including appearance, function, and preservation may be considered. Where multiple examples of an object exist, it is possible to select different examples for different roles. Where there is only a single example, it is necessary to consider which role or balance of roles it will have before commencing work as any decision will affect the extent of cleaning and restoration work and thus the cost. Such decisions should consider rarity, condition, and preservation (the degree of original completeness) (Barclay 2005). It is difficult to change directions later in the process (Mann 1994). The options are:

- Returning the object to its original function. Here the primary goal is seeing or hearing the object work and the approach may be more invasive. It means cleaning and checking that all parts work and are lubricated, ascertaining that they are safe to operate (guard rails are in place, operating instructions exist, users are trained, and parts meet modern safety codes), replacing worn and unsafe components, and obtaining operating licences and insurance for public operation if necessary.

- Preserving the object and retaining any evidence in or on it. Investigation is extensive; each part, when it was added or altered, repainted, etc. is recorded so that the object's history is understood. When the most fragile or at-risk parts of the object (where evidence may be most easily lost) are identified, they can be protected and regularly monitored. Cleaning may be very limited to preserve the evidence of operation. In some cases, preserving the object may mean returning it to use for a short time/single instance to record its sound or action (Case Study 9B: Organised Piano). This may be paired with replication; where the original object is preserved but a careful replica is made, based on the investigation of the original, that can demonstrate the object in action (Hoffmann 2013).
- Focusing on the appearance of the item at a particular point in its working life. Working condition may be a secondary consideration and the object may be static or only occasionally used. Any cleaning and restoration should balance the evidence lost against the improvement in appearance (and thus information for viewer). In this instance a restored finish may be seen as more informative or accurate than a poorly preserved but original finish and invasive surface intervention may be undertaken.

The approach to the object's cleaning and conservation depends on the values of all its parts (tangible and intangible) as well as its condition. Where it is rare, fragile, relatively complete, and has important historic information, greater emphasis may be placed on preserving the material (tangible) nature of the object. Where more common, more robust, and less complete more active cleaning and conservation activities can take place emphasising its intangible characteristics, which are a by-product of function (Barclay 2005; Lithgow *et al.* 2008). It should be noted, that although it is normal to run some types of working objects, others, such as firearms, are returned to working order less frequently. Weapons are often deliberately deactivated by removing the firing pin or filling the barrels for museum display. The benefits and the risks to the object, user, and viewer are all important to consider.

Balancing function, preservation, and appearance results in many different combinations (Figure 9.3). Where an individual object sits within these options is determined by the object, the stakeholders, the professional judgement of the conservators and curators, and the preserving institution's aims. A good example of such a discussion is the National Museum of Australia's decision to retain the *Sundowner*, the car famously driven by Francis Birtles in 1927 from London to Melbourne, in a state 'capable of operation' but uncleaned and not restarted. The museum retained the persistent oil leak the caked-on oil, and the scratches, dents, sand, mud, and grass from the journey arguing that the social history of the journey was every bit as important as the physical machine itself. Thorrowgood and Hallam, who treated the car, justified the decision, likening correcting faults and removing evidence to 'straightening the leaning tower of Pisa' or 'editing Shakespeare' (2004). Although such decisions are made every day, they are less commonly discussed in print.

	State	Actions	Essential Records
1	Working	Device continues to operate normally, though there may be restrictions on time, temperatures and pressures of operation to ensure continues to operate safely. Trained operators where needed, maintenance programme and log of maintenance and use.	O, C, N, A
2	Working occasionally	As above, but only working on a limited number of occasions to minimise wear and slowing decay to low levels. Times of operation advertised to maximise visitation. Worked by alternative means such as compressed air or a hidden electric motor.	O, C, N, A
3	Working once	Conserved / restored so it can run once and be recorded. Thereafter the recording can be played toshow motion / sound etc. Any temporary restoration undertaken to make it usable can be retained or reversed and object is kept in visible static condition. (Powell and Wills 2001)	O, C, N, A
4	Emulation / Pastiche	Original shell, new interior mechanisme.g. computer monitor in old TV showing old programmes, digital speaker in a radio playing music of the periodor an electric motor beneath an old car chassis. (X)	R
5	Replica	Replica of an original working object. Elements may be changed for safety,display and education reasons such as glass windows inserted to allow mechanism to be seen.	Accuracy should be recorded
6	Static (display)	Original shell and mechanism, remains on display. Cleaned and made safe for public viewing (public access controlled, elements of device shielded from public).It may be displayed in restored, partially restoredor unrestored condition.	O, C, N, A
7	Static (stored)	Original working object stored, normallyavailable for approved and trained researchers and requested viewings. Preserves all evidence of operation. Not intended ever to run again.No restoration or safety work undertaken on objectbut notices alert staff and approved researchers to any unsafe element of the device.Emphasis on preserving all the physical evidence rather than some by record.	
8	Spare	Working object to be used for spares to support working objects.	

O – The percentage of original parts should be recorded, key examples given.

C – The percentage of parts cannibalised from other machines should be recorded and key examples given.

N – The percentage of new parts should be recorded and key examples given. Any modern or newly made parts should be marked with date of creation so it is clear they are modern replacements and not original. They should wear at similar rate to the original so that try do not damage surrounding elements. New parts may be custom made to accommodate unusual size, voltage or other characteristics.

A – Any adaptations made for safe working should be recorded.

X – Provided no damage is done to the object carcass being used or the removed parts, and they are saved, this can be an ethical approach preserving both the historic object without damage or wear and giving the aesthetic experience of the working object.

R – Good records of the dismantling and the current location of the different parts shouldbe made.

Figure 9.3 Table of the principal forms in which working objects are displayed and stored in museums.

Many working objects consist of a mechanism (i.e. an action or engine) and a surrounding shell (i.e. the case and face of a clock or the bodywork of a car).

- Mechanism – may be mechanical, electromechanical, or electrical and when working may move and/or produce sound. Respecting the object's working value normally requires the mechanism to continue to operate either through repair or replacement. The original parts have value, and even when replaced, are often retained.
- Shell – protects the mechanism and often has a decorative surface that conveys information and/or appeals to the viewer through its colour and form. It signals attributes such as stylishness and wealth, as well as function, to the viewer. Layers of paint or repairs to the object are a valuable record of the object's history and evolving ideas of taste and economy in that society. Conservation may either preserve the final appearance or restore the colour and decoration to an earlier period in the object's life.

In some instances, different conservators may work on different components. For example, a furniture conservator may work on the shell of a tall-case clock while a metals conservator or a horologist may undertake repairs to the mechanism. Differences in the conservation approaches to the mechanism and the shell are based on the different values of each component. These differences are seen in the conservation of kinetic sculptures (the fusion of modern art with movement devices to add time and motion to artistic expression). The mechanism often fails due to component wear (reminding us that not all working objects are designed or built for long-term repeated use) generating ethical issues regarding replacing original parts (Rivenc and Bec 2018). Conservators approaching such objects recognise the key point of such sculptures is their movement and have consequently been prepared to repair, remake, or replace the functional element. As many electrical components quickly become obsolete and unobtainable, this may result in attempts to emulate their actions with later components rather than true replacement (Wolfe and Wood 2020). The aesthetic element may be treated like other artworks, retaining as much of the original as is present, while restoring areas of damage and loss so that the artist's original intent is recovered and can be experienced.

For non-working objects, simple storage in a benign environment may be appropriate. However, where there are surfaces that move over one another, are under tension, load, or pressure, and contain sealed compartments where corrosion may occur, it is important to consider what is the most appropriate method of 'static' storage. Should things be left under tension? Should the tension be reduced or removed? Should components (especially polymer and rubber components such as tyres) be routinely moved to prevent distortion? A number of measures are necessary to safely store large working objects. For example, aircraft wings should be supported to avoid bending or breaking due to constant static load in one direction, vehicles should be placed on axle stands to allow tires to be rotated and engines with oil in them may need to be hand cranked to lubricate the parts and prevent gaskets and seals from failing (Wain 2017: 84–85). Although it may seem less expensive and even easier to remove working objects from use, it is never as simple as simply placing them on a shelf and leaving them. The decision to place them in storage should be undertaken carefully and thoughtfully and with a recognition that on-going maintenance and engagement will remain a reality of their care (Wain 2017).

Socially Active Objects

Working objects are not the only types of objects where it is important to consider the intangible nature of the pieces. Many collections contain objects that are socially active. These objects express and embody (often literally) the beliefs, identities, traumas, and traditional cultural practices of modern groups and communities. Socially active objects include but are not limited to:

- Sacred Objects – objects created for veneration or imbued with the essence of a divinity or holy individual. Sacred objects may be routinely used in a variety of rituals that can involve wearing, touching, kissing, carrying, and exhibiting the objects and even renewing or remaking them. Many sacred objects are also venerated through prayers and offerings. In some instances, offerings are made at a remove, such as laying flowers in front of a shrine, but in others they are applied directly to the object itself, such as the Hindu tradition of pouring milk on a Shiva Lingam. Sacred objects, and the beliefs they embody, may be linked to other forms of intangible heritage, such as song (chants, hymn), or dance, that are important to consider and preserve as well.
- Objects associated with superstitions – often these are secular objects around which a legend centres (Figure 9.4). Interactions with the object are believed to bring good fortune to individuals or, in some cases, ill fortune to their rivals.
- Objects from Indigenous and World Cultures – although such objects may include ceremonial and sacred objects, they may also include functional, everyday objects that permit identities to be negotiated, maintained, and expressed. Traditional forms of knowledge, information about lineage, or prerogative, may be transmitted through the choice of materials and the patterns and motifs used to decorate the objects. For diasporic populations and for communities where colonial intrusions have disrupted traditional hierarchies and the transfer of traditional knowledge, engagement with objects in collections around the world can facilitate cultural revitalisation (Seip 1999; Case Study 9 C: Tlingit basket). The importance of using the appropriate indigenous terminology for plants and other materials in (conservation) documentation, as a means of supporting language revitalisation efforts and helping to preserve another aspect of intangible culture often associated with objects from these cultures has been noted (Pearlstein 2021).

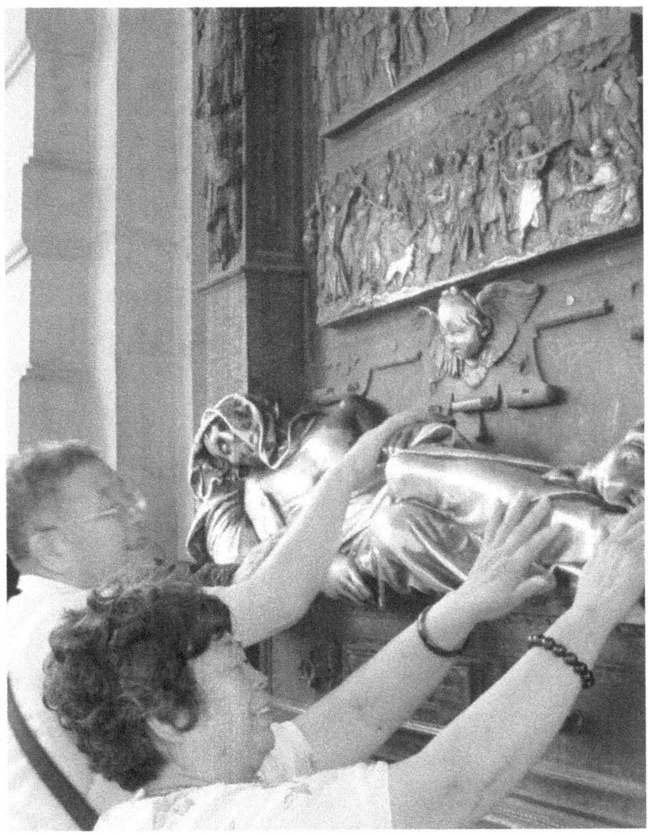

Figure 9.4 Monument to Everard t'Serclaes by Julien Dillens (1902) in Brussels. Touching the statue is said to bring luck and to grant wishes. The wear from countless hands is visible in the loss of patina and the wear on features such as the cherub's face. Emily Williams.

- Ceremonial objects – these objects exemplify the power, status and identities of individuals, nations, or organisations.[8] They often include ornamental items made of precious materials, such as crowns and other regalia, as well as thrones and other seats of power, but may include more vernacular items, such as miners' banners. They are retained for occasional use (often annual but sometimes less frequent) and are stored carefully, meaning that many can be of considerable age. Many are displayed when not in use. For example, the Lord Mayor of London's coach, built in 1757 and considered to be the oldest ceremonial vehicle in regular use in the world, is exhibited at the Museum of London for approximately 50 weeks of the year. In late October, it is taken from the museum, serviced, and used to transport the Lord Mayor of London from Mansion House to the Royal Courts of Justice to swear allegiance to the reigning monarch before being returned to the museum (Boylan 2006).[9] The recent history of the Stone of Scone demonstrates the power that ceremonial objects can hold within a country's national mythos even after hundreds of years.[10] It is important to note that ceremonial objects may embody a mixture of social, political, and spiritual significance and that each element must be considered when approaching their treatment or care.

- Monuments – although not all monuments are socially active, either because the individual or moment they commemorate has been largely forgotten or is uncontested, many are and may serve as lightning rods for controversy. Their presence on landscapes offers physical sites where abstract ideas can be negotiated and power dynamics can be contested and/or reaffirmed (Chidester and Linenthal 1995) (Figure 9.5). Decisions about how to conserve public monuments may involve complex political, social, cultural, or aesthetic considerations as was the case during the lengthy treatment of the statue of Kamehameha I (Wharton 2011) or the Statue of Liberty (Case Study 3A).

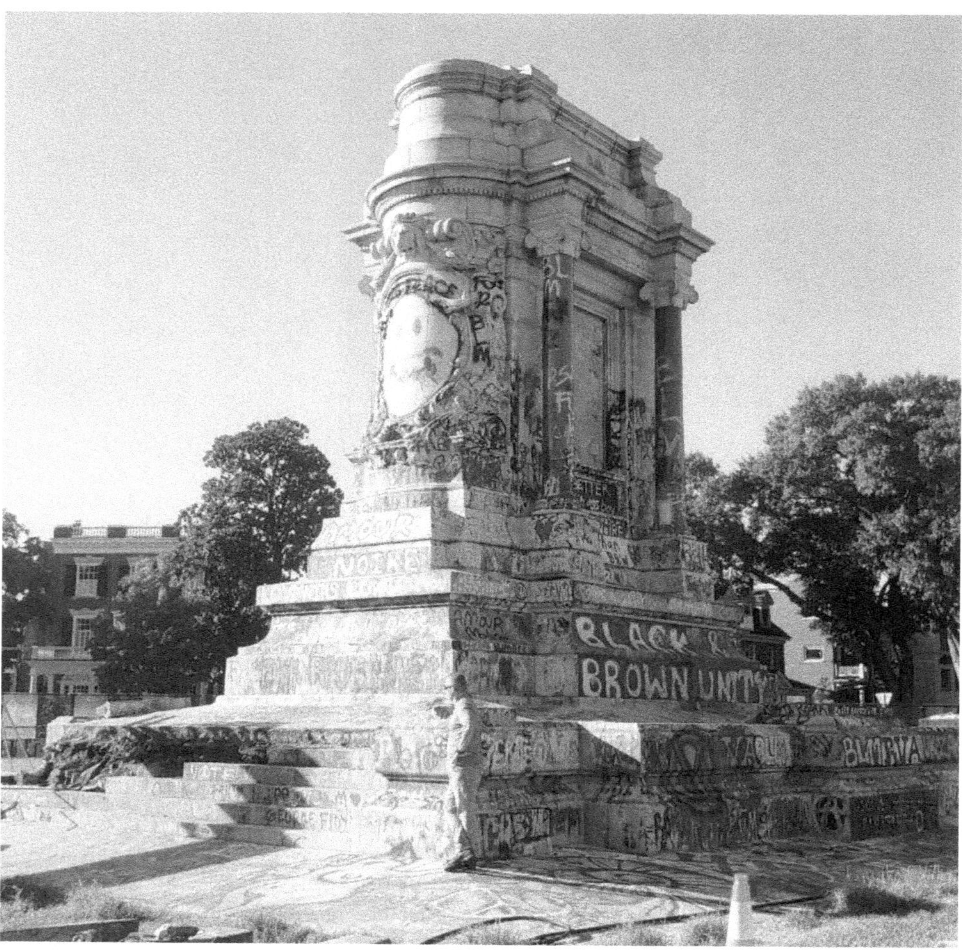

Figure 9.5 Black lives matter themed graffiti on the base of the (removed) Robert E. Lee statue in Richmond, VA. Graffiti such as this poses a challenge for conservators and city managers. It represents a form of social discourse and civic engagement for some but is challenging to others. Should it be retained as evidence of a historic moment or documented and removed as an eye sore? Katherine Ridgway.

- Objects and sites of trauma – such objects and places are the survivors of war, genocide, assassination, terrorist attacks, and natural disasters. They are emotionally laden and engage with viewers calling on them to remember and bear witness. Exhibiting and conserving them requires a careful balance between stabilisation and not removing or altering the damage that gives them power. Discussing the treatment of the Ladder 3 truck in the National September 11 Memorial Museum, which became a symbol of resilience for New York City Firefighters after it was heavily damaged when the North Tower collapsed, Jane Klinger noted that the twinned themes of survival and destruction, reverence, and fear, had to be balanced in all the decision-making (Klinger 2013). The latter were manifest in the 9/11 dust that still coated part of the truck. The dust held the potential to contain toxic chemicals (a source of fear) but also minute quantities of human remains (a cause for reverence). Decisions about cleaning had to weigh both elements but also had to consider how a mangled truck that looked sparklingly clean might read for visitors. Time, location, and the type of trauma may change the delicate balance between pathos and presentation and mean that there is a continual process of renegotiation and rebalancing. At sites associated with World War I and World War II, exposure to the elements and the resultant decay still prompts difficult decisions about whether to retain decaying original (historic) material or to replace it to better support the process of memorialisation and witnessing (Curry 2010).
- Human remains and ancestor objects – death is a biological process, but it is also a social process that is invested with deep spiritual, social, and mnemonic significance. As a result, human remains hold deep fascination for many, spiritual significance for others (Beck 2001; Dahl 2020), and political importance for some (Laroche and Blakey 1997). Humans have used their bodies as canvases for expressing their identities and beliefs for millennia. Practices like tattooing, piercing, tooth modification, and ritual scarification permanently alter bodies while temporary alterations include hairstyles, clothing, and adornment. Diet, disease, past medical practices, kinship, places of origin, labour practices, and burial practices can all be studied through careful analysis of human remains (Case Study 7 A: Lindow Man). Interest in extracting data from human remains has often led other values to be overshadowed, particularly in the Western scientific tradition where a clear distinction between the living and the dead is understood to exist. This has often led human remains to be treated differently from the grave goods found with them (Cassmann 2001) and even curated separately. In non-western and indigenous cultures, the distinction between the dead and the living and the objects buried with them can be more fluid. Kinship and ancestral relationships can be understood in ways that transcend simple genealogical descent. Objects may be imbued with the spirit or essence of an individual (often the maker or primary user) or clan and may be understood to be 'living' embodiments of that ancestor (Sully 2007). Such objects may demand certain levels of care from their descendants while at the same time reinforcing the social ties within those communities (Swieringa 2021).
- Contemporary art – some contemporary artworks seek to challenge public perception, provoke a response from the media and/or develop, and inform public opinion. These socially active objects are often at their most powerful shortly after their creation and may gradually lose their power to challenge

> and engage the viewer in critical discourse as time progresses. For example, Impressionist artists sought to challenge the academy, encouraging new forms of seeing and a focus on movement and ordinary subject matter. Initially their work was derided and heavily critiqued, and the artists were forced to establish alternative exhibits outside the mainstream ones to sell their art. Today many of their works are regarded as part of the artistic canon and Impressionism is so well accepted that package holidays visit the homes of Impressionist painters and Impressionist paintings command eye-watering prices in art sales (Loft 2019).

Socially active objects may require very different levels of conservation depending on why they are active and to whom. For example, some contemporary works of art actively utilise inherent vice[11] to provoke viewer interactions. Dieter Roth created a series of chocolate and birdseed busts in the 1960s to explore the inevitable transformation of the human body. The temporary nature of these works was important to his concept and his intent was that they would be exhibited outside. Many have subsequently been acquired by museums and although they may accept the inevitable transformation and decay of the chocolate, conservation efforts have focused on preventing them from becoming a vehicle for the deterioration of other collections. To this end, pest management strategies have been employed (Assis 2022), but restoration has been avoided. In the case of Janine Antoni's chocolate sculptures, *Lick and Lather* and *Gnaw*, however, desire is part of the message and so Antoni wants viewers to be able to get close, to smell the material, and even potentially to interact with it (Cembalest 2013). She recasts the chocolate busts if they are damaged, and conservators maintain a stock of the same chocolate to effect smaller repairs. Visitor engagement is often a key element of contemporary art. Felix Gonzalez Torres' work *Untitled (Portrait of Ross in LA)* consists of a spill of candy that commemorates the loss of his partner, Ross Laycock, from AIDS. The shape of the spill is less important than its weight, roughly 175 pounds (79 Kg), Laycock's weight when healthy. Visitors are invited to take a piece of candy away and the institution hosting the work is asked to replenish the candy regularly to maintain the same approximate weight.[12] As the spill of candy diminishes, it parallel's Laycock's own weight loss due to the disease while the restocking of the candy metaphorically grants perpetual life but also symbolises the invisibility that many AIDS victims suffered. In this instance, the medium of the work is edible (a potential risk) and the desire for the visitor to interact with it is integral (another risk); therefore, conservation cannot impact either element but may seek to limit the impact of the risks through the placement of the spill within the gallery and increased pest management.

In contrast to this minimalist approach, ceremonial objects often receive more interventive approaches. Frequently, it is important for them to convey a sense of power and prestige. Therefore, such objects are cleaned, polished, and maintained frequently to keep them in a condition that mimics their 'as new' appearance. In Western traditions, this may mean that when, and if, they become damaged or worn, invasive restoration techniques, such as reshaping or replacement, may be routinely undertaken. Additionally, alterations may be made that would not be considered if the piece were merely a historic item. Reinforcing elements have been added to some historic seats of power and some ceremonial vehicles have been retrofitted to permit the addition of bulletproof glass and other safety devices. Since many ceremonial objects are made of precious materials and their loss could cause public humiliation, security may play an outsized role in their care and curation. When such objects are retired or replaced, they are often formally decommissioned in a ceremonial way, and it is common for them to become museum exhibits, if they were not previously. When this occurs, the object begins to transition towards being a historical object and may lose some of its social activity, a process which inevitably changes how the conservator is asked to engage with it and the levels of care that may be seen to be appropriate for it.[13]

This process of museumification[14] may not be appropriate for all socially active objects. Discussing the conservation efforts carried out by the George Floyd Global Memorial, Jeanelle Austin (2021) noted that the end goal is not to create a museum but rather to create a 'rememory', a term taken from Toni Morrison's novel *Beloved*, in which the grief, protest, and hope that motivated people to memorialise Floyd's death are reexperienced and the visitor is commissioned to go out and do something more (to take the protest further and to work to enact change). To serve this goal, the 'street conservation' practised by the caretakers at the site takes a minimalist approach in which damage is accepted and even embraced. Conservation is enacted intentionally but with the preservation of the story taking precedence over the materiality of the piece (Austin 2021). The act of conserving the material is principally seen as a mechanism for continued participation in the protest for racial equity and an act of healing. This emphasis varies from the 'traditional' Western conservation viewpoint, which has tended to be positivist, scientific, and data-driven (and to draw heavily on concepts derived from Enlightenment era thinking as we saw in Chapters 1 and 2). Traditionally, the view of many indigenous groups have also varied from the Western one.[15] For them, the idea of prolonging the existence of an object is not seen as natural (Clavir 2002: 123). Objects were viewed as having a fixed life span in which they fulfilled a purpose and when they are damaged or no longer served the function for which they were created, they were remade and the original was allowed to decay or was buried or burnt. Speaking about Totem Poles, Gloria Cranmer-Webster, Kwakwaka'wakw, noted 'many Indian people feel that once a pole has served its purpose it should be allowed to go back into the ground. I think this attitude has a lot to do with the way Indian people look at the objects. The objects themselves are not important; what matters is what the objects represent. They represent the right to own that thing, and that right remains even if the object decays or is otherwise lost' (Cranmer-Webster 1986). Don Bain, Lheit-lit'en (Carrier) nation, notes that although one object may replace another one, it takes on its own identity – 'the knowledge that is contained within the object is important, but [it] can be transferred to another object' (cited in Clavir 2002: 122). The new version of the object does not have to follow the form of the older object perfectly but rather may draw from a shared decorative language. For a conservator working on such material, it is important to understand the culture and the worldview that created the object and to be thoughtful about how that impacts the conservation approach they may take and how in turn the conservation impacts the object.

Many religious objects remain symbols of belief that are actively used in the present day. If the object is valued for its evidentiary value as well as its intangible values, this can lead to conflict between the care of the object and the needs and desires of the faithful. Molina and Pincemin (1994) recount an example where conservators adopted a minimally interventive approach to the cleaning and restoration of medieval polychrome statues in Northern France, only to face dissatisfaction from congregations who expected to see the surfaces refreshed. Similar disappointments have been documented in Norway (Spaarschuh and Kempton 2020: 365). They reflect a desire by the congregation to honour their deity and to see the objects as items of devotion, contemplation, and beauty. These interactions also stem from an overemphasis by the conservators on the historical/evidentiary values of the items rather than their intangible ones. In some instances, the local community subsequently undertook the repainting of the images themselves (Molina and Pincemin 1994). By working more closely with the community to manage expectations and/or adopting a more people-centred approach that addresses the needs of the community in the treatment design, a more successful outcome might have been achieved.

People-Centred Conservation and Consultation

People-centred approaches to the conservation of sacred items and other socially active objects build on the understanding that the complex biographies that objects often have do not solely spring from their travels through time but also from their interactions with the communities and individuals for whom they are meaningful. People-centred conservation approaches therefore seek to consider how the conservator's work impacts the community that cares about the collections. Instead of relying on the notion that whoever owns heritage decides how it will be conserved, these approaches seek to involve those for whom the heritage is meaningful, empowering communities to participate in substantive decision-making about the care of collections (Clavir 2002; Peters 2008; Krmpotich *et al.* 2013; Sully and Cardoso 2014; Henderson and Nakamoto 2016; Swierenga 2021). Such approaches may seek to understand the significance of the artifact and the beliefs embedded in it and adapt treatments to accommodate them. For example, Drumheller and Kaminitz (1994) note that after recognising that many Native American objects are viewed as living objects led the National Museum of the American Indian to change its approach to pest management leading to the use of more traditional and nature-based approaches (such as cedar and naturally occurring insect repellent plant secretions) and utilised fewer toxic approaches such as fumigation and freezing that might 'kill' the object.[16] At the Museum of Anthropology at the University of British Columbia (MOA), it is understood that many ceremonial objects 'play important roles in expressing family lineages and inherited rights and privileges' that are of importance to the cultural survival of the communities that created them and that as such the non-material, intangible elements should be weighed heavily when considering any risks to the material aspects of pieces that might result from loans or use (Swierenga 2021). The minor alterations that are at times necessary for, or that result from, use (activation) are viewed not as damage but as valued changes demonstrating the continued lives of the objects.[17] Conservators work closely with community members to ensure that the appropriate balance is struck between the tangible and intangible components of the materials and that one is not valued more highly than the other. Careful consultation (Chapter 10), a willingness to listen, and flexibility are at the heart of this work. The conservator does not abandon their duty of care for the objects but rather seeks to find solutions that can accommodate and preserve all the possible meanings of the object. Peters (2008) has noted that conservators engaged in these processes do not represent either the people or the objects but rather aim to work with the outcome of the connections between the people and the objects, strengthening them and ensuring their successful and sustainable development.

Adopting people-centred approaches and undertaking consultations can be difficult for conservators. There are no blueprints for success since each case will be different based on the stakeholders involved, the object under discussion and its needs as well as the history of engagement that may have taken place. For conservators new to the process, it can feel as if their proficiency is being challenged and this can be particularly difficult given the time and training that it can take to build such expertise. Ellen Pearlstein (2021) also notes that reconciling differences between indigenous knowledge and the results of scientific findings can feel problematic at times and that this can strain the process. Interactions with stakeholders who have experience working with conservators and familiarity with conservation approaches will be different from interactions with stakeholders who are unfamiliar with the process. Limited resources and distance from source communities can impose restrictions on the adoption of these sorts of approaches. Although virtual consultations are a possibility, they are dependent on infrastructure to support them, and this may not always be in place. Additionally, building the mutual trust and understanding needed to conduct and sustain meaningful engagements often relies on shared activities and experiences (such as shared meals, workshops, etc.) and this can be difficult to replicate virtually.

The adoption of people-centred approaches recognises that in addition to being a technical and scientific process, conservation is a social one (Eastop 2006; Peters 2008) and that this puts a responsibility on conservators to consider and respond to wider social, economic, and political factors to ensure that their work is relevant, sustainable, and does not harm others. Although people-centred approaches originated in legally mandated consultation processes that sought to address the very disparate power dynamics between museums and collecting bodies and indigenous communities (Wharton 2005; Johnson *et al.* 2005), increasingly, as museums are pushed to broaden access to other marginalised communities and to the public, such approaches are being extended to include other constituencies. For example, the Museum of London has used people-centred approaches to curation and conservation projects aimed at engaging and reskilling homeless and unemployed populations (Ganiaris and Lang 2013). The conservation efforts carried out by the George Floyd Global Memorial is guided by the idea that the people are more sacred than the memorial itself and that every offering (object left at the memorial) is somebody's offering, so it is important to ensure that everyone's voice is heard and that their story is told (Austin 2021). The responsibilities that engaging with the social aspects of conservation brings will be examined in further detail in Chapter 11.

9A Case Study: The Forth Railway Bridge (Paxton 1990, Glen *et al.* 2012)

In the 1880s, the North British Railway needed to bridge the Firth of Forth to complete its railway link between Edinburgh and Dundee. Designed by the engineers Sir Benjamin Baker and Sir John Fowler, the Forth Railway Bridge comprises three huge cantilevers with viaducts at each end, the whole edifice spanning 1.5 miles. It was only the second cantilevered bridge in Europe and is the world's second-longest single cantilever span at 1,709 ft. Construction necessitated the use of steel to withstand the stresses created by the form, rather than cast iron, the normal material for metal bridge construction of this period. The construction of the bridge, between 1882 and 1890, cost approximately £3 million and was undertaken by a consortium led by William Arral of Glasgow. It consumed 740,000 cubic ft. of granite, 48,000 cubic yards of stone, 64,300 cubic yards of concrete, and 54,160 tons of steel held together with 6.5 million rivets (*The Sunday Times* 1995). The monumental structure was deliberately created in such a sturdy form to withstand the ferocious North Sea gales that had collapsed the Tay Railway Bridge in December 1879. The Forth Railway Bridge opened as a functioning railway bridge on 4 March 1890 and continues to be used by over 200 trains a day (Glen *et al.* 2012; Figure 9.6).

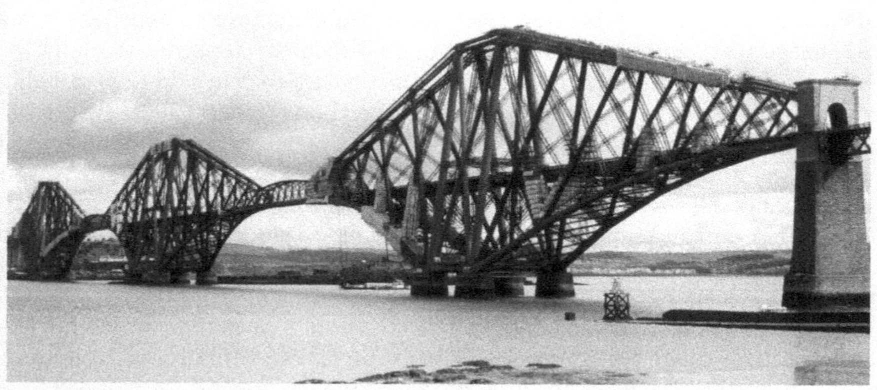

Figure 9.6 The Forth Railway Bridge. Its size and exposed position require a continuous maintenance programme that is funded by the continued use of the bridge as a functioning railway bridge. Chris Caple.

From the outset, a regular routine of repainting was essential to maintain this bridge, particularly its 145 acres of steel. This herculean task involved rubbing down of the metalwork with wire brushes and metal scrappers followed by painting with several coats of the distinctive red lead-based 'Forth Bridge Red' paint manufactured by Craig & Rose of Leith Walk, Edinburgh. By 1993, the maintenance programme consumed 1,000 gallons of paint, employed 16 painters as part of a forty-strong workforce and cost £600,000 per annum

(Bowditch 1993). The idea that the painters started at one end and worked their way to the other end, only to restart at the beginning is a modern myth. Instead, they tackle those areas that are in most urgent need of repainting. The painting of the Forth Railway Bridge has, however, passed into everyday usage as a metaphor for any unending task.

From 1989 onwards, the regime of wire brushing was replaced with shot-blasting, a more effective way to remove the old paint. The metal thus exposed was covered within four hours using a primer followed by two undercoats and finally two topcoats of the distinctive 'Forth Bridge Red' paint. The original lead-based paint was replaced with an iron oxide-based primer and undercoat, and vinyl-alkyl-based topcoat. Where possible the undercoats and topcoats were normally sprayed on to ensure even coverage. In 1993, attempting to save money, the owner of the bridge, British Rail (Railtrack from 1994), was reported in *The Times* as suspending the maintenance programme for a year (Bowditch 1993). Although the bridge was floodlit in 1991 and Railtrack spent £3 million in 1994 strengthening and renewing the railway line running over the bridge to allow trains to traverse the bridge at up to 50 mph rather than the previous 20 mph, by 1996 Railtrack was required by the Health and Safety Executive to start an emergency maintenance programme or risk prosecution (*The Times* 1996). The impression given was that the owner, Railtrack, had cut the maintenance schedule to a minimum. Following a review in 1996–1997, Railtrack announced a £40 million programme of repairs and repainting for the bridge running from 1998 to 2001 (Railway Technology 2012).

In 2002, Network Rail replaced Railtrack as owners of Britain's railways, including the Forth Railway Bridge, and agreed to a £130 million contract with Balfour Beatty to restore and renovate the bridge. This involved working along the bridge, covering it section by section in scaffolding and polymer sheeting to create an enclosure around each original girder to keep it dry and trap waste. Working inside the enclosure, any defective steelwork was replaced, the old lead paint and corrosion were blasted off with abrasive copper slag grit at 120 psi and the clean bare steel surface repainted with a three-coat paint system consisting of (1) zinc phosphate primer, (2) a tough protective 400-micron thick glass-flake epoxy coating capped with an acrylic urethane topcoat giving UV protection, and (3) the traditional 'Forth Bridge Red' colour (manufactured by Leigh Paints now Sherwin-Williams Paints). This paint system is identical to that used on North Sea Oil rigs and is designed to last 20–25 years before replacement is needed. The waste from the process, lead paint dust and grit, was collected and disposed of safely. The shielded environment and spray coating resulted in a faultless protective coating (Andrew 2011; Glen *et al.* 2012). The Victorian steelwork was found to be in excellent condition, virtually no metalwork replacement was required.

Although William Morris described the bridge as 'the supremist specimen of all ugliness' (*The Sunday Times* 1995), more recent critics have seen it as a structure of beauty and merit (Black 1997). It has become a heritage icon in Scotland – appearing in books, TV, films, computer games, advertising, and on banknotes and coins – providing an identity based on engineering achievement rather than tartans or romantic castles. Historic Scotland recognised its importance to the national psyche and listed the structure in 1973. UNESCO inscribed the bridge as a World Heritage Site on July 5, 2015, recognising it as 'an extraordinary and impressive milestone in bridge design and construction during the period when railways came to dominate long-distance land travel'. Its listing as an 'ancient monument' gives protection against deliberate human damage, but it is the bridge's maintenance regime and its paint coating that provide protection against the weather. The importance of the original colour and form of the bridge was acknowledged by British Rail, Railtrack and later Network Rail and Balfour Beatty who retained the original paint colouring in the final coat of their repainting regimes.

Once people begin to treasure any particular part of the past, it ceases to be retained purely for its functionality, it is also retained for its social and historic value, its aesthetic qualities and its value as evidence documenting the historic past. This raises the question: to what extent is the repainting of the Forth Railway Bridge an act of conservation? The repainting of the structure undoubtedly preserves the Forth Railway Bridge. Although the original paint has long since been lost to the effects of wire brushing and shot blasting, the original steelwork is preserved through this process and the original colour and finish of the object is clearly restored through the cleaning and repainting process.

In the case of the Forth Railway Bridge the maintenance costs are huge and at present can only be met whilst this bridge is part of a functioning railway. No heritage agency could fund these repair and repainting costs. Smaller bridges, such as the one at Ironbridge Gorge, are of a scale that they can be successfully conserved purely as monuments. The Forth Railway Bridge's role as a working object is manifest every time a train thunders over it. Only when the bridge ceases to be a functioning railway bridge, which may be well into the future, will we discover whether the Scottish public treasure it sufficiently to see it conserved and are prepared to meet the full (and continuing) costs of preservation.

9B Case Study: The Organised Upright Grand Piano (Watson n.d.; Watson 2014; Bridges 2016)

In 2012, The Colonial Williamsburg Foundation acquired a combination of six-stop pipe organ and upright grand piano, known as an 'Organised Upright Grand Piano'. It was created in 1799 for one of Williamsburg's most prominent families. The instrument was in unaltered condition, untouched by past restoration, but it survived in a disassembled state with loose parts that were too weak and damaged to be assembled without conservation. It was missing its piano action, which had been discarded early in the object's history, and most of the trapwork for switching between the piano and organ. The 256 original lead pipes were mangled and crumpled and had, in some cases, been chewed by rodents. For most people, the boxes of fragments and individual pieces might not have warranted a second look but for John Watson, then Colonial Williamsburg's Curator and Conservator of Instruments, the object was an important item that he had been researching and pursuing for much of his career at the Foundation. In recognising the object's value as a historic document, Watson began a process that helped to define its significance. This is not an uncommon role for curators, conservators, archaeologists, and other knowledgeable individuals to play in ensuring the survival of historic objects. As both the curator and conservator of this object, he was uniquely placed to understand its values and to work to preserve them.

The only surviving example of an organised upright piano,[18] the instrument was a powerful status symbol. St. George Tucker (1752–1827), the scion of a wealthy and influential Bermudian family, came to Williamsburg at age 19 to study law under George Wythe. Tucker fought in the American Revolution and later served as a judge and as a Professor of Law at the College of William and Mary, 'through his cultivation of business and political relationship, maintenance of loyal kinship bonds ... and marriages to widows from other leading families, [he] served as a virtual CEO of a far-reaching enterprise' (Watson 2014). For such a wealthy, powerful, and influential individual, the presence of a complex, fashionable, and unusual instrument, made in England and imported at cost, would have signalled his global connections, while its decoration in the 'neat and plain' style favoured in the new Republic, signalled his loyalties. At nearly 9' tall 7' wide (2.92 m) and 18' deep (0.45 m), the presence of the organised piano would have been hard to miss. It was likely the most complex domestic instrument in the state of Virginia if not the country.

As acquired, the instrument was a powerful document of an unusual and historically important period in instrument manufacture. An inscription on the nameboard tied it to an important firm of 18th-century instrument dealers and additional inscriptions within the instrument itself related it to a significant maker of keyboards and an early 19th-century restorer with links to important figures in the state of Virginia. There was a powerful argument to be made for leaving the instrument as it was and preserving it as an unsullied record. Indeed, this was in keeping with the Foundation's approach to the acquisition of musical instruments, which advocated for the restoration of instruments only when previous restoration had already contributed to the loss of those elements most commonly replaced during refurbishment. On the other hand, as a collection of fragments, the instrument was hard to read and could never be exhibited. Additionally, its 'voice' could not be heard. As the single survivor of its type, this meant that important information about the object's nature including the sounds it produced, which are unique and characteristic of the period, would not be recovered or appreciated.

After careful consideration, the decision was made to restore the instrument using an approach known as 'restorative conservation' (Watson 2010). Restorative conservation seeks to fuse the goals of conventional instrument restoration (which often prioritises form and sound over substance) with preservation (the protection of substance as a bearer of historical information). In this instance, the musical and aesthetic qualities were restored using non-traditional and state-of-the-art conservation methods that aimed to preserve the historical evidence that might otherwise be lost in conventional instrument restoration. The goal was not to make the instrument playable on a daily basis, but rather to put the instrument back together and permit the sound (an intangible aspect) to be recorded and communicated to visitors. As a result, less invasive and less permanent approaches could be taken where warranted.

The work undertaken included careful documentation of every facet of the piece. Most of the crushed pipes were reshaped and the holes in them were filled although several were left unrestored as documents of the object's history. The stop action for the organ was largely intact and was cleaned and repaired. A new piano action was made to replace the missing one using technical information from other upright grand pianos. Luckily, the replication of this element, which would normally take the most wear and tear, insured that the instrument could be played with minimal wear to the most vulnerable elements. Additionally, the bellows were re-leathers, missing knobs and veneers associated with the keyboard were replaced and the cloth front restored (Figure 9.7).

The treatment, which ultimately involved a team of 24 individuals including organ builders, piano restorers, researchers, upholstery conservators, material analysts, and furniture conservators, allowed an important piece of Virginian history to be fully appreciated. Not only could the unusual form of the instrument be viewed and understood but also the unique sound it produced could be experienced. Five different period appropriate pieces of music were recorded, and a video of the instrument being played was also made.[19]

Once treatment was complete, the organised piano was installed in the *Changing Keys* exhibit where it was shown along with other historic instruments. Different approaches to the restoration of each of these instruments were dictated by the condition of the instrument and by its past treatment. As a corpus, they preserve a wealth of important historical information including the changing appearance of historical keyboards, the variety of materials they were made from, evidence of the craftsmanship needed to produce them, and the sounds that they produced.

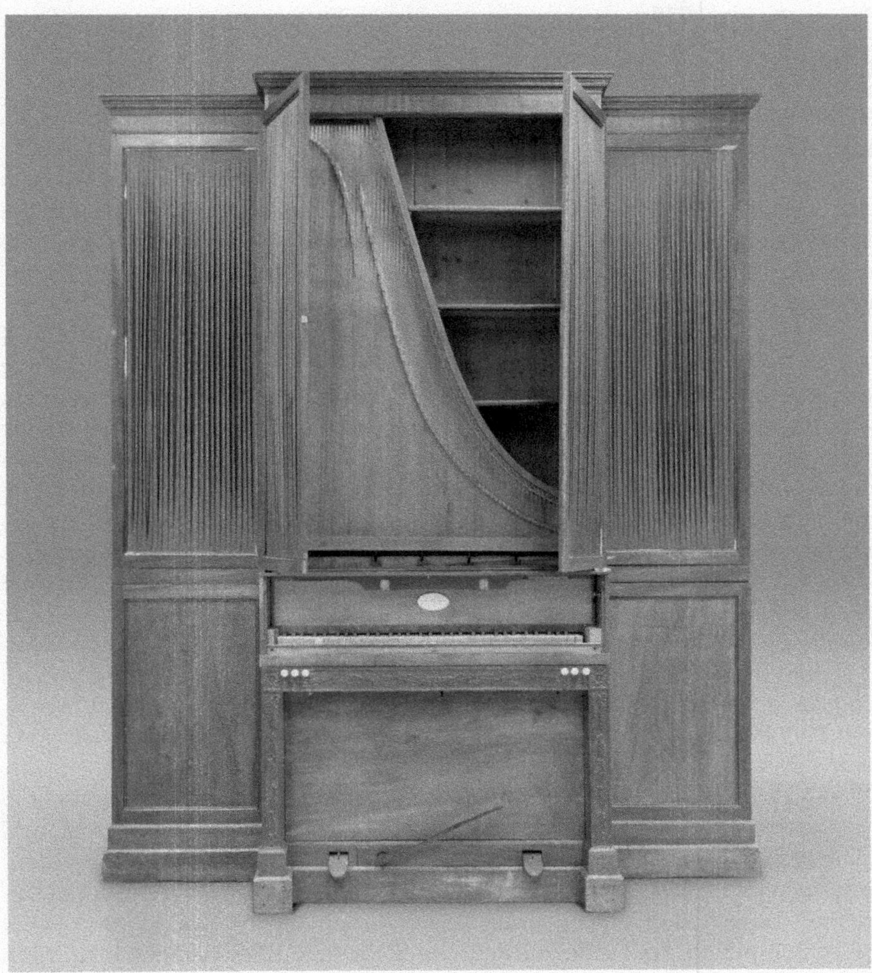

Figure 9.7 Organised Upright Grand Piano, after treatment. The Colonial Williamsburg Foundation. Museum Purchase. Conservation of this instrument is made possible by a gift from Constance Tucker and Marshall Tucker in memory of N. Beverly Tucker Jr.

9C Case Study: Conservation of a Tlingit Basket (Pouliot *et al.* 2017)

'Before me stands an old American Indian basket, it is a production of my own people. As I look and study its dilapidated form I feel as if it recognizes me, and my thoughts flash across thousands of miles, back to the land where we both belong, and then back to the age stained old piece before me. It seems to me that I have seen this before. Is not this the old 'Rest-in-shadow'? It may be that I only heard of it when I was yet too young to remember important things' (Shotridge 1921).

In 2007, a damaged Tlingit basket was sent to Winterthur/University of Delaware Program in Art Conservation (WUDPAC) with a short note expressing a hope that students could practice with it. The basket was in poor condition, which its packing and transport to Delaware had exacerbated. The rim was in several fragments, there were multiple tears throughout the basket, as well as a thick layer of dirt and debris (Figure 9.8). Normally an object in this condition might have been added to WUDPAC's study collection as something for students to sample and practice treatments on; however, Bruno Pouliot, a conservator at Winterthur and a professor in WUDPAC had recently returned from a trip to Alaska and saw a different potential for the object.

A graduate student on the WUDPAC course undertook a careful examination of the object, confirming that it was an older basket and worthy of treatment. During the examination process, the student contacted Teri Rofkar, a well-known Tlingit basket maker based in Sitka. Consultation with Rofkar helped to draw out details about the basket, its weave, and decoration.

When treatment was later undertaken on the basket, Rofkar again helped to guide the work, sharing insights about the behaviour of spruce root, and shaping the conservation goals. She was not averse to the addition of standard conservation materials but felt it was important to understand any products that might have been added in the past and to carefully clean the basket. Analysis of the dyes suggested a potential date for the object and UV examination showed that past owners had made a series of repairs in the past. No traces of the heavy metals associated with pesticides were identified on the basket, supporting a history of retention in private collections. Repairs were made to the basket using Japanese tissue and wheat starch paste to stabilise the tears in the body. The losses to the rim were not repaired as they required the addition of too much new material.

Rofkar dubbed the basket 'the old one' noting that 'we are the ones moving through the lives of these "old ones" rather than the other way around'. For Rofkar one of the key goals of the treatment was to allow 'the old one' to continue to share its experiences and to experience new things itself. Toxic treatments were to be avoided because they would limit both of those goals (Figure 9.8).

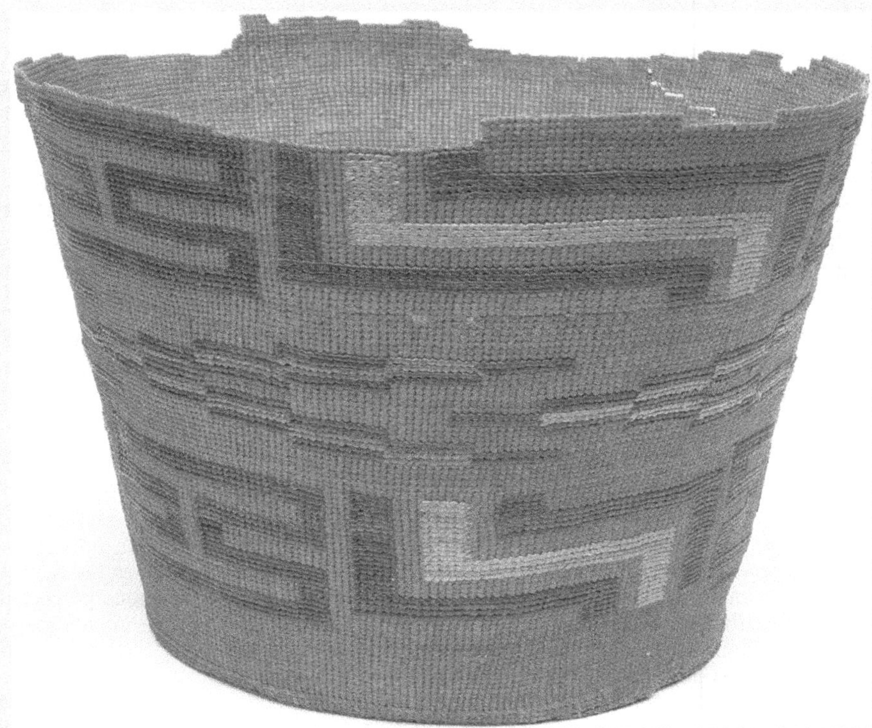

Figure 9.8 Tlingit basket, before treatment. Crista Pack.

In 2016, once the conservation was complete, the basket was given to Rofkar to take back to Sitka, to share with the community and to participate in her teaching about traditional basket weaving techniques. Such teaching helps to revivify cultural traditions and to pass traditional knowledge onto the next generation in indigenous communities. Rofkar used the basket in a series of programs including:

- Summer programs in the Sitka School District designed to deepen the teachers' understanding of traditional arts and traditions and demonstrate how basket making contributes to the skills acquisition in the classroom.
- The Sitka Native Education Program Berry Camp where children were permitted to hold it, learn about it and even place the sorts of berries it was originally designed to hold in it. For Rofkar one of the joys of this experience was watching the connections that modern children built with the old one and the way in which they used contemporary culture to understand and connect with it.
- A residency at the Sheldon Jackson Museum in Sitka in which Rofkar shared the artistry and techniques of basket making and in which the 'the old one' acted as a bridge between the modern weavings being demonstrated and older baskets carefully tended in cases within the museum.

Through the collaboration between conservators and traditional artists, 'the old one' has become an active object once again, building new connections with the people around it, experiencing the world, and creating new bridges between generations. It has served as a teacher both within and without the Tlingit community, and along with other similar objects is helping to revitalise Tlingit culture and to promote dialogues within the community that support and strengthen the Tlingit worldview and identity. Both the material characteristics embodied in its form and decoration and its intangible characteristics – its presence, its experiences, its personality – are vital aspects of its ability to act as a guide and both are worthy of preservation. 'The old one' and other objects like it are also helping to teach conservators how to work in new ways, to share authority and to look beyond simply the materials of which objects are made and consider all their meanings.

Notes

1 Gamelan is the traditional ensemble music of Indonesia. Primarily composed of percussive instruments, it also incorporates bamboo flutes, stringed instruments, such as the Siter and Rebab, and human voice and is traditionally used to accompany religious ceremonies, wayang puppet theatre, dance concerts, and other performances. The instruments are produced in traditional workshops, using craft techniques that are specific to the production of these instruments. The sounds produced by the multi-timbre ensemble are unique and are so deeply rooted in Indonesian culture that a popular saying holds that nothing is final until the final gong is hung. Imbued with spiritual significance, there are also ritually prescribed approaches and treatments to the instruments.

2 The movement, sound, smell, warmth, and vibration produced by machine are also characteristic of living creatures. It is not surprising that machines are often described as living (Wain 2017: 84). Musical instruments are said to have voices and breath (Watson 2010) and often described using anthropomorphised terms such as throat, belly, and mouth. People talk to machines, name them, and often have complex interactive relationships with them similar to those they may have with living creatures.

3 It should be noted that actions like changing the oil and replacing worn parts in working objects are not dissimilar to re-leading stain glass windows or revarnishing a painting. All are actions aimed at retaining the function of the object. However, the frequency and scale with which such actions may be carried out on working objects is what is sometimes seen as problematic.

4 However, it is important to note that while changing the source of power can produce cleaner, quieter experiences it can also fundamentally change the visitor's encounter and the sensory effect of the machine (Wain 2017).

5 The Silver Swan at the Bowes Museum in County Durham, England, an automaton dating to 1773, is only run once a day at a set time. For visitors, whose visits do not coincide with this, videos of the swan in action are available. Interestingly, lack of use during the Covid-19 pandemic in 2020/2021 caused the mechanism to seize up, pointing to the importance of even this limited use to the ongoing functioning of the object.

6 Although it has fewer wheels, a unicycle can still be understood through its similarities to the more familiar bicycle. While the shape and materials of many objects reveal their function, more recent electrical and computational devices often form a 'black box'. The function is not immediately clear and thus there is a greater need to show such devices at work (Newey 2000).

7 A term used by Ernst Van de Wetering to describe the restoration of works of art, but appropriately extended to historic vehicles (Van de Wetering 1996, 193).

8 Such organisations may include civic corporations, academic institutions, regiments, sporting associations, and fraternal orders, such as the Freemasons or Oddfellows.

9 This procession is known as the Lord Mayor's show.

10 Also known as the 'Stone of Destiny' or the 'Coronation stone' and traditionally used to crown the kings of Scotland the stone was forcibly removed from Scone Abbey by Edward I and taken to London in 1296. It was incorporated in a throne on which all subsequent monarchs of England and the United Kingdom were seated during their coronation. In 1950, Scottish nationalists stole the stone from Westminster Abbey. Although the stone was returned to England four months later the theft reinvigorated the nationalist cause. In 1996, the stone was returned to Scotland as a ceremonial response to rising Scottish nationalism.

11 Inherent vice is the tendency of an object to self-destruct or deteriorate due to the instability of the materials it is made of their incompatibility or poor construction that does not respect the character of the materials.

12 Although not necessarily carried out by conservators, this act of restoration may be seen as similar to the restoration carried out on *The Ambassadors* (Case Study 6 A) – a near invisible act that permits the artwork to function as the artist intended.

13 Other socially active objects may undergo similar processes. Writing about tombstones, Harold Mytum (2004) has noted that their social activity begins to diminish rapidly if relatives move or die. Exceptions to this may include war cemeteries, such as those in El Alamein or Normandy, where the massing of graves from a single conflict provides a focal point for memory, engagement, and reflection beyond the lives of those close to the deceased; and National burial sites, such as Arlington National Cemetery in the US or St. Paul's Cathedral in Britain, where the assembled burials and monuments reinforce aspects of the national identity. In the US, Canada, and Ireland, communities have recently re-engaged with African American graveyards (Palmer and Palmer 2015) and graves associated with Native schools and Magdalene laundries leading to recognition of the treatment of individuals and groups at these sites, strengthened community bonds, and in some cases legal redress.

14 Public perception of the museumification process typically consists of cataloguing, preservation actions that limit interaction with the object (i.e. 'please do not touch signs' or wearing white gloves to handle the object) and display in a glass case.

15 It is important to note that as there is a diversity of western views, there is a diversity of views among indigenous groups, First Nations and world cultures.

16 It should be noted that this example predates the formal use of the term 'People-centered conservation' however it clearly relates to this practice and remains an excellent one for showing how conservation practices can be altered to support community beliefs and values.

17 Although some conservators may express discomfort at the idea of a process that tolerates damage, it is something that we must remember occurs every day in museum settings as objects receive light damage from display or experience handling from being on open display. It is also important to note that if we only preserve the material components of objects, then damage is being done to their conceptual and intangible components.

18 Organised pianos were fashionable in the late 18th and 19th century but the ones that survived are all square pianos with a small number of organ pipes inserted below the action. The upright nature of this piano allowed a considerably larger number of pipes to be inserted. Fourteen British organised square pianos survive (Watson 2014:19).

19 An example of the unique sound of the organised piano can be heard at http://update.jrw1.com/top/1%20Haydn_Adagio_CMaj_Sonata%20(piano%20&%20organ%20together).mp3 (Accessed March 1, 2022).

10 Perception, Judgement, and Decision-making

Conservators, like many other professionals, face complex problems with numerous possible solutions. They must identify what the problems are, determine the options for dealing with them, decide on the solutions and then enact them. There are frequently no simple answers; every intervention to a historic or artistic object requires careful judgement. Successful conservation depends on the conservator knowing what the object is, where it comes from, what it relates to (context), the materials it is composed of, how those materials decay, and the various measures that could be implemented to clean, stabilise, and preserve the object. Crucially, successful outcomes also depend on the conservator's ability to determine (or judge) which interventive or preventive measures are most appropriate to implement. Judgement, or the weighing of knowledge leading to a decision, includes considering the ethical issues, the extent to which intervention is warranted, the resources available, the wishes of the object's owner, the risk of damage to the object, and any health and safety implications, as well as other factors, such as the values inherent in the object. This can be challenging for those entering the field, who may seek defined 'rules' or prescriptive approaches, and for allied professionals who may find the variability of approaches demanded challenging.

Perception

It is comforting to think that we all perceive the same thing when looking at the same object; unfortunately, this is not the case. The process of viewing and identifying the object is, in large part, a mental process involving our memories and experiences, meaning that we all perceive what we see slightly differently.

Perception begins when light bounces off an object and enters the eyes. The light is focussed by the cornea and lens onto the light-sensitive retina cells at the back of the eye. These cells act as transducers and convert the photons of light into electrical impulses that pass through the optic nerve to the visual cortex of the brain. Different retinal cells (i.e. rod and cones), are more or less sensitive to different light levels while different photo-pigment particles within the cone cells are receptive to different wavelengths of light giving us colour vision. These signals are processed in the brain in two ways:

- bottom-up processing – where the longer we look the more detail we see, and the more the visual image builds up

DOI: 10.4324/9781003009078-10

- top-down processing – where we draw contextual information, recognise patterns, and draw from memory to suggest hypotheses about what we are seeing.

In the bottom-up process, different light effects are correlated with events in the physical world (Gibson 1966); for example, brighter objects are understood as nearer, objects diminishing in size are perceived as moving away, and where one image is blocked by another, one is understood to be in front of the other. This system evolved in simple organisms to detect what was in the environment to avoid collisions. Such basic capacities allow us to learn about the world around us, even as newborns. Similarly, humans tend not to look at fixed points, our eyes move around scenes, locating interesting parts and building up mental 3D maps of the scene. We unconsciously focus on key aspects of the image such as edges/outlines or the faces of people as we seek to understand what the image is. We probably start our images with a simple 2D outline, then move to fill in light and shade developing a 3D model. The repeated focus on key areas suggests an interactive process gathering and updating information, which is accumulated and interrogated in the brain.

Top-down processing refers to the use of contextual information in pattern recognition. We use partial information and draw on previous images and associated information (schemata) to aid our understanding (Gregory 1970). For example, reading one scrawled word can be difficult but when it is part of a sentence it may be easier because we can use the meaning of the words surrounding it to help us understand. This can lead to misidentifications. Similarly, our perception of colour and shade are relative, influenced by the colour and shade of the things that surround them.

Vision developed in a competitive evolutionary situation. There are benefits to gaining information quickly (such as detecting threats) but also to gathering accurate information, which builds up slowly avoiding misidentification, unnecessary action, and wasted energy. Thus, both a quick system, imparting partial information and seeking correspondence with known information, and a slower checking detail system are desirable. All brain activities consume energy (calories!) and evolution seeks to minimise energy expenditure. Thus, we do not look at all things closely, if we are satisfied with the correspondence between the image and our perception (identification) then we do not pursue the matter further – though we may be left with a misidentification. Where there are visual discrepancies between the image being registered in our brains and what we think we perceive, then the brain works to resolve the problem, focussing on the differences, thus we pay more attention to them. This may well be why we focus on the cracks in a plate or chips in a mug. They do not correspond well with the idea of a whole object, which we perceive in our heads; we therefore focus on the errors and blemishes and try to better understand them.

As we look and perceive, images and cues flood into our short-term memory, which has limited capacity; typically holding between five and nine elements (images and information) for 15–30 seconds (Miller 1956). Information is therefore grouped together; either 'chunked' together (e.g. memories of a given time and place), categorised into groups where similar things are corralled, or run together as complex sequences of actions (schemata, patterns). Humans do not normally see single images; the visual image is part of a continuous stream of information with other associated images (i.e. a context). Thus, when seeking to identify an object, we are selecting from a group of restricted images – those that correspond to the surrounding context. The patterns or schemata carry cues or links to further patterns and thus humans perceive in a sequence of patterns (images, actions, movements) described as cognition sequences. This develops into a series or cascade of existing patterns, one triggering another, with an inhibiting or checking mechanism that registers the degree of correspondence or lack of correspondence and automatically generates the next pattern, which may better correspond with the received image (Margolis 1987). Thus, a small white cylinder in a room could be a cigarette or a wooden stick, but the cue of a blackboard in association with the room identifies the white cylinder as a piece of chalk (Figure 10.1). This type of continuous perceptual hypothesis testing requires constant evaluation of many hypotheses in parallel using information collected over time (Bob Kentridge personal communication). It is, however, through such mechanisms that the conservator identifies the object and in so doing accesses images, actions, information associated with it (Figure 10.1).

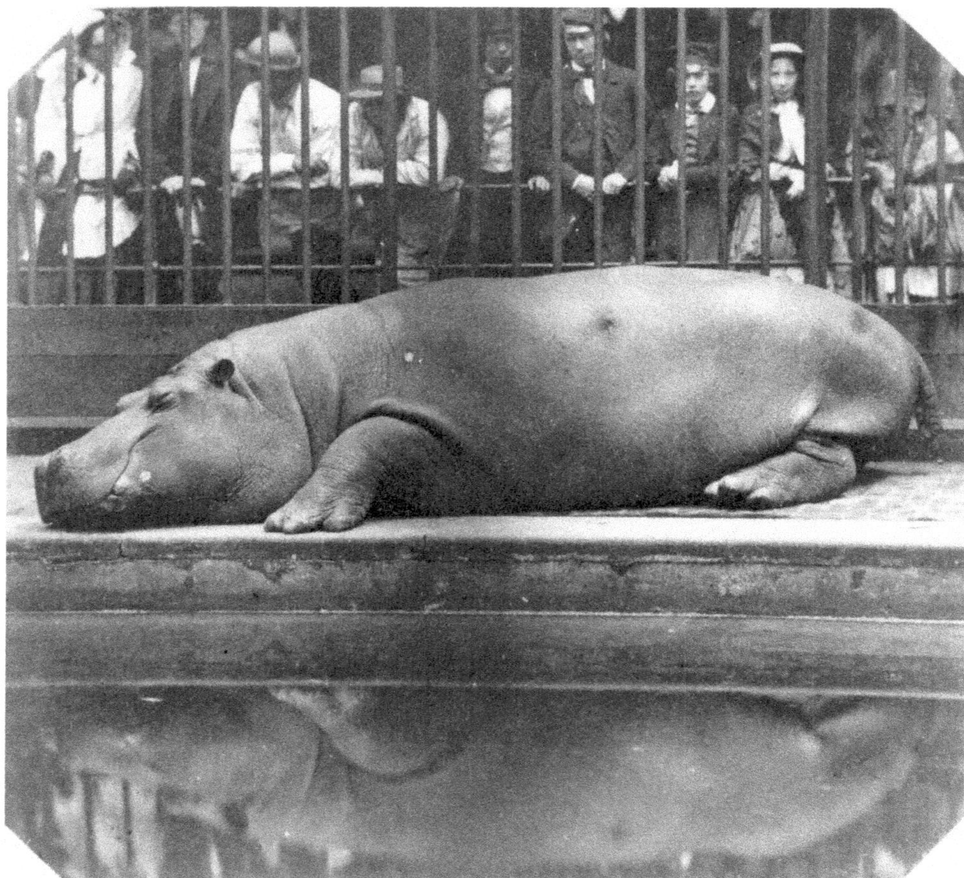

Figure 10.1 The Hippopotamus at the Zoological Gardens, Regent's Park Zoo, London. Photographed by Count de Montizon in 1855. Caged people and a blissful hippo or a caged wild animal and intrepid onlookers? Although we perceive the animal, bars and people, the meaning of the image is entirely derived from our associated information. The Royal Photographic Society.

The pattern (chunks, categories, schemata) with all its cues can lead to unconscious associations e.g. stereotypes. Patterns are learnt slowly in the first place, but repetition (rehearsal) leads to speeding up of the thinking process, as alternatives to the norm are inhibited. Thus, the world becomes an ordered (non-surrealist) place of sequences, such that when watching a game of chess, you expect one move to follow another rather than expecting the chess pieces to become fish. The creation of the patterns by chunking, categorising, and sequencing is rarely even raised to consciousness during operation. They become attention-free, automatic processes and complex actions can be performed while other thinking activities are run in parallel. The patterns are either quickly overwritten or moved to long-term memory.

When humans acquire additional information, it is incorporated into existing patterns of understanding. Additional knowledge is more easily added or assimilated into an area where there is already a significant number of patterns.

Learnt Behaviours

The behaviour of elementary organisms can be explained by simple feedback loops from stimuli; these actions (initially trial and error in response to the stimulus) led to positive outcomes (food, reproduction, survival) and thus evolved into permanent instinctual traits. This reaction sequence can be modified by associating consequences, such as a pleasant or unpleasant stimulus, and the resulting behaviour of the animal can be altered or habituated. These 'learnt' patterns can become more complex and through repetition become unconscious. The acquisition of learnt patterns and responses leads to choices and since there are options there are also different outcomes and different consequences. The more extensive the memory capacity and the greater the level of experience then, theoretically, the wider the range of options and choices and the greater level of consideration attendant on any response.

Judgement

Where there are choices, at higher levels of thought we come to a process, which can be termed judgement. Margolis (1987) defines this in terms of an ability to solve a problem not previously encountered and concludes that it requires some form of imagination for its solution. For example, when chimpanzees are faced with the need to get food suspended high above its head, some can figure out that putting one box onto another will enable them to gain sufficient height to pick the fruit, without having been previously shown. These chimpanzees have run through the possible actions in their heads and building from an existing pattern of reaching food at a lower level by standing on one box have imagined the consequence of standing one box on another.

Human experience suggests that two routes lead to judgement (Kahnemann 2011). In the fast 'seeing that' approach, an intuitive line is drawn through existing facts and extrapolated to form the complete picture, theory, or idea. These intuitive unconscious 'jumps' in understanding, which we all experience, are known as naturalistic decision-making or heuristic thinking (Kahnemann 2003). They are fast, automatic, and effortless and can be both emotionally charged and difficult to modify because they are governed by habit. The slower controlled mode (Kahnemann 2003) or analytic-deliberative (AD) process (Renn 1999) is more deliberate, effortful, and more likely to be consciously monitored and deliberately controlled. The speed of the heuristic process is favoured by evolution, but the exactness, executability, communicability, and reproducibility favoured by our culture demand the reasoned path. There is no guarantee that the AD approach has to define a truth and, though less prone to error than the heuristic approach, it is possible to justify an inaccurate or erroneous thought or action. The AD process can be seen as rationalisation while the heuristic process can be equated with belief and may, in unconscious form, generate emotions and movement. Where reason and belief correspond, we have certainty; where there is belief but no proof or there is proof but no belief there is a paradox and doubt exists. Such states of doubt are frequently encountered in the learning process.

Future potential outcomes (judgements) are communicated through the complex medium of language. It permits concepts to be measured against each other to determine the most effective one. This is the process we refer to as reason and it enables humans to use collective judgements to modify or support their judgement.

Learning

Learning can be understood as a lasting change in perception or behaviour resulting from experience. Initially existing patterns of activity/behaviour/understanding are employed in a new situation and modified based on trial and error. Thus, learning to clean a dirty or corroded object with a scalpel may utilise familiar actions, such as using a knife for paring an apple or for whittling, to guide the movement of the scalpel. As one gains experience with the corroded surface, the patterns are altered by trial and error and improved; actions that are perceived to have improved the situation are slowly improved, retained, and repeated (becoming almost instinctual). When learning new ways of doing things, or re-ordering knowledge in a new way, it is difficult to learn to do things the new 'slow' way rather than using the old 'fast track' pathways and there is a constant problem of sliding back into the old ways of thinking (Margolis 1987). However, once established, the thought process speeds up through repetition (rehearsal). In situations where there are a large variety of activities happening simultaneously, such as stimulating social and changing environments with much to see and do, learning proceeds quickly, whereas in more static environments it proceeds slowly. Where there is external influence (teaching), behaviour can be deliberately modified (learnt), especially where punishments or rewards (operant conditioning) are employed.

An important element within any learning process is not simply establishing a sequence or pattern of thought, but also generating a correct answer. Learnt processes must have some correspondence with reality if they are to be useful to us. Reality testing can take two forms (Abercromby 1960):

- Communication Reality Testing – communicating one's understanding to others and comparing one's judgement with theirs. Since experiential learning is slow, humans have developed technologies such as speech, writing, and imagery to pass on information at an enhanced rate. Complex ideas can be communicated in writing or speech forming a fairly quick and easy method of reality testing, which may only approximate reality since there can be misunderstanding by the individuals involved; the more experienced the group, the less likely this is to occur.
- Physical Reality Testing – the correspondence of one's perception with real objects and real situations. Is what I believe true? For example, if I have worked

out, or simply believe, that this object is light enough for me to lift, I can try lifting it to test my hypothesis. Confidence is gained if the 'learnt' thinking process is proved to be correct. If it is not correct, further facts and information are sought and the thinking process is repeated with the additional information factored in.

A conservator's professional training requires a substantial component of practical work handling, studying, and conserving objects to fully test their developing understanding since there must have a very close correspondence between their understanding and the reality of the objects they handle and conserve if they are to be effective.

The patterns we create through our own experience are strong. They have more associated cues (smells, sounds, touch) than material learned by reading alone; we preferentially image and interpret using our own experience. Although personal experience provides richly cued patterns, it is a slow-learning medium particularly for reasoned ideas. It is far easier to learn a reasoned idea, such as Pythagoras's Theorem, than to derive it for yourself. While it may be imagined that to learn efficiently one can simply read a book or hear a lecture, teachers have lamented throughout time that such communications frequently do not lead to the retention of information. There is a Swedish proverb that states 'What you hear you will forget, what you see you will remember, what you do you know' (Kavanagh 1990; Figure 10.2).

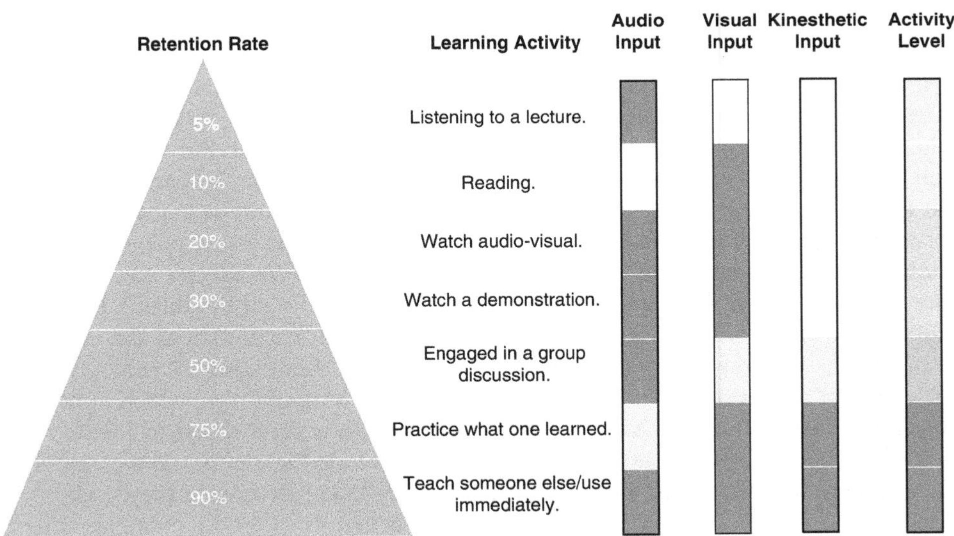

Figure 10.2 The Pyramid of Learning, developed by the National Training Laboratories Institute (Bethel, Maine). Widely used and repeated as it appears to correspond well with human perception of the how well we learn. Redrawn by Chris Caple.

Learning can involve absorbing large amounts of information. Retaining information as a series of separate facts is difficult, therefore it is normally presented (taught) in chunks, categories, or sequences so that relationships between the pieces of information are highlighted, such as through linear narratives of cause and effect. The greater the learner's knowledge of a subject, the more fine grained the chunks of information and the more accurately they are categorised and understood. Many other factors such as motivation, confidence, and the surrounding environment affect learning. Not all taught materials are equally powerful; those that are more recent are more powerful than those that are older. Formal, scientific presentation is often preferentially believed over informal, artistic performance. Dramatic facts and incidents are more readily remembered than the boring or mundane; failure looms large (we all remember our failures) whilst the status quo is unremarkable and is poorly remembered. Therefore, it is not simply the information of images gained that is important, but also the way in which that information was received that influences the power and reliability of the image in the mind.

Limitations and Biases in Perception and Judgement

A series of patterns, such as images, may correspond to the word 'knife.' When associated cues, such as the context or features of the knife, are added, they may allow the knife to be placed in a particular chronological period or associated with an activity, such as eating, hunting, or fighting, or linked to a specific group. In these patterns, evidence (facts) invariably becomes bound up with associated ideas. Although this may be very beneficial for wider understanding, it is important for conservators to distinguish between the facts (the basic image itself) and the assumptions (the ideas or conclusions drawn from it) so that each element can be critically analysed and changed if appropriate. Unless conscious efforts are made to focus on the exact nature of the knife and check every detail, key information such as worn and dirty maker's marks may be missed. Our ability to notice detail, especially changes in detail, is crucial in many human tasks, and has been shown through experimentation to be poor (Gunnell *et al.* 2019). The fact that we fail to spot change when an image is altered (change blindness) shows that our visual perception does not hold a lot of detail, just enough to enable us to function. There is evidence that we overwrite images, fail to reconcile differing images of the same thing, or hang onto an initial image even when things have changed (Simons 2000). We also see what we want to see or expect to see, consequently we miss things (inattentional blindness), this often occurs because we are looking for specific pieces of information and do not look 'outside the box.' Drew *et al.* (2018) illustrated this when they asked CT radiographers with expertise in screening for lung cancer to look for lung nodules, which appear as light circles on chest cavity X-radiographs, 83% of the experts failed to identify the black and white image of a gorilla that had been included in the X-radiograph. The radiographers were so focused on the task that they failed to take in the whole.

Once their minds are made up, humans are generally poor at changing them. Previous experience tends to dominate thinking and lead to the repetition of well-used methods. Experienced individuals use tried and tested methods that they are adept at using, even if it gives a significant bias. A model for reaching or changing a judgement developed by Tversky and Kahneman suggests that judgement is a heuristic process of anchoring and adjustment (Meyer and Booker 1991). The individual starts with an initial decision that is based on previous experience (an intuitive insight based on previous patterns) and this judgement is simply modified with each piece of additional information. This would suggest that a judgement is never wholly recreated from the facts. Having made a judgement, it becomes the dominant fact within the assemblage and cannot be ignored. People are invariably predisposed to weight their own thoughts highly, as well as ideas or facts that they have accepted (Figure 10.3; Case Study 6B: Loch Glashan Satchel). These previous judgements and accepted ideas act as an anchor constraining future consideration of the problem; the final judgement may show a skew or bias towards the original reaction. This unwillingness to embrace a new judgement manifests itself as stubbornness or fear of new ideas. We may even devalue certain pieces of evidence that do not agree with our existing views and overvalue other evidence when it agrees with what we 'know' (confirmation bias).

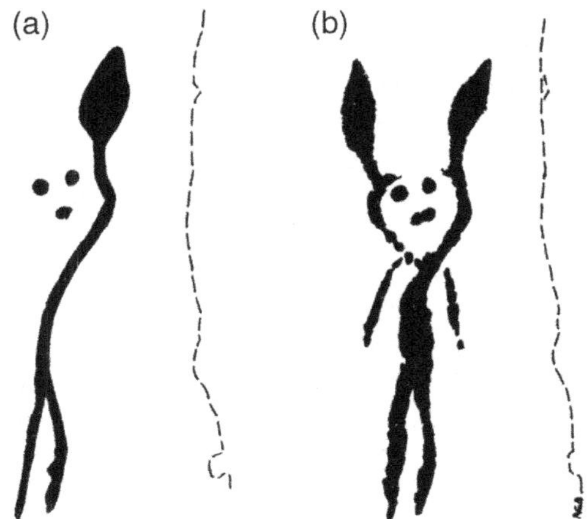

Figure 10.3 The Peterborough petroglyph: (a) as identified and recorded – a snake and three eggs. This image was outlined in wax crayon so subsequent viewers all saw this. (b) The same petroglyph re-examined, crayon removed and photographed in raking light, revealed a figure with raised ears originally pecked into the rock. Even now these markings may be part of a large image which is no longer visible (Bahn *et al.* 1995). Drawn by Robert Bednarick.

Experienced conservators often weigh options unconsciously and only raise them to conscious consideration when there are several options that have similar likelihoods of success or failure. Although it might appear logical to suggest that judgement is based on selecting the best likely result from a range of weighted options, less logical methods are often utilised:

- One or two crucial or higher ranked categories dominate the process.
- A selection is made based on the options that minimise conflict or require lower levels of resources.
- One source of evidence is prioritised over others because we are more familiar with it.

Improving Judgement in Conservation

If judgement is a process of assessing and drawing conclusions based on the available evidence, decision-making is the process where someone chooses between the multiple alternatives. Sound judgement is needed to make optimal decisions. When applying judgement to complex conservation processes, evidence can be understood as individual elements (the object's form, decoration and composition, the extent and nature of the decay mechanism, the extent and nature of preserved evidence, the appropriate ethical considerations, previous treatments), all of which can vary between objects and even in different areas of a single object. This evidence is weighed and contributes to a series of options for conservation processes, such as the extent of cleaning, appropriate stabilisation treatment, appropriate final visual form of the object. These options are also weighed, and a considered decision is reached. Since each object is unique, when deciding what intervention is needed, the conservator should not automatically perform an oft-repeated process that has developed into an unconscious cognition sequence but should seek to follow a conscious judgement process in which a range of options and possible outcomes are considered.

Experts are often highly proficient at making judgements. They perceive more; for example, experienced chess players can remember how 25 pieces are arranged on a board after seeing it for five seconds, whereas novice players will only remember the positions of around five pieces (Chase and Simon 1973). Experts have exercised many more judgements that have been reality tested and thus they can imagine more successful scenarios, automatically discarding unsuccessful ones. However, it is often difficult for an expert to say why one option was chosen rather than another, since much relevant information is perceived and judgement is made unconsciously in a heuristic process. This makes it difficult to accurately describe all the information and factors that were weighed and explain them. For professions where there is a constant stream of problems and data, such as medicine, weather forecasting and conservation, reality provides a natural feedback loop, whose results quickly feed heuristic thinking, and are only occasionally analytically and deliberately analysed.

In areas where there are large amounts of different evidence and many options, judgement is challenging. There is not a single correct answer, but a series of more correct answers and a series of less correct answers. Experiments have shown that a group of experienced doctors confronted with a series of X-radiographs some of which show signs of tuberculosis, will not always pick out the same radiographs, especially in less obvious cases (Abercromby 1960). Confronted with the same set of radiographs a few days later, a doctor may not even pick out the same radiographs as on the previous occasion. The error can be one of observation, failing to see all the important aspects of the image, but is more usually one of judgement where all the aspects of the image were seen but not considered significant. In such cases, shadows seen in the radiograph were considered to be within the natural background variation for human tissue. While errors in observation can be minimised to assemble an accurate understanding (for example by having several experienced observers look at the subject, discuss it and try to consciously strip away their assumptions), it is the nature of judgement that there will always be errors. Good judgement derives from keeping these errors to a minimum. Persistent errors of judgement are called biases and due to their consistency can be detected and counteracted. As mentioned above, one of the most consistent forms of bias is the reluctance to change one's mind.

Many techniques can be used to improve judgement, these include the following:

- Limiting the number of choices. Since only about five to nine elements can be held at one time in the short-term memory, rather than considering many options consider pairs of options and select one as preferable to the other. Continue the process until one option emerges as preferential to all others.

- Breaking the subject down into many smaller questions. When approaching more complex conservation judgements, break it down into a series of smaller judgement steps (Caple and Garlick 2018). Solve each separate stage, then explore the issues imposed by increasing the size or number of objects, adding additional processes or the interactions of one material or technique on another.
- Developing a model of the problem. There has been little exploration or development of this technique within conservation because of the unique nature of most objects, but for managing repetitious tasks it is possible.
- Being aware of engaging in a decision-making process. Through discussing the reasoning behind decisions with colleagues, one engages in thinking at the AD level (Henderson and Waller 2016).
- Communicating and writing down the evidence considered, and the deductions drawn at each stage. After describing and assessing the condition of an object, the next step is generally to propose a conservation treatment. Such conservation proposals can and should be written down to help clarify the various steps that are required. When treating relatively simple objects, experienced conservators may not always write out conservation proposals since the procedures involved are often very familiar but even then, the process of documenting the proposed approach is a useful check against bias. When the conservation of a large and complex object is envisaged, the work can be so multifaceted and involve so many conservators and specialists that written treatment proposals are essential. Treatment proposals are critical when conservation work is done on contract or through a tendering process, so that the client is aware of the work envisaged and its likely outcome and effect. Thus, written conservation proposals support and develop the judgement process.

There is no certainty in a judgement. In conservation, there may be several viable options rather than a single correct answer. However, there are often solutions that are inappropriate or carry significant risk to the object or to the conservator and it is important to weigh these and discard them. There will always be alternate paths and they are an essential part of judgement; good decision-making rests on considering the alternatives and becoming comfortable evaluating the balance of probability.

Optimal Decision-Making

In the 1970s, the development of management theories led to the mathematical modelling of decision-making and methods to aid the process were created. Many of these methods use courses of action (options) supported by weighting factors expressed as probabilities and mathematical models to select the most beneficial course of action based on Bayesian probability.

Although much of the literature concerning 'decision theory' focuses on different mathematical models for evaluating the options (selection process), in practice most of the decision maker's time is spent clearly establishing what the question is, as well as determining what the key options are, finding evidence to support them, establishing the extent of the variables (probabilities), and designing new possible options to consider (Hansen 2005). It would be simpler if this was a linear process; however, in practice it is often circular. As we think about possible options and obtain further information about them, we often return to the question to further clarify it.

The key to good decision-making is asking the right question. Careful phrasing is crucial to ensuring that any answer obtained is meaningful and useful. The question, 'does the RH range in the gallery pose any significant threat to the object,' is not that same as, 'is the RH in the gallery between 50% and 60%.' The first is far harder to answer but more relevant for the object's care than the second, which is far easier to answer. When we are faced with difficult questions, we often unconsciously change them to ones that are easier to answer (attribute substitution) offering a reasonable answer to a question that we have not been actually been asked (Kahnemann 2003).

Like judgement, decision-making depends on heuristic approaches and AD approaches. Heuristic decisions are effective in simple, pragmatic, contextualised situations where there are just a few options to choose from. They draw heavily on personal experience and are frequently influenced by past successes and recent events, especially interesting or alarming incidents (Henderson and Waller 2016: 312). The advantages are that heuristic decision-making can operate when high levels of uncertainty exists and the broad picture (the area in which the right decision must fall) can be appreciated. Experienced practitioners use it extensively since it is very quick (cost effective), and they have a large amount of relevant experience to draw from. Heuristic decisions invariably give 'workable' solutions to the problem, though not always 'the best' answers. However, when there are too many options, heuristic thinking can struggle to reach a decision resulting in decision paralysis and the need to move to an AD process. Analytic deliberate decision-making is slow and takes time and effort. It deals well with a large range of options and enables careful logical decision-making in complex situations. It is aided by decision support tools; however, it is less effective when there is a large amount of uncertainty. AD decision-making processes lend themselves to being written down, which enables the process to be shown to a range of people and is useful when a decision needs to be seen by, and may well be checked by, others (Henderson and Waller 2016: 310). Where there are likely to be strong feelings, the pragmatic evidence-based approach of an AD decision, especially if it is clearly identified and laid out, may allow a decision to be reached in a calmer, less confrontational manner. Whilst AD decisions focus on a set number of options and find the best solution, heuristic decision-making can be broad ranging, can reframe the problem, and can come up with innovative solutions; however, heuristic decisions may fail to quantify things and sometimes may even ignore certain pieces of evidence (Henderson and Waller 2016).

The value of things changes over time, which is not something that can easily be factored into an AD-type decision. Value-based decisions may be better made with heuristic processes (Henderson and Waller 2016). Had the full cost of raising the *Mary Rose*, conserving the recovered artefacts, building a new museum, and putting it all on display (Case study 4B) been known at the start, the project might never have been undertaken (Margret Rule, personal communication) Completed and now celebrated as an important piece of the nation's maritime heritage, most people would now consider the cost of the project worthwhile.

Conservators are expected to justify their decisions when writing up objects for publications and reports, which encourages AD decision-making. Heuristic decisions are rarely reported in print; arguably, they are seen as a less acceptable form of public discourse for conservation, reflecting the increased role of science, ethics, organisational priorities, and 'the need to justify decisions' within the discipline. Prior to the late 1980s, most of the decision-making in conservation was based on previous experience and was largely heuristic. As an increasing number of conservation methods and materials became available but resources became increasingly limited, the need to make decisions more justifiable and balanced became important. Emphasis on preventive conservation approaches, where there was a need to establish the probability associated with a range of risks and consider a range of possible outcomes and their associated costs, led to a greater awareness of AD decision-making processes. Greater access to personal computers from the 1980s onwards also aided AD decision-making to take hold, allowing statistical expression of variability (uncertainty) to be incorporated into the calculations.

In all decision-making, there is an inbuilt bias towards inaction as people have a stronger reaction to action than inaction (Henderson and Waller 2016: 311). The greater the scrutiny of the decision, the more likely inaction is. Since actions often require arguing for additional resources, to avoid the effort, risk of failure, and expenditure of one's valued time, the cheaper option (inaction) is often selected.

Cost-Benefit Analysis

One of the simplest, most widely referenced methods of reaching a decision is cost-benefit analysis (cost-effectiveness analysis). It was first used by the 19th-century French engineer Jules Dupuit to explore the social profitability of constructing a bridge by establishing how much people would pay to use it and how much it would be used, allowing the total potential income to be calculated and compared to the cost of construction. This enabled a social benefit to be expressed in financial terms. Similar calculations have been employed for many major infrastructure developments during the 20th century, especially since the 1950s. It can be used as a hard economic model (the project proceeds if the cost of the income received is greater than the cost of construction) or in non-financial terms where the wider social benefits are considered against the financial outlay. It can also be used as a simple indicative exercise to make stakeholders aware of the money being invested and encourage them to explore how to gain the greatest benefit (effectiveness) out of such development.

Simple decision support tools, such as decision trees, can easily be drawn up (Figure 10.4). The actions within the decision tree may cost money to enact and thus the costs for undertaking a particular course of action can be calculated. The route with the greatest profit or the least investment, or a total that matches the funds available may be selected; however, conservation objectives are invariably more complex and successful outcomes often consist of the greatest increase in value of the object (information, aesthetics, social use, etc.) for the available funding (Caple 2000: 170–175).

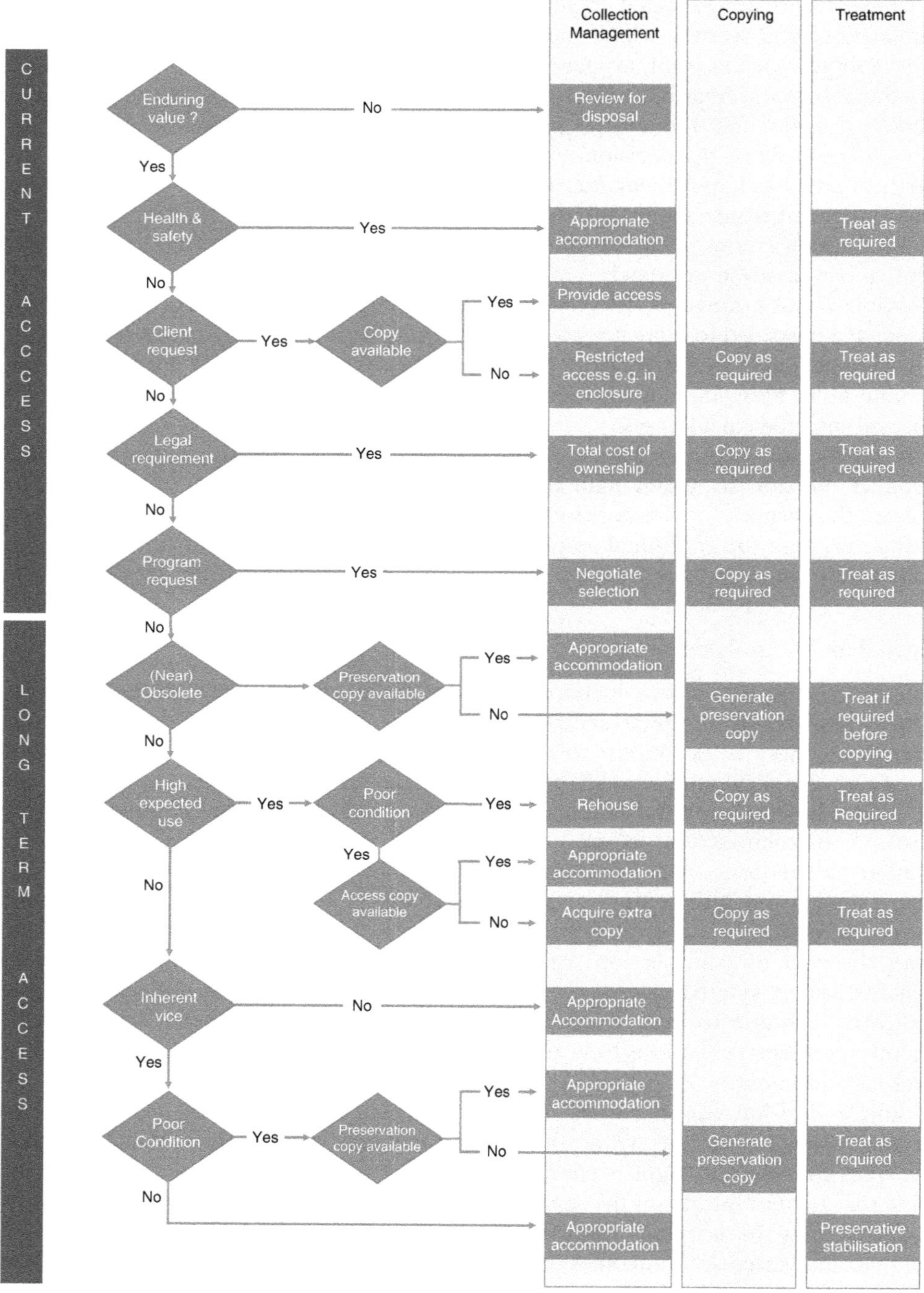

Figure 10.4 A decision tree used at Library and Archives Canada (LAC) to prioritise conservation worksuch as converting media on outdated technology (obsolete software and hardware) as well as traditional book and paper repair, while supporting collection use and meeting legal and health and safety requirements (Clark 2008). Redrawn by Chris Caple.

Adding Complexity

A simple example of the use of cost-benefit analysis in conservation might be the answer to the question 'which technique should I use to clean an object?' If there are three cleaning techniques available in the laboratory and all are equally safe and effective, but the price of the materials used varies (option A is cheap, option B has some cost, option C is expensive), then a simple preference for lower cost might mean that option A is selected. The greatest benefit is achieved for the lowest cost (cost-benefit analysis). If the available options have different cleaning abilities or work at different speeds and with different risks to the object this adds complexity to the question and it may be helpful to introduce numbers to quantify the efficacy, speed, cost, and risk. If the options have many different attributes, the calculation may become very complex. To reach a simple mathematical answer the different options should be considered using the same units, the most widely used is money. Conservator time (salary and laboratory costs) can be converted to monetary values, similarly materials and time can both be expressed as currency; however, choosing between greater or lesser risk of damage to an object (object value) is a difficult unit to work with as it varies between people. Some people may judge that there is a monetary value to an object (you can replace it by buying another one at auction) in which case the calculation can be completed in monetary units. However, if the object contains unique historical evidence from a specific time and place in the past then the decision cannot be accurately reduced to money. One can then use two or more units in a statement to express the options, such as 'the object may be cleaned without any risk of surface damage (value) for X£' or 'cleaned with slight risk of loss of surface (value) for Y£'. Or one can create arbitrary units (i.e. utility or significance), establish a simple relative scale of values, such as 'crucial, important, significant, and limited' that can be given numerical scores (i.e. 1 to 4) then each feature of each cleaning technique is scored. The total value for each technique is calculated and a relative value for each technique is obtained, with the highest/lowest value selected.

The use of realistic monetary values as opposed to arbitrary numbers or statements, helps communicate conservation costs to managers and stakeholders however the results may not always be as nuanced as when other values are incorporated into the decision-making process. Crucially, whichever process is used, it can be checked by heuristic comparison; having made the calculation, does this decision feel right? In cases where the answer feels 'wrong' (counterintuitive), then one may reconsider each step and see what drives the numerical answer. It may be necessary in some cases to revise aspects of the ranking, or to challenge one's own heuristic perception and 'go with the numbers.'

Clarity of thinking can sometimes be achieved by ranking one variable against another for every option or by including more variables and factoring in uncertainty, which can be expressed statistically. A wide range of mathematical models are available, examples include analytic hierarchy process (AHP), multi attribute utility theory (MAUT), multi criteria dimension analysis (MCDA), and Bayesian reasoning. Each technique has its strengths and weaknesses, but it is important to note that many are designed for particular applications. Software packages are available that allow one to input numbers, express preferences, and generate a suggested answer, but it is important to understand the basis of the calculations, else one risks generating an answer that is poorly matched to the circumstances.

Risk Assessment for Museums

The most common use of AD decision-making in conservation is associated with risk assessments of objects and collections (Ashley-Smith 1999; Waller 2003; Brokerhof and Bülow 2016; Pedersoli *et al.* 2016; Rogerson and Garside 2017; Garside *et al.* 2018). For any proposed museum action two factors are considered: the likelihood of detrimental impact and the degree of that impact consequence on a museum object. These are assessed using a simple numerical scale[1], the product of which gives a numerical indication of risk. Using a 1–5 scale (5 = high, 1 = low), a product above 20 represents high risk (i.e. highly likely to have catastrophic impact), scores below 10 represents low risk (i.e. unlikely to have much impact). This tends to produce a table, matrix, or spreadsheet whose cells can be colour coded usually red (high risk), yellow/amber (medium risk), and green (low risk). The traffic light comparison is intentional and allows for a quicker appreciation of risk level than looking through a column of numbers.

- The overall risk level can be obtained by summing the risk factors, or simply looking at the range of coloured cells. The museum can determine the overall level of risk (risk appetite) it is willing to accept for a particular object (related to object value) or across all objects in the institution (consistency). Where objects are rare or unique, institutions may only accept very limited risk, where objects have lower value (several examples exist and the objects are easily replaceable) or there is a benefit to be gained e.g. working objects (widest sense), they may tolerate higher risk levels.
- Risk assessment is relatively transparent because the information is based on specific evidence and can easily be seen and compared with previous assessments. This can lead to consistency in decision-making, which gives senior managers, stakeholders, and colleagues confidence in the system. Loan requests can be approved or rejected based on evidence and subjective discussion in meetings is reduced. The format can be widely understood, which helps communicate the decision to the staff and to stakeholders (such as borrowers).
- Where risks are identified, mitigation strategies can be proposed and the risks re-assessed (Figure 10.5), an approach widely used in health and safety assessment.

Risk Nature	Risk Description	Impact	Likeli-hood	Risk	Mitigation	Impact	Likeli-hood	Risk
Handling	Breakage or loss through improper handling.	5	4	RED	Handling protocol observed. Object only handled by museum staff. Any weakened areas identified and avoided or an alternate object substituted.	3	2	GREEN

Figure 10.5 A single line from a risk assessment for a camera crew coming to film in a museum and the measures that might be employed to mitigate the risks from handling. Subsequent lines assessed the risks of fire, light damage, theft, etc. Chris Caple.

Many natural and economic phenomena describe a Pareto distribution, where a small number of large events make up the bulk of the total, the rest is composed of many small events. Risks such as fire and major structural collapse pose the greatest potential risk to the largest number of objects in a collection while other potential risks, such as handling issues, have lesser impacts on fewer objects (Michalski and Karsten 2018). Reducing the threat posed by fire is a highly effective way of reducing risk to the collections, and thus a cost-effective measure. However, whilst commercial businesses might be able to take out a loan to fix the situation and pay it back annually, public institutions need to obtain a significant grant for such a large investment. Thus, the political, economic, social, cultural, and organisational context in which a museum or heritage institution operates determines its approach to risk management and to decision-making (Pedersoli *et al.* 2016).

The Bigger Picture

Decisions about cultural heritage are made at a series of levels. National priorities, organisational aims, collection requirements, and curatorial interests all impact the preservation and display of individual objects. There is little point in making a decision at a lower level, only to have it overruled at a higher level. So, it is sensible to try and ensure that all decisions fit into the 'bigger picture'. For example, in Britain's National Trust, all decisions, even those around the conservation of objects in historic properties, are considered for their impact on people, finance, and environment (social, economic, and environmental capital). This is intended to ensure the survival and sustainability of both the organisation and the planet (Lithgow 2011). Noting that a number of issues come down to differences between preservation and access, where such issues cannot be resolved (always the initial approach), the Trust invokes the Sandford Principle, placing greater emphasis on preservation (Lithgow 2011). This principle, originally articulated for the UK's National Parks (Lord Sandford chaired their review 1971–1974) was given the weight of law in the 1995 Environment Act 'if it appears that there is a conflict between those purposes, [the legal authority] shall attach greater weight to the purpose of conserving and enhancing the natural beauty, wildlife and cultural heritage of the area comprised in the National Park.' The Trust also tests this principle against the sustainability of the organisation since its continuation is deemed to benefit all the things it cares for and therefore to outweigh the benefits to any one object or property within its care.

Although organisational decision often centres around economic considerations, some decisions are heavily influenced by wider organisational and ethical considerations. When a conservation action is proposed, it is important to assess the action against a series of searching questions to ensure both good judgement and clear answers to the question of why the work must be done. In 1994, the Victoria and Albert (V&A) Conservation Department devised such a list to guide conservators (Richmond 2005). The questions (with clarification for wider use in brackets) that conservation staff were asked to consider include the following:

- Why is conservation needed? (who benefits and how, what happens if nothing is done?)
- Have I consulted existing records?
- Do I need to consult the clients, my peers, other specialists?

- Have I considered all the factors contributing to the identity and significance of the object: historical, technical, associations, sanctity, creator's intention? (what values does it have and to whom?)
- What effects will the conservation have on the evidence of these factors?
- Do I have sufficient skill and information to assess and implement the conservation?
- What are my options for (interventive) conservation which will produce an acceptable result with minimum intervention?
- What are the advantages of each course of conservation?
- Can the use of environment be adapted instead of intervening on the object? (preventive conservation options)
- What are the resource implications of my actions, (do I have the resources?) and does my intended conservation make best use of resources?
- Do established courses of action need to be adapted or new ones developed?
- Are all my actions fully documented to a known and accepted standard?
- Are my records accessible to appropriate users?
- How will my conservation affect subsequent conservation work?
- Have I taken account of the future use and location of the object? (can it be maintained/sustained?)
- How will I assess the success of the conservation and how will I get feedback from owners/curators and peers?

These questions are a useful tool for any conservator faced with designing a conservation treatment, implementing preventive conservation, or managing the care of cultural heritage. By working through them the conservator is forced to consider issues of sustainability (can the treatment be maintained), resourcing, and social valuation (consultation). Furthermore, by carefully answering the questions for themselves, their ability to articulate their decision-making process to stakeholders and to advocate for the object(s) is improved as is the likelihood that their decision will be supported by management and other decision-making bodies.

Consultation

Although successful conservation has always depended on engaging with others to help define the aims of treatment, for much of the field's history this engagement was limited to other professionals, such as architects, curators[2], archaeologists and scientists, and owners. It took place within the context of what Laurajane Smith has dubbed the 'authorised heritage discourse'(AHD), which relies on the 'power/knowledge claims of technical and aesthetic experts and is institutionalised in state cultural agencies and amenity societies' (2007: 11). This discourse tends to privilege monumentality and an innate artefact significance (object truth) that is often tied to age, scientific expert judgement, and grand narratives often tied to nation building projects. Smith and others have argued that there is a performative element of heritage management and preservation that is engaged with the construction and renegotiation of cultural identity, memory, belonging, and serves as a vehicle through which meanings (narratives) and values are rejected or reaffirmed. Within conservation, this important work is carried out through a process known as 'consultation', which serves as a collaborative approach to decision-making and invites a variety of stakeholders to participate in the process alongside owners, conservators, curators, and other specialists. These stakeholders include the following:

- Indigenous communities, traditional landowners, and source communities
- religious leaders
- living artists and after their death the custodians of their vision such as foundations, family, and friends
- members of the public
- those who used dynamic objects such as operating machinery or playing musical instruments.

During the consultation process, a collaborative mode of decision-making is established in which parity is sought between specialists (such as conservators and curators or archaeologists) who can bring certain types of expertise to the table and the collaborating partners who bring other perspectives and expertise to the discussions that may not be available otherwise.

In some instances, consultation is legally mandated[3]; more importantly, however, it has become recognised as a key component of ethical decision-making and is referenced in most conservation codes of ethics. Beyond this, consultation has come to be seen as an important tool for decisions relating to the creation of statements of significance (Russell and Winkworth 2009), the redressing some of the negative impacts of colonialism and racism (Krmpotich and Peers 2013; Swieringa 2021), and also engaging communities in decisions about their heritage (Hughes 2011; Lithgow *et al.* 2018).

Consultation is not always an easy process. Identifying who to consult with is not always straightforward. How wide you throw the net will influence the answers you get and may lead to paralysis due to the volume and potentially contradictory nature of what is said. However, if the consultation is too tightly bounded or those consulted are reduced to tokenistic roles and not accorded parity in the process, there is the risk that valuable time will be spent reaching a decision that is quickly challenged and must be revisited.

It is important to note that it can take time to build the relationships of trust on which successful consultations are based and that patience is needed (Message 2021). Conservators should be aware of the baggage that their institutional affiliations may bring with them and try to find ways to set collaborators at ease and assure them that communication will be open and respectful. Such assurances may come through hospitable gestures or other modes of interaction (Johnson *et al.* 2005: 208). It is advisable to record the consultation where possible, ideally using direct quotes of what was said and by whom. This will help explain what conservation work was done and why, as well as aid future conservators dealing with the object.

Where consultation is undertaken but there is a failure to act on the results, the undertaking should be regarded as unsuccessful (Henderson and Nakamoto 2016). Such outcomes may occur because the conservator did not have the authority to make the final decision or did not involve key decision-makers in the process. Consultation takes time on both the part of the conservator and their collaborators and institutional pressures can create difficulties. Smith and Ngarimu (2021) have shown that despite many institution's aspirations to grant access to collections and to involve indigenous collaborators in the exploration of their collections, access can be stymied by other preservation concerns and workloads, and this can have a detrimental impact on the potential for future consultation. Another reason that the process may breakdown is that conservators, curators, and other specialists may perceive that their technical expertise or the scientific basis of the field is being questioned and feel challenged by that (Henderson and Nakamoto 2016).

Consultative practices can be undertaken with any object. Increasingly consultation has been extended to the general public who have been asked how historic houses interiors should appear (Hughes 2011; Chitty 2018; Lithgow *et al.* 2018), their perception of 'damage' to furniture (Luxford and Thickett 2013), and how illumination levels should be adjusted (Evans and Kaborg 2013). Such efforts have been very beneficial in terms of developing public understanding about the costs associated with conservation and the ways in which deterioration factors act on heritage. The influence that social valuation and aesthetic preferences have on conservation decisions such as cleaning and restoration should not be underestimated. Both the Statue of Liberty and the Acropolis in Athens are World Heritage Sites; however, the Statue of Liberty retains its green corrosion crust (Case Study 3A), whilst the Acropolis' stonework was cleaned of its blackened stone crust, giving it a fresh white marble appearance (Kapelouzou 2012: 177). Neither monument was returned to its original appearance, but in both cases some later alterations to the appearance were removed moving the objects closer to their earlier appearance although, crucially, one which is aesthetically valued by present-day society. The weight placed on such factors in the decision-making process becomes explicit when there is wider (public) consultation. The value placed on the appearance of statues, ruins, and objects of local and national identity is high and influences both decisions and decision makers.

Developing Decision-Making

Interventive (remedial) conservation involves greater risk to the object than other approaches. In universities the focus on health and safety, rising costs for laboratories, less curriculum time for practical work, and fewer teaching support staff, can mean that less interventive conservation is taught and practised. Jonathan Ashley-Smith (2016) has expressed concerns about the loss of practical skilling in conservation training courses and the ways in which the focus on preventive conservation approaches may reinforce a 'hands-off' attitude to conservation. Such factors can contribute to a lack of confidence about using interventive methods for the treatment of important historic and archaeological objects (Child 1994). Educational settings accustom students to undertaking AD-type processes. Although such decision-making takes time, energy, and effort one learns to make reasoned, balanced decisions. Over time and practice, experience is gained and heuristic decision-making improves. As greater experience is gained conservators become increasingly comfortable using whichever decision-making method, heuristic or AD, is most appropriate. Emerging conservators should therefore seek out a broad range of practical experiences. Such experiences enable a broader range of solutions to be considered and may spring from a variety of sources including formal training, structured internships, and continuing professional development (CPD) courses as well as more informal activities such as crafting and volunteer work.

Experimentation offers a way to test and evaluate results before making the final decision regarding the conservation of the object. However:

- It is possible to become too focussed on uncertainty (the things that are not known or understood) and this can lead to inaction. Focus on the things that can be controlled and where progress can be made. It is important that conservators accept that there will be some uncertainty when predicting the future of an object/ treatment while also taking steps to minimise any negative impacts (Henderson 2018).
- The more research is undertaken, the greater the cost and the longer time the decision-making process will take, so it is important to judge when one has information to make a good decision.
- When repeating an experiment, if you get the same result or similar information, the necessity for gaining more information is reduced. If, on the other hand, the information recovered when the experiment is repeated increases the variety of answers, more experimentation/ research may well be required.

Consulting stakeholders and then conserving an object with reference to a client's brief can be a challenging skill to develop. Ellen Pearlstein's innovative solution was to have students conserve heirlooms from each other's families. This gave them experience of consultation: interviewing each other or each other's families, before drawing up statements of significance, agreeing a conservation proposal, and then undertaking the conservation work (Pearlstein 2017). The students became very aware of the value of other people's heritage and were reminded that the conservator's emphasis on preservation or minimal intervention is often not shared by a wider public who want to actively engage with their heritage.

Emerging conservators can also gain useful insights into decision-making processes through hearing or reading more senior conservator's autoethnographic accounts of conservation projects (Stiger 2016). These accounts highlight how different factors are weighted and that there is some uncertainty in any conservation activity. Conservators tend to publish articles that celebrate successful treatments. Although every conservator has at some point in their career experienced a treatment that did not go the way they hoped it would, failures and mistakes are often swept under the carpet. Often the subject of self-deprecating conference coffee-break chatter, these stories are vital learning tools that deserve a wider place in the field. Increasingly their value is being recognised through informal sessions at conferences that are often paired with tips and tricks and the other sorts of useful information infrequently captured in scholarly papers.

10A Case study: The Bush Barrow Gold (Chippindale 1988; Corfield 1988; Kinnes *et al.* 1988; Shell and Robinson 1988)

In 1985, the British Museum was asked to loan objects recovered from Bush Barrow in Wessex to an exhibition entitled 'Symbols of Power' (Clarke *et al.* 1985) at the National Museum of Scotland in Edinburgh. They did this after first reshaping, cleaning, and remounting the large sheet-gold lozenge from Bush Barrow. Subsequently an exchange of views about the merits of this decision was published in the journal *Antiquity* with staff at the British Museum who undertook the restoration, representatives of the Wiltshire Archaeological and Natural History Society, who owned the object, the chairman of the United Kingdom Institute of Conservation (UKIC), and the editor of the journal weighing in. The discussion highlighted the differences in approach and judgement regarding the reshaping of metal objects prevalent in the 1980s, and created a test case, which has shaped subsequent discussions on conservation ethics.

The Bronze Age site at Bush Barrow was excavated by William Cunnington in 1808. He uncovered a human skeleton surrounded with grave goods including several pieces of gold work, amongst which was a 186 mm by 157 mm lozenge made of thin gold alloy foil (0.1–0.2 mm thick). The front surface of the lozenge was decorated with four concentric lozenges outlined by groups of three to four parallel incised grooves. The outermost of the four bands was decorated with an incised zig-zag pattern, the innermost with an incised criss-cross design, the second and third bands were undecorated (see Figure 10.6). The lozenge was bent over along each side forming a 3- to 4-mm ledge and the very edge of the foil was further bent to grip a thin layer of wood that originally formed the object's backing. Brief details about the lozenge and an idealised drawing were published along with full details of the excavation and contents of Bush Barrow in *Ancient History of South Wiltshire* written in 1812 by Sir Richard Colt Hoare, who had financed Cunnington's excavation.

In 1883, The Bush Barrow gold became the property of Wiltshire Archaeological and Natural History Society. It was displayed in their museum in Devizes until 1922 when it was deposited on 'indefinite' loan with the British Museum because of concerns over security in Devises.

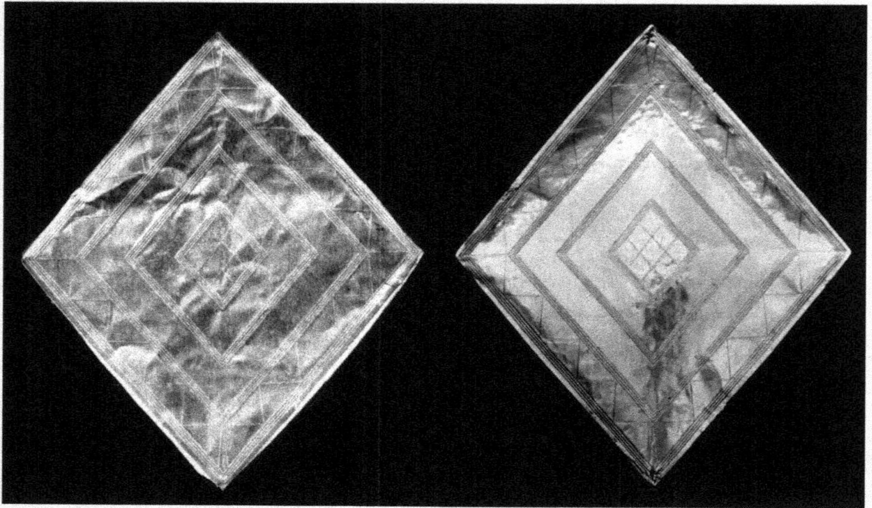

Figure 10.6 The gold lozenge from Bush Barrow, Wiltshire. Left – as photographed in 1912 (Abercromby 1912). Right – current image following reshaping. Wiltshire Archaeological and Natural History Society.

Noting the extremely fragile nature of the object, the continued demand for exhibitions and research and the ease with which thin gold foil is damaged the British Museum staff decided to 'remove the major undulations' (Kinnes *et al.* 1988), clean the lozenge and provide a firm new backing. The cleaning of the object and its fragile nature were discussed with Paul Robinson of the Wiltshire Museum, though no permission to reshape the object was sought or given. The conservation staff of the British Museum had considerable expertise in restoring metal artefacts and believed they were carrying out minor conservation work that was appropriate to the preservation of this object. They noted that the crumpled gold metal of the front surface of the lozenge was almost slack within the more rigid bent sides and that the outer incised lines were in the form of a slight curve. They concluded that the metal had originally had a shallow domed form, with a slight keel at the principal axes. Using fingers, wood, plastic hand tools, and metal tools wrapped in leather, the worst creases were eliminated from the lozenge, which consequently regained a keeled domed form curving 8 mm above the horizontal. Measurements of the incised lines, taken using a series of 90 ° offsets, showed that in the reconstructed domed form, the lines form a very regular straight-lined lozenge design. This restoration helped to bring together the edges of the slight tears in the sides of the lozenge (Oddy 1994). Consequently, the British Museum believed that the object now had the appropriate 'as original' domed profile. An exact Perspex mount was created to fully support this restored form.

The British Museum regarded the distorted shape of the Bush Barrow lozenge as resulting from damage incurred during burial, excavation, and subsequent handling; consequently, they restored it. Following reshaping, the lozenge was cleaned through the gentle application of Goddard's Long Term Silver Foam diluted with water and detergent. This cleaning agent in part cleans using a very fine (1-micron-sized particle) abrasive. While preserving the tool marks and scratches from use or previous cleaning of the object, it has given the surface a reflective shiny finish.

When the object was seen on exhibition in Edinburgh by a member of the Wiltshire Archaeological and Natural History Society, they were surprised by the shiny appearance and reshaped form. Subsequently concerns regarding the reshaping and cleaning were raised by Shell and Robinson (1988) and Chippindale (1988). They questioned:

- The need to undertake any work. Why allow an object to be studied, or go on exhibition if there is a risk of it being damaged by this process?[4]
- The accuracy of the reshaping work and the necessity of cleaning. Measurements taken on a cast of the electrotype of the Bush Barrow lozenge made in 1922, and housed in Devizes Museum, using an Omicron 3-D digitiser which determines surface contours to 0.001 mm, suggested that the dome had originally been very shallow with a maximum height of 3 mm above the horizontal. This raised concerns that the British Museum reshaping had plastically deformed the soft and malleable gold foil.

Shell and Robinson (1988) suggest that the domed form may have been due to distortion from post-excavation care between 1808 and 1922 and that the object may well have originally been flat. They dismissed, the evidence of the gently curved incised lines as a deliberate decorative feature. Additionally, they noted that all the other gold from the Bush Barrow and its surrounding barrows has a matte finish at present and there is no evidence to suggest that it originally had a highly reflective surface.

Corfield (1988), quoting the newly penned 1983 UKIC 'Guidance for Conservation Practice,' described the aim of conservation as 'to reveal the true nature of the object.' Restoring or reshaping metals may reveal one 'truth' while destroying another since almost every object holds many truths. Therefore, a balanced judgement must be made as to what is most important to reveal. It is not normally considered an ethical practice to remove any damage or distortion deliberately enacted upon an object during its life. Occasions where reshaping metal may be considered ethical include:

- Where it can be done without damaging the object. It should be done by an experienced and competent metalworker.
- Where the distortion of the metal results from the burial of the object or its excavation and the distortion clearly did not represent an important aspect of the past history of the object (e.g. the damage caused to the Coppergate helmet by the mechanical excavator (Tweddle 1992), or the crushing experienced by the Anastasius Dish when the Sutton Hoo burial chamber's collapsed (Oddy 1994)).
- Where important information can be uncovered; for example, the unrolling of Roman lead curses (thin sheets of lead on which worshippers scratched messages to the gods) to reveal the inscriptions inside them (Dove 1981). Similarly, the flattened and broken bronze bust of Lucius Aurelius Verus (Smith 1977) was reshaped to identify who was depicted, whilst the Hockwold Treasure was reshaped in order to determine how many objects were present (Oddy 1994). In these examples, the reshaped object provides more information than the flattened, rolled, or distorted form.

Following Colt-Hoare's publication of the lozenge, it appeared in many subsequent publications. Photographs showed that it had a slightly creased or crumpled form that appeared to have changed with time. Although variations in the lighting between the photographs obscured the precise extent of the distortion, Corfield (1988) suggested that handling damage may have occurred, supporting the British Museum's view that the object was at risk if unsupported.

Responding to Shell and Robinson, the British Museum team suggested that shrinkage from the silicone rubber mould and the electrotyping process might have distorted Shell and Robinson's measurements meaning that the derived shape did not accurately reflect the original dimensions of the lozenge. Since the work on the lozenge had already been carried out, no further evidence could be obtained to resolve the issue as to whether the gold was plastically deformed.

The question of the cleaning and degree of reflection from the surface is another area where it is difficult to be certain of the true nature of the object. The degree to which this was the original condition or something that developed during burial (e.g. through etching of the silver from the surface of the metal during the decay of the body) is as yet unresolved. Consequently, the present aesthetic experience, whether shiny or matt, is entirely subjective.

Having decided that the object was to be restored, clearly although the treatment was regarded as 'standard practice' rather than major restoration work by the British Museum, others did not regard it in the same light and greater consultation before the work was undertaken might have eliminated the later controversy. The significant visual change, like that of the wall paintings on the Sistine Chapel ceiling, drew attention to the conservation work, and emphasised the high social value vested in the appearance of objects. It seems likely that the conservation decision by the British Museum was initially a heuristic one, successful previous conservation work on similar objects was quickly cited as a reason for their approach. The subsequent controversy and publication stimulated the AD arguments presented in the papers in *Antiquity*. It remains difficult to judge how far one should go in reshaping. Leaving our museums filled with broken crumpled objects gives a distorted view of the past, as does filling them with beautiful fully restored objects. Whilst all the items on loan from Wiltshire Archaeological and Natural History Society have now been returned to Devizes the most enduring legacy to conservation has been the exposure that this subject received. The high level of research undertaken on this object took place as a result of the controversy and was far greater than would have otherwise occurred. The research highlighted the fragile and easily distorted nature of gold foil. It emphasised the threats posed to objects in museum care and questioned assumptions regarding the original form of objects. It moved the subject of conservation forward with wider awareness and debate on the issue of reshaping metal artefacts. It should be noted that gold sheet artefacts, such as the Ringlemere Cup unearthed in 2001 (Needham *et al.* 2006), which have subsequently entered the British Museum collections, have been left in the 'as found' condition, even when heavily damaged and distorted. In the case of the Ringlemere Cup it remains unclear whether the distortion occurred due to deliberate damage to the cup as part of the burial ritual or through the subsequent collapse of the grave chamber and plough damage.

Notes

1 In the following discussion it is the process that is important, rather than the number of categories, colour, etc. It is important that the same process is consistently used so results are comparable and that clear definitions are created. The National Museum of Australia has some definitions in its *Collection Care and Preservation Policy version 1.0.* Available at: https://www.nma.gov.au/__data/assets/pdf_file/0004/558769/POL-C-042-Collection-care-and-preservation-v1.0.pdf (Accessed June 5, 2022).

2 Stable *et al.* (2021) explored the role the Keeper of Art and Archaeology, a renowned Egyptologist, had in determining the appearance of artefacts in the ancient Egyptian Gallery at the National Museum of Scotland.

3 Examples of laws which mandate consultative processes include but are not limited to the Native American Graves Repatriation and Protection Act-NAGPRA (1990-United States), Treaty of Waitangi Act (1975-New Zealand), and the Aboriginal and Torres Strait Islander Heritage Protection Act (1984-Australia).

4 While this is a valid question, one must also ask, if an object is not accessible is the museum fulfilling its purpose?

11 Responsibilities, Skills, and Sustainable Practices in the 21st Century

The Responsible and Effective Conservator

Conservators do not work in isolation. Their work takes place within a wider context that includes regulatory frameworks, legal obligations, and public perception. To be a responsible and ethical conservator and to ensure that their work remains valued and relevant, a conservator should have many qualities including the following:

- The judgement and practical skills to undertake the conservation of objects. This includes a clear understanding of the aims of conservation, an ability to balance competing treatment needs and make good decisions, as well as the skills to enact the decision reached (Chapters 1–10). The conservator needs to undertake these activities safely and responsibly for the object, themselves, their colleagues, and a wider society.
- An appreciation that they are not simply an individual conservator but are part of a profession and that the reputation of that profession is important in determining its standing (and access to resources) within the heritage community. To be seen as a good professional, there is a need act responsibly, but also to be effective and 'get the job done' well.
- The ability to communicate their work to others and to share its value. This may include working as a team member within an organisation, public outreach, or educating the next generation of conservators.
- Ensuring that the conservation work they undertake is not wasted and that sustainable solutions are enacted. This means considering the implications of everything they do and seeking to preserve both cultural heritage and the planet itself.

Health and Safety

Conservators have a responsibility not to endanger themselves, their colleagues, the public, the objects they treat, or the environment itself. Threats (things likely to cause damage) may come from either the objects themselves or from the conservation processes used and may take many forms including biohazards, toxic chemicals, radioactive materials, using sharp tools and moving heavy objects. The threat posed depends not only on the nature of the material or activity but also on the extent and duration of the activity, the nature of the exposure to the substance and how much is

DOI: 10.4324/9781003009078-11

used; for example, short exposures to dilute acids are less risky to objects than longer exposures to more concentrated acids.

The initial issue in dealing with any risk is the unknown. The next problem may lie in assessing the risk and determining what controls if any should be put in place i.e. identifying what the material is and what risks it poses and how to mitigate them. The expertise needed may be in-house or it may be external. In some cases, correspondence with peers may be sufficient to determine an appropriate course of action, but in others, it may be necessary to hire a consultant.

Objects can present safety issues (Case Study 11A: Danish Vet's Dispensary).[1] Some materials are inherently unsafe, such as radioactive materials (contained in some natural minerals and luminescent dials), or toxic (for example, pigments such as cinnabar or orpiment), while some objects (such as those that emit electricity or those with sharp blades) pose other risks. Some objects pose health hazards because of the ways they were treated in the past; for example, many natural history specimens and ethnographic materials were historically treated with pesticides, which contained arsenic, mercury, chlorine, and other chemicals (Odegaard *et al.* 2005). When examining objects from ethnographic and natural history collections, it is important to know as much about the history of the collection as possible. Simple precautions like wearing personal protective equipment (PPE), such as gloves, dust masks, and laboratory coats, are important. Portable XRF may indicate whether heavy metals (linked to some persistent pesticides) are present. If there are concerns, it is advisable to notify colleagues of any potential threat, bag, or box the object to minimise contact, and then arrange for further testing or analysis.

There has been increasing awareness in recent decades of the threats chemicals pose to human health (i.e. as toxins, carcinogens, mutagens, etc). Many countries have passed laws and regulations to control threats to health and safety and conservators should be familiar with them.[2] If chemicals are used, a risk assessment, which includes awareness of the nature of chemicals being used and the controls that can be put in place to minimise their effects, is often required.[3]

Some conservation treatments used heavily in the 19th and early 20th centuries are no longer safe or appropriate. In reviewing chemical treatments over the past 50 years, the following trends can be noticed:

- There is less bulk use of chemicals and in particular acids. Poultices and spot treatments are frequently preferred over immersion to minimise the quantities of chemicals needed.
- Where chemicals are used, more controls are in place. They are used in minimal quantities, are more dilute, and are used, where possible, in contained environments, such as gloveboxes or fume cabinets.
- Solvent use has been reduced and confined principally to areas with extraction capabilities. Additionally, less carcinogenic solvents and those with higher boiling points have been employed to minimise risk to the conservator.
- Non-toxic approaches, such as freezing and/or high temperature treatments (Xavier-Rowe *et al.* 2000; Carrlee 2003) or anoxia (Child 2002), are now widely used to control pest infestations in historic artefacts instead of biocides.
- A greater emphasis has been placed on the need to label chemicals and to make others aware of the risks posed. Chemicals should be disposed of according to the

local regulations or legal requirements, these may include safe disposal by commercial waste disposal firms.

Chemicals are not the only hazards that may be present in labs. Sharp tools, such as scalpels, pin vices, board shears, guillotines, and even lathes, band saws, and other power tools, require safe storage and an awareness (often acquired through training) of how to work safely around them as well as an understanding of which materials each will cut effectively. Not using such tools when distracted or tired may also be an important control. Repetitive actions, such as scalpel cleaning under a microscope, inpainting, or airbrasion can lead to muscular stress and it may be important to get up and to stretch periodically to avoid strain. Exposure to vibrations and sound should also be limited; in the case of vibrations, this may involve only working for a certain duration and then taking a break, sound abatement may include the addition of architectural baffles or the use of ear protectors. Similarly moving heavy, large, or awkward objects requires both practice and a plan. When moving large or heavy objects, planning the route to minimise periods when one might have to hold rather than carry the object, considering whether one or more people are needed for the move, learning to lift so that stress is not placed on back, using appropriate lifting and moving equipment and seeking advice from others with more experience are all invaluable. New conservation methods and equipment bring the potential for associated risks, each should be assessed for risk, and appropriate regulations consulted, and procedures implemented, as seen in the precautions associated with using lasers in conservation cleaning (Cooper 1998). It is difficult to accurately assess the risks of a process with which you are not familiar, so it is important to talk with others who have experience with the process. Small tips and tricks can enhance the safety of an operation, an effective conservator should strive to be risk aware rather than risk adverse.

Mental Health

Mental health is an important consideration. Stress occurs when there are constant demands that go beyond our ability to cope with them. These can be imposed by others or by oneself. High levels of chronic stress can lead to anxiety and depression as well as physical symptoms. For conservators working in private practice, especially if their lab is in or connected to their home, establishing a work life balance can be a real factor, while conservators working in institutional environments report that paperwork and research often must be done afterhours or at home due to interruptions, meetings, and other responsibilities in the workplace. The boom in virtual meetings, conferences, and activities such as virtual couriering that the COVID-19 pandemic fuelled has meant an increase in work-related activities occurring outside of 'regular' business hours, which can contribute to a sensation of burnout. It is important to balance workload and to be reflective when presented with new opportunities. While it can feel difficult or unwise to turn down opportunities, especially as an emerging conservator, one should carefully consider how they are serving one's practice or career goals. It is important to ask yourself:

- Does this project, no matter how exciting or flattering, help me to learn new material or to advance my practices in the directions I want it to go? Do I have the

skills now to do the work and if not, will I be supported adequately in acquiring the skills needed?
- Do I have the time for this both from a professional and a personal point of view? Can I add this to my current workload without feeling overburdened? If it means doing some of the work in my 'downtime', how will I feel about that?
- Will I be able to meet the deadlines? Are they reasonably spaced? Are they in competition with any other deadlines I already have? How will they impact my work if they alter – is my schedule so tight that any variation will cause an issue?

If the answer to any of these questions is no, it may be appropriate to turn the project down or negotiate different parameters, such as additional training or the spacing of deadlines. One may also need to adjust career goals and the way one works.

Recently the impact on mental health of working with supernatural and sensitive materials has been raised (Pickering 2020). Although the question is raised in relation to the impacts of such objects on indigenous staff members in Australian museums, it is important to note that the issue is broader than this. Conservators working with objects and sites of trauma have noted that such objects can take a mental and emotional toll. The closeness that working with objects requires can compound these effects and teams that discuss their experiences with each other are better able to process them and are thus more resilient (Reeve and Adams 1993).

Professional Competence

The various codes of ethics that govern conservators spell out a number of responsibilities for conservation professionals (AICCM 2002; ICON 2020; AIC 2020). Some are quite specific, related to conservation activities such as the responsibility to document treatments and demonstrate informed respect for the unique character of cultural property and the people or persons who created it. Others speak to personal conduct and the need for self-control such as practicing within the limits of one's own competencies, operating within the laws of the country in which you are practising conservation and avoiding bringing the field into disrepute.

If clients, stakeholders, and allied professionals have a positive experience of working with conservators, perceive the work to be of value and to have been done well, the conservation profession can be justified and sustained. If on the other hand, the experience is negative, the work has little value or is of a poor quality, they will lose faith in the individual conservators and quite possibly in the field itself. Key to retaining stakeholders' confidence is the idea of the conservator working within the bounds of their 'professional competence'. Competence is built through training (awareness of current practice and knowledge about the object and its materials and decay) and hands on experience (experience carrying out similar processes) and is typically communicated through qualifications and referrals. While professional competence is easy to define in certain areas – one is not competent to drive a forklift unless one is trained in its usage – in conservation determining competency can be more nuanced because of the unique nature of many objects and the distribution of conservators. For example, a furniture conservator may know a tremendous amount about wood, but should they take on the treatment of waterlogged archaeological wood? With time and effort, they could presumably research the aspects of waterlogged wood that make it unique and the current approaches to its practice, build a treatment plan, and undertake the work. A more cost effective or optimal result could be gained by referring the object to someone with more experience treating waterlogged wood. However, in regions where there are few archaeological conservators with expertise treating waterlogged wood, it may be necessary for the furniture conservator to stretch their competencies. Careful reflection, research and decision-making will be key to making this decision a success.

Within the conservation field, new skills and techniques are initially gained through training programs, apprenticeships, placements, internships, and fellowships and later through continuing professional development (CPD), the importance of which is underscored by the fact that many professional conservation organisations now include a requirement for individuals to engage with it on a regular (often annual) basis. The definition of CPD is typically broad and may include attending workshops, seminars, and conferences, taking art or craft classes, reading articles, and visiting or working in labs other than one's own for short periods. The experiential demands that building and maintaining competency place on conservators has given rise to a corollary responsibility within the field, which relates to delivering training. Training may take the form of mentoring emerging conservators, supervising placements and internships, or designing and delivering short courses or it can be a more informal approach such as showing a colleague how to carry out a treatment step. Training (like outreach) takes time, thought and energy; however, it is vital to the development of the field. Confidence can be a barrier to sharing skills. Conservators can lack confidence in their 'mastery' of techniques and therefore be protective of their work, reluctant to share and to open it up for potential criticism (Clare 2018). It is important to remember that competence and mastery (or expertise) are not the same thing. They are different points on a scale of skills acquisition (Dreyfus and Dreyfus 1980) with competence implying a good working understand of the skill and its background as well as an ability to work independently to an acceptable standard and mastery suggesting an authoritative knowledge and an ability to easily go beyond existing interpretations and apply the skill in a new and innovative way (ECCO 2011; ICON 2020). In practice, most conservator's work is a mix of the two with areas of competency and areas that approach mastery of a technique or concept occurring simultaneously. Accepting this allows us to be more reflective about our practice, spot knowledge gaps, and communicate better with others. It also permits us to see where we have skills that we can share.

Professional competence is reinforced through good business practices. These include the following:

- Willingness to consult with others to acquire the necessary information to plan and conduct conservation projects and to identify any unusual skills that may be needed.
- Accurately estimating the resources needed to carry out conservation work.
- Successful management and completion of projects i.e. completing the work on time and within budget.
- Problem solving to ensure that both the stakeholder's and the objects' needs are met and successfully communicating those solutions to all involved.
- Crediting and acknowledging the contributions of others to the work.
- Maintaining an awareness of laws and regulations that impact conservation practices including those addressing, health and safety, looted and stolen property

(Tubb 1995; Tubb and Sease 1996), and sacred and religious materials as well as human remains (Hutt and Riddle 2007) and endangered species (Owczarek *et al.* 2015).
- Ensuring that those whose training or activities they supervise are prepared, equipped and appropriately supported to carry out the work.

As the case of the Bush Barrow Gold demonstrates, issues of ownership, permission, and the scope of work to be done need to be resolved prior to any work being initiated (Case Study 10A). Permission for the work must be given and stakeholders should be aware of what will be done (Figure 3.2). If a conservator is asked to carry out work that they consider inappropriate or unethical they can decline to undertake it or advise the owner/curator of why such actions are inappropriate (Balachandran 2007). Prior to discussing conservation measures, conservators, and stakeholders (owners, curators, community members, etc.) should discuss the nature and importance (values) of the object and a formal written contract between the parties for the conservation work should be drawn up. This may vary in scope depending on the scale of the project. Ensuring that the object is appropriately insured and secured when in the care of the conservator, and any subcontractors, may be important parts of such contractual negotiations.

Conservation Outreach

Conservation outreach, where conservators engage with the public, has become an important part of the conservator's responsibilities in the 21st century (Figure 11.1; Pye 2001; Brooks 2008; Williams 2013). Outreach takes many forms including publication, exhibitions, media appearances, social media, tours, lectures, training, and volunteer engagement. There are many reasons for conducting outreach activities, including but not limited to:

- Increasing public awareness and support for conservation. Direct support for conservation, including funding and advocacy for conservation projects or the field in general, may be a by-product of outreach but that should not necessarily be the overriding goal. Indirect support such as name recognition, understanding, and goodwill may be equally important.
- Increased engagement with collections care. There are not nearly enough conservators to care for the world's cultural heritage. Outreach to allied professionals, such as curators, collection managers, and archaeologists can help lift the level of care that both moveable and immoveable heritage receive.[4] Similarly, volunteer projects engage the public and spread the conservator's reach (Ganiaris and Lang 2013). Outreach efforts may also impart valuable information about how to interact with heritage (many museums now include 'please touch' panels or displays to demonstrate the impact of repeated handling and touching on objects). Teaching the public to care for their own objects ensures that objects that might not otherwise get care do.
- As part of an approach to shared decision-making. Outreach may be a part of a consultation process. The Attingham Rediscovered project invited members of the public to help shape the National Trust's approach to the conservation of the building (Hughes 2011).

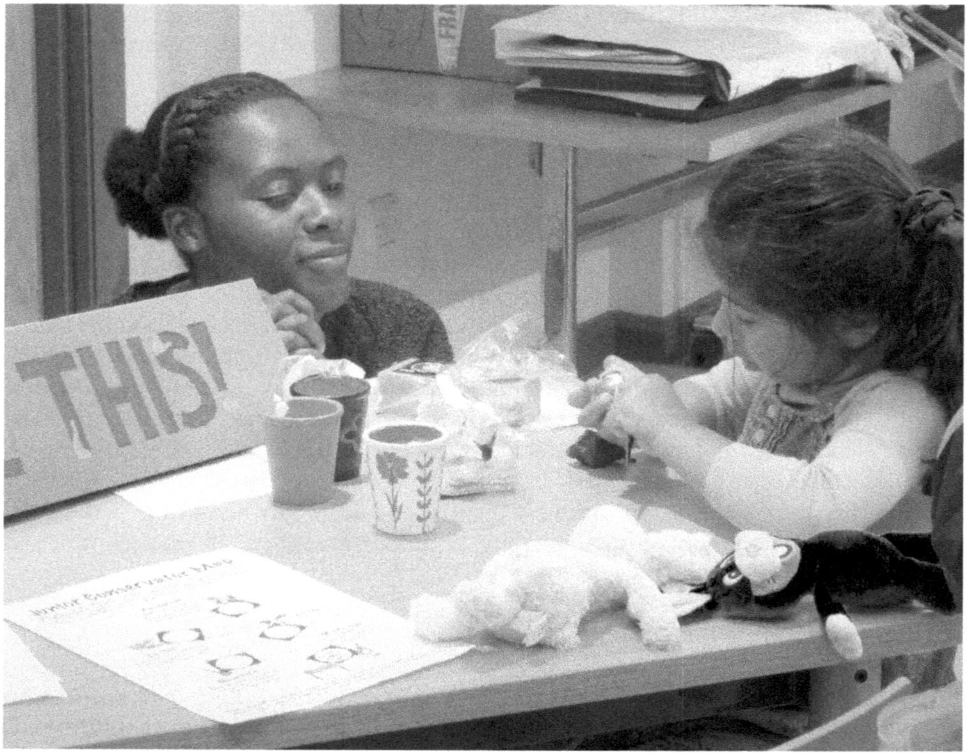

Figure 11.1 A conservation MA student discusses fills with a 'Junior conservator' at an outreach event.

Source: Emily Williams.

Media

There are many different venues through which outreach may be delivered. Radio interviews, television programs, magazines, and newspapers have the advantage of reaching the broadest audiences, but it is important to remember that many of these outlets have their own agendas and their own narratives to advance. If a story fits neatly within these, it may be presented nearly as submitted; however, if it does not it may be edited to create a more dramatic or controversial story. Tropes that the media sometimes employs include the idea of the object transformed, characterised by dramatic before and after imagery, and the 'forensic' investigation, characterised by lots of close ups of conservators in lab-coats peering through microscopes and other high-tech equipment to reveal precious information about the past. Such imagery conforms with how conservators often present themselves; however, Mary Brooks (2008) has pointed out that they do not always serve the field well. Although they focus on aspects of conservation work, they often render the conservator largely invisible (a pair of disembodied hands wielding tools or an operator for an analytical device). What is left out, because it does not generate strong, recognisable images (Podany and Lansing

Maish 1993), is the interpretive decision-making and the social process that adds to an object's value, both of which are key elements of the conservator's job.

Although interventive treatments are reported on with some frequency, preventive conservation attracts less attention. The threat of loss can be a goad to action, but many heritage institutions are wary about suggesting that their collections are not in an ideal state as this can lead to accusations of neglect (Pye 2001: 188). Jones and Holden have noted that despite the importance of collection care, headlines stating that collections are not degrading are not very exciting (2008: 61). An exception occurred during the lockdowns associated with the COVID-19 pandemic when preventive conservation was seen as essential work and one of the few activities for which one could leave home. It therefore became newsworthy as the changes experienced by collections became a way of understanding spaces without humans in them and the magnitude of the disruption caused by the virus (cf. Chilton 2020; Gillett 2021).

Generally, conservators have a positive public image since they have unusual skills, save things from destruction, and make much loved items whole and beautiful again. In 2006, when a visitor fell and broke three Qing dynasty vases at the Fitzwilliam Museum in Cambridge, the museum's careful management of their public relation transformed early criticism into a powerful success story that highlighted their collections care and was picked up by international news agencies, enhancing the museum's reputation worldwide.[5] However, adverse stories fed by criticism from allied professionals (Case Study 6 A: Sistine Ceiling) or journalistic outrage about the cost of heritage may have longer lives than feel-good stories. When dealing with the media it is therefore important to get good advice; many museums and heritage organisations have press and publicity officers who can help with interview preparation.

- Be prepared; know your topic, consider your key points, and learn why you are being interviewed. It is okay to ask the reporter in-depth questions about what they expect from the interview beforehand or to ask for a list of potential questions.
- Be prepared for the reporter to go off topic. Think about how you might redirect them back to your key points.
- Brief answers are more effective. They help to make the dialog in an interview to seem more like a conversation. Avoid the lengthy detail that often forms the core of conservation documentation since time and space are often limited.
- Be careful about using lots of qualifying words; conservators are taught to qualify observations with words like 'almost certainly', 'probably', and 'may be' but the public tends to hear this as uncertainty rather than an indication of probability.
- Avoid the use of jargon and think carefully about how to simplify complex technical details and make them relatable. If the interview is for radio or a podcast, think about how you might describe what the audience is not seeing. Adding a few descriptive metaphors or colourful images will help the audience to 'see' what you are saying and will make your message more memorable.

Conservation Exhibits

When conservators drive the communication, whether in the form of an exhibition, tour, lectures, or social media, they control the message directly and can be subtler and more nuanced. There have been many powerful and effective conservation exhibitions and exhibits that include substantive conservation components.[6] Such exhibits, like behind-the-scenes tours of conservation labs, may offer visitors an opportunity to see objects from unexpected angles, sometimes quite literally but also metaphorically. Visitor numbers often illustrate the popularity of such exhibits, but few formal studies have been carried out to determine how successful the messaging is. Do people learn what we want them to? Does it really lead them to change their behaviour or to look at other cultural heritage in a different way? How well do they read the labels and if they do not is the content clear or somewhat baffling? Many exhibit evaluations are ad-hoc and address enjoyment rather than knowledge gained (Williams 2013b). Some important work has been done in this area (Drago 2011: 33–36; Koutromanou 2017) but more remains to be done to understand how effective such outreach truly is. Although exhibitions are excellent ways of focussing public interest in conservation, one down-side is that they are often short-term and rapidly replaced. Even the Conservation Centre at the National Museums Liverpool, a whole museum devoted to explaining conservation that opened in 1996 and won the 1998 European Museum of the Year award, had a relatively short run closing to the public in 2010 (Watts *et al.* 2013).

Static exhibitions lack the immediacy of seeing work in progress, although video components can inject this aspect to a limited capacity. Consequently, many museums and heritage organisations have built 'open' conservation labs where visitors can see into the lab (Lochhead and Tonkin 2013; Peters 2013; Arista and Drayman Weisser 2013). These labs allow visitors to watch conservation in action but, without explanation, the work can be puzzling; especially, if it involves activities that appear violent, such as hitting an object with a hammer to remove concretion layers, or actions that appear to make the object look worse (such as the removal of overpaint on a painting revealing fields of gesso and primer beneath). How to offer explanation while accommodating changing numbers of objects and their natures has been an area of discussion (Peters 2013; Lochhead and Tonkin 2013).[7] The Penn Museum's Artifact lab successfully addressed these issues. The lab has glass windows through which visitors can look and the surrounding gallery supports its work by presenting conservation case studies. Text panels and video introduce conservation while a reading corner offers interested visitors an opportunity for deeper engagement. Windows into the lab are opened twice a day allowing visitors to interact with conservators and to ask questions about the work. Designed as a short-term answer to the conservation needs of the Museum's Egyptian collections, its popularity has led to its extension. Since there is another conservation lab in the building, conservators can choose which objects are suitable to treat in front of the public and which are not. Due to the size of the museum's conservation team, staff can rotate in the lab allowing a degree of freshness. The conservators working in the Artifact lab have been careful to monitor their impact.[8] Open labs have an added benefit in that they help to make conservation more visible not only to visitors but also to other staff within the host institution (Drago 2011). Where conservation has been viewed as a technical role that is subservient to other heritage professionals, this can be particularly powerful in disrupting the narrative and elevating the conservator's voice.

Social Media

Conservators have successfully presented conservation information through social media. Most heritage organisations have websites. Conservation projects can provide positive stories for these, demonstrating the care and expertise that collections in the organisation receive. Such stories may be the public's first encounter with conservation. Websites and other forms of social media engage audiences who can be very far away as well as much closer to home, but they require frequent updating to ensure they remain relevant and 'fresh'. Social media can draw people interested in specific aspects of the past, or technology, into conservation. The engaging blog run by conservators at the Mariner's Museum has introduced an audience interested in the American Civil War, and more specifically in the USS *Monitor* and her pioneering engineering, to the methods, aims, and ethics of conservation. Institutions or labs may have their own social media presences and it is important to understand whether they have any restrictions about what can be said or posted on the official and platform or shared on employee's personal accounts. When sharing conservation materials on websites and social media, it is important to:

- Share your enthusiasm about your work and the excitement of discovery. This is what grabs others and prompts them to engage.
- Proofread content.
- Check with your institution, clients or stakeholders, or other individuals regarding image permissions and releasing new information.
- Be aware that data protection laws vary in different countries and may impact what you can or cannot post.
- Be certain the image selection supports the message you wish to send; for example, a messy or overcrowded bench space may not convey careful object handling.
- Remember that once something is posted, you lose some control of it since others can share, quote, extract, and copy it.

Volunteer Engagement

Volunteers have worked effectively on archaeological excavations and as room guides in historic homes for many years. Heritage organisations around the world have also involve volunteers in collections care-related capacities including rehousing initiatives (Figure 11.2; Ganiaris and Lang 2013), running and restoring historic working objects,[9] and carrying out preventive conservation tasks, such as light readings and pest monitoring in historic properties (Lithgow and Timbrell 2014; Xavier-Rowe 2018; Lloyd and Lithgow 2021). Volunteers may be most effective when working as a team on a large project or where many small items of a similar nature require simple interventions. Both the volunteers and the organisation should gain from the activity. An enjoyable and sociable workplace, doing meaningful tasks is often important for older volunteers (Lithgow and Timbrell 2014). For younger volunteers, training and work experience opportunities may be crucial elements to help them develop their resumés, gain additional skills, and demonstrate their productivity and reliability to future employers. Good training, a clearly organised activity with support and supervision in a convivial working environment are frequently key to the success of the project. Long-term, regular volunteers frequently become highly skilled and can organise and supervise others making them more valuable to the organisation. Organisations that use volunteers effectively put time, energy, and effort (resources) into planning and managing their activities (Ganiaris and Lang 2013). The resource invested should be smaller than the benefit derived from the work, or there is no advantage to the organisation.[10] If their experience is good, volunteers are frequently passionate advocates for heritage organisations, promoting them at a grass roots level with a credibility that springs from personal experience and is almost impossible to match. Although some conservators have reservations about the appropriateness of using volunteers in conservation, often citing concerns about security, safety, and the potential that volunteer positions will replace paid staff posts, those involved with volunteer programmes rarely express such concerns. In many institutions (both large and small), volunteers are fundamental to accomplishing the collections care agenda.

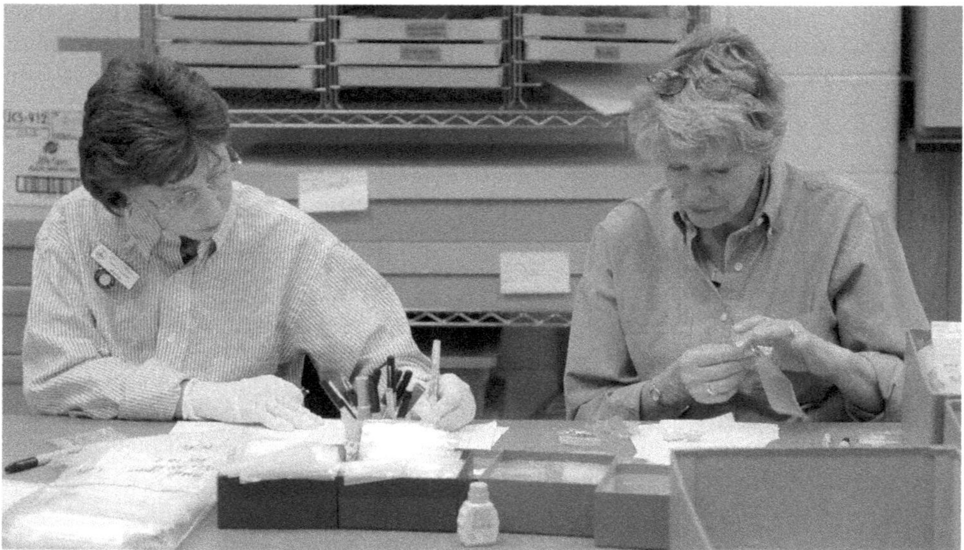

Figure 11.2 Two volunteers rehouse archaeological objects.
Source: Emily Williams.

Impact

Increasingly government funding and research grants are tied to impact (the demonstration of a marked effect or beneficial influence) on the public. Impact can be hard to measure but engagement and outreach provide clear metrics (numbers) that can be used for such purposes. Metrics that can be gathered may include simple information like the total number of participants, or more nuanced information such as the total number of individuals from different socio-economic or ethnic backgrounds reached or the degree to which participants felt the program changed their perception of a topic. Conservation outreach activities generate impact but as has been mentioned it is important to be thoughtful about what data will be collected and disciplined in its collection.

Challenges for the 21st century

Conservation (and the larger heritage sector) face a number of social and environmental challenges in the 21st century. How conservators address them will be dependant on their skills and judgement as well as their ability to recognise, understand, and manage the impact of these changes.

Climate Change

Climate change is the most pressing challenge for both humans and cultural heritage in the 21st century.

- Weather patterns have become more unpredictable, and the severity of storms has increased. Warming ocean waters are fuelling ever more powerful storms[11] that are unleashing more rain on the areas they hit.[12] In 2016, heavy rain and flooding of the Seine, necessitated the emergency relocation of materials from underground storage locations at the Louvre (Muñoz 2021).
- It is predicted that by 2100, sea levels may rise by 80–200 cm (Lindsey 2020) flooding many coastal cities and ports, such as Shanghai, Tokyo, New York, Amsterdam, and Venice as well as cities such as London that are located near tidal estuaries. Large populations will be displaced (potentially leading to conflict for resources) and collections of arts and antiques, as well as immovable cultural heritage, concentrated in these cities will require relocation or face potential loss.
- Wildfires have escalated in both scale and severity due to increasing seasonal temperatures, dry winds and dry vegetation and exacerbated by the impacts of urbanisation and the abandonment of traditional fire management protocols. Archaeological sites which are often covered by vegetation and/or situated close to forests and other flammable plant materials have historically been at the most risk; however, increasingly wildfires are now threatening large urban areas and the cultural heritage that is often massed there.

Recently nearly a third of the objects in the Louvre were relocated to a purpose-built collections care facility in the north of France to protect them from flooding (Muñoz 2021). Such moves are likely to become increasingly common as the impacts of climate change are increasingly felt. They offer opportunities to build in state-of-the-art protections and energy efficiencies and may be shared between heritage institutions creating cost-savings. However, they require long-term sustained planning (on the order of a decade or more), which tests the 3–5-year planning cycles that are common for museums and heritage organisations.

Reducing Environmental Impact

Beginning in the mid-1990s, many businesses began adopting a new framework for measuring their performance. Known as Triple Bottom Line (TBL) accounting, it encouraged businesses to measure not only their profits but also their impact on people and the planet, in order to measure and support the implementation of sustainable practices (Elkington 1994). Additional measures such as cultural sustainability are sometimes added. Museums and heritage organisations are increasingly adopting the TBL framework to guide their practice.[13] New initiatives are often required to demonstrate their potential positive impact in each of these areas prior to adoption (Lithgow 2011).

International efforts aimed at reducing carbon emissions have contributed to the notion that conservation activities should not only be minimally interventive to the objects themselves but also have as minimal an effect on the environment as possible. In addition to the chemicals used, and the impact of their disposal, energy emissions from air-conditioning and lighting storage and display spaces must be carefully considered. A growing awareness of the amount of energy that museums consume in maintaining tight environmental set points has led to the quest for lower energy solutions for environmental control, a growing emphasis on the use of microclimates, revisions to environmental standards, and the search for greener materials and equipment.

Although all conservators have a role to play in achieving environmental sustainability, challenges may be posed by the definitions of conservation practice, time constraints, identifying tools for decision-making, and institutional support. Identifying truly sustainable solutions is time-consuming. A holistic appreciation of the needs is required; for example, recycling is only effective when it is continued beyond the laboratory to the regional collection facility and the material is reused as a raw material and not simply added to landfill. The literature on climate change is prolific and often utilises a variety of models to predict future impacts, which can be confusing. Similarly, what may appear to be an easy win in terms of sustainability can prove to have a hidden tail when one undertakes a Life Cycle Assessment.[14] Manufacturers often make exaggerated claims about the green credentials of their products or the energy-saving benefits that may accrue through their use, a process known as 'greenwashing' that can take time and energy to parse correctly. For some conservators, the process of keeping up to date on all the sustainable options in addition to media specific conservation information feels overwhelming and can lead to inaction; worry about taking the 'wrong' action and difficulty in determining how to weigh environmental sustainability against treatment efficacy are also barriers to action. Recognising the personal and institutional impediments to action is important as it allows the development of strategies to overcome them.

A growing number of tools are being developed to aid conservators in their decision-making. For example, the *Sustainability Tools in Cultural Heritage* (STiCH) project has developed a Carbon Calculator that allows conservators to examine the carbon footprint of treatment alternatives,[15] while ICCROM's *Our Collections Matter* project disseminates resources for museums and cultural heritage institutions to successfully link their initiatives to the United Nations Sustainable Development Goals (SDGs).

Diversifying the Face of Conservation

Conservation can be a tool for social justice, preserving the stories of minority groups and offering counternarratives to dominant histories (Peters 2020; Williams 2020). The more diverse the profession is and the more cultural perspectives, life experiences,[16] and broader social networks it incorporates, the more it is enriched and the better able it is to identify, preserve, and uphold the multiple meanings of objects (Balachandran 2016). Dean Whiting (1995) noted that when members of the Māori community acquired conservation qualifications, the face of conservation in New Zealand changed. They were

> asked by their people to help define the peculiar mix of cultural preservation and conservation philosophy to produce policy and charters that will help guide conservation within tribal and national contexts … [creating] … a degree of

acceptance and relevance that will continue as long as Māori have a role in the development, decision making, and implementation processes.

In North America and Europe, conservators are overwhelmingly white. In a 2018 survey conducted by AIC, 91% of the respondents identified as white, while in the UK, 88% of conservators identified as white in a recent survey (Membership Designation Working Group 2018; Francis 2021). In North America and Europe, conservation is increasingly dominated by women; many of whom come from middle-class backgrounds. Within the American Institute of Conservation, while 34% of the membership identified as male in 1995 and only 18.4% did in 2018 (AIC 1996; Membership Designation Working Group 2018).[17] A disproportionate number of males are in leadership positions, which is reflective of broader museum hiring practices (Davis 2019). Important work is being done to transform the field, to combat gender inequalities, to make salaries more transparent and equitable, to elevate the conservator's 'voice' and to encourage participation from non-traditional backgrounds,[18] although Balachandran (2016) has noted that historically initiatives aimed at raising the number of non-white conservators in the United States have been largely ineffective. Diversifying the profession will continue to be a challenge as the 21st-century progresses. What constitutes success may look quite different from institution to institution and country to country, which can complicate the process.

Digital World

Prior to the late 20th century, information was embedded in books, whereas increasingly, data can be stored and retrieved digitally fundamentally changing its availability. While research has been greatly facilitated by the accessibility of information and the interrogation of 'big data', the challenge is increasingly how to use information meaningfully:

- What questions to ask
- How to create a framework of understanding into which to place data
- Learning to distinguish reliable information from biased, falsified, or poorly collected data.

As museums, libraries, and cultural heritage organisations digitise more collections, communicating the value of the physical object (with all its storage, treatment, and staffing needs) becomes increasingly important. Digitisation projects often provide funding for physical intervention (stabilisation and interventive conservation), but ongoing data storage and migration costs can divert funds from collections storage (especially if there is a perception that the digital version is more 'visited' than the original). For conservators, one of the challenges of the 21st century may centre on striking a balance between the needs of the physical copy and the digital record. Negotiating this balance may be further tried by concept of versioning. Many modern works of art, such as installations and performance art change each time they are presented. Such presentations, authorised (licensed) by the artist and created to their specifications, are considered 'versions' of the artwork and must be documented fully to create a record of their existence. Full recording can be substantial to capture the complexity of placement, audio-visual and technological change. As there are slight variations between each recreation/performance, they are often recorded as a numbered version of the artwork so that they can be accurately referenced.[19] The more a piece is shown the larger and more complex the dataset associated with it becomes.

Expanding Heritage and Diminishing Resources

Increasing wealth and the facility of travel combined with urban development has led to a significant rise in cultural tourism in the 21st century. The number of museums worldwide has increased from 22,000 in 1975 to 95,000 today (UNESCO 2020). In China alone, the number of museums has increased, from 349 in 1978 to over 5,100 in 2019 (Zuo 2019). At the same time, there has also been a tremendous rise in the number of sites, monuments and buildings that are deemed worthy of preservation, retention, and public access. On the one hand, this growth is an asset for the cultural heritage sector providing opportunities for new narratives, preserving a more diverse and relevant record of the past and creating new employment opportunities. However, resourcing the world's museums and cultural heritage is a challenge. Many heritage institutions begin as private initiatives (a collector choosing to make their collection accessible or a local interest group preserving a building or site) but, as broader communities engage with the site, pressure may be put on local government or national government to support these projects. To accomplish this, funds may be diverted from other collections or sites and the 'pie' sliced ever more thinly. In the UK and other countries, small regional museums funded by local governments, which also deal with a wide range of social issues, are struggling financially. Budgets are being cut and museums are being pushed to show their societal value by supporting an increasing number of educational and societal programs that often divert staff from collections care. To reduce core costs, some museums have laid off specialist curators and conservators and shut conservation laboratories and administrators rely on buying in conservation services on a commercial basis. In such arrangements, because conservators may only have 'keyhole' visions of the collection that centres on a single object or small group of objects that need conservation, the long-term views of how both collections materials and conservation materials interact with each other in 'real world' scenarios may be lost. These longitudinal studies have in the past provided critical tests to treatment and storage approaches and highlighted areas where the complexity of material and environmental interactions has prompted unexpected reactions. An important example is in waterlogged wood conservation where long-term observations of ship's timbers highlighted the degradative effects of sulphur and alum salts. It is also worth noting that for many conservators working commercially, participating in conferences and writing papers for publication represents a loss in income since few contracts include disseminating the treatment information meaning that creative solutions to conservation problems may also be lost.

Larger museums are also coming under increasing public pressure to deaccession collections. When this issue is raised it is often the museum's highlights that are targeted rather than the bulk collections that support study. Whether such recommendations are fuelled by the astronomic prices that art can command or the ongoing costs of collections storage, they pose an issue for museums and conservators. That museum collections cannot continue to grow unceasingly moving from storage site to ever larger storage site like some form of hermit crab is understood, but divesting collections of attractive assets that bring in visitors and resources is also unwise.

Conservators may need to become more engaged with conversations about how deaccessioning may be a collections care tool in the decades to come (Swain 2010; Williams 2020).

Neutrality

The focus in the last decade of the 20th and the first two decades of the 21st century on why we conserve what we conserve has led to a focus on the narratives that animate objects and give them significance. Where conservators previously saw themselves as neutral actors focused primarily on material questions such as what should be conserved and how that can be achieved technically, there is a growing awareness that our actions are not neutral. We contribute to how others perceive objects and thus to the value(s) of objects (Cane 2009; Genbrugge 2017; Williams 2020). Conservators, as well as conservation organisations, have biases (both conscious and unconscious) that play a role in their decision-making processes (Chapter 10) and that can influence their responses to situations and cause unintentional harm.[20] Durant (2020) and Henderson (2022) have shown that in attempting to maintain a position of neutrality the field is in fact making decisions that may work to support structural inequalities and negative narratives. As conservation increasingly prioritises the interactions between humans and objects and works to facilitate them, it is increasingly active in giving a voice to subaltern narratives and communities and in challenging ingrained positions. However, conservators should also be cognizant about their power and the privilege that their work with objects grants them. Choosing not to preserve certain materials because they do not agree with one's politics or beliefs may be as problematic as not examining the positions those objects reinforce. There is a balance to be threaded between professional activism and personal activism and the conservation profession must be more reflective about its approach. Internal guidance may need to be developed addressing whether there are situations in which conservators can and should remain neutral. For example, are there situations in which individual conservators can and should recuse themselves from working on objects? How do we ensure that our personal views do not drown out or unduly influence the views of the communities with which we work? Since the values vested in objects are not static and will change as society transforms around them, conservators and the conservation profession must engage in an iterative process of self-reflection.[21]

Conclusion: Judgement, Skills, and Decision-Making in the 21st Century

The more holistic appreciation of 'collections care' that manifested itself in the last decade of 20th century and the first quarter of the 21st century is being combined with longer term concerns about the planet's environment and diminishing resources. Conservators are being challenged to seek more sustainable solutions for both interventive conservation activity (increasing recycling and reducing chemical usage) and storage of museum artefacts (lowering energy costs). The increased involvement of a wider range of people in heritage decision-making and the availability of funding demand more transparent prioritisation systems and that conservation actions are tied to significance and value. Conservators have the technical tools needed to help them negotiate these challenges. The implementation of risk management systems, carefully defined decision-making protocols, and assessment frameworks that naturally prioritise object biographies and the connections that objects and people all form will help to meet these challenges. Conservators are skilled at understanding and managing change, however they will be required to continue developing and extending their communication skills to position their expertise at the centre of heritage decision-making. Teamwork will continue to be a part of the conservator's toolkit but 21st-century conservators will increasingly rely on (and need to develop) a broad range of soft skills including leadership skills (Clare 2018; Wickens and Norris 2018; Davis 2019). The conservator's dedication to preserving the past and making it accessible to both the people of the present day and those of the future and the unique insight that multi-temporal perspective grants them will remain constants.

11A Case Study: The Contents of a Danish Vet's Dispensary (Arnsby 2017)

A collection of 153 labelled containers (tins, porcelain jars, and glass bottles, all with lids or stoppers) owned by the Østfyns Museum were sent to the Bevarings Center Fyn (a regional conservation centre) for treatment (Figure 11.3). Dating from the 1950s to the 1970s, they held pharmaceutical compounds. Previously displayed as part of a traditional veterinary surgery belonging to Carl Nielsen of Nyborg, the collection was slated for storage but uncertainty over the toxicity of the contents prompted a curatorial request to remove and safely dispose of the contents, retaining the containers. Additionally, the museum was unable to meet new legal requirements regarding licensing and security for drugs and there were concerns about the safety of visitors and staff.

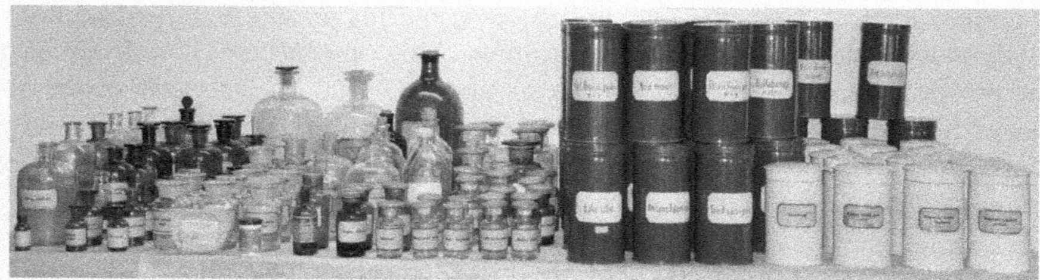

Figure 11.3 The contents of a Danish Vet's Dispensary, Østfyns Museum. Jenny Arnsby.

The dispensary project presented conflicting responsibilities for the conservator. Disposing of the contents would remove the potential to study them later. While the 20th century does not seem very distant and it may be expected that little can be added to our understanding of such recent medicines, research has shown this not to be true. Many historical medicines have an unexpected range of compounds beyond what is listed on the label (Fischel *et al.* 2016). Therefore, the only evidence of what was administered may come from the compound itself. On the other hand, retaining such materials, even in sealed containers, represented a potential threat to museum staff and to the public. It is essential to know what is present and to ascertain the risk to staff and public. To truly determine risk, chemical analysis is necessary, but the costs associated with such analysis may be beyond the budget of a small museum. Retaining the contents of containers can also pose a risk to the object, as the contents may exacerbate corrosion and other forms of chemical breakdown. Following discussions with the curators, the conservator identified the compounds, arranged for their safe disposal, cleaned the containers so no compound remained, and cleaned and conserved the containers and labels so that they could continue to function as a useful museum display.

Contents

It was essential to know what was present – both to ensure safe disposal and to form an accurate historical record of what such a collection contained. The conservator was English, and the labels were written in Danish and Latin. To ensure all information was retained and understandable, it was necessary to work in all three languages. Two spreadsheets were created one inventorying the materials and their usage and the other containing additional details about their form and their toxicity and the requirements for handling them (Figure 11.4):

Label	Danish	English	Usage
Creolin	Udtræk fra stenkulstjære	Coal tar distilate	Disinfectant, cleaner, flea remedy

Chemical Kemikalie	Toxicity Giftighed	Form Form	Weight (g) Vegt + container	Details Bemærkinger	Precautions Forholdregler	Protective Equipment Værnemidler	Toxicity – current data Giftighed ud fra nutidig data
Lead nitrate (crude)	+	Powder	442	Almost empty	Avoid contact with skin, eyes and clothing. Avoid ingestion and inhalation (see data sheet)	Goggle, gloves, mask / fume hood	Heavy metal harmful to health, environmentally harmful
Plumbi nitras venal	+	Pulver	442	Naesten tom	Undgå kontakt med hud øjne og tøj. Undgå indtagelse og indånding (se datablad)	Beskyttelsesbrillier, handsker, maske / stinkskab	Tungmetal, sundhedsskadeligt, miljøskadeligt

Figure 11.4 Data excerpts from the spreadsheets. Jenny Arnsby.

When completed these allowed the museum to retain details of the collection's contents and provided information about the threats posed to health. Following consultation with local authorities, a range of disposal options was agreed:

- Plant material was disposed with usual lab waste.
- A local pharmacy accepted and disposed of all medicinal compounds except acids, alkalis, and heavy metals.

- The local authority (*Kommune*) collected and disposed of the remaining hazardous wastes.

Exceptions were made to this. For example, powdered plant material incorporating foxglove which contains digitalis (a heart stimulant that is toxic in large doses) was disposed of with other pharmaceuticals rather than the plant material.

Containers

The contents of metal containers, normally powders or dried plant materials, were scooped or brushed out and the material disposed of. Any rust was removed from internal and external surfaces using a Dremel tool with various abrasive heads. As much original surface was retained as possible. The tins were degreased and given a coating of microcrystalline wax to give some protection.

The contents of paper bags, normally powders or dried plant materials, were scooped and brushed out and the material disposed of.

The contents of ceramic jars, normally ointments, were scooped out. The interior was wiped down using paper towelling and the material disposed of. Solvents or heat were used (in a fume cupboard if required) to ensure all the residue was removed. If the ceramics were broken, they were re-adhered with HMG Paraloid adhesive. No further restoration was undertaken.

The contents of glass bottles, normally liquids, were poured into a plastic container for disposal. The interior was wiped down using solvents (in fume cupboard) if required to ensure all residue removed. Solids were broken up in to powders and poured out or dissolved in the appropriate solvent. Where the stoppers created problems, they were drilled out and cut away (cork) or loosened with lubricating oil, tools, heat, and force in combination (glass stoppers). If the glass was broken, the pieces were re-adhered with Hxtal NYL adhesive.

Labels were dry cleaned with an eraser. If they were loose or contaminated, they were detached using humidification (Navarro 2011) washed in warm mater to remove adsorbed chemicals and acidity, then dried under weights between sheets of blotting paper. If they were fragile, they were backed with Japanese tissue. The labels were reattached to the container exterior with wheat starch paste. Some tins contained internal labels, these were also removed with humification, washed, dried, and returned loose to the tin. All deliberate markings were carefully preserved. The containers were then packed in suitable boxes for museum storage

Considerations

The approach taken raises the question of what is being conserved and where the conservator's responsibility lies. Is the appearance (of a mid-20th-century veterinary assemblage) or the contents (the materials used) what should be valued? The collection remains an accurate image of what the contents of a mid-20th-century Danish veterinary clinic dispensary looked like, though it is now a poorer historical document and has reduced research potential. It is safe to store and display both now and for the foreseeable future. The approach is a good compromise in which health and safety and didactic values have been served as well as the organisational needs of the collecting institution (removing a legal requirement for expensive testing and controls). The Østfyns Museum is not unique in making such decisions, many museums have chosen to remove 'dangerous' materials from their collections and many others have policies prohibiting the collection of such material. Other organisations, such as Museums and Galleries of New South Wales, have argued that it is impossible to remove all risk and therefore prefer to ensure there is an accurate awareness of risk and that it is effectively managed (Arnsby 2017: 30).

When one institution makes such the decision to deaccession material, there is informational loss but if such material is present in other collections the loss may be limited. In the case of the veterinary collection, it was felt that the action could be justified because other collections within Denmark retained representative samples of some of the plant materials.[22] However, without discussion and information sharing between organisations, there is the risk that the collections that one institution is relying on to serve as a repository may make similar decisions to deaccession materials resulting in total loss.

11B Case Study: Tullio Lombardo's Adam (Metropolitan Museum of Art 2014; Riccardelli et al. 2014)

On October 6, 2002, at 5:59 pm, the pedestal supporting Tullio Lombardo's *Adam* (ca. 1490–1495), one of the sculptural masterpieces of the Renaissance, collapsed. Security camera footage suggests that the collapse occurred within an eight-second window. The life-sized Carrara marble statue toppled onto a stone floor in The Metropolitan Museum of Art's Vélez Blanco Patio (a 16-century period room used to display Renaissance statuary) shattering into 28 large pieces and hundreds of smaller fragments. The arms and lower legs were most damaged while the head, face, and torso were relatively unharmed.

The statue, carved circa 1490–1495, was commissioned for the tomb of the Venetian Doge Andrea Vendramin (1398–1478) but was removed from the tomb in 1819 and acquired by The Met in the 1930s. It is recognised as the first monumental nude from the Renaissance to closely follow the idealism of classical Roman statuary and one of the 'most profound contemplations of divine and artistic creation, of human beauty and frailty, of temptation and sin and redemption ever realized' (Syson and Cafà 2014) The museum's director at the time of the accident, Phillipe de Montebello, described the collapse and damage as 'about the worst thing that could happen in a museum' (Syson and Cafà 2014) and determined that the statue should be returned to its original appearance. Recognising that the project required a variety of expertise (from management, to recovery, mending and aesthetic aspects as well as material selection and 3D imaging and media relations), a multidisciplinary team of conservators, curators, engineers, designers, media specialists, and administrators was assembled to tackle the project.

The first step towards the statue's reassembly was to recover all the fragments. To this end, a grid was established on the patio floor and each fragment was mapped and given its grid location as it was collected. Over the course of several years, the team carefully studied every fragment to determine its condition and position within the sculpture. Initially it had been hoped that the position of fragments on the floor might provide clues to their position within the statue, but this was not the case, and it took years to piece all the fragments back together in even a single area of damage. Fragments were not adhered together at this point to avoid locking pieces out. Care was taken in handling and piecing the fragments together to prevent degradation of the fresh break edges.

While undertaking this work, the team also evaluated the traditional methods for stone sculpture reconstruction. They found that few fundamental studies existed and set out to:

- understand the nature of the forces acting on each element of the sculpture
- test specific reassembly and restoration materials and methods
- evaluate the feasibility of implementation.

To do this, the team undertook a complete three-dimensional laser-scan of all the major fragments, which allowed full and one-fifth scale physical models to be created (minimising handling of the originals) and permitted finite element analysis (FEA) to be carried out. FEA, a computer-based structural analysis technique, is used to assess the distribution of force, stress, and strain in an object, while taking into consideration its material characteristics. This analysis provided graphical stress plots that described the nature and magnitude of the force on each join in the sculpture. The information gleaned from this analysis helped the team determine the necessary strength of adhesive and which parts of the sculpture might require pinning (dowelling), a traditional but invasive technique designed to help strengthen joins. The development of additional focused FEA models allowed the team to virtually evaluate several pinning scenarios including their size, location, orientation, and method of insertion.

A literature review suggested that although thermosetting adhesives (such as polyester and epoxy resins) had previously been favoured in stone reconstruction, other thermoplastic adhesives (such as acrylic resins and in particular Paraloid B-72) had the potential to provide sufficient strength to bond large marble sculpture while providing other benefits, such as greater potential for reversibility. Tests were conducted on marble disks to gauge the strength of a number of adhesives, their bond-line thickness (i.e. how much space is added by the adhesive film between the two marble fragments), and the deformation experienced when the adhesive was placed under a load over time (adhesive creep). Additionally, pinning materials were tested under a variety of scenarios. Combining the results of physical materials testing of materials with the insights obtained from virtual FEA pinning models, the Tullio team chose a 3:1 mixture of

Paraloid B-72 and Paraloid B-48N as an adhesive and to use fiberglass pins but to limit their usage to only the joins most vulnerable to shear stress.

The experiments indicated the importance of pressure in minimising bond line thickness, permitting the reconstruction of the sculpture with nearly invisible gaps between the fragments. Given the contours of the sculpture it was impossible to deliver this pressure using traditional clamping methods alone and the team felt that a 'self-clamping' method where the weight of the sculpture itself was used to create the pressure on each join was required. To accommodate this decision, a custom-made rig was constructed consisting of an external armature composed of carbon fibre straps, ball joints and a rigid framework that could be used in tandem with an overhead bridge crane and a custom-designed lifting table. Once the armature was created, an initial dry run was carried out, permitting the overall alignment of the fragments to be assessed and allowing conservators to plan the safest order in which to mend the fragments. FEA analysis determined that three pins were needed: one in the left knee and one in each ankle. The holes for the pins were carefully drilled using custom-built rigs to hold the pieces steady and maintain the correct alignment of the fragments and the drill bit. Drilling was carried out using custom-fabricated diamond core bits and a bench lathe. During drilling water was used to cool the bit and the stone and to flush the marble dust generated from the hole. Later, when it was time to mend the left knee and the ankles, the insides of the holes were coated with a thin barrier layer of Paraloid B-72 and then epoxy sleeves were cast into the holes. Fiberglass pins were inserted into the sleeves prior to bonding the fracture surfaces with the acrylic resin mixture.

Adhering the statue together was carried out over months. Rather than simply start from the bottom and work upward, a strategic approach was adopted taking into account the adhesive setting times, the complex shapes of the fragments, and the stress that would come to bear on each join as it was bonded. Using a 'dry stacking' method, the conservators bonded only one join at a time, each time assembling all of the remaining leg fragments without adhesive. Once the fragments were fully assembled, the sculpture was left alone, immobile for at least one month, because acrylic resins set by the slow process of solvent evaporation. Only then were the remaining unbonded fragments disassembled and the process repeated for a different join. This approach allowed the conservators to monitor the alignment of the fragments with each join that was mended. The slow and painstaking process of making *Adam* stand again started with the left arm, then moved to the upper left thigh, progressed to the ankles, and then to the remaining leg fragments. The fragmentary right arm was mostly assembled independently from the torso and was attached only after the sculpture was freestanding, unencumbered by its external assembly armature. The final pieces – the head, and a branch held in *Adam*'s right hand – were attached two and a half years after the first fragment was bonded.

Once the sculpture had been reconstructed, the next step in its treatment was cleaning. Past surface applications, including fats and oils to impart gloss, and dust accumulation had yellowed and darkened the surface over time in an uneven manner. Cleaning was undertaken using vinyl eraser strips that were slightly moistened with saliva. Once cleaned, the losses associated with the breaks were filled using a mixture of B-72, a bulking agent (powdered alumina) and colouring agents such as white earth, pumice sepiolite and rottenstone, which created a translucent, dough-like material that could be worked into the losses and emulated the look of marble. Once hardened, the fills could be shaped. Archival photos, from the statue's accession in 1936, informed reconstruction of the areas of most profound loss. Pains were taken to match the tool marks in adjoining areas of the marble and the final step was to tone the fills with pigments in a polyvinyl acetate medium to match the colour of these areas (Figure 11.5).

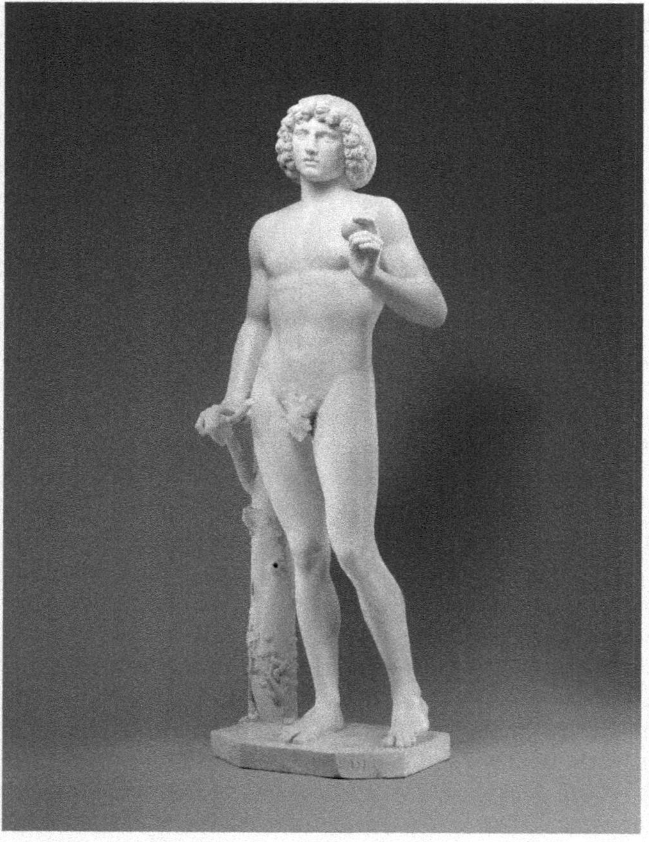

Figure 11.5 The reassembled statue of Adam by Tullio Lombardo. Fletcher Fund, 1936, The Metropolitan Museum of Art.

The statue's fall was shocking for the museum and its staff. For conservators and curators whose careers are dedicated to the care and preservation of objects, such an event can be traumatic and emotional. For an institution as storied as The Metropolitan Museum, such an event can be embarrassing. However, the careful and thoughtful approach of the museum and the Tullio team permitted many positive elements to be extracted from the experience. It was transformed into an opportunity to learn more about the statue, about Tullio's working practices, to contribute to the conservation field and to highlight the museum's commitment to its collections. Petrographic study was carried out to determine the provenance of the marble, careful analysis of the tool marks revealed information about Tullio's working technique and surface analysis provided information about the presence of past surface finishes. Additionally, curatorial research focused on the classical sources that Tullio had used revealing new insights about the statue and its art historical significance (Syson and Cafà 2014; Cafà 2014). The careful and deliberate assessment and evaluation of the conservation approaches available has resulted in the publication of at least five academic publications (Jorjani *et al*. 2009; Rahbar *et al*. 2010; Riccardelli *et al*. 2010, 2014; Rosewitz *et al*. 2016), several masters theses and provided valuable learning experiences for a number of conservation interns. As a result, the findings will continue to inform other treatments and contribute to the development of new approaches to the conservation of sculpture. Throughout the process the conservation work was carefully documented, resulting in a number of videos (cf. *After the Fall: The Conservation of Tullio Lombardo's* Adam available at https://www.youtube.com/watch?v=3oznnP6SkSc) and articles in popular publications. When *Adam* did return to public view in a bespoke gallery for the exhibition *Tullio Lombardo's* Adam*: A Masterpiece Restored,*[23] all aspects of the conservation project were featured in carefully crafted videos describing decision-making, research, and the hands-on process accomplished by the team. Few institutions would have had the resources to carry out this treatment in that manner that The Met could; staffing a project for nearly 12 years, commissioning specialist equipment and committing to research are all costly endeavours. However, when shared, high profile projects, such as this one, tend to benefit not just the institution that carried them out but the entire field as well. The public's interest is seized by the artistry and skill involved. Sharing the decisions made involved also permits both the public and other professionals to understand the complexity and care necessary, while sharing the results helps to inform and advance future conservation undertakings.

Notes

1 Details of hazardous materials in museum collections and the appropriate steps to take to minimise the threat they pose can be found at https://hazardsincollections.org.uk.

2 These regulations require employers to provide safe working conditions, ensure all equipment and practices meet the regulations, and supply relevant safety equipment, employees are required to comply with instructions and use the supplied equipment. Many large organisations

employ Health and Safety officers who help to ensure compliance, but conservators working in small museums or in private practice may need to do more of this work themselves.

3 Chemical data sheets can be obtained from https://www.hse.gov.uk/coshh/basics/datasheets.htm

Key terms used include: Pathogen – causes disease; Carcinogen – causes cancer; Toxic – poisonous, potentially lethal; OES – Occupational Exposure Standard; MEL – Maximum Exposure Limit (this must not be exceeded); LD50 – Lethal Dose 50% (when 50% of a test population of animals died after exposure to this chemical at the stated level of concentration); LEV – Local Exhaust Ventilation; PRE – Protective Respiratory Equipment; PPE – Personal Protective Equipment; TWA – Time Weighted Average; REL – Recommended (maximum) Exposure Limit (long term = 8 hours exposure, short term = 15 minutes); TLV – Threshold Limit Value (normally applied to dangerous dusts and expressed in mg/m^3 e.g. $<0.005\ mg/m^3$).

4 An excellent example of this is the Connecting to Collections Care (C2C Care) program run by the Foundation for the American Institute of Conservation (FAIC), which provides resources and professional development to staff working at small and mid-sized museums that might not otherwise have access to conservators in their institutions. C2C Care offers webinars on a variety of topics relating to collections care and also an on-line community in which people can ask questions and seek advice.

5 https://stories.fitzmuseum.cam.ac.uk/kangxi-vases-conservation/

6 A list of many of these is maintained on the Conservation Wiki site and in many cases there are also links to exhibit content. https://www.conservation-wiki.com/wiki/PR_and_Outreach-Exhibiting_Conservation, accessed March 31, 2021.

7 Other issues that conservators have faced in such labs are the fact that critical parts of a conservator's work like documentation, report writing, and even preventive conservation largely involve sitting at a computer which visitors do not find engaging. Some conservators have reported that visitor interactions, tapping on the glass, pulling faces, etc. …, can be distracting and/or irritating and make the conservator feel a little like an exhibit in a zoo.

8 By 2020, eight years after it had opened, conservators in the artefact lab had spoken to over 40,000 visitors, created programs for 500 summer campers, treated over 700+ objects (many of which required at least 100 hours of treatment time) and 13 human mummies, spent 12 hours on the front page of Reddit.com and given formal presentations about work in the lab at five professional conferences and eight other professional events.

9 The North Yorkshire Moors Historic Railway Trust (NYMHRT) rely on approximately 550 volunteers to help maintain and run steam trains on 24 miles of track. https://www.nymr.co.uk/north-york-moors-historical-railway-trust

10 Unskilled and untrained volunteers doing a few hours here and there are of limited use and projects that seek to utilise them may need to put a lot of energy into clearly defining and supporting their work, which makes the benefit even smaller.

11 Particularly hurricanes (Atlantic Ocean), typhoons (Pacific Ocean), and cyclones (Indian Ocean). Such storms form when water temperatures are over 80 F (26 C) and there is sufficient moisture in the system and uniform winds to fuel them. The frequency and size of other storms has also increased, and a growing number have been christened 'superstorms.'

12 In 2017, Hurricane Harvey drenched southeast Texas with 60 inches (1.52 m) of rain. Since the late 20th century, there has been a six-fold increase in the probability of a rainmaker of Harvey's magnitude and a study suggests that in Texas, hurricane rains of 20 inches will evolve from once-in-100-year events to once-in-5.5-year events (Emmanuel 2017). Another study suggests that a global rain increase of 14% may occur by the end of the 21st century (Knutson *et al.* 2015). In England.

13 In 2003, the Western Australian Museum was the first museum to employ TBL action plan reporting following a call from Museums Australia that urged museums to apply TBL performance metrics to their overall performance (Graham-Taylor 2003), while in England the National Trust had begun employing TBL indicators to guide their approach to conservation (Lithgow *et al.* 2008).

14 Life Cycle Analysis (LCA) is a method of quantifying environmental impacts associated with a given product by creating an inventory of resources used and pollutants generated in the production (cradle to gate) and use of a particular product from the gathering of the raw materials needed to create the product to the point where all residual materials are returned

to the earth (cradle to grave). The Sustainability Tools in Cultural Heritage (STiCH) website https://stich.culturalheritage.org/ offers examples of LCAs in conservation.

15 https://stich.culturalheritage.org/carbon-calculator/#browse. Other tools that have been developed include a series of free books on waste and materials, energy, and social sustainability (https://www.kiculture.org/ki-books/).

16 In addition to gender and race/ethnicity other areas where diversity is desirable include religion, sexual orientation, gender reassignment and identity, socio-economic background, education, age, and disability.

17 The results of both surveys need to be approached with some caution as to the final numbers. Neither survey was a comprehensive survey of the entire membership. Instead, both surveys allowed members to opt in. As a result, they may be more indicative of general trends than as a set of hard and fast numbers.

18 For example, the UCLA's Andrew W Mellon Opportunity for Diversity in Conservation (mellondiversityconservation.org) and the Winterthur University of Delaware collaborations with historically black universities and colleges in the United States (https://www.artcons.udel.edu/outreach/diversity-initiatives/tipc-c-program).

19 The notion of versioning can also be usefully applied to working objects that have spent a substantial time in one restored form and then been restored to another form or appearance or to long standing structures that have been much altered through time.

20 When Kim Kardashian wore the dress in which Marilyn Monroe famously sang Happy Birthday to President Kennedy to the Met Gala in 2022, ICOM Costume critiqued the owner of the dress for permitting this, saying 'historic garments should not be worn by anybody, public or private figures.' This response was criticised in turn as being Eurocentric and focusing too much on the associated historic and material values of such textiles. Puawei Cairns, director of audience and insight at Te Papa in New Zealand, wrote 'Some textiles in museums should be worn if they are of use in ritual ceremonies or continuing the connections between object and kin. Conservation is increasingly about becoming the bridge to enable that to happen, not the block. Good Ol' ICOM. Only thinking of its own eurocentric cultural bubble' (https://camd.org.au/icom-apology-prompted-by-maori-curator/).

21 It is important to note that continued discussion and engagement with a wide range of communities should be considered an important ingredient in this process.

22 The National Medicine Museum, part of Copenhagen University, retains a collection of plant material used in Danish folk medicine.

23 https://www.metmuseum.org/press/exhibitions/2014/tullio-lombardos-adam

Bibliography

AAIB (Air Accidents Investigation Branch) (2014) *De Havilland DH98 Mosquito T3*. Available at: https://assets.publishing.service.gov.uk/media/542301dce5274a1317000b69/dft_avsafety_pdf_501355.pdf (Accessed Jan 3, 2022).

Abd El Gawad, H., Balachandran, S., Elgharably, A., Parent, C. and Stevenson, A. (2020) 'Your mummies, their ancestors.' *Caring for and about Ancient Human Remains. Online panel*. Available at: https://www.youtube.com/watch?v=CLGUhS2qUi8 (Accessed May 10, 2022).

Abercromby, J. (1912) *A Study of Bronze Age Pottery of Great Britain and Ireland and Its Associated Grave Goods in Two Volumes*. Oxford: Clarendon Press.

Abercromby, M. (1960) *The Anatomy of Judgement*. Harmondsworth: Penguin.

ABTEM (Association of British Transport and Engineering Museums) (2018) *Guidelines for the Care of Larger and Working Historic Objects*. Available at: http://online.fliphtml5.com/wffb/bclk/#p=1 (Accessed May 25, 2022).

Abousnnouga, G. and Machin, D. (2010) 'Analysing the language of war monuments.' *Visual Communication* 9: 131–149.

Adkins, L. and Adkins, R. (1989) *Archaeological Illustration*. Cambridge: Cambridge University Press.

Agnew, N. (2001) 'Methodology, Conservation Criteria and Performance Evaluation for Archaeological Site Shelters.' *Conservation and Managements of Archaeological Sites* 5 (1-2): 7–18.

Agnew, N. and Demas, M. (1998) 'Preserving the Laetoli footprints.' *Scientific American* September 1988: 26–37.

Agnew, N. and Levin, J. (1996) 'Adapting technology for conservation.' *Conservation, The GCI Newsletter 11(3)*: 16–18.

Agrawal, O. (1981)'"Appropriate" Indian Technology for the conservation on museum collections.' In *"Appropriate technologies" in the Conservation of Cultural heritage*. Paris: UNESCO press. pp. 70–77.

AIC (American Institute of Conservation) (n.d.) *Conservation Terminology*. Available at: https://www.culturalheritage.org/about-conservation/what-is-conservation/definitions#.W2mGqNgzrMI. (Accessed May 28, 2022).

AIC (American Institute of Conservation) (1994) 'Code of Ethics and Guidelines for Practice.' *AIC News* May 1994: 17–20.

AIC (2020) *American Institute of Conservation: Our Code of Ethics*. Available at: https://www.culturalheritage.org/about-conservation/code-of-ethics (Accessed June 3, 2020).

AICCM (2002) *Code of ethics and Code of Practice*. Available at: https://aiccm.org.au/wp-content/uploads/2020/01/CODE-OF-ETHICS-AND-CODE-OF-PRACTICE-Australian-Institute-for-Conservation-of-Cultural-Material-1.pdf#:~:text=AICCM%20Members%20shall%20strive%20to,%2C%20treatment%2C%20training%20and%20education.&text=AICCM%20Members%20have%20the%20obligation,to%20this%20Code%20of%20Ethics. (Accessed June 27, 2021).

Akagawa, N. and Smith, L. (2019) *Safeguarding Intangible Heritage: Practices and Politics*. London: Routledge.

Alcock, L. (2003) *Kings and Warriors, Craftsmen and Priests*. Edinburgh: Society of Antiquaries Scotland.

Aleppo, M. (2003) '160 years of conservation documentation at the National Archives, UK.' *The Paper Conservator* 27: 97–99.

Allfrey, M. (1999) 'Brodsworth Hall: the preservation of a country house,' in G. Chitty and D. Baker (eds.) *Managing Historic Sites and Buildings*. London: Routledge, pp. 115–125.

Allfrey, M. and Xavier Rowe, A. (2012) 'Conserving and Presenting Brodsworth Hall: New Approaches for a Sustainable Future,' in *Proceedings of "The Artifact, Its Context and Their Narrative," Joint Conference of ICOM-DEMHIST and Three ICOM-CC Working Groups*. Paris: International Council of Museums.

Allington-Jones, L. (2013) 'The phoenix: The role of conservation ethics in the development of St. Pancras Railway Station. *JCMS Journal*. 10.5334/jcms.1021205.

Al Quntar, S., *et al.* (2015) 'Responding to a Cultural Heritage Crisis: the example of the safeguarding the heritage of Syria and Iraq Project.' *Near Eastern Archaeology* 78 (3): 154–160.

ALVA (Association of leading Visitor Attractions) (2021) Visits made in 2021 to Visitor Attractions in Membership w. ALVA. https://www.alva.org.uk/details.cfm?p=616 (Accessed June 4, 2022).

Ames, M. (1994) 'Cannibal tours, glass boxes and the politics of interpretation,' in S.M. Pearce (ed.) *Interpreting Objects and Collections*. London: Routledge.

Andrew, J (2011) 'Restoration of the Forth Bridge.' *Ingenia* 49: 15–20. Available at: https://www.ingenia.org.uk/Ingenia/Articles/75cfa009-7fd8-4f82-b41b-0d07f0b1d5e2 (Accessed April 26, 2021).

Andrews, T., Andrews, W. and Baker, C. (1992) 'An investigation into the removal of enzymes from paper following conservation treatment: Reversibility.' *Journal of the American Institute of Conservation* 31 (3): 313–323.

Anglove, L., Ormsby, B., Townsend, J. and Wolbers, R. (2017) *Gels in the Conservation of Art*. London: Archetype.

Antoine, D. and Taylor, E. (2014) 'Handling, Storing and Transporting Human Remains,' in A. Fletcher, A. and Antoine, D., and Hill, J. (eds.) *Regarding the Dead: Human Remains in the British Museum*. London: The British Museum Press, pp. 43–48.

Applebaum, B. (1987) 'Criteria for Treatment: reversibility.' *Journal of the American Institute for Conservation* 26 (2): 65–73.

Applebaum, B. 2007. *Conservation Treatment Methodology*. London: Butterworth Heinemann.

Applebaum, B. (2013) 'Conservation in the 21st Century: will a 20th century code of ethics suffice?' in P. Hatchfield (ed.) *Ethics and Critical Thinking in Conservation*. Washington, DC: The American Institute of Conservation.

Arista, J. and Drayman Weisser, T. (2013) 'The conservation window at the Walters Art Museum: Building conservation support by creating public value,' in E. Williams (ed.) T*he Public Face of Conservation*. London: Archetype Publication in association with Colonial Williamsburg.

Arnsby, J. (2017) 'Project One - Veterinary Kit,' Portfolio of Professional Practice, unpublished portfolio of work for MA in Conservation of Archaeological and Museum Objects, Dept. of Archaeology, Durham University.

Artifact Lab. (2021) 'Respecting human remains: edit to past blog posts.' Available at: https://www.penn.museum/sites/artifactlab/2021/05/06/respecting-human-remains-edits-to-past-blog-posts/ (Accessed May 10, 2022).

Artioli, G. (2010) *Scientific Methods and Cultural Heritage. An Introduction to the Application of Materials Science to Archaeometry and Conservation Science*. Oxford: Oxford University Press.

Ashley-Smith, J. (1994) 'A constant approach to a mixed collection,' in A. Oddy (ed.) *Restoration: Is It Acceptable? British Museum Occasional Paper No. 99*. London: British Museum Press.

Ashley-Smith, J. (1999) *Risk Assessment for Object Conservation*. Oxford: Butterworth-Heinemann.

Ashley-Smith, J. (2016) 'Losing the edge: the risk of decline in practical skills.' *Journal of the Institute of Conservation* 39 (3): 119–132.

Ashley-Smith, J. (2017) 'A role for bespoke codes of ethics,' in J. Bridgland (ed.) *ICOM-CC 18th Triennial Conference Preprints, Copenhagen, 4–8 September 2017*. Paris: International Council of Museums.

Ashley-Smith, J., Umney, N. and Ford, D. (1994) 'Let's be honest – realistic environmental parameters for loaned objects.' In A. Roy and P. Smith (eds.) *Preventive Conservation Practice, Theory and Research: 1994 IIC Ottawa Congress*. London: IIC.

Ashurst, J. (2007) *Conservation of Ruins*. London: Butterworth Heinemann.

Assis, V. (2022) 'A Sweet Result: Saving a Dieter Roth Chocolate Sculpture from becoming Food.' Available at: https://www.iiconservation.org/content/sweet-result-saving-dieter-roth-chocolate-sculpture-becoming-food (Accessed February 28, 2022).

Atalay, S. Camurouglu, D., Hodder, I., Moser, S., Orbasu, A. and Pye, E. (2010) 'Protecting and exhibiting Çatalhöyük.' *Turkish Academy of Sciences Journal of Cultural Inventory* 8: 155–166.

Austin, J. (2021) *A Sankofa Moment: Heritage, Conservation and Racial Justice at the George Floyd Global Memorial*. Available at: https://www.youtube.com/watch?v=r47PW__wWqU (Accessed June 13, 2022).

Australia ICOMOS (2013) *Practice note: Understanding and assessing cultural significance. Version 1*. Available at: https://australia.icomos.org/wp-content/uploads/Practice-Note_Understanding-and-assessing-cultural-significance.pdf (Accessed July 27, 2020).

Babbington, C. and Hughes, H. (1992) 'Conservation of the Painted Decoration at Brodsworth Hall.' *English Heritage Conservation Bulletin* 17, *supplement: Scientific and Technical Review* Issue 1, 3–6.

Baboian, R., Cliver, E. and Bellante, E. (eds.) (1990) *The Statue of Liberty Restoration*. Houston, Texas: National Association of Corrosion Engineers.

Baines, J. (1994) 'Ancient Egyptian concepts and uses of the past: 3rd and 2nd millennium BC evidence,' in R. Layton (ed.) *Who Needs the Past? Indigenous Values and Archaeology*. London: Routledge. pp. 131–149.

Baglioni, P., Chelazzi, D. and Giorgi, R. (2015) *Nanotechnologies in the Conservation of Cultural Heritage: A compendium of materials and techniques*. Netherlands: Springer.

Baker, M. and McManus, E. (1992) 'History, care and handling of America's spacesuits: problems in modern materials.' *Journal of the American Institute for Conservation* 31 (1): 77–85.

Balachandran, S. (2007) 'Edge of an ethical dilemma.' *Archaeology Magazine* 60 (6): 18–20.

Balachandran, S. (2009) 'Among the dead and their possessions: a conservator's role in the death, life and afterlife of human remains and their associated objects.' *Journal of the American Institute for Conservation* 48 (3): 199–222.

Balachandran, S (2016) *Race, Diversity and Politics in Conservation: Our 21st century Crisis*. Available at: https://resources.culturalheritage.org/conservators-converse/2016/05/25/race-diversity-and-politics-in-conservation-our-21st-century-crisis-sanchita-balachandran/ (Accessed May 8, 2022).

Baldwin, A. (2017) 'Conservation techniques,' In A. Baldwin and J. Joy (eds.) *A Celtic Feast: The Iron Age Cauldrons from Chiseldon, Wiltshire*. London: Trustees of the British Museum.

Ball, S. and Winsor, P. (1997) *Larger and Working Objects: A Guide to Their Preservation and Care*. London: Museums and Galleries Commission.

Ballard, G. (2004) *Portland Cement at the Capitol: a non destuctive investigation.* Available at: https://www.buildingconservation.com/articles/portland/portland-cement.htm. Accessed May 30, 2022.

Balogh, C. and Grayburn, R. (2019) 'Technical Study of an Attic Skyphos with Ancient Lead Repairs,' In J. Mandrus and V. Schussler (eds.) *Recent Advances in Glass and Ceramics Conservation 2019: Interim Meeting of the ICOM-CC Glass and Ceramics Working Group and Icon Ceramics and Glass Group Conference, 5-7 September 2019*, London, United Kingdom Available at: https://www.icom-cc-publications-online.org/3588/Technical-Study-of-an-Attic-Skyphos-with-Ancient-Lead-Repairs (Accessed February 24, 2021).

Barcilon, P. (2001) *Leonardo, The Last Supper*. Chicago: University of Chicago Press.

Barclay, R. (2005) *The Preservation and Use of Historic Musical Instruments, Display Case and Concert Hall.* Abingdon: Earthscan.

Barnes, A. (2010) 'Roman helmet found in field sells for £2.3m.' *The Independent*. October 7, 2010. Available at: https://www.independent.co.uk/news/uk/home-news/roman-helmet-found-in-field-sells-for-ps2-3m-2100601.html. (Accessed December 6, 2021).

Baumeister, M., *et al.* (2020) 'Digital 3-D reproduction and CNC milling: putting the final touches on an architectural highlight, the Cassiobury House Staircase.' *Wooden Artifacts Group Postprints* 34: 39–57. (Available at: https://www.culturalheritage.org/docs/default-source/publications/papers/039-058-wag2020-baumeister_et_al.pdf?sfvrsn=78b31420_4 (Accessed June 2, 2020).

Bearss, Edwin C. (1980) *Hardluck Ironclad: The Sinking and Salvage of the Cairo*. Baton Rouge: Louisiana State University Press.

Beck, J. and Daley, M. (1993) *Art Restoration, the Culture, the Business, and the Scandal.* New York: W.W. Norton and Co.

Beck, E. (2001) '"Es ist alles to Ding"!? Considerations in dealing with Relics,' in E. Williams (ed.) *Human Remains: Conservation, Retrieval and Analysis. BAR International Series 934.* Oxford: Archaeopress.

Beck, L. (2013) 'Digital documentation in the conservation of cultural heritage: finding the practical in best practice.' *International Archives of the Photogrammetry, Remote Sensing and Spatial Information Sciences* XL-5/W2: 85–90.

Beeton, I. (1859) *Mrs Beetons's Household Management*. London: Ward Lock.

Belk, R. (1994) 'Collectors and collecting,' in S. Pearce (ed.) *Interpreting Objects and Collections*. London: Routledge.

Belk, R. (2014) 'Ownership and collecting,' in R. Frost and G. Steketee (eds.) *The Oxford Handbook of Hoarding and Acquiring*. Oxford: Oxford University Press. pp. 33–42.

Berducou, M. (1996) 'Introduction to archaeological conservation,' in N. Stanley Price, M. Kirby Talley and A. Vaccaro (eds.) *Historical and Philosophical Issues in the Conservation of Cultural Heritage*. Los Angeles: The Getty Conservation Institute.

Berkouwer, M. and Church, D. (1993) 'Textiles at Brodsworth Hall deep freezing against insect infestation.' *English Heritage Conservation Bulletin* 19: 12–14.

Bernard-Maugiron, H. and Courboulès, M.-L. (2018) 'Is it possible and reasonable to treat a 31-metre waterlogged Roman boat in just two years?' in E. Williams and E. Hocker (eds.) *Proceedings of the 14th ICOM-CC Group on Wet Organic Archaeological Materials Conference, Portsmouth 2019*. Paris: ICOM.

Bertholon, R. (2002) 'To get rid of the crust or not: emergence of the idea of "original surface" in the conservation of metal archaeological objects in the first half of the 20th century,' in A. Oddy and S. Smith (eds.) *Past Practice, Future Prospects, BM Occasional Paper 145*. London: British Museum.

Bertholon, R. (2004) 'The location of the original surface: a review of the conservation literature,' in I. MacLeod, J. Theile and C. Degrigny (eds.) *Metal 2001: Proceedings of the International Conference on Metals Conservation, Santiago, Chile 2-6 April 2001*. Perth: Western Australia Museum, pp. 167–179.

Bewer, F. (2010) *A Laboratory for Art: Harvard's Fogg Museum and the Emergence of Conservation in America, 1900-1950*. Cambridge, MA: Harvard Art Museum.

Bewer, F., Eremin, K. and Chang, A. (2017) 'Chemistry Revisited in a Laboratory for Art,' in N. Owczarek, N, Gleeson, M. and Grant, L. (eds.) *Engaging Conservation, Collaboration across Disciplines*. London: Archetype. pp. 190–198.

Bickersteth, J., Clayton, S. and Tennant, F. (2008) 'Conserving and Interpreting the Historic Huts of Antarctica,' in Saunders, D., Townsend, J. and Woodcock, S. (eds.) *Conservation and Access, Contributions to the London Congress 15-19 September 2008*. London: International Institute of Conservation. pp. 218–220.

Bickersteth, J. (2014) 'Environmental Conditions for Safeguarding Collections: What should our set points be?' *Studies in Conservation* 59 (4): 218–224.

Big Pit National Coal Museum (n.d.) *Big Pit National Coal Museum*. https://museum.wales/bigpit/ (Accessed April 29, 2021).

Bill, J. (2007) *Welcome on Board! The Sea Stallion from Glendalough: A Viking Longship Recreated*. Roskilde-Denmark: Viking Ship Museum.

Bilz, M., *et al.* (1993) 'A study of the thermal breakdown of polyethylene glycol,' in P. Hoffmann (ed.) *Proceedings of the 5th ICOM Group on Wet Organic Archaeological Materials Conference, Portland, Maine 1993*. Bremerhaven: ICOM-CC.

Bilz, M. and Grattan, D.W. (1996) 'The ageing of Parylene: difficulties with the Arrhenius approach,' in J. Bridgland (ed.) *11th Triennial Meeting, Edinburgh 1-6 September 1996*. Edinburgh: ICOM-CC.

Bintliff, J. (1988) 'A review of contemporary perspectives on the 'meaning' of the past,' in J. Bintliff (ed.) *Extracting Meaning from the Past*. Oxford: Oxbow.

Black, J. (1997) 'Letter: The Forth Bridge as a work of art,' *The Times*, 26 June 1997: 23.

Blackshaw, S. and Daniels, V. (1979) 'The testing of materials for use in storage and display in museums.' *The Conservator 3*: 16–19.

Blake, E and Zelinsky, D. (2018) *National Hurricane Center Tropical Cyclone Report Hurricane Harvey*. Available at: https://www.nhc.noaa.gov/data/tcr/AL092017_Harvey.pdf (Accessed March 26 2022).

Blouin, V.Y., Mardikian, P. and Watters, C. (2010) 'Finite Element Analysis of the H.L. Hunley Submarine: A turning point in the projects history,' in P. Mardikian, C. Chemello, C. Watters and P. Hull (eds.) *Metal 2010*. Paris: ICOM. pp. 393–399.

Bloomfield, T. (2008) 'Pupuru te mahara – preserving the memory working with Maori communities on preservation projects in Aotearoa, New Zealand.' In J. Bridgland (ed.) *ICOM-CC New Delhi Triennial Meeting*. Available at: https://www.icom-cc-publications-online.org/PublicationDetail.aspx?cid=de918c1f-b80f-46e5-b1f5-163e61a6d4e2 (Accessed July 26, 2008).

Blyth, V. and Hillyer, L. (1993) 'Carpet beetle – A pilot study in detection and control.' *The Conservator* 16: 65–77.

Bockhoff, F., *et al* (1984) 'Infrared studies of the kinetics of stabilisation of soluble nylon,' in Bromelle, N., *et al.* (eds.) *Adhesives and Consolidants: 1984 IIC Paris Congress*. London: IIC.

Bomford, D. (1994) 'Changing taste in the restoration of paintings,' in A. Oddy (ed.) *Restoration: Is It Acceptable?* British Museum Occasional Paper No. 99. London: British Museum Press.

Bomford, D. (2003) 'The conservator as narrator: changed perspectives in the conservation of paintings,' in M. Leonard (ed.) *Personal Viewpoints: thoughts about Painting Conservation*. Malibu: The John Paul Getty Trust.

Bowditch, G. (1993) 'Painting the Forth Bridge halts at last.' *The Times*, 2 February 1993: 3.

Bowman, A., Thomas, J. and Wright, R. (1974) 'The Vindolanda writing-tablets.' *Britannia* 5: 471–480.

Boylan, P. (2006) 'The intangible heritage: a challenge and an opportunity for museums and museum professional training.' *International Journal of Intangible Heritage* 1: 53–66.

Bradley, S. (1983) 'Conservation recording in the British Museum.' *The Conservator* 7: 9–12.

Brand, S. (1994) *How Buildings Learn*. London: Orion.

Brandi, C. (1996) 'Theory of restoration I,' in N. Price, M. Kirby Talley and A. Vaccaro (eds.) *Historical and Philosophical Issues in the Conservation of Cultural Heritage*. Los Angeles: Getty Conservation Institute.

Brandt, K. (1987) 'Twenty-five questions about Michelangelo's Sistine Ceiling.' *Apollo* 126: 392–400.

Breeze, D. (1993) 'Ancient Monuments Legislation.' in J. Hunter and I. Ralston (eds.) *Archaeological Resource Management in the UK*. Stroud: Alan Sutton Publishing. pp. 44–55.

Breeze, D. and Bishop, M. (2013) *The Crosby Garrett Helmet*. The Armatura Press.

Brewster, D. (1861) 'Optical phenomena of ancient decomposed glass.' *Transactions of The Royal Society of Edinburgh* 23: 193–204.

Bridges, H. (2016) 'Revealing the maker's hands: curator John Watson finds the humanity in additions to Changing Keys.' *The Virginia Gazette*, August 31, 2016.

Brimblecombe, P., Thickett, D. and Yoon, Y.H. (2009) 'The cementation of coarse dust to indoor surfaces.' *Journal of Cultural Heritage* 10: 410–414.

Brinch Madsen, H. (1987) 'Artefact conservation in Denmark at the beginning of the last century,' in J. Black (ed.) *Recent Advances in the Conservation and Analysis of Artefacts*. London: Summer Schools Press.

Brinch-Madsen, H. (2009) 'Repairs in antiquity illustrated by examples from Prehistory in Denmark,' in J. Ambers *et al.* (eds.) *Holding it All Together; Ancient and Modern Approaches to Joining, Repair and Consolidation*. London: Archetype Publications.

Brinch-Madsen, H., Meyer, I. and Jacobson, T. (2001) 'Conservation of waterlogged wood: an obsolete method,'' in A. Oddy and S. Smith (eds.) P*ast Practice-Future Prospects. The British Museum Occasional Paper Number 145*. London: British Museum. pp. 33–39.

Brokerhof, A. and Bülow, A. (2016) 'The QuiskScan – a quick risk Scan to identify value and hazard in a collection.' *Journal of the Institute of Conservation* 39 (1): 18–28.

Bromelle, N. and Thomson, G. (eds.) (1982) *Science and Technology in the Service of Conservation: 1982 IIC Washington Congress*. London: IIC.

Brooks, H. 2000. *A Short History of IIC: Foundation and Development*. London: IIC.

Brooks, M. (1998) 'International conservation codes of ethics and practice and their implications for teaching and learning ethics in textile conservation education with special reference to the Diploma in textile conservation taught at the Textile Conservation Centre,' in D. Eastop and A. Timar–Balazsy (eds.) *International Perspectives in Textile Conservation*. London: Archetype.

Brooks, M. (2008) 'Talking to ourselves: why do conservators find it so hard to convince others of the significance of conservation,' in J. Bridgeland (ed.) *Preprints of the ICOM-CC 15th Triennial Conference, New Delhi, 22-26 September 2008*. New Delhi: Allied Publishers. pp. 1135–1140.

Brooks, M and Eastop, D. (2006) 'Matter out of place: paradigms for analyzing textile cleaning.' *Journal of the American Institute of Conservation* 45 (3): 171–181.

Brooks, M. and Eastop, D. (2011) *Changing Views of Textiles Conservation*. Los Angeles: Getty Conservation Institute.

Brooks, M., *et al.* (1994) 'Restoration or conservation – issues for textile conservators, a textile conservation perspective,' in A. Oddy (ed.) *Restoration: Is It Acceptable? British Museum Occasional Paper No. 99*. London: British Museum Press.

Brooks, M., *et al.* (1996) 'Artefact or information? Articulating the conflicts in conserving archaeological textiles,' in A. Roy and P. Smith (eds.) *Archaeological Conservation and Its Consequences: IIC 1996 Copenhagen Congress*. London: IIC.

Brooks, M., *et al.* (2020) 'Fragments of faith: unpicking Archbishop John Morton's vestments' *The Antiquaries Journal* 100: 274–303.

Brostoff, L. (1995) 'Investigation into the interaction of benzotriazole with copper corrosion minerals and surfaces,' in I. MacLeod, S. Pennec and L. Robbiola (eds.) *Metal 95, Proceedings of the International Conference on Metals Conservation*. London: James & James.

Bruce-Mitford, R. (1972) 'The Sutton Hoo helmet: a new reconstruction.' *The British Museum Quarterly* 36 (3/4): 120–130.

Bruce-Mitford, R. (1978) *The Sutton Hoo Ship Burial: Vol. 2, Arms, Armour and Regalia*. London: British Museum Publications.

BS 4971:2017 - *Conservation and care of archive and library collections*. Available at: https://www.thenbs.com/PublicationIndex/documents/details?DocID=319706 (Accessed October 1, 2021).

BS EN 15898: 2019 (2019) *Conservation of cultural heritage — Main general terms and definitions*. London: British Standards Institute.

Buys, S. and Oakley, V. (1993) *The Conservation and Restoration of Ceramics*. Oxford: Butterworth-Heinemann.

Burden, L., *et al.* (2004) 'The reconstruction of 105 Bronze Age ceramics.' *The Conservator* 28: 37–46.

Byrne, A., and Cook, I. (1976) 'The preparation and examination of cross sections,' in C. Pearson and G. Pretty (eds.) Proceedings of the National Seminar on the Conservation of Cultural Material, Perth, 1973. Perth: ICCM (Institute for the Conservation of Cultural Material).

Cafà, V. (2014) 'Ancient sources for Tullio Lombardo's *Adam*.' *Metropolitan Museum Journal* 49: 32–47.

Caldararo, N. (1987) 'An outline history of conservation in archaeology and anthropology as presented through its publications.' *Journal of the American Institute for Conservation* 26(2): 85–104.

Cane, S. (2009) 'Why do we conserve? Developing Understanding of Conservation as a Cultural Construct.' in A. Richmond and A. Bracker (eds.) *Conservation Principles, Dilemmas and Uncomfortable Truths*. Oxford: Butterworth Heinemann. pp. 163–177.

Caple, C. (1999) 'The Cathedral doors.' *Durham Archaeological Journal* 14-15: 131–140.

Caple, C. (2000) *Conservation Skills: Judgement, Method and Decision Making*. London: Routledge.

Caple, C. (2006) *Objects: Reluctant Witnesses to the Past*. London: Routledge.

Caple, C. (2007) *Excavations at Dryslwyn Castle 1980-1995*, Society for Medieval Archaeology Monograph. London: Society for Medieval Archaeology No. 26.

Caple, C. (2011) *Preventive Conservation in Museums*. London: Routledge.

Caple, C. (2016) *Preservation of Archaeological Remains In Situ*. Abingdon: Routledge.

Caple, C. (2020a) 'Introduction: the challenges of archaeological conservation,' in C. Caple and V. Garlick (eds.) *Studies in Archaeological Conservation*. London: Routledge. pp. 3–27.

Caple, C. (2020b) 'The Yarm Helmet.' *Medieval Archaeology* 64 (1): 31–64.

Caple, C. (2020c) 'Appendix: analyses of mortar samples from Castell Carndochan,' in D. Hopwell (ed.) 'Castell Carndochan: survey and excavation 2014–17,' *Archaeologia Cambrensis* 169 (2020): 177–207.

Caple, C. and Garlick, V. (2018) 'Identification and valuation of archaeological artefacts: developments using digital x-radiography.' *Journal of the Institute of Conservation* 41: 128–141.

Caple, C. and Garlick, V. (2020) *Studies in Archaeological Conservation*. London: Routledge.

Carradice, I. and Campbell, S. (1994) "The Conservation of lead communion tokens by potentiostatic reduction.' *Studies in Conservation* 39 (2): 100–106.

Carrlee, E. (2003) 'Does low temperature pest management cause damage? Literature review and observational study of ethnographic artifacts.' *Journal of the American Institute of Conservation* 42 (2): 141–166.

Carr-Whitworth, C. 2009 *Brodsworth Hall and Gardens*. London: English Heritage.

Cassmann, V. (2001) 'Artifacts associated with human remains,' in E. Williams (ed.) *Human Remains: Conservation, Retrieval, and Analysis*. BAR International Series 934. Oxford: Archaeopress.

Cassman, V., Odegaard, N., and Powell, J., (eds.) (2007) *Human Remains: Guide for Museums and Academic Institutions*. Oxford: Altamira Press.

Cather, S. (2003) 'Assessing causes and mechanisms of detrimental change to wall paintings,' in W. Gowing and A. Heritage (eds.) *Conserving the Painted Past: Developing Approaches to Wall Painting Conservation*. London: James and James. pp. 64–71.

Cellini, B. (1878) *Memoirs of Benvenuto Cellini, A Florentine Artist*, trans. T. Roscoe. London: G. Bell.

Cembalest, R. (2013) 'Self Portrait of the artist as a self-destructing chocolate head.' *Art News*, February 21, 2013. Available at: https://www.artnews.com/art-news/news/chocolate-self-portraits-by-janine-antoni-and-dieter-rot-2190/ (Accessed February 28, 2022).

Chadwick, A., Benko, A. and Schofield, E. (2012) 'Application of microfocus x-ray beams from synchrotrons in heritage conservation.' *International Journal of Architectural Heritage* 6: 228–258.

Chamberlin, E. (1979) *Preserving the Past*. London: Dent.

Champion, T. (1996) 'Protecting the monuments: archaeological legislation from the 1882 Act to PPG 16,' in M. Hunter (ed.) *Preserving the Past*. Stroud: Alan Sutton Publishing.

Chapman, J. (2000) *Fragmentation in Archaeology*. London: Routledge.

Chapman, J. and Gaydarska, B. (2007) *Parts and wholes: fragmentation in prehistoric context*. Oxford: Oxbow Books.

Chase, W. and Simon, H. (1973) 'The minds' eye in chess,' in W. Chase (ed.) *Visual information Processing*. New York: Academic Press. pp. 215–281.

Charteris, L. (1999) 'Reversibility-myth and misuse,' in A. Oddy and S. Carroll (eds.) *Reversibility does it exist? British Museum Occasional Paper no. 135*. London: British Museum.

Chemello, C., *et al.* (2019) *Aluminum: History, Technology, and Conservation (Proceedings from the 2014 International Conference)*. Washington DC: Smithsonian. 10.5479/si.1949-2367.9

Child, R. (1994) 'Putting things in context – The ethics of working collections,' in A. Oddy (ed.) *Restoration: Is it Acceptable? British Museum Occasional Paper No. 99*. London: British Museum Press.

Child, R. 1997. 'Ethics and museum conservation,' in G. Edson (ed.) *Museum Ethics*. London: Routledge.

Child, R. (2002) 'Anoxic environments in archive conservation.' *Journal of the Society of Archivists* 23 (2): 171–178.

Child, R. (2006) 'Conserving a coal mine,' in C. Buttler and M. Davis (eds.) *Things Fall Apart … Museum Conservation in Practice*. Cardiff: National Museum of Wales.

Child, R. and Pinniger, D. (1987) 'Insect pest control in UK museums,' in J. Black (ed.) *Recent Advances in Conservation and Analysis of Artefacts*. London: Summer Schools Press.

Child, R. and Pinniger, D. (1994) 'Insect trapping in museums and historic houses.' in A. Roy and P. Smith (eds.) *Preventive Conservation Practice, Theory and Research: 1994 IIC Ottawa Congress*. London: IIC.

Chilton, L. (2020) *British Museum undergoes biggest deep clean in decades to remove lock-down dust*. Available at: https://www.independent.co.uk/arts-entertainment/art/news/british-museum-open-lockdown-coronavirus-clean-dust-tickets-when-closed-a9676056.html (Accessed April 2, 2022).

China ICOMOS (2004) *Principles for the Conservation of Heritage Sites in China*. Los Angeles: Getty Conservation Institute. Available at: https://www.getty.edu/conservation/publications_resources/pdf_publications/pdf/china_prin_heritage_sites.pdf (Accessed Nov 13, 2021).

Chippindale, C. (1983) *Stonehenge Complete*. London: Thames & Hudson.

Chippindale, C. (1988) 'Editorial.' *Antiquity* 62: 207–208.

Chitty, G. (2018) 'Caring for Brodsworth: an impact study of the 'conservation in action' project at Brodsworth Hall 2016-17.' Research Report Available at: https://eprints.whiterose.ac.uk/134819/1/Final_report_31072018.pdf

Cimino, D., *et al.* (2018) '3d printing technologies: are their materials safe for conservation treatments?' *IOP Conference Series: Materials Science and Engineering*. Doi: 364. 012029. 10.1088/1757-899X/364/1/012029.

Clare, H. (2018) 'Vision and vulnerability: thoughts on leadership and conservation.' *Studies in Conservation* 63 (sup 1): 64–69.

Clarke, D., Cowie, T., and Foxon, A. (1985) *Symbols of Power, at the Time of Stonehenge*. Edinburgh: HMSO.

Clavir, M. (2002) *Preserving What is Valued: Museums, Conservation and First Nations*. Vancouver: UBC Press.

Cleere, H. (ed.) (1984) *Approaches to the Archaeological Heritage*. Cambridge: Cambridge University Press.

Cleere, H. (2002) 'Preserving archaeological sites and monuments,' in *Encyclopaedia of Life Support Systems*. Paris: UNESCO.

Cleland, H. (1932) 'The crime of archaeology – a study of weathering.' *The Scientific Monthly* 35 (2): 169–173.

Cobb, K. and Evans, T. (2009) 'Rivets: connections and repair in Mississippian period copper artifacts,' in J. Ambers, *et al.* (eds.) *Holding it All Together; Ancient and Modern Approaches to Joining, Repair and Consolidation*. London: Archetype Publications.

Colalucci, G. (1991) 'The frescoes of Michelangelo on the vault of the Sistine Chapel: Original technique and conservation,' in S. Cather (ed.) *The Conservation of Wall Paintings*. Los Angeles: Getty Conservation Institute.

Colalucci, G. (2017) 'Michelangelo Buonarroti: restoration of the frescoes on the vaulted ceiling and the *Last Judgement* in the Sistine Chapel.' *Conservation Science in Cultural Heritage* 16 (1): 89–108.

Colalucci, G. (2018) "Michelangelo and I.' *Conservation Science in Cultural Heritage* 18: 165–175.

Coles, J. (1987) 'The preservation of archaeological sites by environmental intervention,' in H. Hodges (ed.) *In-Situ Archaeological Conservation*. Mexico: Instituto Nacional de Antropologia e Historia and J. Paul Getty Trust. pp. 32–55.

Conti, A. (trans. H. Glanville) (2007) *History of Conservation of Works of Art*. Oxford: Butterworth-Heinemann.

Cook, J. (2018) *Ice Age Art, Arrival of the Modern Mind*. London: British Museum Press.

Coon, C., *et al.* (2016) 'Preserving rapid prototypes: a review.' *Heritage Science* 4, 40. 10.1186/s40494-016-0097-y

Cooper, M. (1998) *Laser Cleaning in Conservation*. Oxford: Butterworth-Heinemann.

Coppack, G. (1999) 'Setting and structure: the conservation of Wigmore Castle,' in G. Chitty and D. Baker (eds.) *Managing Historic Sites and Buildings*. London: Routledge. pp. 61–70.

Coremans, P. (1969) 'The training of restorers.' In ICOM (ed.) *Problems of Conservation in Museums*. London: Allen & Unwin.

Corfield, M. (1983) 'Conservation records in the Wiltshire Library and Museums Services.' *The Conservator* 7: 5–8.

Corfield, M. (1988) 'Towards a conservation profession,' in V. Todd (ed.) *Conservation Today, Papers Presented at the UKIC 30th Anniversary Conference 1988*. London: UKIC.

Corfield, M. (1988b) 'The reshaping of archaeological metal objects: some ethical considerations.' *Antiquity* 62: 261–265.

Corfield, M. (1992) 'Conservation documentation.' in J. Thompson (ed.) *The Manual of Curatorship*. Oxford: Butterworth-Heinemann.

Corfield, M., *et al.* (eds.) (1998) *Preserving Archaeological Remains in Situ, Proceedings of the Conference of 1st-3rd April 1996*. London: Museum of London.

Costain, C. (1994) 'Framework for preservation of museum collections.' *CCI Newsletter* No. 14, 1–4.

Craddock, P. (1978) 'The composition of the copper alloys used by the Greeks, Etruscan and Roman civilizations: 3 The origins and early use of brass' *Journal of Archaeological Science* 5: 1–16.

Cranmer-Webster, G (1986) Conservation and cultural centers: U'mista Cultural Center, Alert Bay, Canada. in R. Barclay, *et al.* (eds.) *Symposium 86: The Care and Preservation of Ethnological Materials*. Ottawa: CCI. pp. 77–79.

Crone, A. and Campbell, E. (2005) *A Crannog of the First Millennium AD: Excavations by Jack Scott at Loch Glashan, Argyll, 1960*. Edinburgh: Society of Antiquaries Scotland.

Cronyn, J. (1990) *The Elements of Archaeological Conservation*. London: Routledge.

Ctein. (2010) *Digital Restoration from Start to Finish: How to repair old and damaged photographs*. Waltham, MA: Focal Press.

Cunliffe, B. (ed.) (1988) *The Temple of Sulis Minerva at Bath, Vol 2: The Finds from the Sacred Spring*. Oxford: Oxford University Committee for Archaeology.

Cuno, J. (2012) *Whose Culture? The Promise of Museums and the Debate over Antiquities*. Princeton: Princeton University Press.

Cutajar, D.J., *et al.* (2016) 'A significant statement: new outlooks on treatment documentation.' *Journal of the Institute of Conservation* 39 (2): 81–97.

Curry, A. (2010) 'Can Auschwitz Be Saved?' Smithsonian Magazine.

Dahl, S. (2020) 'Buddhist mummy or 'living Buddha'? The politics of immortality in Japanese Buddhism.' *Anthropological Forum* 30 (3): 292–312.

Daniel, V. (2019) 'The Conservation of Lindow Man and subsequent changes.' *Journal of Wetland Archaeology* 19 (1-2): 57–66.

Daniel, V., Hanlon, G. and Maekawa, S. (1994) 'The use of nitrogen anoxia to eradicate museum insect pests.' *Studies in Conservation* 39 (S1): 11.

Daniel, V. and Ward, S. (1982) 'A rapid test for the detection of substances that will tarnish silver.' *Studies in Conservation* 27 (2): 58–60.

Daniel, V., *et al.* (2008) 'Australian Museum-Pacific Island museums and communities: a partnership approach,' In *ICOM Committee for Conservation 15th Triennial Meeting New Delhi India 22-26 September 2008*. Available at: https://www.icom-cc-publications-online.org/1836/Australian-Museum-Pacific-Island-museums-and-communities--a-partnership-approach (Accessed June 11, 2022).

Darvill, T. and Fulton, A. (1998) *The Monuments at Risk Survey of England 1995*. London: Bournemouth University and English Heritage.

Dauma, M. and Henchman, M. (1997) 'The scientific evaluation of images,' in S. Bradley (ed.) *The Interface Between Science and Conservation, British Museum Occasional Paper No. 116*. London: British Museum Press.

Davies, M. and Rawlins, I. (1946) *The War-Time Storage in Wales of Pictures from the National Gallery*. London: Transactions of the Honourable Society of Cymmrodorion.

David, R. (2008) "The International Ancient Egyptian Mummy Tissue Bank: A 21st century contribution to palaeopathological and paleo-pharmacological studies," in Z. Hawass and J. Richards (eds.) *The Archaeology and Art of Ancient Egypt: Essays in Honour of David B. O'Connor*. Egypt: Conseil Suprême des Antiquités Egyptiennes. pp. 214–216.

Davis, S.L. (2019) Understanding and improving gender equity in conservation. *Journal of the American Institute for Conservation* 58: 202–216.

Davis, S. and Chemello, C. 'CSI Abydos: conservation and scientific investigation of wood funerary artifacts at the Abydos Middle Cemetery,' *Bulletin of the American Research Center in Egypt* 204: 13–20.

Davy, H. (1821) 'Some observations and experiments on the papyri found in the ruins of Herculaneum.' *Philosophical Transactions of the Royal Society of London* 111: 191–208.

Davy, J. (1826) 'Observations on the changes that have taken place in some ancient alloys of copper.' *Philosophical Transactions of the Royal Society of London 116*: 55–59.

Demas, M., *et al.* (1996) 'Preservation of the Laetoli hominid trackway in Tanzania,' in A. Roy and P. Smith (eds.) *Archaeological Conservation and Its Consequences: 1996 IIC Copenhagen Congress*. London: IIC.

Demas, M., *et al.* (2010) 'Sustainable visitation at the Mogao Grottoes: a methodology for visitor carrying capacity,' in N. Agnew (ed.) *Conservation of Ancient Sites on the Silk Road: Proceedings of the Second International Conference on the Conservation of Grotto Sites*. Los Angeles: Getty Conservation Institute, pp. 160–169.

Dempwolf, T. (2006) 'Industrial heritage conservation: the historic diesel power station in Wustermark,' in D. Saunders, J. Townsend, and S. Woodcock, (eds.) *The Object in Context: Crossing Conservation Boundaries, Contributions to the IIC Munich Congress 28 August-1 September 2006*. London: IIC, 76–81.

Dickens, C. (1861) *Great Expectations*. London: Chapman and Hall.

Diebold, W. (1995) 'The politics of derestoration: the Aegina pediment and the German confrontation with the past.' *Art Journal* 54 (2): 60–66.

Dillon, J. (2006) 'In the News .... the Fitzwilliam smashed porcelain vases,' *Icon News* 4: 27–29.

Dollery, D. (1994) 'A methodology of preventive conservation for a large, expanding and mixed archaeological collection,' in A. Roy and P. Smith (eds.) *Preventive Conservation Practice, Theory and Research: 1994 IIC Ottawa Congress*. London: IIC.

Dollery, D. and Henderson, J. (1996) 'Conservation records for the archaeologist?' in A. Roy and P. Smith (eds.) *Archaeological Conservation and Its Consequences, 1996 IIC Copenhagen Congress*. London: IIC.

Dollery, D. and Henderson, J. (eds.) (1997) *Industrial Collections: Care and Conservation*. Cardiff: Council for Museums in Wales and UKIC.

Dooijes, R and Nieuwenhuyse, O. (2007) 'Ancient repairs: techniques and social meaning,' in M. Bentz and X. Kastner (eds.) *Konservieren Oden Restaurierung Griechischer Vasen von der Antike bis heute*. Munich: Verlag CH Beck.

Dooijes, R and Nieuwenhuyse, O. (2009) 'Ancient repairs in archaeological research: a Near Eastern perspective,' in J. Ambers *et al.* (eds.) *Holding it All Together; Ancient and Modern Approaches to Joining, Repair and Consolidation*. London: Archetype Publications.

Dorrell, P. (1989) *Photography in Archaeology and Conservation*. Cambridge: Cambridge University Press.

Doumas, D. (2010) 'Reconstructing the image: A discussion on the effectiveness of restoration methods for painted surface: theory and practice at the Benaki Museum.' *ΜΟΥΣΕΙΟ ΜΠΕΝΑΚΗ* 10: 83–101. Available at: https://ejournals.epublishing.ekt.gr/index.php/benaki/article/viewFile/1777/1766.pdf (Accessed February 21, 2021).

Dove, S. (1981) 'Conservation of glass-inlaid bronzes and lead curses from Uley, Gloucestershire.' *The Conservator* 5: 31–35.

Dowman, A. (1970) *Conservation in Field Archaeology*. London: Methuen & Co. Ltd.

Down, J. (1995) 'Adhesion projects at the Canadian Conservation Institute,' in M. Wright and J. Townsend (eds.) *Resins: Ancient and Modern*. Edinburgh: SSCR.

Down, J. (2015) 'Evaluation of selected poly(vinyl acetate) and acrylic adhesives" *Studies in Conservation* 60 (1): 33–54.

Down, J., *et al.* (2002) 'Analysis of the Archimedes Palimpsest.' *Studies in Conservation* 47 (sup 3): 52–58.

Drago, A. (2011) '"I feel included:" the *Conservation in Focus* exhibition at the British Museum.' *Journal of the Institute of Conservation* 34 (1): 28–38.

Drayton Hall Preservation Trust (2018) 'Drayton Hall: The Creation and Preservation of an American Icon.' Charleston, SC. The History Press.

Drew, T., Vo, M. and Wolfe, J. (2013) 'The invisible gorilla strikes again: sustained inattentional blindness in expert observers.' *Psychological Science* 24 (9): 1848–1853.

Drews, M., *et al.* (2010) 'Conservation of waterlogged cork using supercritical CO_2 drying,' in E. Williams and C. Peachey (eds.) *The Conservation of Archaeological Materials: Current trends and future directions. BAR international Series 2116*. Oxford: Archaeopress.

Drews, M., *et al* (2013) 'The application of subcritical fluids for the stabilization of marine archaeological iron.' *Studies in Conservation* 58(4): 314–325.

Dreyfus, S. and Dreyfus, H. (1980) *A Five Stages Model of the Mental Activities Involved in Directed Skill Acquisition*. Washington, DC:Storming Media.

Drysdale, L. (1987) 'Me and my object – a very special relationship.' *Conservation News* 33: 9.

Drysdale, L. (1988) 'The eternal triangle: relationships between conservators, their clients and objects,' in V. Todd (ed.) *Conservation Today, Papers Presented at the UKIC 30th Anniversary Conference 1988*. London: UKIC.

Drumheller, A. and Kaminitz, M. (1994) 'Traditional care and conservation, the merging of two disciplines at the National Museum of the American Indian,' in A. Roy and P. Smith (eds.) *Preventive Conservation Practice, Theory and Research: 1994 IIC Ottawa Congress*. London: IIC.

Durant, F. (2020) "Conservation is not neutral (and neither are we)." Invited presentation for Conservation Together at Home Webinar Series, The Institute for Conservation (UK), online: June 14, 2020. https://youtu.be/bFKS12TYTEg

Dyer, J., *et al.* (2011) 'Reassessment of Anoxic Storage of Ethnographic Rubber Objects,' in J. Bridgland (ed.) *Preprints of 16th Triennial Conference, ICOM-CC, Lisbon, Portugal, 19–23 September 2011*. Paris: ICOM-CC.

Eastop, D. (1998) 'Decision making in conservation: determining the role of artefacts,' in A. Timar Balazsy and D. Eastop (eds.) *International Perspectives on Textile Conservation*. London: Archetype.

Eastop, D. (2006) 'Conservation as material culture,' in C. Tilley, *et al.* (eds.) *The Handbook of Material Culture*. London: SAGE Publications, pp. 516–533.

Eastop, D. and Brooks, M. (1996) 'To clean or not to clean: the value of soils and creases, in J. Bridgland (ed.) *11th Triennial Meeting, Edinburgh 1-6 September 1996*. Edinburgh: ICOM-CC.

Eastop, D. and Gill, K. (2001) *Upholstery Conservation: Principles and Practice*. London: Routledge.

ECCO (2002) *Professional Guidelines I*. Available at: http://www.ecco-eu.org/fileadmin/user_upload/ECCO_professional_guidelines_I.pdf. (Accessed on June 3rd, 2020).

ECCO (2011) *Competencies for access to the conservation restoration profession*. Available at: https://www.ecco-eu.org/wp-content/uploads/2021/01/ECCO_Competences_EN.pdf. (Accessed on July 25, 2022).

Edensor, T. (2011) 'Entangled agencies, material networks and repair in a building assemblage: the mutable stone of St. Ann's Church, Manchester.' *Transactions of the Institute of British Geographers NS* 36: 316–334.

Edge, D. (1994) 'The armourer's craft: restoration or conservation?' in A. Oddy (ed.) *Restoration: Is It Acceptable? British Museum Occasional Paper No. 99*. London: British Museum Press.

Edson, G. (1997) *Museum Ethics*. London: Routledge.

Edwards, B. (2004) 'Changing Avebury.' *The Regional Historian* Issue 12 (spring 2004). Available at: https://www2.uwe.ac.uk/faculties/CAHE/Documents/Research/Regional-history/RHCissue12.pdf (Accessed July 26, 2020).

Edwards, E. (2019) 'Survey of audience reception in the Sistine Chapel: decoding the message of Sacred art.' *Church Communication and Culture* 3 (3): 260–282.

Egan, G. (2012) 'Marked window leads.' *Post Medieval Archaeology* 46 (2): 291–303.

Eggert, P. (2009) *Securing the Past*. Cambridge: CUP.

Ekserdjian, D. (1987) 'The Sistine Ceiling and the critics.' *Apollo 126*: 401–404.

Elkington, J. (1994) 'Towards the Sustainable Corporation: Win-Win-Win Business Strategies for Sustainable Development.' *California Management Review* 36 (2): 90–100.

Emmanuel, K. (2017) 'Assessing the present and future probability of Hurricane Harvey's rainfall.' *PNAS* 114 (48): 12681–12684.

English Heritage (1995) *Brodsworth Hall.* London: English Heritage.

English Heritage (2008) *Conservation Principles Policies and Guidance.* London: English Heritage Available at: www.english-heritage.org.uk/professional/advice/conservation-principles/ConservationPrinciples/ (Accessed August 1, 2020).

Erhardt, D. and Mecklenburg, M. (1994) 'Relative humidity re-examined,' in A. Roy and P. Smith (eds.) *Preventive Conservation Practice, Theory and Research: 1994 IIC Ottawa Congress.* London: IIC.

Evans, A. (1986) *The Sutton Hoo Ship Burial.* London: British Museum Publications.

Evans, H. and Kaborg, H. (2013) 'The Nationalmuseum lighting lab.' *Art Bulletin of Nationalmuseum Stockholm* 20: 139–146.

FAIC (Foundation for the American Institute of Conservation) (2021) *Sustainability in Cultural Heritage Website.* Available at: https://stich.culturalheritage.org/ (Accessed May 1, 2022).

Faraday, M. (1843) *On the Ventilation of Lamp Burners*, Royal Institution Lecture, 7 April 1843, London.

Fell, V. (1996) 'Washing away the evidence,' in A. Roy and P. Smith (eds). *Archaeological Conservation and Its Consequences*, 1996 IIC Copenhagen Congress. London: IIC.

Feller, R.L. (1978) 'Standards in the evaluation of thermoplastic resins,' in *ICOM-CC Fourth Triennial Conference, Zagreb 1978.* Zagreb: ICOM-CC.

Fjaestad, M., *et al.* (1998) 'Are recently excavated bronze artefacts more deteriorated than earlier finds?' in W. Mourey and L. Robbiola (eds.) *Metal 98: Proceedings of the International Conference on Metals Conservation.* London: James and James, 71–79.

Ford, D., *et al.* (2004) 'Chaco Canyon reburial program.' *Conservation and Management of Archaeological Sites* 6 (3-4): 177–202.

Foster, S. and Jones, S. (2019) 'Untold heritage values and significance of replicas.' *Conservation and Management of Archaeological Sites* 21 (1): 1–24.

Foster, S and Jones, S. (2020) *New Futures for Replicas: principles and guidance for museums and heritage.* Available at: https://replicas.wordpress.stir.ac.uk/files/2020/07/NewFutureReplicas-leaflet-proof6-spreadslow-res.pdf (Accessed June 2, 2022).

Foundling Museum (n.d.) *The Tokens.* Available at: https://foundlingmuseum.org.uk/collections/whats-on-display/the-tokens/ [Accessed August 8, 2020]

Fowler, J. (1880) 'On the processes of decay and, incidentally, on the composition and texture of glass at different periods, and the history of its manufacture.' *Archaeologia* 46: 65–162.

Fowler, P. (1992) *The Past in Contemporary Society: Then, Now.* London: Routledge.

France-Lanord, A. (1996) 'Knowing how to question the object before restoring it,' in N. Stanley Price, M. Kirby Talley Jr and A. Vaccaro (eds.) *Historical and Philosophical Issues in the Conservation of Cultural Heritage.* Los Angeles: The Getty Conservation Institute.

Francis, K. (2021) 'The absence of black and ethnic minority representation in UK heritage conservation and the value of including diverse voices.' *Journal of the Institute of Conservation* 44(3): 183–196. 10.1080/19455224.2021.1974066

Fulcher, K. (2014) 'The diverse use of AJK dough in conservation.' *Journal of the Institute of Conservation* 37 (1): 1–11.

Galliano, F., Werner, G., and Menzel, K. (1998) 'Monitoring of metal corrosion and soil solution at two excavation sites and in the laboratory,' in W. Mourey and L. Robbiola (eds.) *Metal 98, Proceedings of the International Conference on Metals Conservation.* London: James and James, pp. 87–91.

Ganiaris, H., Keene, S. and Starling, K. (1982) 'A comparison of some leather treatments for excavated leather.' *The Conservator* 6: 12–23.

Ganiaris, H. and Lang, R. (2013) 'Lifting the barriers: widening involvement in conservation at the Museum of London,' in E. Williams (ed.) *The Public Face of Conservation.* London: Archetype, pp. 212–221.

Ganiaris, H. and Sully, D. (1998) 'Showcase construction: materials and methods used in the Museum of London.' *The Conservator* 22: 57–67.

Gao, Q. and Jones, S. (2020) 'Authenticity and heritage conservation: seeking common complexities beyond the Eastern and Western dichotomy.' *International Journal of Heritage Studies* 27 (1): 90–106.

Garfinkle, A., *et al.* (1997) 'Art conservation and the legal obligation to preserve artistic intent.' *Journal of the American Institute for Conservation 36(2)*: 151–163.

Garside, P., Bradford, K. and Hamlyn, S. (2018) 'The use of risk management to support preventive conservation.' *Studies in Conservation* 63 (Sup 1): 94–100.

Genbrugge, S. (2017) "The effects on conservation of the changing appreciation of Central African Objects," in N. Owczarek, M. Gleeson and L. Grant (eds.) *Engaging Conservation Collaboration across Disciplines*. London: Archetype Publications, pp. 138–147.

Geneste, J.M. and Mauriac, M. (2014) 'The conservation of Lascaux cave, France' in C. Saiz-Jimenez (ed.) *The Conservation of Subterranean Cultural Heritage*. London: T&F?/Routledge, pp. 165–172.

George, G. (1984) 'The Great Drayton Hall Debate.' *History News* (January 1984): 7–12.

Gessler, C. and McEnroe, K. (2019) 'Just when you thought you knew how to polish silver: an analysis of silver polish applicators,' in C. Chemello, E. Brambilla and E. Joseph (eds.) *Metal 2019. Proceedings of the Interim Meeting of the ICOM-CC Metals Working Group September 2-6, 2019 Neuchâtel, Switzerland.* Available at: https://www.icom-cc-publications-online.org/3482/Just-When-You-Thought-You-Knew-How-to-Polish-Silver--An-Analysis-of-Silver-Polish-Applicators. (Accessed December 6, 2021).

Gibson, J. (1966) *The Senses Considered as Perceptual Systems*. Boston: Houghton Mifflin.

Giesen, M. (2013) *Curating Human Remains: Caring for the Dead in the United Kingdom*. Woodbridge: Boydell Press.

Gilardoni, A., Orsini, R. and Taccani, S. (1994) *X-Rays in Art* (2nd Edition). Lecco, Italy: Gilardoni SpA.

Gilberg, M. (1987) 'Friedrich Rathgen: The father of modern archaeological conservation.' *Journal of the American Institute for Conservation* 26(2): 105–120.

Gilberg, M. (1991) 'The effects of low oxygen atmospheres on museum pests.' *Studies in Conservation* 36(2): 93–98.

Gilchrist, R. (2012) *Medieval Life, Archaeology and the Life Discourse*. Woodbridge: The Boydell Press.

Gillings, M. and Pollard, J. (1999) 'Non-portable stone artefacts and contexts of meaning: the tale of Grey Wether (www.museums.ncl.ac.uk/Avebury/stone4.htm),' *World Archaeology*, 31(2), 179–193. doi:10.1080/00438243.1999.9980440.

Gillett, F. (2021) Covid-19: the secret life of museums. Available at: https://www.bbc.co.uk/news/uk-55755740 (Accessed April 2, 2022).

Giusti, A. (1994) 'Filling lacunae in Florentine mosaic and tessera mosaic: reflections and proposals,' in A. Oddy (ed.) *Restoration: Is It Acceptable? British Museum Occasional Paper No. 99*. London: British Museum Press.

Gleeson, M. (2014) *Analysis of the shabti box varnish*. Available at: https://www.penn.museum/sites/artifactlab/tag/shabti-box/ Accessed Nov 30, 2021.

Glen, A., Bowman, C. and Andrew, J. (2012) *Forth Bridge: Restoring an Icon*. Ramsey, Isle of Man: Lily.

Glob, P. (1969) *The Bog People: Iron-Age Man Preserved*. London: Faber.

Godley, J. (2015) *Master Art Forger the Story of Han Van Meegeren*. Andesite Press (originally printed 1950).

Gombrich, E. (1962) 'Dark varnishes: variations on a theme from Pliny.' *Burlington Magazine* 104: 51–55.

Goodburn-Brown, D. (1996) 'Surface studies on metals from waterlogged sites.' in I. MacLeod, *et al.* (eds.) *Metal 95*. London: James and James.

Goodburn-Brown, D. and Jones, J. (eds.) (1998) *Look After the Pennies: Numismatics and Conservation in the 1990s*. London: Archetype.

Gordon, R., Hermens, E. and Lennard, F. (2014) *Authenticity and Replication: The 'Real Thing' in Art and Conservation*. London: Archetype Press.

Gosden, C. and Marshall, Y. (1999) 'The Cultural Biography of Objects.' *World Archaeology* 31: 169–178.

Graham-Taylor, S. (2003) *Museums and Sustainability: Guidelines for Policy and Practice in Museums and Galleries*. Melbourne: Museum Australia.

Grant, D. (2010) 'David Ascalon and the Visual Artists Rights Act.' *The Wall Street Journal*, Aug 31, 2010.

Graves, C. (2008) 'From an archaeology of iconoclasm to an anthropology of the body.' *Current Anthropology* 49 (1): 35–60.

Graves, L. (2015) *Early Seating Upholstery: Reading the evidence*. Williamsburg: The Colonial Williamsburg Foundation.

Graves, L. and C. Howlett (1997) 'Leather bottoms, satin haircloth and Spanish beard: conserving Virginia upholstered seating furniture,' in L. Beckerdite (ed.) *American Furniture*. Hanover, NH: University: Press of New England, Chipstone Foundation, pp. 267–297.

Grayson, A. (1973) *Papyrus and Tablet*. Englewood Cliffs, NJ: Prentice Hall.

Greaves, P., Fuller, K. and Miller, L. (2019) 'The conservation programme,' in C. Fern, T. Dickinson, and L. Webster (eds.) *The Staffordshire Hoard: An Anglo-Saxon Treasure*. London: Society of Antiquaries of London. pp. 16–24.

Greene, V. (2006) 'Using case studies for examining the decision-making process for cleaning ethnographic objects.' *Journal of the American Institute for Conservation* 45 (3): 183–199.

Green, L. (1991) 'Microchemical test.' *Conservation News* 45: 35.

Green, L. and Thickett, D. (1993) 'Interlaboratory comparison of the Oddy Test,' in N. Tennant (ed.) *Conservation Science in the UK*. London: James & James.

Green, L., and Thickett, D. (1995) 'Testing materials for use in the storage and display of antiquities: a revised methodology.' *Studies in Conservation* 40 (3): 145–152.

Gregory, R. (1970) *The Intelligent Eye*. London: Weidenfeld and Nicholson.

Griffiths, N., Jenner, A. and Wilson, C. (1990) *Drawing Archaeological Finds: A Handbook*. London: Archetype.

Gunnell, D., *et al.* (2019) 'The hazards of perception: evaluating a change blindness demonstration within a real-world driver education course.' *Cognitive Research* 4 (15). 10.1186/s41235-019-0165-4

Haines, B. (1985) 'Identification of leather,' in S. Fogle, *et al.* (eds.) *Recent Advances in Leather Conservation*. Washington, DC: AIC.

Hamilton, D. (2010) *Methods of Conserving Archaeological Material from Underwater Sites*. Available at: https://nautarch.tamu.edu/CRL/conservationmanual/ (Accessed December 29, 2020).

Hansen, S. (2005) *Decision Theory: A Brief Introduction*. Available at; https://people.kth.se/~soh/decisiontheory.pdf (Accessed January 2, 2022).

Hanssen-Bauer, F. (1996) 'Stability as a technical and an ethical requirement in Conservation,' in J. Bridgland (ed.) *11th Triennial Meeting, Edinburgh 1-6 September 1996*. Edinburgh: ICOM-CC.

Harder, S. (2007) *The Current State of Archaeological Ironwork Storage in North-East England*, unpublished MA Dissertation.

Harrison, R. (2013) *Heritage. Critical Approaches*. London: Routledge.

Haynes, M.L. (1993) 'Buried treasures: Wartime and recent uses of underground space for artefact storage,' unpublished MA dissertation, Department of Archaeology, University of Durham.

Hedley, G. (1986) 'Cleaning and meaning: The ravished image reviewed.' *The Conservator* 10: 2–6.

Hedley, G. (1990) 'Long lost relations and newfound relativities: Issues in the cleaning of paintings,' in V. Todd (ed.) *Appearance, Opinion, Change: Evaluating the Look of Paintings*. London: UKIC.

Henderson, J. (2001) 'New skills new influence,' in A. Oddy and S. Smith (eds.) *Past Practice-Future Prospects. The British Museum Occasional Paper Number 145*. London: British Museum, pp. 103–108.

Henderson, J. (2022) 'Inconvenient questions and the question of neutrality,' in P. Murray et al. (eds.) *Contemporary Issues in Book and Paper Conservation (Proceedings of Mod Cons BPG conference 2021)*. London: Archetype Publications.

Henderson, J. (2018) 'Managing Uncertainty for Preventive Conservation.' *Studies in Conservation* 63 (Sup 1): 108–112.

Henderson, J. (2020) 'Beyond Lifetimes: who do er exclude when we keep things for the future?' *Journal of the Institute of Conservation* 43 (3): 195–212.

Henderson, J. and Nakamoto, T. (2016) 'Dialogue in conservation decision making.' *Studies in Conservation* 61 (Suppliment) 2: 67–78.

Henderson, J. and Waller, R. (2016) 'Effective preservation decision strategies.' *Studies in Conservation* 61 (6): 308–323.

Heuman, J. (ed.) (1995) *From Marble to Chocolate: the Conservation of Modern Sculpture*. London: Archetype.

Hickey-Friedman, L. (2002) 'A review of ultra-violet light and examination techniques.' *Objects Specialty Group Postprints* 9: 161–168.

Hicks, B. and Kropf, S. (2002) *Raising the Hunley*. New York: Random House.

High, K., *et al.* (2016) 'Fading star: towards understanding the effects of acidification on the preservation of organic remains (wood) at Star Carr,' in T. Grant and C. Cook (eds.) *Proceedings of the 12th ICOM-WOAM conference, Istanbul 2013*. Paris: ICOM-CC, pp. 62–71.

High, K., *et al.* (2018) 'An assessment of post-excavation changes observed in bone and wood artifacts from Star Carr,' in E. Williams and E. Hocker (eds.) *Proceedings of the 13th ICOM-CC Group on Wet Organic Archaeological Materials Conference Florence 2016*. Paris: ICOM-CC.

Hindin, S. (2014) 'How the west was won: Charles Muskavitch, James Roth, and the arrival of 'scientific' art conservation in the western United States.' *Journal of Art Historiography* 11: 1–50.

Historic England (English Heritage) (2008) *Conservation Principles, Policies and Guidance, for the Sustainable Management of the Historic Environment*. London: English Heritage. Available at: https://historicengland.org.uk/images-books/publications/conservation-principles-sustainable-management-historic-environment/conservationprinciplespoliciesandguidance april08web/ (Accessed August 2, 2020).

Historic England. (2019) Heritage and the Economy. Available at: https://historicengland.org.uk/content/heritage-counts/pub/2019/heritage-and-the-economy-2019/ (Accessed August 3, 2020).

Hoadley, R. (1991) *Identifying Wood: Accurate Results with Simple Tools*. Newton, CT: The Taunton Press.

Hoare, R. (1812) *Ancient History of South Wiltshire*. Llandrindod Wells: Castle Hill.

Hodder, I. (1987) 'The contextual analysis of symbolic meanings,' in I. Hodder (ed.) *The Archaeology of Contextual Meanings*. Cambridge: Cambridge University Press.

Hodder, I. (2012) *Entangled: An Archaeology of the Relationships between Humans and Things*. Oxford: Wiley-Blackwell.

Hodges, H. (1975) 'Problems and ethics of the restoration of pottery,' in D. Leigh, , *et al.* (eds.) *Conservation in Archaeology and the Applied Arts: 1975 IIC Stockholm. Congress*. London: IIC.

Hoffman, P. (1983) 'A rapid method for the detection of polyethylene glycols(PEG) in wood.' *Studies in Conservation* 28: 189–193.

Hoffmann, W. (2013) 'Bringing history to life: reproducing a Worthington steam pump from the USS Monitor.' *Objects Specialty Group Postprints* 20. Available at: https://resources.culturalheritage.org/osg-postprints/v20/hoffmann/ (Accessed Dec 20, 2021).

Horie, C.V. (1983) 'Reversibility of polymer treatments,' in *Resins in Conservation: Papers given at the Proceedings of the Symposium, Edinburgh 1982*. Edinburgh: SSCR. pp. 3.1–3.6.

Horie, C.V. (1987) (1st ed) *Materials for Conservation*. London: Butterworth.

Horie, C.V. (2010) (2nd ed) *Materials for Conservation, organic consolidants, adhesives and coatings*. London: Routledge.

Hoskins, J. (1998) *Biographical Objects: How Things Tell the Stories of People's Lives*. New York, NY: Routledge.

Hucklesby, C. (2005) 'Changing values: exploring the aetiology behind the nature of conservation among different cultural groups,' in I. Verger (eds.) *ICOM Committee for Conservation 14th Triennial meeting Preprints, The Hague, 12-16 September 2005*. London: James & James, pp. 1022–1027.

Hughes, C. (2011) 'The Attingham Re-discovered Project, National Trust, Shropshire UK.' Available at: https://www.icom-cc-publications-online.org/1067/The-Attingham-Re-discovered-Project-National-Trust-Shropshire-UK (Accessed March 31, 2021).

Hunt, D. (2001) 'The value of human remains for research and education,' in E. Williams (ed.) *Human Remains: Conservation, Retrieval and Analysis BAR International Research Series 934*. Oxford: Archaeopress, pp. 129–135.

Hunter, K. and Foley, K. (1984) 'The Lincoln Hanging Bowl,' in L. Bacon and B. Knight (eds.) *From Pinheads to Hanging Bowls, UKIC Occasional Paper 7*. London: UKIC.

Hutt, S. and Riddle, J. (2007) 'The law of Human Remains and Burials,' in V. Cassman, N. Odegaard, and J. Powell (eds.) *Human Remains: Guide for Museums and Academic Institutions*. Oxford: Atlamira Press.

Hurcombe, L. (2007) *Archaeological Artefacts as Material Culture*. Abingdon: Routledge.

ICOM (International Council of Museums) (2021) *Museums, Museum Professionals and Covid-19: Third Survey*. Available at: https://icom.museum/wp-content/uploads/2021/07/Museums-and-Covid-19_third-ICOM-report.pdf (Accessed Nov 14, 2021).

ICOM-CC (International Council of Museums Conservation Committee) (1984) *The Conservator-Restorer: A Definition of the Profession*. Copenhagen: ICOM-CC.

ICOM-CC (2009) *Terminology to characterize the conservation of tangible cultural heritage Resolution adopted by the ICOM-CC membership at the 15th Triennial Conference, New Delhi, 22-26 September 2008*. Available at: http://www.icom-cc.org/54/document/icom-cc-resolution-terminology-english/?id=744#.YQZsAI5KjIU (Accessed August 1, 2021).

ICOM-CC (2014) *Environmental Guidelines ICOM-CC and IIC Declaration*. Available at: http://www.icom-cc.org/332/-icom-cc-documents/declaration-on-environmental-guidelines/#.YQkdKY5KjIU (Accessed August 3, 2021).

ICOMOS (1965) *The Venice Charter*. Available at: https://www.icomos.org/charters/venice_e.pdf (accessed November 11, 2021).

ICOMOS (1994) *The Nara Charter*. Available at: https://www.icomos.org/charters/nara-e.pdf (Accessed November 11, 2021).

ICOMOS Australia (1979) *The Burra Charter 1979*. Available at: https://australia.icomos.org/wp-content/uploads/Burra-Charter_1979.pdf (Accessed November 11, 2021).

ICOMOS Australia (1999) *The Burra Charter 1999*. Available at: https://australia.icomos.org/wp-content/uploads/BURRA_CHARTER.pdf (Accessed November 11, 2021).

ICOMOS, Australia (2013) The Burra Charter-2013. Available at: http://openarchive.icomos.org/id/eprint/2145/ (Accessed January 9, 2023).

ICON (2014) *The Institute of Conservation's Code of Conduct*. Available at: http://www.tankerdale.co.uk/wp-content/uploads/2016/01/ICON-Code-of-Conduct.pdf#:~:text=The%20Code%20of%20Conduct%20states%20the%20general%20principles,who%20are%20volunteering%20or%20in%20training.%20The%20Code (Accessed November 11, 2021).

ICON (2020) Icon Ethical Guidance. Available at: https://www.icon.org.uk/resources/standards-and-ethics/icon-ethical-guidance.html (Accessed November 11, 2021).

ICON (2020) Professional Standards and Judgements and Ethics. Available at: https://www.icon.org.uk/resources/resources-for-conservation-professionals/standards-and-ethics/icon-professional-standards.html. (Accessed July 25, 2022).

Idelson, A. and Severini, L. (2018) 'Inpainting,' in *Encyclopaedia of Archaeological Sciences*. Available at: https://onlinelibrary.wiley.com/doi/full/10.1002/9781119188230.saseas0330 (Accessed April 2, 2021).

IMLS (2019) *Protecting America's Collections Results from the Heritage Health Information Survey*. Available at: https://www.imls.gov/sites/default/files/publications/documents/imls-hhis-report.pdf (Accessed August 29, 2021).

Ireland, T. and Lydon, J. (2005) *Object Lessons: Archaeology and Heritage in Australia*. Melbourne: Australian Scholarly Publishing.

Iten, C. (2008) 'Ceramics mended with lacquer: fundamental aesthetic principles, techniques and artistic concepts,' in *Flickwerk: The Aesthetics of Mended Japanese Ceramics*, 18–24. Ithaca, NY: Herbert F. Johnson Museum of Art, Cornell University and Münster: Museum für Lackkunst. Available at: http://annacolibri.com/wp-content/uploads/2013/02/Flickwerk_The_Aesthetics_of_Mended_Japanese_Ceramics.pdf. (Accessed September 1, 2020).

Jacobsen, E., van Hasselt, J and Toth, A. (1975) 'The manufacture of gongs in Semarang.' *Indonesia* 19: 127–172.

Jacobsen, M., Blouin, V. and Shirley, W. (2012) 'Does erosion corrosion account for intriguing damage to the Civil War submarine H.L. Hunley.' *Marine Technology Society Journal* 46 (6), 38–48.

Jaeschke, R. (1996) 'When does history end,' in A. Roy and P. Smith (eds.) *Archaeological Conservation and Its Consequences: 1996 IIC Copenhagen Congress*. London: IIC.

James, N. (2017) 'Our fourth Lascaux.' *Antiquity* 91 (359): 1367–1374.

Jedrzejewska, H. (1976) *Ethics in Conservation*. Stockholm: Kungel Konsthögskolan Institutet för Materialkunskap.

Jenkins, S. (2003) *England's Thousand Best Houses*. London: Penguin.

Johns, D. (2018) 'Conserving 14th and 15th century canoes in satellite treatment facilities in Aotearoa, New Zealand - 'Getting by' down under,' in E. Williams and E. Hocker (eds.) *Proceedings of the 13th ICOM-CC Group on Wet Organic Archaeological Materials Conference Florence 2016*. Florence: ICOM-CC.

Johnson, A., Hannen, W. and Zuccari, F. (2013) 'Vibration control during museum construction projects.' *Journal of the American Institute for Conservation* 52 (1): 30–47.

Johnson, J. (1993) 'Conservation and archaeology in Great Britain and the United States: A comparison.' *Journal of the American Institute of Conservation* 32: 249–269.

Johnson, J., *et al.* (2005) 'Practical aspects of consultation with communities.' *Journal of the American Institute of Conservation* 44 (3): 302–215.

Johnson, R. (2001) 'The "Boy-learner' and the 'quiet American': Arthur Trotman and Bill Rector's contribution to the preservation of London's Material Heritage,' in A. Oddy and S. Smith (eds.) *Past Practice-Future Prospects. The British Museum Occasional Paper Number 145*. London: British Museum, pp. 137–142.

Jokilehto, J. (1999) *A History of Architectural Conservation*. Oxford: Butterworth-Heinemann.

Jones, A. (2019) *A Portable Cosmos: Revealing the Antikythera Mechanism, Scientific Wonder of the Ancient World*. Oxford: Oxford University Press.

Jones, M. (1990) *Fake? The Art of Deception*. London: British Museum Publications Ltd.

Jones, M. (2003) *For Future Generations, Conservation of a Tudor Maritime Collection, The Archaeology of the Mary Rose Vol. 5*. Portsmouth: The Mary Rose Trust.

Jones, S. (2018) 'How Monkey Christ brought new life to a quiet Spanish Town.' *The Guardian*, December 28, 2018.

Jones, S. and Holden, J. (2008) *It's a Material World: Caring for the Public Realm*. London: Demos.

Jones-Amin, H., Tan, H. and Tee, A. (2006) 'Gamelan: can a conservation-conceived protocol protect it spiritually and physically in a museum?' in D. Saunders, J. Townsend and S. Woodcock (eds.) *The Object in Context: Crossing Conservation Boundaries, Contributions to the IIC Munich Congress 28 August-1 September 2006*. London: IIC. pp. 138–143.

Jorjani, M., *et al.* (2009) 'An evaluation of potential adhesives for marble repair,' in J. Ambers, *et al.* (eds.) *Holding it all together: Ancient and Modern Approaches to joining, repair and consolidation*. London: Archetype in association with the British Museum.

Joy, J. and Farley, J. (2019) 'The curation and display of Lindow Man.' *Journal of Wetland Archaeology* 19 (1-2): 172–185.

Kahnemann, D. (2003) 'A perspective on judgement and choice: mapping bounded rationality.' *American Psychologist* 58(9): 697–720.

Kahnemann, D. (2011) *Thinking Fast and Slow*. New York: Farrar, Straus, and Giroux.

Kamba, N., *et al.* (2008) 'Measurement and analysis of the global transport environment for packing cases for artifacts.' *Studies in Conservation* 53(sup1): 60–63.

Kapelouzou, I. (2012) 'The inherent sharing of conservation decisions,' *Studies in Conservation* 57 (3): 172–182.

Kavanagh, G. (1990) *History Curatorship*. Washington DC: Smithsonian Institution Press.

Keene, S. (1991) 'Audits of care: framework for collections condition survey,' in M. Norman and V. Todd (eds.) *Storage, preprints for the UKIC Conference 'Restoration '91.'* London: UKIC.

Keene, S. (1994) 'Real time survival rates for treatments of archaeological iron,' in D. Scott, J. Podany and B. Considine (eds.) *Ancient and Historic Metals, Conservation and Scientific Research*. Marina del Rey, CA: Getty Conservation Institute, pp. 250–264.

Keene, S. (1996) *Managing Conservation in Museums*. London: Butterworth-Heinemann.

Keene, S. (2002) *Managing Conservation in Museums*. 2nd Edition. Oxford: Butterworth-Heinemann.

Keene, S. and Orton, C. (1985) 'Stability of treated archaeological iron: an assessment.' *Studies in Conservation* 30: 136–142.

Keepax, C. (1975) 'Scanning electron microscopy of wood replaced by iron corrosion products.' *Journal of Archaeological Science* 2: 145–150.

Keepax, C. and Robson, M. (1978) 'Conservation and associated examination of a Roman chest: evidence for woodworking techniques.' *The Conservator* 2: 35–40.

Kennedy, M. (2017) 'Secret painting of Mary Queen of Scots lost for centuries goes on display.' *The Guardian*, October 27, 2017. Available at: https://www.theguardian.com/artanddesign/2017/oct/27/secret-portrait-of-mary-queen-of-scots-lost-for-centuries-goes-on-display. (Accessed November 30, 2021).

Khatchadourian, L. (2019) 'Life among the ruins: the vibrant afterlife of Socialist modernity.' Paper presented at the Theoretical Archaeology Group Conference. Available at: https://www.academia.edu/39368594/LIFE_IN_RUINS_THE_VIBRANT_AFTERLIFE_OF_SOCIALIST_MODERNITY. (Accessed December 20, 2021).

Kilian, M. (2002) 'Smithsonian lost trust over donor flap, report says.' *Chicago Tribune*, May 8 2002. Available at: https://www.chicagotribune.com/news/ct-xpm-2002-05-08-0205080211-story.html. (Accessed Oct 31, 2021).

Kinnes, I., Longworth, I., McIntyre, I., Needham, S. and Oddy, A. (1988) 'Bush Barrow Gold.' *Antiquity* 62: 24–39.

Kirby Atkinson, J. (2014) 'Environmental conditions for the safeguarding of collections: a background to the current debate on the control of relative humidity and temperature,' *Studies in Conservation* 59 (4): 205–212.

Kirby Talley, M. Jr (1998) 'Miscreants and hotentots: restorers and restoration attitudes and practices in seventeenth and eighteenth century England,' in C. Sitwell and S. Staniforth (eds.) *Studies in the History of Painting Restoration*. London: Archetype.

Kirby Talley, M. (1999) 'The Delta Plan: a nationwide rescue operation.' *Museum International* 51 (1): 11–15.

Kitamura, K. (1988) 'Some thoughts about conserving Urushi art objects in Japan, and an example of conservation work,' in N. Brommelle and P. Smith (eds.) *Urushi*. Marina del Rey, CA: The Getty Conservation Institute.

Klinger, J. (2013) 'Objects of trauma, finding the balance,' in P. Hatchfield (ed) *Ethics and Critical Thinking in Conservation*. Washington, DC: American Institute for Conservation.

Knell, S. (1994) Care of Collections (*Leicester Readers in Museum Studies*).

Koob, S. (1998) Obsolete Fill Materials Found on Ceramics. *Journal of the American Institute for Conservation* 37 (1): 49–67.

Koob, S. (2006) *Conservation and Care of Glass Objects*. London: Archetype Books.

Kopytoff, I. (1986) 'The cultural biography of things: commoditization as process,' in A. Appadurai (ed.) *The Social Life of Things: Commodities in Cultural Perspective*. Cambridge: Cambridge University Press, pp. 84–94.

Korenberg, C., *et al.* (2018) 'Refinements introduced in the Oddy test methodology.' *Studies in Conservation* 63 (1): 2–12.

Kosek, J. (1994) 'Restoration of Art on Paper in the West: A consideration of changing attitudes and values,' in A. Oddy (ed.) *Restoration: Is It Acceptable? British Museum Occasional Paper No. 99*. London: British Museum Press.

Kousser, R. (2015) 'Monument and memory in ancient Greece and Rome: a comparative perspective,' in K. Galinsky and K. Lapatin (eds.) *Cultural Memories in the Roman Empire*. Los Angeles: Getty Publications, pp. 33–48.

Koutromanou, D. (2017) 'Developing evaluation strategies for engagement projects in museum conservation,' in G. Chitty (ed.) *Heritage Conservation and Communities; Engagement, Participation and Capacity Building*. London: Routledge. pp. 122–140.

Knight, M., Boughton, D. and Wilkinson, R. (2019) *Objects of the Past in the Past: Investigating the Significance of Earlier Artefacts in Later Contexts*. Oxford: Archaeopress.

Knutson, T., *et al.* (2015) 'Global projections of intense tropical cyclone activity for the late twenty-first century from dynamical downscaling of CMI P5/RCP4.5 scenarios. *Journal of Climate* 28 (18): 7203–7224.

Krmpotich, C., *et al.* (2013) *This is Our Life: Haida Material Heritage and Changing Museum Practice*. Vancouver: University of British Columbia Press.

Lambert, S. (2014) 'The early history of preventive conservation in Great Britain and the United States 1850-1950.' *CeROArt* 9. Available at: https://journals.openedition.org/ceroart/3765. (Accessed November 18, 2020).

Lambert-Zazulak, P. (2000) "The International Ancient Egyptian Tissue Bank at the Manchester Museum." *Antiquity* 74: 44–48.

Lang, J. and Middleton, A. (2005) *Radiography of Cultural Material*. 2nd Edition. Amsterdam: Elsevier.

Lance, R., *et al.* (2017) 'Air blast injuries killed the crew of the submarine H.L. Hunley.' *PloS one* 12(8): e0182244.

LaRoche, C. and Blakey, M. (1997) 'Seizing intellectual power: the dialogue at the New York African Burial Ground.' *Historical Archaeology* 31 (3): 84–106.

Laurenson, P. (2006) 'Authenticity, change and loss in the conservation of time-based media installations,' *Tate Papers* 6 (Autumn 2006). Available at: https://www.tate.org.uk/research/publications/tate-papers/06/authenticity-change-and-loss-conservation-of-time-based-media-installations. (Accessed April 26, 2021.

Lawson, L. and Cane, S. (2016) 'Do conservators dream of electric sheep? Replicas and replication.' *Studies in Conservation* 61 (2): 109–113.

Layton, R. (ed) (1994) *Who Needs the Past? Indigenous Values and Archaeology*. London: Routledge.

Lee, L. R. and Thickett, D. (1996) *Selection of Materials for the Storage or Display of Museum Objects, British Museum Occasional Paper No. 111*. London: British Museum Press.

Lepie, H. and Minkenberg, G. (2013) *The Cathedral Treasury of Aachen*, 3rd Edition. Regensburg: Schnell & Steiner.

Lewis, R. (2005a) 'Interpretation in conservation: A rare leather find from an early historic crannog,' *The Conservator* 29: 87–94.

Lewis, R. (2005b) 'The history, conservation and re-interpretation of SF105, the satchel,' in A. Crone and E. Campbell (eds.) *A Crannog of the First Millennium AD: Excavations by Jack Scott at Loch Glashan, Argyll, 1960*. Edinburgh: Society of Antiquaries Scotland, pp. 81–85.

Lindgren, J. (1996) '"A new departure in historic and patriotic work" personalism, professionalism and conflicting concepts of material culture in the late nineteenth and early twentieth centuries.' *The Public Historian* 18 (2): 41–60.

Lindsey, R. (2019) Climate change: Global sea level. Available at: https://www.climate.gov/news-features/understanding-climate/climate-change-global-sea-level. (Accessed July 25, 2022).

Lipe, D. (1987) 'Value and meaning in cultural resources,' in H. Cleere (ed.) *Approaches to the Archaeological Heritage*. Cambridge: Cambridge University Press.

Lipkowitz, G., *et al.* (2021) 'Numerical modelling of moisture loss during controlled drying of marine archaeological wood.' *Forests* 12 (12): 1662. 10.3390/f12121662

Lister, D. (1991) 'Restoration "ruins ceiling,"' *The Independent*, 20 March 1991: 12

Lithgow, K. (2011) 'Sustainable decision making - change in National Trust collections conservation.' *Journal of the Institute of Conservation* 34 (1): 128–142.

Lithgow, K., Golfomitsou, S. and Dillon, C. (2018) 'Coming clean about cleaning. Professional and public perspectives: are conservators truthful and visitors useful in decision making?' *Studies in Conservation* 63 (Sup 1): 392–396.

Lithgow, K., Staniforth, S., and Etheridge, P. (2008) 'Prioritizing access in the conservation of National Trust collections. *Studies in Conservation* 53 (S1): 178–185.

Lithgow, K. and Timbrell, H. (2014) 'How better volunteering can improve conservation: why we need to stop wondering whether volunteering in conservation is a good thing and just get better at doing it well.' *Journal of the Institute of Conservation* 37 (1): 3–14.

Lloyd, H., *et al.* (2002) 'The effects of visitor activity on dust in historic collections.' *The Conservator* 26: 72–84.

Lloyd, H. and Lithgow, K. (2021) 'For whose benefit? Integrating people and conservation In Transcending Boundaries: Integrated Approaches to Conservation,' in J. Bridgland (ed.) ICOM-CC 19th Triennial Conference Preprints, Beijing, 17–21 May 2021. Paris: ICOM.

Lochhead, V. and Tonkin, L. (2013) 'Preserving ideas that are worth fighting for: Textile conservation in the public eye at the People's History Museum, Manchester, UK', in E. Williams (ed.) *The Public Face of Conservation.* London: Archetype Publication in association with Colonial Williamsburg.

Loft, H. (2019) 'Record-breaking $110.7 Million Monet leads Impressionist and Modern Art Evening Sales.' Available at: https://www.sothebys.com/en/articles/record-breaking-110-7-million-monet-shatters-records-at-impressionist-modern-art-evening-sale. (Accessed February 28, 2022).

Lord, B., Lord, G. and Nicks, J. (1989) *The Cost of Collecting*. London: HMSO.

Lowenthal, D. (1992) 'Counterfeit art and authentic fakes?' *International Journal of Cultural Property* 1 (1): 79–103.

Lowenthal, D. (1996) *Possessed by the Past*. New York: The Free Press.

Luxford, N. and Thickett, D. (2013) 'Change or damage? Using dissemination to encourage public involvement in conservation research,' in E. Williams (ed.) *The Public Face of Conservation*. London: Archetype Publications, pp. 66–75.

MacGregor, N. (2012) *A History of the World in 100 Objects*. London: Penguin Books.

Malkogeorgou, T. (2006) The ethics of conservation practice: a look from within. *V&A Conservation Journal* Issue 52. Available at: http://www.vam.ac.uk/content/journals/conservation-journal/issue-52/the-ethics-of-conservation-practice-a-look-from-within/ (Accessed November 19, 2019).

Mancinelli, F. (1991) 'The frescoes of Michelangelo on the vault of the Sistine Chapel: Conservation methodology, problems, and results,' in S. Cather (ed.) *The Conservation of Wall Paintings*. Los Angeles: Getty Conservation Institute.

Mancinelli, F. (1992) 'Michelangelo's frescoes in the Sistine Chapel,' in Oddy, A. (ed.) *The Art of the Conservator*. London: British Museum Press.

Mann, P. (1994) 'The restoration of vehicles for use in research, exhibition, and demonstration,' in A. Oddy (ed.) *Restoration: Is It Acceptable? British Museum Occasional Paper No.99*. London: British Museum Press.

Marçal, H. (2019) 'Contemporary Art Conservation,' published as part of the research project Reshaping the Collectible: When Artworks Live in the Museum, Tate. Available at: https://www.tate.org.uk/research/reshaping-the-collectible/research-approach-conservation (Accessed November 28, 2020).

Marcon (2011) 'Six steps to safe shipment,' in C. Caple (ed.) *Preventive Conservation in Museums*. London: Routledge, pp. 63–78.

Mardikian, P. (2004) 'Conservation and management strategies applied to post recovery analysis of the American Civil War submarine H.L. Hunley (1864).' *The International Journal of Nautical Archaeology* (2004) 33 (1): 137–148.

Mardikian, P., *et al.* (2009) 'New perspectives regarding the stabilization of terrestrial and marine archaeological iron,' in M. McCarthy (ed.) *Iron, Steel and Steamship Archaeology*. Fremantle: Australian National Centre of Excellence for Maritime Archaeology, pp. 113–118.

Mardikian, P., *et al.* (2010) 'New perspectives on the stabilization of terrestrial and marine archaeological iron,' in E. Williams and C. Peachey (eds.) *The Conservation of Archaeological Materials: Current Trends and Future Directions. BAR International Series 2116*. Oxford: Archaeopress.

Mardikian, P. (2013) 'The use of subcritical fluids for the stabilisation of archaeological iron: an overview,' In J. Dillmann *et al.* (eds.) *Corrosion of Metallic Heritage Artefacts: Investigation, Conservation and Prediction of Long Term Behaviour*, 434–465. 10.1533/9781782421573.5.434

Margolis, H. (1987) *Patterns, Thinking, and Cognition: A Theory of Judgement*. Chicago: University of Chicago Press.

Mariac, M. (2011) 'Lascaux: the history of the discovery of an outstanding decorated cave.' *Adoranten 2011*. Available at: https://www.rockartscandinavia.com/adoranten-vv4.php (Accessed August 29, 2022).

Marsden, P. (2003) *Sealed by Time, The loss and Recovery of the Mary Rose. The Archaeology of the Mary Rose Vol. 1*. Portsmouth: The Mary Rose Trust.

Maryon, H. (1947) 'The Sutton Hoo Helmet,' *Antiquity* 21: 137–144.

Mason, R. and Avrami, E. (2000) 'Heritage values and challenges of conservation planning,' in J. Teutonico and G. Palumbo (eds), *Management Planning for Archaeological Sites*. Los Angeles: GCI, pp. 13–26.

Mathias, C., Ramsdale, K. and Nixon, D. (2004) 'Saving archaeological iron using the Revolutionary Preservation System,' in J. Ashton and D. Hallam (eds.) *Metal 2004*. Canberra: National Museum of Australia.

Mauriac, M. (2011) *Lascaux: the history of the discovery of an outstanding decorated cave, Adoranten 2011*. https://www.rockartscandinavia.com/adoranten-vv4.php

McClure, I. (1992) 'Henry Prince of Wales on Horseback by Robert Peake the Elder,' in A. Oddy (ed.) *The Art of the Conservator*. London: British Museum Press.

McCrone, W. and Delly, J. (1973) *The Particle Atlas*. 2nd Edition. Michigan: Ann Arbor Science Publishers.

McGhee, R. (1994) 'Ivory for the Sea Woman: the symbolic attributes of prehistoric technology,' in S. Pearce (ed.) *Interpreting Objects and Collections*. London: Routledge.

MDA (Museum Documentation Association) (1997) *The MDA Archaeological Objects Thesaurus*. Cambridge: MDA.

Mealings, B. (2009) 'If at first you do not succeed! The conservation of Holland I 1982-2003,' in M. McCarthy (ed.) *Iron, Steel and Steamship Archaeology*. Fremantle: Australian National Centre of Excellence for Maritime Archaeology, pp. 110–112.

Means, B. (2017) 'A digital passport to the past: the 'accidental' public archaeology of the virtual curation laboratory.' *Public Archaeology* 16 (3-4): 230–238.

Measday, D. (2017) 'A summary of ultraviolet fluorescent materials relevant to conservation.' *AICCM National Newsletter* No. 137. Available at: https://primastoria.files.wordpress.com/2017/03/uv-relevant-to-conservation.pdf (Accessed December 20, 2020).

Mecklenburg, M. and Merrill, R. (1997) 'Shock and vibration hazards,' in M. Richards, M. Mecklenburg, and R. Merrill (eds.) *In Art in transit: Handbook for packing and transporting paintings*. Washington, D.C.: National Art Gallery.

Meehan, B. (2005) 'Book satchels in medieval Scotland and Ireland,' in A. Crone and E. Campbell (eds.) *A Crannog of the First Millennium AD: Excavations by Jack Scott at Loch Glashan, Argyll, 1960*. Edinburgh: Society of Antiquaries Scotland, pp. 85–92.

Mellar, S. (1992) 'The exhibition and conservation of African objects: considering the non-tangible.' *Journal of the American Institute for Conservation* 31(1): 3–16.

Membership Designation Working Group (2018) '2018 Member Designation Survey: Preliminary Report.' Available at: https://www.culturalheritage.org/docs/default-source/publications/reports/survey-reports/member-designation-survey—preliminary-reportb3996e46946d640d929bff00002fd16b.pdf?sfvrsn=c6f40a20_6. (Accessed August 1, 2022).

Message, B. (2021) *Designing for Specific Audiences: Working with Indigenous Cultures*. Available at: https://www.museums.ca/site/designing_audiences. (Accessed June 22, 2022).

Metropolitan Museum of Art. (2014) *After the Fall: The Conservation of Tullio Lombardo's Adam* Available at: https://www.youtube.com/watch?v=3oznnP6SkSc. (Accessed January 5 2022).

Meyer, M. and Booker, J. (1991) *Eliciting and Analysing Expert Judgement: A Practical Guide*. London: Academic Press.

MGC (Museums and Galleries Commission) (1992) *Standards in the Museum Care of Archaeological Collections*. London: MGC.

MGC (Museums and Galleries Commission) (1993a) *Standards in the Museum Care of Biological Collections*. London: MGC.

MGC (Museums and Galleries Commission) (1993b) *Standards in the Museum Care of Geological Collections*. London: MGC.

MGC (Museums and Galleries Commission) (1994) *Standards in the Museum. Care of Larger and Working Objects*. London: MGC.

MGC (Museums and Galleries Commission) (1995a) *Standards in the Museum. Care of Musical Instruments*. London: MGC.

MGC (Museums and Galleries Commission) (1996) *Standards in the Museum Care of Photographic Collections*. London: MGC.

MGC (Museums and Galleries Commission) (1998a) *Standards in the Museum Care of Costume and Textile Collections*. London: MGC.

MGC (Museums and Galleries Commission) (1998b) *Levels of Collection Care: a self- assessment checklist for UK Museums*. London: MGC.

Michalski, S. (1993) 'Relative humidity: A discussion of correct/incorrect values,' J. Bridgland (ed.) *ICOM-CC 10th Triennial Meeting, Washington, DC, USA 1993*. Washington: ICOM-CC.

Michalski, S. (1994) 'A systematic approach to preservation: description and integration with other museum activities.' in A. Roy and P. Smith (eds.) *Preventive Conservation, Theory and Research: preprints of the Ottawa Congress, 12-16 September 1994*. London: IIC, pp. 8–11.

Michalski, S. (1997) 'The Lighting Decision,' in CCI (eds.) *Fabric of an Exhibition: An Interdisciplinary Approach – Preprints*. Ottawa: CCI, pp. 97–104.

Michalski, S. (2007) 'The Ideal climate, risk management, the ASHRAE chapter. Proofed fluctuations, and toward a full risk analysis model,' in *Experts' Roundtable on Sustainable Climate Management Strategies. Tenerife, Spain* 2007. Available at: http://www.getty.edu/conservation/science/climate/climate_experts_roundtable.html (Accessed January 30, 2022).

Michalski, S. and Karsten, I. (2018) 'The cost effectiveness of preventive conservation actions.' *Studies in Conservation* 63 (Sup 1): 187–194.

Milanese, A. (2013) 'Exhibit and experiment: a history of the Real Museo Borbonico,' in E. Risser and D. Saunders (eds.) *The Restoration of Ancient Bronzes: Naples and Beyond*. Los Angeles: J. Paul Getty Museum.

Miller, G. (1956) 'The magical number 7, plus or minus 2.' *Psychological Review* 63: 81–97.

Miller, G., *et al.* (eds.) (1991) *Approaches to Material Culture Research for Historical Archaeologists*. California, PA: The Society for Historical Archaeology.

Minolta (1988) *Precise Colour Communication*. Osaka: Minolta.

Modestini, D. (2005) John Brealey and the cleaning of paintings. *Metropolitan Museum Journal* 40: 27–36.

Molina, T. and Pincemin, M. (1994) 'Restoration acceptable to whom?,' in A. Oddy (ed.) *Restoration: Is It Acceptable? British Museum Occasional Paper No. 99*. London: British Museum Press.

Moody, J. (2015) 'Heritage and history,' in E. Waterton and S. Watson (eds.) *The Palgrave Handbook of Contemporary Heritage Research*. London: Palgrave MacMillan, pp. 113–129.

Moore, M. (2001) Conservation documentation and the implications of digitisation. *Journal of Conservation and Museum Studies* 7, 1–19.

Moore, P., Webb, J. and Collinson, M. (1991) *Pollen Analysis*. Oxford: Blackwell.

Mora, P., Mora, L. and Philippot, P. (1984) *Conservation of Wall Painting*. Oxford: Butterworth-Heinemann.

Mora, P., Mora, L. and Philippot, P. (1996) 'Problems of presentation,' in N. Stanley Price, M. Kirby Talley Jr and A. Vaccaro (eds.) *Historical and Philosophical Issues in the Conservation of Cultural Heritage*. Los Angeles: The Getty Conservation Institute.

Morris, W. (1996) 'Manifesto of the society for the protection of ancient buildings,' in N. Stanley Price, M. Kirby Talley Jr and A. Vaccaro (eds.) *Historical and Philosophical Issues in the Conservation of Cultural Heritage*. Los Angeles: The Getty Conservation Institute.

Mullhall, I. (2020) 'Banking for the future: the National Museum of Ireland Bog Body Tissue Samples Bank' *Journal of Wetland Archaeology* 19 (1-2): 89–114.

Munoz, J. (2021) 'How the Louvre is protecting its cultural treasures against extreme weather.' *Smithsonian Magazine*. Available at; https://www.smithsonianmag.com/smart-news/how-louvre-protecting-its-cultural-treasures-against-extreme-weather-180977063/ (Accessed May 1, 2022).

Muñoz, J. (2021) How the Louvre is protecting its cultural treasures against extreme weather' Smithsonian Magazine, February 19, 2021. Available at: How the Louvre Is Protecting Its Cultural Treasures Against Extreme Weather | Smart News| Smithsonian Magazine (Accessed August 1, 2022).

Muñoz Viñas, S. (2005) *Contemporary Theory of Conservation*. Oxford: Elsevier.

Muñoz Viñas, S. (2020) *On the Ethics of Cultural Heritage Conservation*. London: Archetype Publications.

Murray Pease Committee (1964) 'The Murray Pease Report.' *Studies in Conservation* 9 (3): 116–121.

Mytum, H. (2004) 'Artefact biography as an approach to material culture: Irish gravestones as a material form of genealogy.' *Journal of Irish Archaeology* 12-13: 111–127.

Näsänen, L., *et al.* (2013) 'The applicability of subcritical fluids to the conservation of actively corroding iron artifacts of cultural significance' *The Journal of Supercritical Fluids*, 79: 289–298. 10.1016/j.supflu.2012.12.033.

Navarro, J. (2011) 'Removing and re-attaching paper labels.' *Conservation Journal* 59 (Spring 2011). Available at: http://www.vam.ac.uk/content/journals/conservation-journal/spring-2011-issue-59/removing-and-re-attaching-paper-labels/ (Accessed August 28, 2022).

Needham, S., Parfitt, K. and Varndell, G. (eds.) (2006) *The Ringlemere Cup: Precious Cups and the Beginning of the Channel Bronze Age. British Museum Research Publication 163*. London: British Museum.

Netz, R., *et al.* (2011a) *The Archimedes Palimpsest. Volume 1: Catalogue and Commentary*. Cambridge: Cambridge University Press.

Netz, R., *et al.* (2011b) *The Archimedes Palimpsest. Volume 2: Images and Transcriptions*. Cambridge: Cambridge University Press.

Newbery, E. and Fecher, S. (1990) *In the Nick of Time: A Practical Guide to Teaching about Conservation of Objects*. London: Resource.

Newey, H. (2000) 'Conservation and preservation of scientific and industrial collections.' *Studies in Conservation* 45 (Sup 1): 137–139.

Nimmrichter, J., Kautek, W. and Schreiner, M. (eds.) (2006) *Lasers in the Conservation of Artworks: LACONA VI Proceedings*, Vienna, Austria, Sept. 21–25, 2005. New York: Springer.

Norman, M. (1988) 'Early conservation techniques and the Ashmolean Museum,' in S. Watkins and C. Brown (eds.) *Conservation of Ancient Egyptian Materials*. London: Institute of Archaeology Publications.

Norman, M. (2001) 'It is surprising that things can be preserved as well as they are: conservation and the Ashmolean since before 1683,' in A. Oddy *et al.* (eds.) *Past Practice, Future Prospects*. London: British Museum.

Nunberg, S., and Sutton, S. (2018) *What is Life Cycle Assessment (LCA) and How Does it Help Heritage Professionals*. Available at: https://community.culturalheritage.org/blogs/sarah-nunberg/2018/08/24/what-is-life-cycle-analysis-lca-and-how-does-it-he (Accessed April 18, 2020).

Nylander, J. (1990) *Fabrics for Historic Buildings. A Guide to Selecting Reproductions Fabrics*. 4th Edition. Chichester: Preservation Press (Wiley).

NZCCM (New Zealand Conservators of Cultural Material) (2006) *Code of Ethics*. Available at: https://www.nzccm.org.nz/resources/Documents/codeofethics.pdf (Accessed June 20, 2022).

O'Connor, S. and Brooks, M. (2007) *X-radiography of Textiles, Dress and Related Objects*. Abingdon: Routledge.

Oddy, A. (1973) 'An unsuspected danger in display.' *Museums Journal* 73(1): 27–28.

Oddy, A. (1975) 'The corrosion of metals on display,' in D. Leigh, A. Moncrieff, A. Oddy and P. Pratt (eds.) *Conservation in Archaeology and the Applied Arts: 1975 IIC Stockholm Congress*. London: IIC.

Oddy, A. (1994) 'Restoration – Is it acceptable?' in A. Oddy (ed.) in *Restoration: Is It Acceptable?, British Museum Occasional Paper No. 99*. London: British Museum Press.

Oddy, A. (1996) 'The Forbes Prize Lecture 1996.' *IIC Bulletin* 5 (October 1996): 1–5.

Oddy, A. (1997) 'Obituary for Harold James Plenderleith.' *IIC Bulletin* 6 (December 1997): 1–2.

Oddy, A. (2002) 'The conservation of marble sculptures in the British Museum before 1975.' *Studies in Conservation* 47: 145–154.

Odegaard, N. (1995) 'Artist's intent: material culture studies and conservation.' *Journal of the American Institute for Conservation* 34(3): 187–197.

Odegaard, N., Carroll, S. and Zimmt, W. (2005) *Materials Characterization Tests: For Objects of Art and Archaeology*. 2nd Edition. London: Archetype.

Odegaard, N and Sadongei, A. (2005) *Old Poisons, New Problems: A Museum Resource for Managing Contaminated Cultural Materials*. Walnut Creek, CA: Altamira Press.

Ogilvie, T. (2020) 'Conserving bog bodies: the key questions.' *Journal of Wetland Archaeology* 19 (1-2): 67–88.

O'Hern, R., Pearlstein, E. and Gagliardi, S. (2016) 'Beyond the surface: where cultural contexts and scientific analyses meet in museum conservation of West African power association helmet masks.' *Museum Anthropology* 39 (1): 70–86.

Omar, S., McCord, M. and Daniels, V. (1989) 'The conservation of bog bodies by freezedrying.' *Studies in Conservation* 34(3): 101–109.

Orlofsky, P. and Trupin, D. (1993) 'The role of connoisseurship in determining the textile conservator's treatment options.' *Journal of the American Institute for Conservation* 32: 109–118.

Orwell, G. (1949) *Nineteen Eighty-Four*. London: Penguin.

Owczarek, N., *et al.* (2015) *The Preservation of Cultural Property with Respect to the US Government Regulation of African Elephant Ivory*. Available at: https://www.culturalheritage.org/docs/default-source/resources/administration/governance/position-papers-and-statements/position-paper-on-government-regulation-of-ivory-(november-2015).pdf?sfvrsn=65969176_6 (Accessed July 14, 2022).

Oxley, I. (1998) 'The in-situ preservation of underwater sites,' in M. Corfield, P. Hinton, T. Nixon and M. Pollard (eds.) *Preserving Archaeological Remains in Situ. Proceedings of the Conference of 1st-3rd April 1996*. London: Museum of London.

Painter, T. (1995) 'Chemical and microbiological aspects of the preservation process in sphagnum peat,' in R. Turner and R. Scaife (eds.) *Bog Bodies: New Discoveries and New Perspectives*. London: British Museum Press.

Palmer, B. and Palmer, E. (2015) 'Reclaiming black history, one grave at a time.' *The Nation*, October 15, 2015. Available at: https://www.thenation.com/article/archive/reclaiming-black-history-one-grave-at-a-time/ (Accessed June 10, 2022).

Parent, C. (2021) 'Other peoples' secrets and the all-seeing eye of the conservator.' *News in Conservation* 83: 52–55.

Paterakis, A. and Hickey-Friedman, L. (2011) 'Stabilization of iron artifacts from Kaman-Kalehöyük: a comparison of chemical and environmental methods.' *Studies in Conservation* 56(3): 179–190.

Patterson, K., Barker, B. and Walsh, F. (2002) 'Electrochemical and physical techniques in support of the conservation of historic vessels in the Solent.' Paper presented at the UK Corrosion 2002 Conference, October 22-24, Cardiff.

Paxton, R. (ed.) (1990) *100 Years of the Forth Bridge*. London: Thomas Telford.

Payne, E. (2019) '3D imaging of the Parthenon sculptures: an assessment of the archaeological value of nineteenth century plaster casts.' *Antiquity* 93 (372): 1625–1642.

Peacock, E. (2005) 'Investigation of conservation methods for a textile recovered from the American Civil War submarine H.L. Hunley (1864),' in P. Hoffmann, *et al.* (eds.) *ICOM Committee for Conservation (ICOM-CC) Working Group on Wet Organic Archaeological Materials. Conference, 9th, Copenhagen, Denmark, 2004*. Bremerhaven: Verlag H.M. Hauschild for ICOM-CC, pp. 497–509.

Peacock, E. and Callanan, M. (2018) 'The challenges of developing sustainable heritage management and preservation strategies for perennial snow patch artefacts,' in E. Williams and E. Hocker (eds.) *Proceedings of the 13th ICOM-CC Group on Wet Organic Archaeological Materials Conference Florence 2016*. Paris: ICOM-CC, pp. 22–26.

Pearce, S. (1990) *Archaeological Curatorship*. London: Leicester University Press.

Pearce, S. (ed.) (1994) *Interpreting Objects and Collections*. London: Routledge.

Pearlstein, E. (2017) 'Conserving ourselves: embedding significance into conservation decision-making in graduate education.' *Studies in Conservation* 62 (8): 435–444.

Pearlstein, E. (2021) *Curriculum Shifts: Humility in Conservation*. Available at: https://markk-hamburg.de/from-conservation-to-conversation/workshop-contributions/ (Accessed May 1, 2022).

Pearson, D., Butler, H. and Schofield, E. (2018) 'Discussion on the practicalities and effectiveness of re-treating a wooden gun carriage with DTPA,' in E. Williams and E. Hocker (eds.) *Proceedings of the 13th ICOM-CC Group on Wet Organic Archaeological Materials Conference Florence 2016*. Florence: ICOM-CC, pp. 256–262.

Pearson, D. and Schofield, E. (2021) 'The Mary Rose: larger than life,' in E. Williams (ed.) *Proceedings of the 14th ICOM-CC Group on Wet Organic Archaeological Materials Conference, Portsmouth 2019*. Paris: ICOM.

Pedersoli, L., Antomarchi, C. and Michalski, C. (2016) *A Guide to Risk Management of Cultural Heritage*. Ottawa: CCI. Available at: https://www.iccrom.org/sites/default/files/2017-12/risk_management_guide_english_web.pdf (Accessed May 10, 2022).

Peek, M (2011) *Theft and vandalism in museums facts and figures to support collection risk management*. Available at: https://www.icom-cc-publications-online.org/1193/Theft-and-Vandalism-in-museums---facts-and-figures-to-support-Collection-Risk-Management (Accessed June 20, 2022).

Peers, L. (1999) '"Many tender ties" the shifting contexts and meanings of the S. Black bag.' *World Archaeology* 31(2): 288–302.

Penn, K. (2000) *Excavations on the Norwich Southern Bypass 1989-1991 part 2. The Anglo-Saxon Cemetery at Harford Farm, Caistor St. Edmund, Norfolk*. Gressenhall: East Anglian Archaeological Report No. 92.

Peters, K. (1981) 'The conservation of a living artefact. A Maori meeting house at Makahae. A preliminary report,' in *ICOM-CC 6th Triennial Meeting, Ottawa 1981*. Ottawa: ICOM-CC.

Peters, R. (2008) *The brave new world of conservation*. 10.13140/2.1.2900.0961.

Peters, I. (2013) 'Through the looking glass: guest experience and the wonderous world of conservation at the Musical Instrument Museum' in E. Williams (ed.) *The Public Face of Conservation*. London: Archetype Publication in association with Colonial Williamsburg.

Peters, R. (2020) 'Conservation and engagement: transforming and being transformed,' in R. Peters, *et al.* (eds.) *Heritage Conservation and Social Engagement*. London: UCL Press.

Pettifer, A. (2002) *English Castles: A Guide by Counties*. Woodbridge: Boydell and Brewer.

Philippot, P. (1996) 'Restoration from the perspective of the humanities,' in Stanley Price, N., M. Kirby Talley Jr, M. and Vaccaro, A. (eds.) *Historical and Philosophical Issues in the Conservation of Cultural Heritage*. Los Angeles: The Getty Conservation Institute.

Pinelli, O. (2003) 'From the need for completion to the cult of the fragment: how tastes, scholarship and museum curator's choices changed our views of ancient sculptures,' in J. Grossman, J. Podany and M. True (eds.) *History of Restoration of Ancient Stone Sculptures*. Malibu: J. Paul Getty Trust, pp. 61–74.

Pintus, S. (2009) 'An account of the flood and the days that followed,' in H. Spande (ed.) *Conservation Legacies of the Florence Flood of 1966*. London: Archetype, pp. 10–15.

Pitt Rivers, A. (1875) 'On the Evolution of Culture.' *Proceedings of the Royal Institution* VII: 496–520.

Plenderleith, H. J. (1932) 'The examination and preservation of paintings: a digest.' *Museums Journal* 32: 308–389.

Plenderleith, H. (1998) 'A history of conservation.' *Studies in Conservation* 43(3): 129–143.

Plenderleith, H. and Werner, A. (1971) *Conservation of Antiquities and Works of Art*. Oxford: Oxford University Press.

Plutarch (1914) *Lives Volume I: Theseus and Romulus. Lycurgus and Numa. Solon and Publicola*. Loeb Classical Library 46. Translated byB. Perrin. Cambridge, MA: Harvard University Press.

Podany, J. and Lansing Maish, S. (1993) 'Can the complex be made simple? Informing the public about conservation through museum exhibitions.' *Journal of the American Institute for Conservation* 32(2): 101–108.

Podany, J. (1994) 'Restoring what wasn't there: reconsideration of the eighteenth-century restorations to the Lansdowne Herakles in the collection of the J. Paul Getty Museum,' in A. Oddy (ed.) *Restoration: Is It Acceptable? British Museum Occasional Paper No. 99*. London: British Museum Press.

Podany, J. (2003) 'Lessons from the past' in J. Grossman, J. Podany and M. True (eds.) *History of Restoration of Ancient Stone Sculptures*. Malibu: J. Paul Getty Trust, pp. 13–24.

Podany, J., Risser, E. and Sanchez, E. (2009) 'Never forever: assembly of sculpture guided by the demands of disassembly,' in J. Ambers, *et al.* (eds.) *Holding it all Together: Ancient and Modern Approaches to Joining, Repair and Consolidation*. London: Archetype Publications in Association with the British Museum.

Pollard, M. and Heron, C. (1996) *Archaeological Chemistry*. Cambridge: Royal Society of Chemistry.

Pollard, M., *et al.* (2004) 'Assessing the influence of agrochemicals on the rate of copper corrosion in the vadose zone of arable land. Part 1: field experiments.' *Conservation and Management of Archaeological Sites* 6: 363–376.

Pollard, M., *et al.* (2004) 'Assessing the influence of agrochemicals on the rate of copper corrosion in the vadose zone of arable land. Part 2: laboratory simulations.' *Conservation and Management of Archaeological Sites* 7: 225–239.

Pollard, A.M., *et al.* (2006) Assessing the influence of agrochemicals on the rate of copper corrosion in the vadose zone of arable land Part 1: field experiments. *Conservation and Management of Archaeological Sites*, 7, 225–239.

Pollard, M., *et al.* (2007) *Analytical Chemistry in Archaeology*. Cambridge: Cambridge University Press.

Pomian, K. (1994) 'The collection: between the visible and the invisible,' in S. Pearce (ed.) *Interpreting Objects and Collections*. London: Routledge.

Pouliot, B., *et al.* (2017) 'Learning from an "old one': a Tlingit basket makes its journey home,' in N. Owczarek, M. Gleeson and L. Grant (eds.) *Engaging Conservation Collaboration across Disciplines*. London: Archetype Publications, pp. 115–122.

Pretzel, B. (2000) 'Determining the colour fastness of the Bullerswood carpet.' *Studies in Conservation*, 45 (Sup 1): 150–154.

Pye, E. (2001) *Caring for the Past: Issues in Conservation for Archaeology and Museums*. London: James & James.

Pye, E. (ed.) (2008) *The Power of Touch: Handling Objects in Museums and Heritage Contexts*. Walnut Creek, California: Left Coast Press.

Pye, E. (2016) 'Challenges of conservation: working objects.' *Science Museum Group Journal* Autumn 2016, Issue 06. 10.15180/160608

Pye, E. and Cronyn, J. (1987) 'The archaeological conservator reaexamined: A personal view,' in J. Black (ed.) *Recent Advance in the Conservation and Analysis of Artefacts*. London: Summer Schools Press.

Quant, A. (2002) 'The Archimedes Palimpsest: conservation treatment, digital imaging and transcription of a rare medieval manuscript.' *Studies in Conservation* 47 (sup 3): 165–170.

Quirke, S. and Spencer, J. (1992) *The British Museum. Book of Ancient Egypt*. London: Thames & Hudson.

Quye, A and Williamson, C. (1999) *Plastics: Conserving and Collecting*. Edinburgh: National Museum of Scotland.

Rahbar, N., *et al.* (2010) 'Mixed mode fracture of marble/adhesive interfaces.' *Materials Science and Engineering* A527 (18-19): 4939–4946.

Renn, O. and Schweizer, P. (2009) 'Inclusive risk governance: concepts and application to environmental policy making.' *Environmental Policy and Governance* 19: 174–184.

Railway Technology. (2012) Forth Rail Bridge, Firth of Forth. Available at: https://www.railway-technology.com/projects/forth-rail-bridge-firth-scotland/ (Accessed August 28, 2022).

Rainbird, P. (1999) 'Entangled biographies: Western Pacific ceramics and the tombs of Pohnpei.' *World Archaeology* 31(2): 214–224.

Rathgen, F. (1898) *Die Konservierung von Altertumsfunden*. Berlin: W. Spemann.

Rathgen, F. (1905) *The Preservation of Antiquities. A Handbook for Curators* (trans. G.A. Auden and H. Auden). Cambridge: Cambridge University Press.

Reedy, C. (1992) 'Religious and ethical issues in the study of conservation of Tibetan sculpture.' *Journal of the American Institute for Conservation* 31(1): 41–50.

Reedy, C. (2008) *Thin-section Petrography of Stone and Ceramic Cultural Materials*. London: Archetype.

Reeve, J. and Adams, M. (1993) *The Spitalfields Project. Volume 1: across the Styx*. 10.5284/1081789.

Remer, A. (2020) 'Editorial.' *Museum International* 72 (1-2): 1–7.

Renfrew, C. and Bahn, P. (1991) *Archaeology: Theories, Methods and Practice*. London: Thames & Hudson.

Renn, O. (1999) 'A model for an Analytic-Deliberative process in risk management.' *Environmental Science and Technology*, 33(18): 3049 -3055.

Re:source (2002) *Benchmarks in Collections Care for Museums, Archives and Libraries*. London: Resource.

Rhyl-Svendsen, M., *et al.* (2010) *Does a standard temperature need to be constant?* Available at: https://www.conservationphysics.org/standards/standardtemperature_mrs.pdf (Accessed August 29, 2021).

Riccardelli, C., *et al.* (2014) 'The treatment of Tullio Lombardo's *Adam*: a new approach to the conservation of monumental marble sculpture.' *Metropolitan Museum Journal* 49: 49–115.

Riccardelli, C., *et al.* (2010) 'An examination of pinning materials for marble sculpture.' *Objects Specialty Group Postprints* 17: 95–112.

Richmond, A. (2005) 'The Ethics checklist:10 years on.' *Conservation Journal* 50. Available at: http://www.vam.ac.uk/content/journals/conservation-journal/issue-50/the-ethics-checklist-ten-years-on/ (Accessed June 27, 2021).

Riedlmayer, A. (1994) 'Killing memory: the targeting of libraries and Archives in Bosnia-Herzegovina.' *MELA Notes* 61: 1–6.

Riegl, A. (1996) 'The modern cult of monuments: its essence and its development,' in N. Stanley Price, *et al.* (eds.) *Historical and Philosophical Issues in the Conservation of Cultural Heritage*. Los Angeles: The Getty Conservation Institute.

Rimmer, M.B. and Caple, C. (2008) 'Estimating artefact loss: a comparison of metal artefact loss rates through in-situ decay and loss of ancient monument sites in England,' in H. Kars and R. van Heeringen (eds.) *Preserving Archaeological Remains In Situ? Proceedings of the 3rd Conference 7-9 December 2006, Amsterdam*. Geoarchaeological and Bioarchaeological Studies 10. Amsterdam: Vrije Universiteit Amsterdam, pp. 65–74.

Rimmer, M., *et al.* (2013) *Guidelines for the Storage and Display of Archaeological Metalwork*. Swindon: English Heritage.

Risdonne, V., *et al.* (2021) 'A multi-analytical study of historical coated plaster surfaces: the examination of a nineteenth century V & A cast of a tombstone.' *Heritage Science* 9. Available at: https://heritagesciencejournal.springeropen.com/articles/10.1186/s40494-021-00533-0 (Accessed June 2, 2022).

Risser, E. and Saunders, D. (2013) *The Restoration of Ancient Bronzes: Naples and Beyond*. Los Angeles: J. Paul Getty Museum.

Rivenc, R. and Bek, R. (2018) *Keep it Moving? Conserving Kinetic Art*. Los Angeles: Getty Conservation Institute. Available at: http://www.getty.edu/publications/keepitmoving/ (Accessed November 15, 2021).

Rivera, J. (2017) 'The use of refurbished marine containers as a permanent storage solution for the maritime collection of the H.L. Hunley submarine.' *Journal of the American Institute of Conservation* 56 (2): 161–168.

Rivera, J. and Scafuri, M. (2017) 'The sea, the sub and maritime collaboration: how conservators and archaeologists worked together to recover and conserve the *H.L. Hunley* submarine,' in N. Owczarek, M. Gleeson and L. Grant (eds), *Engaging Conservation, Collaborating Across Disciplines*. London: Archetype and University of Pennsylvania Museum of Archaeology and Anthropology.

Rivers, S. and Umney, N. (2003) *Conservation of Furniture*. London: Butterworth-Heinemann.

Robb, J. (2009) 'People of stone: stelae, personhood and society in prehistoric Europe.' *Journal of Archaeological Method and Theory* 16: 162–183.

Roberts, M. (1994) *Durham*. London: Batsford and English Heritage.

Robertson, J., Roux, C., and Wiggins, K., (2018) *Forensic Examination of Fibers*. 3rd Edition. Boca Raton, FL: CRC Press.

Rodgers, B. (2004) *The Archaeologist's Manual for Conservation*. Heidelberg: Springer.

Rogerson, C. and Garside, P. (2017) 'Increasing the profile and influence of conservation: an unexpected benefit of risk assessments.' *Journal of the Institute of Conservation* 40 (1): 34–48.

Rosenberg, G. (1917) *Antiquités en Fer et en Bronze: Leur Transformation dans la Terre Contenant de l'Acide Carbonique et des Chlorures et Leur Conservation* (trans A. Husson). Copenhagen: Gyldendal.

Rosenberg, G. (1933) 'Antiquities and humidity.' *Museum Journal* 1933: 307–314.

Rosewitz, J., *et al.* (2016) 'A multimodal study of pinning selection for restoration of a historic statue.' *Materials and Design* 98: 294–304.

Roy, A. (1994) *Artists Pigments: A Handbook of Their Histories and Characteristics, Vol. 2*. Washington: National Gallery of Art.

Roy, A. and Smith, P. (eds.) (1994) *Preventive Conservation Practice, Theory and Research: 1994 IIC Ottawa Congress*. London: IIC.

Rodwell, W. (2013) *The Coronation Chair and Stone of Scone*. Oxford: Oxbow.

Russel, R. and Winkworth, K. (2009) *Significance 2.0: A guide to Assessing the Significance of Collections*. Rundle Mill, SA: Collections Council of Australia.

Sanchez, G. and Allen, D. (1990) 'Seismic strengthening of historic adobe structures in California: an overview,' in N. Agnew, M. Taylor and A. Balderramma (eds.) *Adobe 90, Preprints 6th International Conference on the Conservation of Earthen Architecture, Las Cruces, New Mexico*. Los Angeles: Getty Conservation Institute. pp. 348–356.

Sand, J. (2015) 'Japan's monument problem: Ise Shrine as metaphor.' *Past and Present* (Supplement 10): 126–152.

Savage, A. (2019) *Adam Savage Meets Neil Armstrong's Apollo 11 Spacesuit*. Available at: https://www.youtube.com/watch?v=m2esyN4fuiA (Accessed November 14, 2021).

Schamberger, K., *et al.* (2012) 'Chapter 17: Living in a material world: object biography and transnational lives.' Available at: http://epress.anu.edu.au/anu-lives/transnational/mobile-devices/ch17.htm. (Accessed December 23, 2020).

Schmisseur, A. (2016) *Archaeological Conservation in the United Kingdom: Development, History and Diffusion of Knowledge*. Unpublished PhD, University of York.

Schutz, A., Braun, D. and Gegenfurtner, K. (2011) 'Eye Movements and Perception: A Selective Review.' *Journal of Vision* 11 (5): 9: 1–30.

Schwartz, G. (2013) 'Memory and its demolition. Ancestors, animals and sacrifice at Umm el Marra, Syria.' *Cambridge Archaeological Journal* 23 (3): 495–522.

Science Museum Group. (2018) *Science Museum Group Human Remains Policy*. Accessed June 2020. Available at: https://www.sciencemuseumgroup.org.uk/wp-content/uploads/2018/10/Human-remains-policy-updated-10-18.pdf. (Accessed May 10, 2022).

Scott, D. (1991) *Metallography and Microstructure in Ancient and Historic Metals*. Marina del Rey: Getty Conservation Institute and J. Paul Getty Trust.

Scott, D. (2016) *Art: Authenticity, Restoration, Forgery*. Los Angeles: UCLA Cotsen Institute of Archaeology Press.

Schiffer, M. (1999) *The Material Life of Human Beings*. London: Routledge.

Sease, C. (1981) 'The case against using soluble nylon in conservation work.' *Studies in Conservation* 26(3): 102–110.

Sease, C. (1994) *A Conservation Manual for the Field Archaeologist*. Los Angeles: Institute of Archaeology, University of California.

Sease, C. (1996) 'A short history of archaeological conservation,' in Roy, A. and Smith, P. (eds.) *Archaeological Conservation and its Consequences: 1996 IIC Copenhagen Congress*. London: IIC.

Seeley, N. (1987) 'Archaeological conservation: The development of a discipline.' *Institute of Archaeology Bulletin* 24: 161–176.

Seip, L. (1999) Transformations of meaning: The life history of a Nuxalk mask. *World Archaeology* 31: 272–287.

Serpico, M. and White, R. (2001) 'The use and identification of varnish on New Kingdom funerary equipment,' in W. Davies (ed.) *Color and Painting in Ancient Egypt*. London: British Museum Press.

Shashoua, Y. (2008) *Conservation of Plastics: Materials Science, Degradation and Preservation*. London: Routledge.

Shashoua, Y. (2014) 'A safe place, storage strategies for plastics.' *GCI Newsletter* 29: 1.

Shashoua, Y., Schnell, U. and Young, L. (2002) 'Deterioration of plasticized PVC components in Apollo spacesuits,' in T. van Oosten, Y. Shashoua, and F. Waentig (eds.) *Plastics in Art - History, Technology, Preservation*. Munich: Siegl, pp. 69–79.

Shell, C. and Robinson, P. (1988) 'The recent reconstruction of the Bush Barrow Lozenge Plate.' *Antiquity* 62: 248–260.

Shotridge, L. (1921) 'Tlingit Woman's Root Basket.' *The Museum Journal* XII (3): 162–178.

Shugar, A. and Mass, J. (eds.) (2012) *Handheld XRF for Art and Archaeology*. Leuven: Leuven University Press.

Simons, D. (ed.) (2000) *Change Blindness and Visual Memory*. Hove: Psychology Press Ltd.

Sirén, O. (1914) The importance of the antique to Donatello. *American Journal of Archaeology* 18 (4): 438–461.

Sitwell, C. and Staniforth, S. (1998) *Studies in the History of Painting Restoration*. London: Archetype.

Skowranek, H. (2007) 'Should we reproduce the beauty of decay? A *Museumsleben* in the work of Dieter Roth,' in *Tate Papers* 8 (Autumn 2007). Available at: https://www.tate.org.uk/research/publications/tate-papers/08/should-we-reproduce-the-beauty-of-decay-a-museumsleben-in-the-work-of-dieter-roth (Accessed November 23, 2020).

Smedemark, S., Ryhl-Svendsen, M. and Toftum, J. (2020) 'Removal of organic acids from indoor air in museum storage rooms by active and passive sorption techniques.' *Studies in Conservation* 65 (5):251–261.

Smith, B. (1990) 'Shared responsibility: welcome and introduction,' in B. Ramsay-Jolicoeur and I. Wainwright (eds.) *Shared Responsibility*. Ottawa: National Gallery of Canada.

Smith, C. and Ngarimu, R. (2021) 'Artefact access: the gulf between theory and practice,' in J. Bridgland (ed.) *Transcending Boundaries: Integrated Approaches to Conservation. ICOM-CC 19th Triennial Conference Preprints. Beijing, 17-21 May 2021*. Paris: ICOM.

Smith, G. and Johnson, R. (2008) 'Strip "Teas": solubility data for the removal (and application) of low molecular weight synthetic resins used as inpainting media and picture varnishes.' *WAAC Newsletter* 30 (1): 11–19.

Smith, L. (2007) *The Uses of Heritage*. Oxford: Routledge.

Smith, P. (1977) 'Some aspects of commercial restoration and conservation.' *The Conservator* 1: 32–34.

Smith, S. (1992) 'The Portland Vase,' in A. Oddy (ed.) *The Art of the Conservator*. London: British Museum Press.

Smith, S. (2016) 'The submarine H.L. Hunley: confederate innovation and Southern icon,' in A. King (ed.) *Archaeology in South Carolina: Exploring the Hidden Heritage of the Palmetto State*. Columbia: University of South Carolina Press.

Smyth, H. (1989) 'The Conservation Center: origins and early years,' in N. Baer (ed.) *Training in Conservation a Symposium on the Occasion of the Dedication of the Stephen Chan House*. New York: Institute of Fine Arts.

Soressi, M. and Geneste, J.-M. (2011) 'The history and efficacy of the Chaîne Opératoire approach to lithic analysis: studying techniques to reveal past societies in an evolutionary perspective.' *PaleoAnthropology* 2011: 334–350.

Sousa, M., *et al.* (2007) 'The art of CO_2 for art conservation: a green approach to antique textile cleaning.' *Green Chemistry* 9: 943–947.

Spaarschuh, C. and Kempton, H. (2020) 'Acting on behalf of objects? Conservator's reflections on their professional role.' *Studies in Conservation* 65 (6): 358–374.

Spicer, G. (2013) 'Conservation treatment of a Hunziger cantilevered armchair including the use of magnets to create tufting.' *Journal of the American Institute of Conservation* 52 (2): 107–122.

Stable, C., *et al.* (2021) 'Rediscovering Ancient Egypt: consideration of the legacy, ethics and aesthetics of previously restored Egyptian artifacts.' *Journal of Institute of Conservation* 44 (2): 1–19.

Stanco, F., Battiato, S. and Gallo, G. (eds.) (2011) *Digital Imaging for Cultural Heritage Preservation: Analysis, Restoration, and Reconstruction of Ancient Artworks*. Boca Raton, FL: CRC Press.

Staniforth, S. (1990) 'Benefits versus costs in environmental control,' in S. Keene (ed.) *Managing Conservation*. London: UKIC.

Staniforth, S. (2013) *Historical Perspectives on Preventive Conservation*. Readings in Conservation. Los Angles: Getty Conservation Institute.

Stanley Price, N., Kirby Talley, M. and Vaccaro, A. (eds.) (1996) *Historical and Philosophical Issues in the Conservation of Cultural Heritage*. Los Angeles: The Getty Conservation Institute.

Stead, I., Bourke, J. and Brothwell, D. (eds.) (1986) *Lindow Man: The Body in the Bog*. London: British Museum Publications.

Stein, M. (1903) *Sand-Buried Ruins of Khotan*. London: T. Fisher Unwin.

Stephens, C., Buscarino, I. and Breitung, E. (2018) 'Updating the Oddy test: comparison with volatiles identified using chromatographic techniques.' *Studies in Conservation* 63 (S1): 425–427.

Stewart, N.-A. (2007) 'Conserving the sacred.' *ICON News* (8): 30–31.

Stiger, S. (2016) 'Autoethography as a new approach in conservation.' *Studies in Conservation* 61 (Sup 2): 227–232.

Stoner, J. (2015) 'Vignettes of interdisciplinary technical art history investigation.' *CeROArt HS*. Available at: https://journals.openedition.org/ceroart/4508. (Accessed November 11, 2020).

Stout, G. (1931) 'The technical conference at Rome.' *Fogg Art Museum Notes* 2 (6): 330–332.

Street, R. (2008) 'Projecting the UK's changing climate.' *Conservation Bulletin* 57 (Spring 2008): 3–5.

Strlic, M., *et al.* (2013) 'Damage functions in heritage science.' *Studies in Conservation* 58 (2): 80–87.

Strong, D. (1973) 'Roman Museums,' D. Strong (ed.) *Archaeological Theory and Practice*. London: Seminar Press.

Stuart, B. (2007) *Analytical Techniques in Materials Conservation*. Chichester: Wiley.

Stubbs, J.H. (1995) 'Protection and presentation of excavated structures,' in N. Stanley Price (ed.) *Conservation on Archaeological Excavations*. Rome: ICCROM, pp. 73–90.

Stukeley, W. (1743) *Avebury, a Temple of the British Druids with some others described. London: William Stukeley*. Available at: http://www.avebury-web.co.uk/AburyWS/AburyWS.html (Accessed July 26, 2020).

Sully, D. and Cardoso, I. (2014) 'Painting Hinemihi: people based conservation and the paint analysis of Hinemihi's carvings.' *Studies in Conservation* 59 (3): 180–193.

Sully, D. (2007) *Decolonizing Conservation: Caring for Māori meeting Houses outside New Zealand*. Walnut Creek, CA: Left Coast Press.

Sully, D. and Suenson-Taylor, K. (1996) 'A condition survey of glycerol treated freeze-dried leather in long term storage,' in A. Roy and P. Smith (eds) *Archaeological Conservation and its Consequences, 1996 IIC Copenhagen Congress*. London: IIC.

Swain, H. (2010) 'A change in philosophy for the care of archaeological collections,' in E. Williams and C. Peachey (eds.) *The Conservation of Archaeological Materials: Current trends and Future directions*. BAR International Series 2116. Oxford: Archaeopress, pp. 145–150.

Sweetnam, E. and Henderson, J. (2021) 'Disruptive conservation: challenging conservation orthodoxy.' *Studies in Conservation* 67 (1-2): 63–71. 10.1080/00393630.2021.1947073

Swieringa, H. (2021) 'A subtle shift: the care and use of Indigenous belongings after the calls to action.' in J. Bridgland (ed.) *Transcending Boundaries: Integrated Approaches to Conservation. ICOM-CC 19th Triennial Conference Preprints. Beijing, 17-21 May 2021*. Paris: ICOM.

Syson, L and Cafà, V. (2014) '*Adam* by Tullio Lombardo.' *Metropolitan Museum Journal* 49: 8–31.

Szrajber, T. (1997) *The British Museum Materials Thesaurus*. Cambridge: MDA and British Museum.

Taylor, J. (2013) 'Causes and extent of variation in collection condition survey data.' *Studies in Conservation* 58 (2): 95–106.

Taylor, J. (2017) 'Improving reliability in collection condition surveys by utilizing training and decision guides.' *Journal of the American Institute of Conservation* 56 (2): 126–141.

Tejedor, C. (2010) 'Re-conservation of wood samples from the Vasa with alkoxysilanes: preliminary assessment.' in K. Straetkvern and E. Williams (eds.) *Proceedings of the 11th ICOM-CC Group on Wet Organic Archaeological Materials Conference, Greenville 2010*. Paris: ICOM, pp. 439–462.

Te Marvelde, M. (1999) 'Research into the history of conservation-restoration: remarks on relevance and method,' in *Preprints of the ICOM-CC 12th Triennial Meeting, Lyon 29 August - 3 September 1999*. London: James and James.

Te Marvelde, M. (2011) 'Two treatment approaches to one militia painting a critical analysis of recent developments in Dutch conservation,' in J. Bridgland (ed.) *Preprints of the ICOM-CC 16th triennial Meeting, Lisbon, Portugal, 19-23 September 2011*. Almada: Criterio.

Teppo, E. (2020) 'Intro Er: YAG lasers in the conservation of artworks.' *Journal of the Institute of Conservation* 43: 2–11.

Tétreault, J. (2003) *Airborne Pollutants in Museums, Galleries and Archives: Risk Assessment, Control Strategies and Preservation Management*. Ottawa: Canadian Conservation Institute.

The Sunday Times (1995) 'Red Hot, the issue made from girders,' *The Sunday Times*, 22 January 1995: SC/8.

The Times (1996) 'Forth Rail Bridge Neglected,' *The Times*, March 1996: 6.

Thickett, D. (2018) 'Frontiers of preventive conservation.' *Studies in Conservation* 63 (sup 1): 262–267.

Thickett, D. and Lee, L. (2004) *Selection of materials for the storage or display of museum objects. (Revised edition.) British Museum Occasional Paper 111*. London: British Museum, pp. 1–30.

Thomas, S. and Stone, P. (2009) *Metal Detecting and Archaeology*. Woodbridge: Boydell Press.

Thompson, M. (1977) *General Pitt-Rivers*. Bradford-on-Avon: Moonraker Press.

Thompson, M. (1979) *Rubbish Theory: Creation and Destruction of Value*. First Edition. Oxford: Oxford University Press.

Thompson, M. (2006) *Ruins Reused: Changing Attitudes to Ruins Since the Late Eighteenth Century*. Kings Lynn: Heritage Marketing and Publications Ltd.

Thompson, M. (2017) *Rubbish Theory: The Creation and Destruction of Value*. New Edition. London: Pluto Press.

Thomson, G. (1978) *The Museum Environment*. London: Butterworth.

Thorrowgood, D. and Hallam, D. (2004) 'Preserving the significance: why the journey mattered more than the car.' Available at: https://bigstuff.omeka.net/items/show/66/ (Accessed December 20, 2021).

Thunberg, J., Watkinson, D. and Emmerson, N. (2021) 'Desiccated microenvironments for heritage metals: creation and management.' *Studies in Conservation* 66 (3): 127–153.

Thurley, S. (2013) *Men from the Ministry: How Britain Saved its Heritage*. New Haven, CT: Yale University Press.

Tilley, C. (1994) 'Interpreting material culture,' in S. Pearce (ed.) *Interpreting Objects and Collections*. London: Routledge.

Tilley, C., *et al.* (2006), *Handbook of Material Culture*. London: Sage Publications.

Townsend, J. and Tennent, N. (1993) 'Color transparencies: Studies on light fading and storage stability,' in J. Bridgland (ed.) *Preprints of the ICOM-CC 10th Triennial Meeting, Washington 1993*. Washington: ICOM-CC.

Trutty-Coohill, P. (2005) 'The restored Sistine Chapel ceiling: the transcendent made immanent,' in A. Tymieniecka (ed.) *Human Creation between Reality and Illusion. Analecta Husserliana* (The Yearbook of Phenomenological Research) 87. Dordrecht: Springer.

Tubb K. (1995) *Antiquities Trade or Betrayed. Legal, Ethical and Conservation Issues*. London: Archetype Publications, Ltd.

Tubb, K. and Sease, C. (1996) 'Sacrificing the wood for the trees-should conservation have a role in the antiquities trade?' in A. and P. Smith (eds.) Archaeological Conservation and Its Consequences. Preprints of the Contributions to the Copenhagen Congress, 26-30 August 1996. London: International Institute for Conservation.

Turnbull, P. and Pickering, M. (eds.) (2010) *The Long Way Home: The Meaning and Values of Repatriation*. Oxford: Berghan Books.

Turgoose, S. (1982) 'Post Excavation changes in Iron Antiquities.' *Studies in Conservation* 27 (3): 97–101.

Turner, R. and Scaife, R. (eds.) (1995) *Bog Bodies: New Discoveries and New Perspectives*. London: British Museum Press.

Turner, S. (2020) *Conserving Medusa*. Available at: https://www.museums.cam.ac.uk/blog/2020/11/16/conserving-medusa/ (Accessed June 2, 2020).

Tversky, A. and Kahneman, D. (1974) 'Judgement under uncertainty: heuristics and biases.' *Science* 185: 1124–1131.

Tweddle, D. (1992) *The Anglian Helmet from Coppergate*. London: York Archaeological Trust and CBA.

UKIC (United Kingdom Institute for Conservation) (1983) *Guidance for Conservation Practice*. London: UKIC.

UNESCO (1989) *Recommendation on the Safeguarding of Traditional Culture and Folklore*. Available at: http://www.un-documents.net/folklore.htm (Accessed June 21, 2022).

UNESCO (2001) *Universal Declaration on Cultural Diversity*. Available at: http://www.unesco.org/new/fileadmin/MULTIMEDIA/HQ/CLT/pdf/5_Cultural_Diversity_EN.pdf (Accessed May 28th, 2020).

UNESCO (2003) *Convention for the Safeguarding of the Intangible Cultural Heritage*. Available at: https://ich.unesco.org/en/convention (Accessed June 21, 2002).

UNESCO (2020) *What is meant by cultural heritage*. Available at: www.unesco.org/new/en/culture/themes/illicit-trafficking-of-cultural-property/unesco-database-of-national-cultural-heritage-laws/frequently-asked-questions/definition-of-the-cultural-heritage/ (Accessed on June 4th, 2020).

UNESCO (2020) *Museums around the World in the Face of COVID-19*. Available at: https://unesdoc.unesco.org/ark:/4822 3/pf0000373530. (Accessed July 25, 2020).

Unruh, J. and Harbeck, C. (2021) 'Conservation decision-making in the field: a case study.' *Journal of the Institute of Conservation* 44 (1): 3–24.

Uring, P., *et al.* (2020) 'Assessment of indoor air quality for a better preventive conservation of some French museums and monuments.' *Environmental Science and Pollution Research* 27: 42850–42867.

Vaccaro, A. (1996) 'Reintegration of losses,' in N. Stanley Price, M. Kirby Talley Jr, and A. Vaccaro (eds.) *Historical and Philosophical Issues in the Conservation of Cultural Heritage*. Los Angeles: The Getty Conservation Institute.

Van de Wetering, E. (1996) 'The autonomy of restoration: ethical considerations in relation to artistic concepts' in C. Price *et al.* (eds.) *Historical and Philosophical Issues in the Conservation of Cultural Heritage*. Los Angeles: GCI, pp. 193–199.

van Schoute, R. and Verougstraete-Marcq, H. (1986) *Scientific Examination of Easel Paintings, PACT 13*. Strasbourg: Council of Europe.

Vlasatý, T. (2019) 'Origins of the "St Wenceslas Helmet."' Available at: http://sagy.vikingove.cz/on-the-origins-of-the-st-wenceslas-helmet/ (Accessed August 4, 2020).

Wain, A. (2011) 'A many-headed axe: originality in large technology heritage.' *Journal of Australian Studies* 35 (4): 495–510.

Wain, A. (2017) 'The importance of movement and operation as preventive conservation strategies for heritage machinery.' *Journal of the American Institute for Conservation* 56 (2): 81–95.

Walden, S. (1985) *The Ravished Image*. London: Weidenfeld and Nicholson.

Walden, S. (2006) *The Ravished Image: An Introduction to the Art of Restoring Paintings*. 2nd Revised Edition. London: Gibson Square Books Ltd.

Walker, K. and Bacon, L. (1987) 'A condition survey of specimens in the Horniman Museum: a progress report,' in J. Black (ed.) *Recent Advances in the Conservation and Analysis of Artifacts*. London: Summer Schools Press.

Waller, R. (1994) 'Conservation risk assessment: A strategy for managing resources for preventive conservation,' in A. Roy and P. Smith (eds.) *Preventive Conservation Practice, Theory and Research: 1994 IIC Ottawa Congress*. London: IIC.

Waller, R. (1995) 'Risk management applied to preventive conservation.' In C. Rose, C. Hawks and H. Genoways (eds.) *Storage of Natural History Collections: A Preventive Conservation Approach*. Society for the Preservation of Natural History Collections.

Waller, R. (2003) *Cultural Property Risk Analysis Model, Development and Application to Preventive Conservation at the Canadian Museum of Nature*. Goteborg: Acta Universitatis Gothoburgensis.

Walmsley, E., Fletcher, C. and Delaney, J. (1992) 'Evaluation of system performance of near infrared imaging devices.' *Studies in Conservation* 37: 120–131.

Ward, C., Ambers, J. and Cook, J. (2009) 'A 13,000 year old repair: new observations on a Late Magdalenian spear-thrower from Montastruc, Tarn-et-Garonne, France,' in J. Ambers, *et al.* (eds.) *Holding it All Together; Ancient and Modern Approaches to Joining, Repair and Consolidation*. London: Archetype Publications.

Warda, J. (2011) *The AIC Guide to Digital Photography and conservation Documentation*. 2nd Edition. Washington DC: American Institute for Conservation.

Watkins, S. (1997) 'Science and conservation at the British Museum: a nineteenth century legacy' in S. Bradley (ed.) *The Interface Between Science and Conservation, British Museum Occasional Paper No. 116*. London: British Museum Press.

Watkinson, D. (1982) 'Making a large-scale replica of the Pillar of Eliseg.' *The Conservator* 6: 6–11.

Watkinson, D. (1996) 'Chloride extraction from archaeological iron: comparative treatment efficiencies,' in A. Roy and P. Smith (eds.) *Archaeological Conservation and its Consequences: 1996 IIC Copenhagen Congress*. London: IIC.

Watkinson, D. (2008) 'SS Great Britain: conservation and access - synergy and cost,' in G. Saunders, J. Townsend and S. Woodcock (eds.) *Conservation and Access; contributions to the London Congress 15-19 September 2008*. London: IIC, pp. 109–114.

Watkinson, D. (1996) 'Defining the contribution of non-conservators to conservation: the role of the conservation technician,' in J. Cronyn and K. Foley (eds.) *A Qualified Community: Towards Internationally Agreed Standards of Qualification for Conservation*. London: ICOM-CC Working Group on Training in Conservation and Restoration.

Watkinson, D. and Lewis, M. (2005) 'Desiccated storage of chloride contaminated archaeological iron objects.' *Studies in Conservation* 50 (4): 241–252.

Watkinson, D. and Rimmer, M. (2014) 'Quantifying effectiveness of chloride desalination treatments for archaeological iron using oxygen measurement,' in E. Hyslop, *et al.* (eds.) *Metal 2013. Interim Meeting of the ICOM-CC Metal Working Group Edinburgh, Scotland, 16-20 September 2013*. Paris: ICOM-CC, pp. 95–102.

Watkinson, D., Rimmer, M. and Emmerson, N. (2019) 'The Influence of Relative Humidity and intrinsic chloride on post-excavation corrosion rates of archaeological wrought iron.' *Studies in Conservation* 64 (8): 456–471.

Watson, A. (2008) 'Adapt and Conserve.' *Conservation Bulletin* 57 (Spring 2008): 12–13.

Watson, J. (nd) *Longman, Clementi and Co. Organized upright Grand Piano*. Available at: http://update.jrw1.com/top/default.html. (Accessed January 4, 2022).

Watson, J. (2010) *Artifacts in Use: the Paradox of Restoration and the Conservation of Organs*. Richmond, VA: OHS Press in association with Colonial Williamsburg.

Watson, J. (2014) 'The 1799 Organized Upright Grand Piano in Williamsburg: a preliminary report.' *Journal of the American Musical Instrument Society* 40: 9–28.

Watts, S., *et al.* (2013) 'Liverpool's Conservation Centre: fourteen years of public access,' in E. Williams (ed.) *The Public Face of Conservation*. London: Archetype, pp. 16–25.

Wei, W., *et al.* (2018) 'Protecting museum collections from vibrations due to construction: vibration statistics, limits, flexibility and cooperation.' *Studies in Conservation* 63 (supl): 293–300.

Wellman, H. (2010) 'A Tale of three surveys: creating a flexible condition survey for mixed archaeological collections.' in E. Williams and C. Peachey (eds.) *The Conservation of Archaeological Materials: Current trends and Future directions*. BAR International Series 2116. Oxford: Archaeopress, pp. 169–181.

Wessex Archaeology (2015) *HMS Victory Management Plan volume 1*. Available at: https://www.nmrn.org.uk/sites/default/files/victory_cmp_volume_01-.pdf (Accessed October 31, 2021).

Westheimer, F. (1994) 'Preservation of books and electronic storage,' in W. Krumbein *et al.* (eds.) *Durability and Change*. Chichester: Wiley.

Wharton, G. (2005) 'Indigenous claims and heritage conservation: an opportunity for critical dialog.' *Journal of Public Archaeology* 4: 199–204.

Wharton, G. (2011) *The Painted King: Art, Activism and Authenticity in* Hawaii. Honolulu: University of Hawaii Press.

Wharton, G. (2013) 'The challenges of conserving contemporary art,' in B. Altshuler (ed.) *Collecting the New: Museums and Contemporary Art*. Princeton NJ: Princeton University Press, pp. 163–178.

Wharton, G. (2018) 'Bespoke ethics and moral casuistry in the conservation of contemporary art.' *Journal of the Institute of Conservation* 41 (1): 58–70.

Whitley, J. (2002) 'Objects with attitude: biographical facts and fallacies in the study of late Bronze Age and early Iron Age warrior graves." *Cambridge Archaeological Journal* 12 (2): 217–232.

Wickens, J. and Hess Norris, D. (2018) 'The imperative of soft skill development in preventive conservation practice and training' in A. Nevin et al. (eds.) *Preventive Conservation: The State of the Art*. London: IIC.

Willems, W. (2008) 'Archaeological resource management and preservation,' in H. Kars and R. van Herringen (eds.) *Preserving Archaeological Remains In-Situ, proceedings of the 3rd Conference, 7-9 December 2006, Amsterdam*. Amsterdam: Vrije Universiteit Amsterdam, pp. 283–290.

Williams, R. (1986) 'The Beilstein test.' *Canadian Conservation Institute Notes*, 17: 1.

Williams, C. (2002) 'Transforming the old: Cairo's medieval city.' *Middle East Journal* 56 (93): 457–475.

Williams, E. 2000. 'Sixty-five years of history: archaeological conservation at Colonial Williamsburg.' *North American Archaeologist* 21 (2): 107–113.

Williams, E. (ed.) (2001) *Human Remains: Conservation, Retrieval and Analysis Conference*, Williamsburg, VA, November 1999, BAR International Series 943. Oxford: British Archaeological Reports.

Williams, E. (2004) 'Assessing the past: Colonial Williamsburg's archaeological collection.' *Objects Specialty Group Postprints* 10: 72–80. Available at: http://29aqcgc1xnh17fykn459grmc.wpengine.netdna-cdn.com/osg-postprints/wp-content/uploads/sites/8/2015/02/osg010-08.pdf. (Accessed December 21, 2020).

Williams, E. (ed.) (2013) *The Public Face of Conservation*. London: Archetype.

Williams, E. (2020) *Stories in Stone: Memorialization, the creation of History and the Role of Preservation*. Wilmington, DE: Vernon Press.

Williams, E. (2021) "Framing the questions that matter: the relationship between archaeology and conservation," in Y. Edwards-Ingram and A. Edwards (eds.) *Historical Archaeology in the Twenty-first Century: Lessons from Colonial Williamsburg*. Gainesville: University of Florida Press, pp. 195–205.

Williams, J. (2012) 'Thirty years of monitoring in England: what have we learnt.' *Conservation and Management of Archaeological Sites* 14 (1-4): 442–457.

Williams, N. (1989) *The Breaking and Remaking of the Portland Vase*. London: British Museum Publications.

Williams, N. (1992) 'The Sutton Hoo Helmet,' in A. Oddy (ed.) *The Art of the Conservator*. London: British Museum.

Williams, R. (1989) 'The Beilstein test.' *Canadian Conservation Institute Notes* 17: 1.

Wilmering, A. (2004) 'Traditions and trends in furniture conservation.' *Reviews in Conservation* 5: 22–37.

Wilson, P., *et al.* (2017) 'Evaluation of touchable 3D-printed replicas in museums.' *The Museum Journal* 60 (4): 445–465.

Whiting, D. (1995) 'The conservator's approach to sacred art,' *WAAC Newsletter* 17 (3): Sept 1985.

Woodward, C. (1888) 'The action of gas on leather bookbindings: a preliminary experimental enquiry.' *Library Chronicle* 5.

Wolfe, J. and Wood, C. (2020) 'Restoring Stephan Von Huene's Tap Dancer: finding logic within integrated circuits.' *Journal of the American Institute for Conservation* 60 (1): 50–60.

Wollny, K. (1996) Investigation and analysis of copper alloy helmets from the De Walden collection. Unpublished MA dissertation. Department of Archaeology, University of Durham.

Wong, L., Rickerby, S. and Bedair, R. (2017) 'Conserving the wall paintings in the tomb of Tutankhamen: How the past informs the future,' in J. Bridgland (ed.) *ICOM CC 18th Triennial preprints, Copenhagen 2017*. Available at: https://www.icom-cc-publications-online.org/PublicationDetail.aspx?cid=b68834ee-b2eb-4ef1-b7c5-ccc8a0e34c90 (Accessed December 20, 2020).

Würst, H. *et al.* (2016) 'The dustfall collector – a simple passive tool for long-term collection of airborne dust. A project under the Danish mould in buildings program (DAMID).' *Indoor Air* 15: 33–40.

Wyld, M. (1998) 'The restoration of Holbein's *Ambassadors*.' *National Gallery Bulletin* 19: 4–25.

Xavier-Rowe, A., *et al.* (2000) 'Using heat to kill museum insect pests-is it practical and safe?' *Studies in Conservation* 45 (sup 1): 206–211.

Xavier Rowe, A., *et al.* (2018) 'Operation Clothes Moth: where preventive conservation and public engagement meet.' *Studies in Conservation* 63 (Sup 1): 445–450.

Xavier-Rowe, A., Lankester, P., Lauder, D. and Pinniger, D. (2018) 'Operation clothes moth: Where preventive conservation and public engagement meet' in A. Nevin *et al.* (eds.) *Preventive Conservation: The State of the Art*. London:IIC.

Yagihashi, S. (1988) 'The preservation and handing down of traditional Urushi art techniques in Japan,' in N. Brommelle and P. Smith (eds.) *Urushi*. Marina del Rey: The Getty Conservation Institute.

Yourcenar, M. (1996) 'That mighty sculptor time,' in N. Stanley Price, M. Kirby Talley Jr, and A. Vaccaro (eds.) *Historical and Philosophical Issues in the Conservation of Cultural Heritage*. Los Angeles: The Getty Conservation Institute.

Young, L. and Avino, M. (2013) 'A picture is worth a thousand words: using x-radiographs of the National Air and Space Museum's collection to promote preservation,' in E. Williams (ed.) *The Public Face of Conservation*. London: Archetype Publications, pp. 49–56.

Young L. and Young, A. (2001) *The Preservation, Storage and Display of Spacesuits. Collections Care Report No. 5*. Washington: The Smithsonian National Air and Space Museum.

Zhang, J., Thickett, D. and Green, L. (1994) 'Two tests for the detection of volatile organic acids and formaldehyde." *Journal of the American Institute of Conservation* 33 (1): 47–53.

Zuo, M. (2019) 'China has opened thousands of new museums but who wants them?' *South China Morning Post*, January 20, 2019.

Index

Milton Keynes UK
Ingram Content Group UK Ltd.
UKHW030841121223
434203UK00021B/318